Advance Praise for David Ray Griffin's
9/11 Ten Years Later

"Our civilization cannot survive if we do not confront the unanswered questions about 9/11. David Ray Griffin does that with the same clarity and meticulous documentation that characterized his preceding books. Frightening as the enormity of the truth about 9/11 may be, we should also bear in mind that it is a window of opportunity for addressing a whole range of problems threatening the lives of our children and grandchildren. I am sure those who follow will recognize David Ray Griffin's body of work as one of the most important contributions of the last decade."
—*Niels Harrit, Associate Professor Emeritus, Nano-science Center, Department of Chemistry, University of Copenhagen*

"Anyone who has actually studied Griffin's writings on 9/11 knows that the evidence against the truth of the official account is overwhelming. It is not surprising that the mainstream response has been to ridicule and ignore rather than to engage in reasoned discussion. What is disappointing is that leading liberals and responsible journalists have joined in by affirming ideas that contradict basic science and condescendingly rejecting solid research without examining it. In this book, Griffin describes the behavior of these journalists and attempts, in a remarkably charitable spirit, to understand it."
—*John B. Cobb, Jr., author of* The Earthist Challenge to Economism *and (with Herman Daly)* For the Common Good

"Why yet another book on 9/11? Because, as David Ray Griffin points out clearly and persuasively, 9/11 continues to be not only the greatest crime in American history, but also the most strenuously covered up, and certainly the crime with the greatest political consequences. He shows how over a decade the events of 9/11 and the reports on them have been used to attack the American democratic system. Above all, he documents the success of this attack—by the refusal of the media, the academy, and religious institutions to openly discuss these matters, and by the numbers of critics who at one extreme have made fools of themselves in echoing the Orwellian official version, and at the other extreme have been either fired or silenced after their dissent from it."
—*Peter Dale Scott, poet, former Canadian diplomat, professor at the University of California (Berkeley) and author of* American War Machine

9/11 TEN YEARS LATER

WHEN STATE CRIMES AGAINST DEMOCRACY SUCCEED

DAVID RAY GRIFFIN

OLIVE
BRANCH
PRESS

An imprint of Interlink Publishing Group, Inc.
www.interlinkbooks.com

First published in 2011 by

OLIVE BRANCH PRESS
An imprint of Interlink Publishing Group, Inc.
46 Crosby Street, Northampton, Massachusetts 01060
www.interlinkbooks.com

Library of Congress Cataloging-in-Publication Data

Griffin, David Ray, 1939-
  9/11 ten years later : when state crimes against democracy succeed / by David Ray Griffin.
    p. cm.
  Includes bibliographical references and index.
  ISBN 978-1-56656-868-5 (pbk.)
  1. September 11 Terrorist Attacks, 2001. 2. Terrorism--Government policy--United States.
  3. Conspiracies--United States. 4. United States--Politics and government--2001-2009. I.
  Title.
    HV6432.7.G7457 2011
    973.931--dc23
                          2011029603

Printed and bound in the United States of America

Cover image: The World Trade Center stands out against a blackened New York City skyline
after a power failure struck the city July 14, 1977. © AP Photos

To request our complete 40-page full-color catalog, please call us toll free at
1-800-238-LINK, visit our website at www.interlinkbooks.com, or write to
Interlink Publishing, 46 Crosby Street, Northampton, MA 01060
e-mail: info@interlinkbooks.com

CONTENTS

ACKNOWLEDGMENTS

I must begin by thanking two people without whom I would not be here to write these acknowledgments.

My wife, Ann Jaqua, nursed me through a series of life-threatening crises, brought on by a staph infection, that almost took my life in 2010.

It only *almost* did so because of a superb team of physicians in Santa Barbara, especially my heart surgeon, Dr. Phillip West. After working on me for two hours—the aortic valve, having become infected, had become largely separated from my heart—Dr. West had an assistant warn my wife that he might not be able to save me. But after five more hours of extraordinarily tedious work, he did so.

Whereas I was brought to the point where I could write again by Dr. West and Ann, along with her daughters—Jennifer, Alison, and Sara Jaqua—and many others, this book also would not have been possible without the help of several other people. Here I must especially lift up two: Tod Fletcher and Elizabeth Woodworth. Besides proofreading the entire manuscript, both of them helped the writing of this book in many other ways. I owe Elizabeth special thanks for checking all the references as well as preparing the index.

I also wish to thank several others from whom I received significant assistance: Matthew Everett, Mark Gaffney, Richard Gage, Niels Harrit, Jim Hoffman, Barbara Honegger, Frank Legge, Massimo Mazzucco, Dennis McMahon, Aidan Monaghan, and John Wyndham.

Chapter 1 is based on a lecture delivered during a 15-city May–June 2010 tour, which was organized by Matthew Naus of Milwaukee.

Chapter 2 is based on an essay entitled "Left-Leaning Despisers of the 9/11 Truth Movement: Do You Really Believe in Miracles?" posted July 6, 2010, at Global Research and 911Truth.org.

A lecture in Seattle on May 27, 2011, arranged by Ben Collet, Richard Curtis, and Mark Snyder, provided the basis for Chapter 3.

Chapter 4 is based on a lecture, "Building What? How SCADs Can Be Hidden in Plain Sight," delivered at a conference called

"Understanding Deep Politics" held May 14–16, 2010, in Santa Cruz, California, which was organized by Gabriel Day, Cheryl Curtiss, Jason King, and Kevin Zenzie. This lecture was posted at 911Truth.org on May 27, 2010, and reprinted as "Building What? How State Crimes against Democracy (SCADs) Can Be Hidden in Plain Sight" in *Censored 2011: The Top 25 Censored Stories*, edited by Mickey Huff and Peter Phillips with Project Censored (New York: Seven Stories, 2010).

Chapter 7 is based on an essay entitled "Tim Russert, Dick Cheney, and 9/11," which was posted June 17, 2008, at Information Clearing House.

Chapter 8 is based on a lecture entitled "9/11 and Nationalist Faith," which was delivered October 19, 2007, at the Iliff School of Theology in Denver, Colorado. This lecture was sponsored by the Veterans of Hope Project, located at Iliff and led by Professor Emeritus Vincent Harding, and by Colorado 9/11 Visibility, led by Fran Shure.

Introduction: 9/11 Ten Years Later

The words in the title of this book—"9/11 Ten Years Later"—are often followed with an exclamation point. The exclamation point may be a way of expressing, by members of the 9/11 Truth Movement, amazement that the truth has not already been publicly revealed. The exclamation point might be used by detractors of this movement—perhaps along with an expletive—to express their feeling that it is time for these people to "get a life." The exclamation point might reflect a position somewhat in the middle—of spouses of members hoping that no more years of their family life will be oriented around the work of trying to get the truth revealed.

In any case, for reasons discussed in this book (especially the final two chapters), there is nothing surprising about the fact that the 9/11 crime has not been revealed. Those who have gained control of a state in an ostensible democracy have many means not only for orchestrating major crimes, but also for preventing those crimes (including their crimes against democracy itself) from being publicized.

What *is* somewhat surprising, perhaps to the perpetrators themselves, is the fact that the 9/11 Truth Movement is still alive and, in fact, continues to grow. The first professional 9/11 organization, Scholars for 9/11 Truth, was formed in 2005, and since then a dozen professional organizations have been created. It was not until 2006 that architect Richard Gage started Architects and Engineers for 9/11 Truth with one member—himself—but now over 1,500 architects and engineers have signed its petition. Some of the organizations, such as Scientists for 9/11 Truth and Actors and Artists for 9/11 Truth, have started up only in the past two years.

This tenth anniversary marks a milestone in my own work: The present book is my tenth book about 9/11. I have been pleased to see, as indicated by sales, that my books on this topic have continued to seem helpful—including my oldest book, *The New Pearl Harbor*.[1]

Unfortunately, "ten years later" also applies to the war in Afghanistan, which began on October 7, 2001. The first chapter of this book deals with the still widely-held belief that this war was justified by 9/11. For people new to the issues, this chapter can serve as a summary of the evidence against the view that Osama bin Laden in particular, or al-Qaeda in general, was responsible for the 9/11 attacks. The tenth anniversary of the 9/11 attacks is also the tenth anniversary of the new onslaught of the (Christian and Jewish) West against the Muslim world—an onslaught that now includes not only the US-NATO attacks on Afghanistan, Iraq, and Libya, but also support for Israel's 2006 war on Lebanon/Hezbollah and its continued oppression of Palestine, along with US provocations in Iran, Yemen, and Syria. How can anyone think that 9/11 is ancient history, which no longer matters?

For most people, "9/11" is virtually synonymous with the title of this book's second chapter: "The Destruction of the World Trade Center." However, rather than simply rehearsing the arguments against the official view—according to which these buildings were brought down by the airplane strikes and the resulting fires—this chapter asks: "Why Have Otherwise Rational Journalists Endorsed Miracles?"—with "miracles" understood to be events that violate well-established laws of science. Dealing with a number of left-leaning journalists, I ask why these people, who in other contexts would ridicule miracles, have endorsed them in relation to the destruction of the World Trade Center. They do not, to be sure, speak in terms of miracles. But they affirm events that require violations of fundamental scientific principles.

In the following chapter, I deal with this question in relation to two of our best and deservedly respected journalists in particular, Bill Moyers and Robert Parry. (Although Parry is not nearly as well known as Moyers, who long hosted what many considered the best hour on television every week, Parry is well respected by people who know his writings.) I ask: Why do Moyers and Parry endorse the official 9/11 story about the World Trade Center, even though one cannot endorse this story without implying a belief in miracles? I suggest that their endorsement can only be understood in terms of the psychological dynamics of the "Big Lie."

In the fourth chapter, I focus on Building 7 of the World Trade Center, taking the name of this chapter from a New York City judge who, while getting ready to rule on a petition to allow the people of the city to vote on whether they want their own investigation of 9/11, asked in response to a statement about Building 7: "Building *what?*" Given the fact that this building was *so big*, and that the demolition of it was *so obvious*, I discuss "How State Crimes against Democracy Can Be Hidden in Plain Sight." I thereby introduce the language of "state crimes against democracy," abbreviated SCADs, which was in 2010 brought into the discussion of 9/11 by means of a symposium in a leading social science journal (this being another example of the continued expansion of the 9/11 Truth Movement). As this language indicates, 9/11 was not simply a crime against the people of the United States and the world, especially the people who were murdered on 9/11 or who had loved ones who were murdered. It was also a crime against democracy itself.

Chapter 5 turns to the chief method through which the perpetrators convinced the American people that the attacks had been orchestrated by Muslims: the apparent phone calls from the 9/11 planes, through which Americans were first told that Middle Eastern men had hijacked four airliners. This information was provided by a leading member of the Bush-Cheney administration, the Department of Justice's solicitor general, Theodore "Ted" Olson, who told CNN and hence the world that his wife, well-known CNN correspondent Barbara Olson, informed him that her plane, American Airlines 77, had been hijacked by men armed with knives and box-cutters. In 2006, it became public knowledge (by means of the FBI's evidence provided for the trial for Zacarias Moussaoui) that Ted Olson's report—that his wife had talked to him twice from AA 77—was not true. This could hardly have been more important, given the fact that the alleged phone calls had provided *the* evidence that the planes had been hijacked, combined with the fact that the first and most important conveyor of this reported evidence was Ted Olson. And yet the American media, which have the responsibility of reporting the information the American public needs to function as a democracy,[2] have never reported the FBI's acknowledgment that the Olson calls never happened. This chapter also treats other evidence that the "phone calls from the planes" never happened.

In Chapter 6, we begin a transition to the official story about the attack on the Pentagon. This chapter is based on an essay that was written the week that Tim Russert, the well-known moderator of *Meet the Press*, suddenly died. Titled "Tim Russert, Dick Cheney, and 9/11," this article pointed out that Cheney, in a discussion with Russert on his program only a few days after 9/11, had revealed something about his actions on 9/11 that contradicted what the 9/11 Commission later claimed—something that strongly suggested that Cheney had given "stand-down" orders prior to the Pentagon attack. I wrote this chapter because I thought that, given the respect and grief for Russert in the news media, there was a chance—not much of one, but more than usual—that someone in the mainstream media might pick up this story. But there was no breach of the general policy: Stories that challenge any important part of the official account of 9/11 are not to be covered. Nevertheless, I turned that essay into a chapter for the present work, both for its intrinsic interest and for its importance for the following chapter.

The title of that following chapter—"A Consensus Approach to the Pentagon"—alludes to the widespread sense, both in and outside the 9/11 Truth community, that, whereas there is a lot of consensus within this community about the destruction of the World Trade Center, there is no such consensus about the attack on the Pentagon. In this chapter, I argue that, although there is indeed much disagreement on the issue that has received the most debate—was the Pentagon hit by a Boeing 757?—this is a relatively trivial point in comparison with an issue about the Pentagon attack on which the 9/11 Truth Movement has reached consensus.

The title of Chapter 8 employs an expression that may seem strange to most readers: "Nationalist Faith." We normally think of the primary form of faith in the United States as Christian. But I suggest, in agreement with theologian John Cobb, that the primary form of faith in America is the American version of nationalism, which could be called "Americanism." To illustrate how this nationalist faith can trump Christian faith, I explain how the one book I wrote on 9/11 from an explicitly Christian point of view, *Christian Faith and the Truth behind 9/11*,[3] led to the removal of Westminster Press's president and vice-president, who had given the go-ahead for the publication of my book. As I explain, people in the church who complained about my book, including members of the board who censured my book, did not raise any theological objections. What was objectionable was that I had provided evidence that the 9/11 attacks, rather than having been carried out by foreign Muslims, were orchestrated by members of the US government.

The final chapter expounds the idea expressed in the book's subtitle: "When State Crimes against Democracy Succeed." Having introduced the notion of SCADs in the fourth chapter, I deal in this final chapter with the dangers to our country and, indeed, to the whole world, when American SCADs succeed and are not quickly reversed. When President Kennedy and then Bobby Kennedy were assassinated, wise commentators at the time warned that if the truth about these murders were not revealed, then more, perhaps greater, state-sponsored crimes would be committed. That prediction came true on 9/11.

Ten years have elapsed since 9/11, and this greatest of all SCADs has not been reversed. So anyone who cares about the future of this country, and of the world as a whole, should be working to expose the state crime against democracy that occurred on 9/11.

1. DID 9/11 JUSTIFY THE WAR IN AFGHANISTAN?

There are many questions to ask about the war in Afghanistan. One that has been widely asked is whether it would turn out to be President Obama's Vietnam. This question has implied several others, such as: Is this war winnable, or has it become a quagmire? And this question is partly motivated by the widespread agreement that the Afghan government under Hamid Karzai is at least as corrupt and incompetent as the government we tried to prop up in South Vietnam for 20 years. Also, just as the American people turned increasingly against the war in Vietnam, they have now turned increasingly against the war in Afghanistan. Commentators have increasingly been referring to it as a "purposeless war."

Although there have been many similarities between these two wars, there has also been a big difference: This time, there has been no draft. For this reason, as anti-war writers often comment, no strong anti-war movement has developed. If there were a draft, so that college students and their friends back home were being sent to Afghanistan, there would have been huge demonstrations against this war all across this country. If the sons and daughters of wealthy and middle class parents had been coming home in boxes, or with permanent injuries, or with post-traumatic stress disorder, which might lead them to commit suicide—this war would have been stopped long ago. People have often asked, did we learn any of the "lessons of Vietnam"? Our government learned one: If you're going to have an unpopular war, don't have a draft.

However, even though there has not been a draft, the American people have said that the war should be brought to an end. An ABC/*Washington Post* Poll in June of 2011 showed that only 43 percent of the American people consider the war "worth fighting," and this figure reflected a bump from the announcement of the killing of Osama bin Laden: In March, only 31 percent marked "worth fighting." A CNN poll showed that 74 percent of the American people wanted US troops to come home partly or totally.[1]

There are many other questions that have been asked about the war in Afghanistan, but in this essay, I focus on only one: Did the 9/11 attacks justify the war in Afghanistan?

This question has thus far been considered off-limits, not to be raised in polite company, and certainly not in the mainstream media. It has been permissible, to be sure, to ask whether the war during the past several years has been justified by those attacks so many years ago. But one has not been allowed to ask whether the original invasion was justified by the 9/11 attacks.

Various commentators, to be sure, have raised some pretty fundamental questions about the effectiveness and affordability of the "counterinsurgency strategy" and even whether American fighting forces should remain in Afghanistan at all. But I will ask an even more fundamental question: Whether this war was ever really justified by the publicly given reason: the terrorist attacks of September 11, 2001.

This question has two parts: First, did these attacks provide a legal justification for the invasion of Afghanistan? Second, if not, did they at least provide a moral justification? I will begin with the question of legal justification.

I Is the War in Afghanistan Legally Justified?

Since the founding of the United Nations in 1945, international law with regard to war has been defined by the UN charter. It is widely agreed by international lawyers that, measured by this standard, the US-led war in Afghanistan has been illegal from the outset.

Marjorie Cohn, a well-known professor of international law, wrote in November 2001:

> [T]he bombings of Afghanistan by the United States and the United Kingdom are illegal. This bombardment violates both international law and United States law.[2]

In 2008, Cohn repeated this argument in an article entitled "Afghanistan: The Other Illegal War." The point of the title was that, although by then it had become widely accepted that the war in *Iraq* was illegal, the war in Afghanistan was *equally* illegal.[3]

According to international law as codified in the UN Charter, she pointed out, disputes are to be brought to the UN Security Council, which alone may legally authorize the use of force. Without this authorization, any military activity against another country is illegal.

However, there are two exceptions to this principle: One of these is that, if your nation has been subjected to an armed attack by another nation, you may respond militarily in self-defense. This condition was not fulfilled by the 9/11 attacks, however, because they were not carried out by another nation. Afghanistan did not attack the United States. Indeed, the 19 men charged with the crime were not Afghans; most of them were from Saudi Arabia.

The other exception occurs when a nation has certain knowledge that an armed attack by another nation is imminent—*too* imminent for the matter to be brought to the Security Council. The need for self-defense must be "instant, overwhelming, leaving no choice of means, and no moment for deliberation." Although the US government claimed that its military operations in Afghanistan were justified by the need to prevent a second attack, this need, even if real, was clearly not urgent, as shown by the fact that the United States waited almost a month to launch its attack on Afghanistan.

US political leaders have claimed, to be sure, that the UN did authorize the US attack on Afghanistan. This claim, originally made by the Bush-Cheney administration, was repeated by President Obama in his West Point speech of December 1, 2009, in which he said that the "United Nations Security Council endorsed the use of all necessary steps to respond to the 9/11 attacks," so that US troops went to Afghanistan "[u]nder the banner of . . . international legitimacy."[4]

However, the language of "all necessary steps" is from UN Security Council Resolution 1368, in which the Council, taking note of its "responsibilities under the Charter," expressed its *own* readiness "to take all necessary steps to respond to the terrorist attacks of 11 September 2001."[5]

Of course, the UN Security Council might have determined that one of these necessary steps was to authorize an attack on Afghanistan by the United States. But it did not. Resolution 1373, which is the only other Security Council resolution about this matter, laid out various responses, but these included matters such as freezing assets, criminalizing the support of terrorists, exchanging police information about terrorists, and capturing and prosecuting terrorists. The use of military force was not mentioned.[6]

The US war in Afghanistan was not authorized by the UN Security Council in 2001 or at any time since, so this war began as an illegal war and has remained an illegal war. Our government's claim to the contrary is false.

This war is illegal, moreover, not only under international law, but also under US law. The UN Charter is a treaty, which was ratified by the United States, and, according to Article VI of the US Constitution, any treaty ratified by the United States is part of "supreme law of the land."[7] The war in Afghanistan, therefore, has been in violation of US law as well as international law. It could not be more illegal.

II IS THE WAR IN AFGHANISTAN MORALLY JUSTIFIED?

The American public for the most part probably does not realize that this war is illegal, because this is not something our political leaders have been anxious to point out, and our press has for the most part also ignored this issue. So most people simply do not know.

If they were informed, however, many Americans would be inclined to argue that, even if technically illegal, the US military effort in Afghanistan has been morally justified by the attacks of 9/11. For a summary statement of this argument, we can turn again to the West Point speech of President Obama, who has taken over the Bush-Cheney account of 9/11. Seeking to provide an answer to the question of "why America and our allies were compelled to fight a war in Afghanistan in the first place," Obama said:

> We did not ask for this fight. On September 11, 2001, nineteen men hijacked four airplanes and used them to murder nearly 3,000 people. They struck at our military and economic nerve centers. They took the lives of innocent men, women and children without regard to their faith or race or station. . . . As we know, these men belonged to al Qaeda—a group of extremists who have distorted and defiled Islam, one of the world's great religions, to justify the slaughter of innocents. . . . [A]fter the Taliban refused to turn over Osama bin Laden—we sent our troops into Afghanistan.

This standard account can be summarized in terms of three points:

- The attacks were carried out by 19 Muslim members of al-Qaeda.
- The attacks had been authorized by the founder of al-Qaeda, Osama bin Laden, who was in Afghanistan.

- The US invasion of Afghanistan was necessary because the Taliban, which was in control of Afghanistan, refused to turn bin Laden over to US authorities.

On the basis of these three points, our political leaders concluded that the United States had the moral right, arising from the universal right of self-defense, to attempt to capture or kill bin Laden and his al-Qaeda network to prevent them from launching another attack on our country.

The only problem with this argument is that all three points are false. I will show this by looking at these three points in reverse order, beginning with the claim that we invaded Afghanistan because the Taliban refused to hand over bin Laden.

1. First Claim: Afghanistan Attacked for Taliban's Refusal to Turn Over bin Laden

The claim that the Taliban refused to turn over bin Laden was repeatedly made by political leaders and our mainstream media. For example, Robert Reid, writing for the Associated Press, said in 2009 that the war "was launched by the Bush administration after the Taliban government refused to hand over Osama bin Laden for his role in the Sept. 11, 2001 terror attacks in the United States."[8] Reports from the time, however, show the truth to be very different.

Who Refused Whom?

Ten days after the 9/11 attacks, CNN reported:

> The Taliban . . . refus[ed] to hand over bin Laden without proof or evidence that he was involved in last week's attacks on the United States. . . . The Taliban ambassador to Pakistan . . . said Friday that deporting him without proof would amount to an "insult to Islam."

CNN also made clear that the Taliban's demand for proof was not made without reason, saying:

> Bin Laden himself has already denied he had anything to do with the attacks, and Taliban officials repeatedly said he could not have been involved in the attacks.

Bush, however, "said the demands were not open to negotiation or discussion."[9]

With this refusal to provide any evidence of bin Laden's responsibility, the Bush administration made it impossible for the Taliban to turn him over. As Afghan experts quoted by the *Washington Post* pointed out, the Taliban, in order to turn over a fellow Muslim to an "infidel" Western nation, needed a "face-saving formula." Milton Bearden, who had been the CIA station chief in Afghanistan in the 1980s, put it this way: While the United States was demanding, "Give up bin Laden," the Taliban were saying, "Do something to help us give him up."[10] But the Bush administration refused.

After the bombing began in October, moreover, the Taliban tried again, offering to turn bin Laden over to a third country if the United States would stop the bombing and provide evidence of his responsibility for the 9/11 attacks. But Bush replied: "There's no need to discuss innocence or guilt. We know he's guilty." An article in London's *Guardian*, which reported this development, was entitled: "Bush Rejects Taliban Offer to Hand Bin Laden Over."[11] So it was the Bush administration, not the Taliban, that was responsible for the fact that bin Laden was not turned over.

In August of 2009, President Obama, who had criticized the US invasion of Iraq as a war of choice, said of the US involvement in Afghanistan: "This is not a war of choice. This is a war of necessity."[12] It appears, however, that it was a war of choice, every bit as much as the war in Iraq.

What Was the Motive for the Invasion?

This conclusion is reinforced by reports indicating that the United States had made the decision to invade Afghanistan *two months before* the 9/11 attacks. The background to this decision was the fact that the United States had been supporting a pipeline project proposed by UNOCAL that would transport oil and gas from the Caspian Sea region through Afghanistan and Pakistan to the Indian Ocean.[13] This project had been on hold through the 1990s because of the civil war that had been going on in Afghanistan since the withdrawal of the Soviet Union in 1989.

In the mid-1990s, the US government had supported the Taliban with the hope that it would be able to unify the country through its military strength and provide a stable government. By the late 1990s, however, the Clinton administration had given up on the Taliban.[14]

When the Bush administration came to power, it decided to give the Taliban one last chance. During a four-day meeting in Berlin in July 2001, representatives of the Bush administration insisted that the Taliban must create a government of "national unity" by sharing power with factions friendly to the United States. The US representatives reportedly said to the Taliban: "Either you accept our offer of a carpet of gold, or we bury you under a carpet of bombs."[15]

After the Taliban refused this offer, the Americans said: "[M]ilitary action against Afghanistan would go ahead . . . before the snows started falling in Afghanistan, by the middle of October at the latest."[16] Indeed, given the fact that the attacks on the World Trade Center and the Pentagon occurred on September 11, the US military was able to mobilize to begin its attack on Afghanistan by October 7.

It appears, therefore, that the United States invaded Afghanistan for reasons far different from the official rationale, according to which we were there to capture or kill Osama bin Laden.

2. Second US Claim: Good Evidence Exists of bin Laden's Responsibility for 9/11 Attacks

I turn now to the second point: the claim that Osama bin Laden had authorized the attacks. Even if the Bush administration refused to give the Taliban evidence for this claim, it surely, most Americans probably assume, *had* such evidence and provided it to those who needed it. Again, however, the reports from the time indicate otherwise.

The Bush Administration

Two weeks after 9/11, Secretary of State Colin Powell said that he expected "in the near future . . . to put out . . . a document that will describe quite clearly the evidence that we have linking [bin Laden] to this attack."[17] But at a joint press conference with President Bush the next morning, Powell withdrew this pledge, saying that "most of [the evidence] is classified."[18]

Is this not remarkable? The Bush administration asked the American people to support an attack on Afghanistan on the basis of its claim that Osama bin Laden, who was in Afghanistan at the time, had authorized those attacks. But it said that the evidence for this claim could not be shared with us.

Seymour Hersh, citing officials from both the CIA and the Department of Justice, said that the real reason why Powell withdrew the pledge to share the evidence was a "lack of solid information."[19]

The British Government

The following week, British Prime Minister Tony Blair tried to help out, issuing a document purportedly showing that "Osama Bin Laden and al-Qaeda, the terrorist network which he heads, planned and carried out the atrocities on 11 September 2001." Blair's report, however, began by saying: "This document does not purport to provide a prosecutable case against Osama Bin Laden in a court of law."[20] So, the case was good enough to go to war, but not good enough to take to court. The next day, the BBC emphasized this weakness, saying: "There is no direct evidence in the public domain linking Osama Bin Laden to the 11 September attacks."[21]

The FBI

What about our own FBI? Surely, people would assume, it has an iron-clad case against bin Laden. But the FBI's "Most Wanted Terrorist" webpage on "Usama Bin Laden" never listed 9/11 as one of the terrorist acts for which he was wanted. This webpage did mention Nairobi (Kenya) and Dar es Salaam (Tanzania) as terrorist acts for which he was wanted. But it made no mention of 9/11.[22] When asked in 2006 why not, Rex Tomb, the FBI's chief of investigative publicity replied: "The reason why 9/11 is not mentioned on Usama Bin Laden's Most Wanted page is because the FBI has no hard evidence connecting Bin Laden to 9/11."[23]

After this story started flying around the Internet and was even covered by a TV station in Louisiana,[23] Dan Eggen of the *Washington Post* tried to downplay its significance in an article entitled "Bin Laden, Most Wanted For Embassy Bombings?"[25] Complaining about "conspiracy theorists" who claimed that "the lack of a Sept. 11 reference [on the FBI's "Most Wanted" webpage for bin Laden] suggests that the connection to al-Qaeda is uncertain," Eggen quoted the explanation offered by a former US attorney, who said that the FBI could not appropriately "put up a wanted picture where no formal charges had been filed."

But that explanation, while true, simply pushes the issue back a step to this question: Why have such charges not been filed? Rex Tomb's fuller statement, which Eggen failed to mention, had answered this question the previous June, saying:

> The FBI gathers evidence. Once evidence is gathered, it is turned
> over to the Department of Justice. The Department of Justice then

decides whether it has enough evidence to present to a federal grand jury. In the case of the 1998 United States Embassies being bombed, Bin Laden has been formally indicted and charged by a grand jury. He has not been formally indicted and charged in connection with 9/11 because the FBI has no hard evidence connecting Bin Laden to 9/11.[26]

Most Americans, however, were never told by the press that the Department of Justice has never formally indicted Osama bin Laden for the 9/11 attacks, because its FBI never provided it with any hard evidence.

The 9/11 Commission

What about the 9/11 Commission? Its entire report is based on the un-questioned premise that bin Laden was behind the attacks. When we look closely, however, we see that the Commission's own co-chairs, Thomas Kean and Lee Hamilton, later admitted that this assumption was not supported by any reliable evidence. Insofar as the 9/11 Com-mission's report did give evidence of bin Ladin's responsibility for the 9/11 attacks, it consisted of testimony that had reportedly been elicited by the CIA from al-Qaeda operatives. The most important of these operatives was Khalid Sheikh Mohammed—generally known as simply "KSM"—who has been called the "mastermind" of the 9/11 attacks.

If you read the 9/11 Commission's account of how bin Laden planned the attacks, and then check the notes, you will find that almost every note says that the information came from KSM.[27]

But Kean and Hamilton, in a 2006 book giving "the inside story of the 9/11 Commission," said that we cannot rely on this information. They had no success, they reported, in "obtaining access to star witnesses in custody . . . , most notably Khalid Sheikh Mohammed."[28] Besides not being allowed by the CIA to interview KSM, they were not permitted to observe his interrogation through one-way glass. They were not even allowed to talk to the interrogators.[29] Therefore, Kean and Hamilton complained:

> We . . . had no way of evaluating the credibility of detainee information. How could we tell if someone such as Khalid Sheikh Mohammed . . . was telling us the truth?[30]

Moreover, it is now known that KSM and the other al-Qaeda lead-ers had been tortured, and it is widely acknowledged that statements elicited by torture lack credibility. "At least four of the operatives whose interrogation figured in the 9/11 Commission Report," an NBC report pointed out, "have claimed that they told interrogators critical information as a way to stop being 'tortured.'"[31]

Accordingly, neither the Bush administration, the British government, the FBI, nor the 9/11 Commission ever provided reliable evidence of bin Laden's responsibility for the attacks.

The Claim that bin Laden Confessed to the 9/11 Attacks

Granted that "hard evidence" of bin Laden's responsibility for 9/11 has never been provided, it is often claimed that evidence is no longer needed, because bin Laden admitted his responsibility. This claim has been made primarily about a videotape that was released on December 13, 2001, by the Pentagon, claiming that the videotape, dated November 9, 2001, had been found in Jalalabad. But doubts have been raised from the beginning. BBC News said in a report entitled "Could the Bin Laden Video Be a Fake?"

> Washington calls it the "smoking gun" that puts Bin Laden's guilt beyond doubt, but many in the Arab world believe the home video of the al-Qaeda chief is a fake.[32]

Reporting "growing doubt in the Muslim world about the authenticity of the film," *Guardian* writer Steven Morris pointed out that "the White House had provided no details about how the Pentagon came to be in possession of the tape. Some opponents of the war theorise that the Bin Laden in the film was a look-alike."[33] The BBC and *Guardian* writers also stated that, without more details, it would be impossible to determine whether the video was authentic.[34]

Bin Laden's Statements about 9/11: Another reason to consider the "confession video" a fake is that, in the days leading up to November 9, bin Laden consistently denied that he planned the 9/11 attacks. He made this statement on September 12, in which bin Laden said that, although he "thanked Almighty Allah and bowed before him when he heard this news [about the attacks]," he had "had no information or knowledge about the attack."[35] He continued to make essentially the same point on September 16,[36] September 17,[37] September 28,[38] and October 7, 2001.[39]

Bin Laden's Appearance: To believe that bin Laden confessed to orchestrating the attacks of 9/11, moreover, one would also need to believe that there was a sudden change not only in bin Laden's testimony but also in his appearance. In videos made on October 7 and November 3, there is a considerable amount of white in bin Laden's beard, but in the latter, his health appears to have deteriorated somewhat.[40] We would expect the bin Laden of the video dated November 9 (the so-called "confession video") to have looked about the same, or even somewhat worse, than the bin Laden in the November 3 video. However, the bin Laden of this video seems darker than previous videos,[41] and seems to be heavier, with fuller cheeks than the bin Laden of a video known to have been made after November 16. Also, the bin Laden of the "confession video" also seemed to have a differently shaped nose[42] and shorter, heavier hands.[43]

Things the Real bin Laden Would Not Have Said: Still another problem is that the bin Laden of this "confession video" made some statements that the real bin Laden, if he were confessing to having planned the attacks, would not have made. For example, "bin Laden," discussing the collapse of the towers, said:

> [D]ue to my experience in this field, I was thinking that the fire from the gas in the plane would melt the iron structure of the building and collapse the area where the plane hit and all the floors above it only. This is all that we had hoped for.[44]

Given his "experience in this field," as a contractor, the real bin Laden would have known that the buildings were framed with steel, not with iron, and he also would have known that none of the buildings' steel (or iron) would have been melted by the "fire from the gas in the plane." He would have known that a building fire fed by jet-fuel could not have gotten above 1,800 degrees Fahrenheit, whereas iron and steel do not begin to melt until they are heated to at least 2,700 degrees. Osama bin Laden, therefore, would not have expected any iron or steel to melt.

The Opinion of Professor Bruce Lawrence: In February 2007, Bruce Lawrence, a Duke University history professor who is widely considered the country's leading academic bin Laden expert,[45] was asked what he thought about this so-called confession video. He said: "It's bogus." Adding that he had friends in the US Department of Homeland Security assigned to work "on the 24/7 bin Laden clock," he said that "they also know it's bogus."[46]

"The Killing of Osama bin Laden"

On May 1, 2011, President Barack Obama announced that a team Navy SEALs had killed Osama bin Laden in Pakistan that day. Although the corporate press simply reported the president's statement as if there were no serious questions to be raised about it, the discussion in the alternative press showed otherwise.

One kind of question raised the morality and even legality of the reported raid, in which a defenseless bin Laden was assassinated, hence murdered.[47] Indeed, later reports indicated, the goal "was never to capture bin Laden," but simply to kill him.[48] Noam Chomsky, for one, argued that bin Laden, who after all was merely a suspect, deserved a trial.[49]

Another kind of question dealt with the reported treatment of the body: No Muslim was invited to perform the last rights, and the body was buried at sea[50]—which is definitely not proper.

Another kind of question was whether the person killed by the SEALs was actually Osama bin Laden.[51] After all, the body, reportedly, was quickly buried at sea; no Muslim friends or acquaintances were asked to confirm the man's identity; we were told that one of his wives was there, but there has not been (as of this writing) an interview with her with a translator. Also there was the question of how Osama bin Laden, who was close to death in 2001, according to many reports (including one by CNN's Sanjay Gupta),[52] could have survived another ten years. Many authorities had even stated that bin Laden died—either definitely or probably—in 2001.[53]

The most important question, however, was one that was not raised in the mainstream press and was only occasionally raised in the alternative media. Obama famously said, in announcing the killing of Osama bin Laden, that "justice was done." This claim presupposed that people had been given good evidence that bin Laden was responsible for the 9/11 attacks. As we have seen, however, no evidence of bin Laden's responsibility had ever been provided.[54] So Chomsky was correct: bin Laden was merely a suspect.

This point was well stated in 2009 by a German federal judge, Dieter Deiseroth, who said:

> To date, more than 8 years after 9/11, no independent authority, no independent court, has reviewed available evidence, alleged or actual, and established verifiable procedures, satisfying constitutional requirements, as to who was responsible for the attacks of 9/11. What

in no case is to be said is that the argumentation is difficult - that it is for us too arduous to identify the perpetrators and possible masterminds and take them into custody: therefore, we avoid these constitutional difficulties and start a war to kill possible suspects by military force directly. It is not acceptable in a constitutional state to omit the necessary steps in identifying suspects and bringing them to trial before an independent court, but instead proclaim a war, bomb a foreign country in which possible suspects or perpetrators may reside, and occupy it militarily.[55]

So if Osama bin Laden was indeed killed on May 1, 2011, the claim that "justice was done" is emphatically *not* true.

3. The Third US Claim: There Is Good Evidence of al-Qaeda's Responsibility

I turn now to the third claim—that, even if there is no proof that Osama bin Laden authorized the attacks, we have abundant evidence that the attacks were carried out by Muslims belonging to his al-Qaeda organization. The main basis for this claim has been evidence that Muslim hijackers were on the airliners. The remainder of this chapter shows that no good evidence exists for this claim. There is even evidence against this claim, suggesting that 9/11 was instead a false-flag attack—an attack that people within our own government orchestrated while planting evidence to implicate Muslims. I will look at various types of evidence that were used to convince Americans that the 9/11 attacks were orchestrated by al-Qaeda Muslims.

Devout Muslims?

The 9/11 Commission portrayed the 19 men who (allegedly) took over the planes as devout Muslims, ready to meet their Maker—a "cadre of trained operatives willing to die."[56]

However, the *San Francisco Chronicle* reported that Atta and other hijackers had made "at least six trips" to Las Vegas, where they had "engaged in some decidedly un-Islamic sampling of prohibited pleasures." The *Chronicle* quoted the head of the Islamic Foundation of Nevada as saying: "True Muslims don't drink, don't gamble, don't go to strip clubs."[57]

Mohamed Atta: The contradiction is especially strong with regard to Mohamed Atta. On the one hand, Professor Dittmar Machule, who was Atta's thesis supervisor at a technical university in Hamburg in the 1990s, said that Atta was "very religious," prayed regularly, and never touched alcohol.[58] (Professor Machule, incidentally, says that he knew this student only as Mohamed al-Emir—although his full name was the same as his father's: Mohamed al-Emir Atta.) The 9/11 Commission says that Atta was very religious, even "fanatically so."[59] (The Commission wrote that when Atta arrived in Germany, he was not fanatically religious at first, but "[t]his would change.") Although Machule did not describe Atta as fanatically religious, he and the 9/11 Commission agreed that Atta was very religious. According to the American press, on the other hand, Mohamed Atta drank heavily. After downing five glasses of vodka, wrote *Newsweek*, Atta shouted an Arabic word that "roughly translates as 'F—k God.'"[60] Investigative reporter Daniel Hopsicker, who wrote a book about Atta, stated that Atta regularly went to strip clubs, hired prostitutes, drank heavily, and took cocaine. Atta even lived with a stripper for several months and then, after she kicked him out, came back and disemboweled her cat and dismembered its kittens.[61]

Could this be the same individual as Professor Machule's student Mohamed al-Emir, who would not even shake hands with a woman upon being introduced, and who never touched alcohol? "I would put my hand in the fire," said the professor, "that this Mohamed El-Amir I know will never taste or touch alcohol." Could the Atta described by Hopsicker and the American press be the young man whom this professor described as not a "bodyguard type" but "more a girl looking type"?[62] Could the man who disemboweled a cat and dismembered its kittens be the young man known to his father as a "gentle and tender boy," who was nicknamed "nightingale"?[63]

We are clearly talking about two different men. This is confirmed by the differences in their appearance. The American Atta was often described as having a hard, cruel face, and the standard FBI photo of him bears this out. The face of the Hamburg student was quite different, as photos available on the Internet show.[64] Also, his professor described him as "very small," being "one meter sixty-two" in height[65]—which means slightly under 5'4"—whereas the American Atta has been described as 5'8" and even 5'10" tall.[66]

One final reason to believe that these different descriptions apply to different men: The father of Mohamed al-Emir Atta reported that on September 12, before either of them had learned of the attacks, his son called him and they "spoke for two minutes about this and that."[67]

Other Members of al-Qaeda: There are also problems in relation to many of the other alleged hijackers. For example, the BBC reported that Waleed al-Shehri, who supposedly died along with Atta on American Flight 11, spoke to journalists and American authorities in Casablanca the following week.[68] Moreover, there were clearly two men going by the name Ziad Jarrah—the name of the alleged hijacker pilot of United Flight 93.[69] Accordingly, besides the fact the men labeled "the hijackers" were not devout Muslims, they may not have even been Muslims of any type.

And if that were not bad enough for the official story, evidence that purportedly shows that they hijacked the planes does not even prove that they were on the planes. All the evidence for this claim falls apart upon examination. I will illustrate this point with a few examples.[70]

Incriminating Evidence in Atta's Luggage?

Proof that al-Qaeda hijacked the planes was reportedly found in luggage belonging to Mohamed Atta that was discovered inside the Boston airport after the attacks. Why was the luggage there? Because, we were told, although Atta was already in Boston on September 10, he and another al-Qaeda operative, Abdul al-Omari, rented a blue Nissan and drove up to Portland, Maine. After staying overnight, they caught a commuter flight back to Boston early the next morning in order to transfer to American Airlines Flight 11. Although these men got to Boston in time to make the transfer, Atta's luggage did not make it.

This luggage, according to an FBI affidavit, contained much incriminating material, including a handheld flight computer, flight simulator manuals, two videotapes about Boeing aircraft, a slide-rule flight calculator, a copy of the Koran, and Atta's last will and testament.[71] This material was widely taken as proof that al-Qaeda was behind the attacks. When examined closely, however, the Atta-to-Portland story loses all credibility.

One problem is the very idea that Atta would have included these items in baggage that was to be transferred to Flight 11. What good would a flight computer and other flying aids do inside a suitcase in the plane's luggage compartment? Why would Atta have planned to take his will on a plane he planned to crash into the World Trade Center?

Another problem with the Atta-to-Portland story was the question of why he would have taken this trip. Atta was supposedly the ringleader of the hijackers as well as the intended pilot for Flight 11. If the commuter flight had been late, Atta would have had to call off the whole operation, which he had reportedly been planning for two years. Why in the world would Atta have taken the overnight trip to Portland? Both the FBI and the 9/11 Commission admitted that they had no answer to this question.[72]

We can see why those unanswerable questions exist by examining news stories that appeared immediately after the 9/11 attacks. According to these stories, the incriminating materials were found in a rented white Mitsubishi, which Atta had left in the Boston airport parking lot (not in Atta's luggage inside the airport). As reported in these news stories, two al-Qaeda members indeed drove the rented blue Nissan to Portland, stayed overnight, and then took the commuter flight back to Boston the next morning, in time to board Flight 11. But they—as material left in the car reportedly showed—were named Adnan and Ameer Bukhari (not Mohamed Atta and Abdul al-Omari).[73]

This story fell apart on the afternoon of September 13, when it was discovered that the Bukharis could not have been on Flight 11, because neither of them had died on 9/11: Ameer Bukhari had died the year before, whereas Adnan Bukhari was still alive.[74]

By the next day—September 14—the Associated Press started saying that Atta and a companion drove a blue Nissan to Portland, stayed overnight, and then took the commuter flight back to Boston. By September 16, a *Washington Post* story added the detail that the incriminating material had been found in Atta's luggage inside the Boston airport (rather than in a white Mitsubishi).[75] Within three days, in other words, the story had been transformed into what has remained the official story to this day.

Given the way in which the Atta-to-Portland story emerged, we cannot take seriously the idea that Atta's luggage provided reliable evidence about al-Qaeda's responsibility for 9/11.

Al-Qaeda Operatives on Airport Security Videos?

Frames from videos taken by airport security cameras supposedly showed al-Qaeda operatives checking into the airports at Boston and Washington, DC. But this photographic evidence was deceptive.

Shortly after the attacks, photos showing Mohamed Atta and Abdul al-Omari at an airport "were flashed round the world."[76] It was widely assumed that these photos were from the airport at Boston, whereas they were really from the airport in Portland, Maine. No photos showing Atta or any of the other alleged hijackers at Boston's Logan Airport were ever produced. We at best have photographic evidence that Atta and al-Omari were at the Portland Jetport. Moreover, a photo showing Atta and al-Omari passing through the security checkpoint is marked both 05:45 and 05:53[77]—which means that the photo could not be genuine.

On the day in July 2004 that *The 9/11 Commission Report* was published, the official story was said to have been corroborated by an airport video, about which the Associated Press wrote:

> Hijacker Khalid al-Mihdhar . . . passes through the security checkpoint at Dulles International Airport in Chantilly, Va., Sept. 11 2001, just hours before American Airlines Flight 77 crashed into the Pentagon in this image from a surveillance video.[78]

However, this video contains no evidence that it was taken by a security camera at Dulles on September 11. As Rowland Morgan and Ian Henshall pointed out:

> [A] normal security video has time and date burned into the integral video image by proprietary equipment according to an authenticated pattern, along with camera identification and the location that the camera covered. The video released in 2004 contained no such data.[79]

Also, although this so-called Dulles video contained a man who was identified by the 9/11 Commission as Hani Hanjour,[80] this man had a muscular build and a full head of hair, with no receding hairline, whereas Hanjour was thin and had a receding hairline (as shown by a photo taken six days before 9/11).[81]

Besides the fact the videos purportedly showing hijackers for Flights 11 and 77 are clearly inauthentic, there are no videos even purportedly showing the hijackers for the other two flights—even though, if the 19 "hijackers" had really checked into the Boston and Dulles airports, authentic security videos would exist to prove this claim.

A Hijacker's Voice on a Radio Transmission

Still more evidence for the existence of hijackers on the planes, the public was told, was provided by a message transmitted by a man on American 11. The man said:

> We have some planes. Just stay quiet, and you'll be okay. We are returning to the airport. . . . Nobody move. Everything will be okay. If you try to make any moves, you'll endanger yourself and the airplane. Just stay quiet. . . . Nobody move please. We are going back to the airport. Don't try to make any stupid moves.[82]

The 9/11 Commission Report, employing the first line of this message ("We have some planes") as the title of its first chapter, stated that this transmission came from "American 11."

However, there was no evidence that this transmission came from American Flight 11 (or any of the other 9/11 planes). According to the FAA's "Summary of Air Traffic Hijack Events," published September 17, 2001, these messages came "from an unknown origin."[83] Bill Peacock, the FAA's air traffic director, said: "We didn't know where the transmission came from."[84] This transmission, in other words, provided no evidence that hijackers had taken control of American Flight 11.

Passports at the Crash Sites

The public's belief that there were al-Qaeda terrorists on the planes was bolstered by the claim that some of their passports had been found at crash sites. But were these reports believable? For example, the FBI claimed that, while searching the streets after the destruction of the World Trade Center, they discovered the passport of Satam al-Suqami, one of the (alleged) hijackers on American Airlines Flight 11, which had (reportedly) crashed into the North Tower.[85] For this to be true, the passport would have had to survive not only the fire ignited by the plane's jet fuel, but also the disintegration of the North Tower, which evidently pulverized much of the building's contents into fine particles of dust. But this claim was too absurd to pass the giggle test: "[T]he idea that [this] passport had escaped from that inferno unsinged," remarked a British commentator, "would [test] the credulity of the staunchest supporter of the FBI's crackdown on terrorism."[86]

By 2004, the claim had been modified to say that "a passer-by picked it up and gave it to a NYPD detective shortly before the World Trade Center towers collapsed."[87] So, rather than needing to survive the destruction of the North Tower, the passport merely needed to escape from al-Suqami's pocket or luggage, then from the plane's cabin, and then from the North Tower without being destroyed or even singed by the giant fireball that erupted when this building was struck. (In *Flat Earth News*, Nick Davies reported the opinion of some senior British sources that "the discovery of a terrorist's passport in the rubble of the Twin Towers in September 2001 had been 'a throwdown,' i.e. it was placed there by somebody official."[88])

An al-Qaeda Headband at a Crash Site?

Some of the "phone calls from the planes" described the "hijackers" as wearing red headbands. For example, the *Washington Post*, discussing United Airlines Flight 93, said:

> [P]assenger Jeremy Glick used a cell phone to tell his wife, Lyzbeth, . . . that the Boeing 757's cockpit had been taken over by three Middle Eastern-looking men. . . . The terrorists, wearing red headbands, had ordered the pilots, flight attendants and passengers to the rear of the plane.[89]

According to the FBI, one of these headbands was found at the Flight 93 crash site along with Ziad Jarrah's passport.[90] But former CIA agent Milt Bearden, who helped train the Mujahideen fighters in Afghanistan, pointed out that it would have been very unlikely that members of al-Qaeda would have worn such headbands: Al-Qaeda is a Sunni movement, whereas the red headband is "a uniquely Shi'a Muslim adornment," dating "back to the formation of the Shi'a sect."[91] Does it not seem likely that the headband was planted by people who failed to understand the difference between Shi'a and Sunni Muslims?

Passenger Manifests

The public has widely assumed, due to misleading claims, that the names of the alleged hijackers were on the passenger manifests for the four flights.[92] However, the manifests for the four airliners did not contain the names of any of the alleged hijackers. They, in fact, contained no Arab names whatsoever.[93]

It might appear that this problem had been rectified in 2005, thanks to the claim by *Los Angeles Times* reporter Terry McDermott that he had received passenger manifests that contain the names of the (alleged) hijackers.[94] However, the evidence presented by the FBI to the Moussaoui trial in the following year (2006) did not include these purported manifests.[95] And there would have been good reason to consider them inauthentic. Although the FBI claimed that it had received flight manifests from the airlines by the morning of 9/11, the "manifests" that appeared in 2005 had names that were not known to the FBI until a day or more after 9/11.[96] These 2005 "manifests," therefore, could not have been the original manifests for the four 9/11 flights.

The American Airlines Flight 77 Autopsy Report

The absence of Arab names on the flight manifests led Dr. Thomas Olmsted—a psychiatrist and former Navy officer—to wonder if there were any Arab names on the autopsy list for American Airlines Flight 77, which reportedly struck the Pentagon. Having sent a FOIA request to the Armed Forces Institute of Pathology, which carried out the autopsy, he received, after a considerable wait, the autopsy list for AA 77. What he discovered was indicated by the title of his report: "Still No Arabs on Flight 77."[97] Claims to the contrary cannot survive scrutiny.[98]

Failure to Squawk the Hijack Code

The public has been led to believe that all the evidence about what happened on board the four airliners supported the claim that they were taken over by hijackers. This claim, however, was contradicted by something that did *not* happen. If pilots have any reason to believe that a hijacking may be in process, they are trained to enter the standard hijack code (7500) into their transponders to alert controllers on the ground. This is called "squawking" the hijack code. But controllers on 9/11 did not receive the code. Why not?

Two months after 9/11, a *Boston Globe* story said that "it appears that the hijackers' entry was surprising enough that the pilots did not have a chance to broadcast a traditional distress call."[99] The very day after 9/11, however, CNN had pointed out: "The action takes seconds."[100] Squawking the hijack code would have taken much less time than hijackers would have required to break into the pilots' cabins. A reporter at the Moussaoui trial, where the (purported) tapes from United 93 had been played, wrote:

> In those tapes, the pilots shouted as hijackers broke into the cockpit. "Mayday! Mayday! Mayday!" a pilot screamed in the first tape. In

the second tape, 30 seconds later, a pilot shouted: "Mayday! Get out of here! Get out of here!"[101]

According to these tapes, therefore, the pilots were still alive and coherent 30 seconds after realizing that hijackers were breaking into the cockpit.

So why did neither of the two pilots on United 93 squawk the hijack code while al-Qaeda hijackers were breaking into the cabin? And why did none of the pilots on any of the other 9/11 flights squawk the code? The fact that the hijack code was not squawked provides very strong evidence that the official story about the 9/11 planes, according to which the cabins were taken over by hijackers, is false.

The Reported Phone Calls from the Planes

It has been widely believed that we knew about the existence of hijackers on the airliners by means of numerous phone calls from passengers and crew members, in which they reported the hijackings. According to the 9/11 Commission: "Reports from two flight attendants [on American 11] tell us most of what we know about how the hijacking happened."[102] As we will see in Chapter 5, however, the reported phone calls from passengers and flight attendants on the 9/11 flights were evidently faked.

CONCLUSION

It appears, therefore, that 9/11 was the most elaborate example yet of a false-flag attack, which occurs when a country, wanting to attack another country, orchestrates attacks on its own people while planting evidence to implicate the other country. Hitler did this when he was ready to attack Poland, which started the European part of World War II; Japan did it when it was ready to attack Manchuria, which started the Asian part of that war. In 1962, the Pentagon's Joint Chiefs of Staff proposed false-flag attacks killing American citizens to provide a pretext for invading Cuba.[103] This proposal was not put into effect because it was vetoed by President Kennedy. But in 2001, the White House wanted to attack Afghanistan, Iraq, and several other predominantly Muslim countries—including Libya, which is the latest country to be attacked by America.[104] And so, it appears, evidence was planted to implicate Muslims.

In any case, the official rationale for our presence in Afghanistan is a lie. The government has been there for other reasons. Critics have offered various suggestions as to the most important of those reasons.[105] Whatever be the answer to that question, however, we have not been there to apprehend the terrorists responsible for the 9/11 attacks. Besides never being legally justified, the war in Afghanistan has not even been morally justified.

This war has been an abomination. In addition to the thousands of US and other NATO troops who have been killed or impaired for life, physically and/or mentally, the US-led invasion-and-occupation of Afghanistan has resulted in a huge number of Afghan casualties, with estimates of death running from several hundred thousand to several million.[106] But whatever the true number, the fact is that the United States has produced a great amount of death and misery—sometimes even bombing funerals and wedding parties—in this poor country, which had already suffered terribly and that, even if the official story were true, had not attacked America. The fact that the official story is a lie makes our war crimes even worse.

Besides the fact that the war in Afghanistan has been a crime against peace—which American leaders at the end of World War II declared to be "the supreme crime"—it should also be understood to be a crime against democracy. This point will be introduced in Chapter 4 and developed more fully in Chapter 9.[107]

2. The Destruction of the World Trade Center: Why Have Otherwise Rational Journalists Endorsed Miracles?

It has now been ten years since the 9/11 attacks. From the beginning, a few people started arguing that the official account of the attacks—that they were carried out by foreign Muslims in other countries—was false, and that 9/11 was an inside job, carried out by people and agencies in our own government. An emerging movement to make this case came to be called "the 9/11 Truth Movement."

According to several left-leaning critics of the 9/11 Truth Movement, some of its central claims, especially about the destruction of the World Trade Center, show its members to be scientifically challenged. In the opinion of some of these critics, moreover, claims made by members of this movement are sometimes unscientific in the strongest possible sense, implying an acceptance of magic and miracles.

After documenting this charge in the first part of this chapter, I show in the second part that the opposite is the case: On the one hand, these left-leaning critics have endorsed the official account of the destruction of the World Trade Center, even though it implies many miracles. On the other hand, the 9/11 Truth Movement, in developing an alternative hypothesis, has done so under the assumption that the laws of nature did not take a holiday on 9/11. In the third part of this chapter, I ask these left-leaning critics some questions raised by the fact that it is they, not members of the 9/11 Truth Movement, who have endorsed a conspiracy theory replete with miracle stories as well as other absurdities.

I The Charge that 9/11 Truth Theories Rest on Unscientific, Even Magical, Beliefs

Several left-leaning critics of the 9/11 Truth Movement charge its members with relying on claims that are contradicted by good science and, in some cases, reflect a belief in magic. By "magic," they mean miracles, understood as violations of basic principles of the physical sciences.

For example, Alexander Cockburn, who has referred to members of the 9/11 Truth Movement as "9/11 conspiracy nuts,"[1] quoted with approval a philosopher who, speaking of "the 9-11 conspiracy cult," said that its "main engine . . . is . . . the death of any conception of evidence," resulting in "the ascendancy of magic over common sense, let alone reason."[2] Also, Cockburn assured his readers: "The conspiracy theory that the World Trade Centre towers were demolished by explosive charges previously placed within them is probably impossible."[3] With regard to Building 7 of the World Trade Center, Cockburn claimed (in 2006) that the (2002) report by FEMA was "more than adequate."[4]

Likewise, George Monbiot, referring to members of the 9/11 Truth Movement as "fantasists," "conspiracy idiots," and "morons," charged that they "believe that [the Bush regime] is capable of magic."[5]

Matt Taibbi, saying that the "9/11 conspiracy theory is so shamefully stupid" and referring to its members as "idiots," wrote with derision about the "alleged scientific impossibilities" in the official account of 9/11; about the claim that "the towers couldn't have fallen the way they did [without the aid of explosives]"; of the view (held by "9/11 Truthers") that "it isn't the plane crashes that topple the buildings, but bombs planted in the Towers that do the trick"; and of "the supposed anomalies of physics involved with the collapse of WTC-7." He had been assured by "scientist friends," he added, that "[a]ll of the 9/11 science claims" are "rank steaming bullshit."[6]

Chris Hayes, writing in *The Nation* in 2006, did not stoop to the kind of name-calling employed by Cockburn, Monbiot, and Taibbi. He also knew, he admitted, of "eyewitness accounts of [people] who heard explosions in the World Trade Center." And he was aware that "jet fuel burns at 1,500 degrees Fahrenheit [whereas] steel melts at 2,500." He asserted, nevertheless, that "the evidence shows [a 9/11 conspiracy] to be virtually impossible," so that the 9/11 Truth Movement's conspiracy theory is "wrongheaded and a terrible waste of time."[7]

Noam Chomsky has also declared that the available facts, when approached scientifically, refute the 9/11 Truth Movement. Speaking of evidence provided by this movement to show that 9/11 "was planned by the Bush Administration," Chomsky declared: "If you look at the evidence, anybody who knows anything about the sciences would instantly discount that evidence."[8] In spite of his dismissive attitude, however, Chomsky in 2006 gave some helpful advice to people who believe they have physical evidence refuting the official account:

> There are ways to assess that: submit it to specialists . . . who have the requisite background in civil-mechanical engineering, materials science, building construction, etc., for review and analysis. . . . Or, . . . submit it to a serious journal for peer review and publication. To my knowledge, there isn't a single submission.[9]

In These Times writer Terry Allen, in a 2006 essay entitled "The 9/11 Faith Movement," assured her readers that "the facts [do not] support the conspiracists' key charge that World Trade Center buildings were destroyed by pre-positioned explosives."[10]

In an essay posted at AlterNet a few months after 9/11, David Corn used a purely a priori argument to demonstrate—at least to his own satisfaction—that 9/11 could not have been an inside job: "U.S. officials would [not have been] . . . good [capable] enough, evil enough, or gutsy enough." In 2009, after having been silent about 9/11 for the intervening years, he addressed the issue again. Referring to "9/11 conspiracy silliness," "9/11 conspiracy poison," and "9/11 fabulists," Corn declared:

> The 9/11 conspiracy . . . was always a load of bunk. You don't have to be an expert on skyscraper engineering . . . to know that [this theory] make[s] no sense.[11]

Corn thereby implied that, whereas anyone can know that the 9/11 Truth Movement's conspiracy theory is false, those people who *are* "expert[s] on skyscraper engineering" would have even more certain knowledge of this fact.

As to how people (such as himself) who are not experts on such matters could know this movement's conspiracy theory to be "a load of bunk," Corn again employed his three-point a priori argument, as re-worded in a 2009 *Mother Jones* essay, according to which the Bush administration was "not that evil," "not that ballsy," and "not that competent."[12] Corn even referred to his three-point argument as "a tutorial that should persuade anyone that the 9/11 theory makes no sense." Although this "tutorial" does *not*, of course, convince members of the 9/11 Truth Movement, Corn explained this fact by saying: "I have learned from experience that people who believe this stuff are not open to persuasion."[13]

In any case, although his argument against the inside-job theory was almost entirely a priori, he did make the above-mentioned suggestion that one's a priori certitude would be reinforced by people, such as "expert[s] on skyscraper engineering," who have relevant types of expertise to evaluate the empirical evidence.

A fuller statement of the general claim made by these authors—that the 9/11 Truth Movement is based on unscientific claims—was formulated by Matthew Rothschild, the editor of *The Progressive*. In an essay entitled "Enough of the 9/11 Conspiracy Theories Already," Rothschild wrote:

> Here's what the conspiracists believe: 9/11 was an inside job. . . . [T]he Twin Towers fell not because of the impact of the airplanes and the ensuing fires but because [of] explosives. Building 7, another high-rise at the World Trade Center that fell on 9/11, also came down by planted explosives. . . . I'm amazed at how many people give credence to these theories. . . . [S]ome of the best engineers in the country have studied these questions and come up with perfectly logical, scientific explanations for what happened. . . . At bottom, the 9/11 conspiracy theories are profoundly irrational and unscientific. It is more than passing strange that progressives, who so revere science on such issues as tobacco, stem cells, evolution, and global warming, are so willing to abandon science and give in to fantasy on the subject of 9/11.[14]

However, in spite of the confidence with which these critics have made their charges, the truth is the complete opposite: It is the official account of the destruction of the World Trade Center, which has been endorsed by the National Institute of Standards and Technology (NIST), that is profoundly unscientific (partly because it ignores a massive amount of evidence pointing to the use of explosives[15]), and it is precisely for this reason that the 9/11 Truth Movement has come up with an alternative explanation—namely, that the WTC buildings were brought down in the procedure known as "controlled demolition."

II Miracles Implied by NIST's Explanation of the WTC's Destruction

The main reason why NIST's theory of the destruction of the World Trade Center is profoundly unscientific is that it cannot be accepted without endorsing miracles, in the sense of violations of fundamental principles of physics and chemistry. The fact that such violations are ruled out by science has been treated with humor in a cartoon involving a mathematical proof on a chalkboard. Most of the steps consist of mathematical equations. But the second step simply says: "Then a miracle happens."[16] This is funny, because it is universally understood in the scientific community that a scientific explanation of some phenomenon cannot include the affirmation of a miracle, even implicitly.

And yet this is what NIST does. NIST's theory of the destruction of the World Trade Center, in fact, includes the affirmation of several miracles. I will demonstrate this point in terms of nine miracles implied by NIST's accounts of the destruction of Building 7 of the World Trade Center (WTC 7) and the Twin Towers (WTC 1 and 2).

1. The Fire-Induced Collapse of WTC 7: An Apparent Miracle

WTC 7 was a 47-story building that came down at 5:21 PM that day. In discussing the miracles implied by NIST's account of this building's collapse, I begin with a fact about WTC 7's collapse that at least *appears* to entail a miracle: that it was (according to the official account) the first steel-framed high-rise building in the known universe to be brought down solely by fire. The Twin Towers were hit by airliners, so the official account could attribute their collapses to the airplane impacts as well as to the ensuing fires. But WTC 7 was not hit by a plane, so its collapse apparently had to be attributed to fire alone.

The unprecedented nature of a fire-induced collapse of a steel-framed high-rise building was expressed a couple of months after 9/11 by *New York Times* reporter James Glanz. Calling the collapse of WTC 7 "a mystery," Glanz reported that "experts said no building like it, a modern, steel-reinforced high-rise, had ever collapsed because of an uncontrolled fire." Glanz also quoted a structural engineer as saying: "[W]ithin the structural engineering community, [WTC 7] is considered to be much more important to understand [than the Twin Towers]," because engineers had no answer to the question, "why did 7 come down?"[17]

The mystery was not lessened in 2002 when FEMA issued the first official report on this building's collapse. Saying that its "best hypothesis" was that flaming debris from the collapse of the North Tower had ignited diesel fuel stored in the building, resulting in large, steel-weakening fires that made the building collapse, FEMA admitted that this hypothesis had "only a low probability of occurrence"[18] (although Alexander Cockburn years later, as we saw above, would declare this report to be "more than adequate").

This cautionary statement by FEMA did not, however, prevent defenders of the official account from claiming that WTC 7's collapse was not really very mysterious after all. In a 2006 book, *Popular Mechanics* told its readers what they could probably expect to find in the report on this building to be put out by NIST—which had taken over from FEMA the responsibility for issuing the official reports on the Twin Towers and WTC 7. Citing NIST's "current working hypothesis," *Popular Mechanics* said that WTC 7's diesel fuel had probably fed the fires "for up to seven hours."[19]

Also, using NIST's then-current thinking in order to claim that "WTC 7 was far more compromised by falling debris than the FEMA report indicated," *Popular Mechanics* argued that critics could not reject the official account on the grounds that it would make WTC 7 the first steel-framed high-rise to have failed "because of fire alone," because, *Popular Mechanics* claimed, the causes of WTC 7's collapse were analogous to the causes of the collapses of WTC 1 and WTC 2: "A combination of physical damage from falling debris [analogous to the damage caused in the Twin Towers by the airplane impacts] and prolonged exposure to the resulting [diesel-fuel-fed] fires [analogous to the jet-fuel-fed fires in the Twin Towers]."[20]

Popular Mechanics called this twofold explanation a "conclusion" that had been reached by "hundreds of experts from academia and private industry, as well as the government." This claim evidently impressed many people, including Chris Hayes and Matthew Rothschild, both of whom said that *Popular Mechanics* had disproved the claims of the 9/11 Truth Movement. Rothschild, repeating *Popular Mechanics'* twofold explanation, wrote:

> Building 7 . . . is a favorite of the conspiracy theorists, since the planes did not strike this structure. But the building did sustain damage from the debris of the Twin Towers. "On about a third of the face to the center and to the bottom—approximately ten stories—

about 25 percent of the depth of the building was scooped out," Shyam Sunder, the lead investigator for the National Institute of Standards and Technology, told *Popular Mechanics*. What's more, the fire in the building lasted for about eight hours, in part because there were fuel tanks in the basement and on some of the floors.[21]

Hayes, saying that "*Popular Mechanics* assembled a team of engineers, physicists, flight experts and the like to critically examine some of the Truth Movement's most common claims," reported that these experts "found them almost entirely without merit." This claim by *Popular Mechanics* evidently settled the matter for Hayes.[22]

Also, although Terry Allen did not mention *Popular Mechanics*, her article clearly depended on it. Assuring her readers that she had found it "relatively easy" to undermine the "facts" employed by the 9/11 Truth Movement, she wrote:

> Many conspiracists offer the collapse of WTC Building 7 as the strongest evidence for the kind of controlled demolition that would prove a plot. Although not hit by planes, it was damaged by debris, and suffered fires eventually fueled by up to 42,000 gallons of diesel fuel stored near ground level.[23]

Like Rothschild, therefore, she gave the same twofold explanation for WTC 7's collapse that had been provided by *Popular Mechanics*.[24]

However, when NIST finally issued its WTC 7 report in 2008, it did not affirm either element in the twofold explanation that had been proffered by *Popular Mechanics*. With regard to the first element, NIST said: "[F]uel oil fires did not play a role in the collapse of WTC 7."[25] With regard to the second element, NIST said: "Other than initiating the fires in WTC 7, the damage from the debris from WTC 1 [the North Tower] had little effect on initiating the collapse of WTC 7."[26]

This second point means that, contrary to what *Popular Mechanics* had claimed it would say, NIST actually asserted that WTC 7 was brought down by fire, at least primarily. In NIST's words, the collapse of WTC 7 was "the first known instance of the total collapse of a [steel-framed] tall building primarily due to fires."[27]

One ambiguity needs clearing up: Although in these just-quoted statements NIST seemed to indicate that the debris damage had "little effect" on initiating the collapse, so that this collapse was only *primarily* (rather than *entirely*) due to fire, NIST generally treated fire as the *sole* cause: Besides repeatedly speaking of a "fire-induced" collapse,[28] a press release by NIST in August 2008 referred to the collapse of WTC 7 as "the first known instance of fire causing the total collapse of a tall building." This press release, moreover, quoted lead investigator Shyam Sunder as saying: "Our study found that the fires in WTC 7 . . . caused an extraordinary event."[28] The brief version of NIST's final report said: "Even without the structural damage, WTC 7 would have collapsed from fires having the same characteristics as those experienced on September 11, 2001."[30] The long version said: "WTC 7 sustained damage to its exterior as a result of falling debris from the collapse of WTC 1, but this damage was found to have no effect on the collapse initiating event."[31]

It is not wrong, therefore, to say that NIST portrayed WTC 7 as the first (and thus far only) steel-framed high-rise building to have come down because of fire alone. NIST said, in other words, precisely what *Popular Mechanics*, knowing that claims about unprecedented physical events are deeply suspect, had assured people it would *not* say.

In doing so, moreover, NIST contradicted both parts of *Popular Mechanics'* explanation for WTC 7's collapse, which, according to Rothschild and Allen, had provided the basis for discounting the 9/11 Truth Movement's claims about this collapse. To review: Rothschild said that the official account was credible, contrary to the Truth Movement's claims, because "the building did sustain damage from the debris of the Twin Towers" and the "fire in the building lasted for about eight hours," due to the "fuel tanks in the basement and on some of the floors."[32] Allen likewise said the official account was believable because, although WTC 7 was not hit by a plane, "it was damaged by debris, and suffered fires eventually fueled by up to 42,000 gallons of diesel fuel stored near ground level."[33]

But then, when NIST later denied that either the debris-damage or the diesel fuel played a role in the collapse of WTC 7, Rothschild and Allen did not retract their prior assurances. It seems that they, in effect, simply said—like Gilda Radner on *Saturday Night Live* in the 1970s—"Never mind." Their attitude seemed to be, in other words, that whatever the government says, that is what they will believe. Whatever kind of journalism this is, it is certainly not critical, truth-seeking journalism.

In any case, NIST's claim that WTC 7 suffered an unprecedented, fire-induced collapse is made even more problematic by the fact that the fires in this building were relatively unimpressive, compared with fires in some other steel-framed high-rises. In 1991, a huge fire in

Philadelphia's One Meridian Plaza lasted for 18 hours and gutted eight of the building's 38 floors.[34] In Caracas in 2004, a fire in a 50-story building raged for 17 hours, completely gutting the building's top 20 floors. In neither case, however, did the building, or even a single floor, collapse.[35]

In WTC 7, by contrast, there were long-lasting fires on only six of the building's 47 floors, according to NIST, and by "long-lasting," NIST meant only that they lasted up to seven hours.[36] It would be exceedingly strange, therefore, if fire had produced a total collapse of this building. The claim becomes even stranger when one discovers that NIST had no evidence that the fires on any of the floors lasted for much over three hours.[37]

Accordingly, besides undermining the confident explanations of WTC 7's collapse offered by *Popular Mechanics*, NIST's conclusion about this building—that it was the first steel-framed high-rise building ever to be brought down by fire—appears to constitute a rather remarkable miracle-claim.

2. WTC 7's Collapse: A Perfect Imitation of an Implosion

More clearly miraculous, given the official account, was the *precise way* in which WTC 7 collapsed: symmetrically (straight down, with an almost perfectly horizontal roofline), into its own footprint. In order for this symmetrical collapse to occur, the top section of all the (vertical) steel columns supporting the building had to fail simultaneously. There were 82 of these columns, so the fire theory of WTC 7's collapse entails that the fires in this building caused the top section of all 82 of these columns to fail at the same instant.

Such a symmetrical failure would have been essentially impossible even if the building had been entirely engulfed by fire, so that all the floors would have been uniformly covered with fire. As it was, however, there were fires on only a few floors, and these fires never covered an entire floor. The official account implies, therefore, that a very asymmetrical pattern of fires produced an entirely symmetrical collapse. If that is not a genuine miracle, it will do until one comes along.

Another problem is the fact that, even if a symmetrical, total collapse could be caused by an asymmetrical pattern of fires, a fire theory could not explain the *sudden onset* of WTC 7's collapse. *Popular Mechanics*, which is unreliable on every aspect of 9/11 (as I showed in my 2007 book, *Debunking 9/11 Debunking*[38]), apparently misled Chris Hayes on this point by suggesting otherwise. Attempting to illustrate his claim that *Popular Mechanics* had shown the core ideas of the 9/11 Truth Movement to be "almost entirely without merit," Hayes wrote:

> To pick just one example, steel might not melt at 1,500 degrees [Fahrenheit], the temperature at which jet fuel burns, but it does begin to lose a lot of its strength, enough to cause the support beams to fail.[39]

However, even if the fire could have heated the steel up to this temperature in the time available (which would have been impossible[40]), the fire would have weakened the steel gradually, causing it to start sagging. Videos would, therefore, show deformations in the building before it came down. But they do not. One moment the building was perfectly immobile, and the next moment, as videos show,[41] it was accelerating downward in free fall (the significance of free fall will be discussed below). As Australian chemist Frank Legge has observed: "There is no sign of the slow start that would be expected if collapse was caused by the gradual softening of the steel."[42]

Because of these two features of the collapse, people knowing anything about such things can tell, simply by seeing a video of WTC 7's collapse, that it was brought down in the procedure known as "controlled demolition." For example, Daniel Hofnung, an engineer in Paris, has written:

> In the years after [the] 9/11 events, I thought that all I read in professional reviews and French newspapers was true. The first time I understood that it was impossible was when I saw a film about the collapse of WTC 7.[43]

Kansas City civil engineer Chester Gearhart wrote:

> I have watched the construction of many large buildings and also have personally witnessed 5 controlled demolitions in Kansas City. When I saw the towers fall on 9/11, I knew something was wrong and my first instinct was that it was impossible. When I saw building 7 fall, I *knew* it was a controlled demolition.[44]

Jack Keller, emeritus professor of engineering at Utah State University (who had been named by *Scientific American* as one of the world's leaders in using science and technology to benefit society), wrote simply of WTC 7's collapse: "Obviously it was the result of controlled demolition."[45]

In revealing the collapse of WTC 7 to be an example of controlled demolition, moreover, the videos show it to be the type of controlled demolition known as "implosion," in which explosives and/or incendiaries are used to slice the building's steel support columns so as to cause the building to collapse into its own footprint.

In 2006, for example, a Dutch filmmaker asked Danny Jowenko, the owner of a controlled demolition company in the Netherlands, to comment on a video of the collapse of WTC 7, without telling him what it was. (Jowenko had been unaware that a third building had collapsed in New York on 9/11.) After viewing the video, Jowenko said: "They simply blew up columns, and the rest caved in afterwards. . . . This is controlled demolition." When asked if he was certain, he replied: "Absolutely, it's been imploded. This was a hired job. A team of experts did this."[46]

Moreover, the reason to implode a building, rather than simply causing it to fall over sideways, is to avoid damaging nearby buildings, and engineering an implosion is no mean feat. An implosion, in the words of a controlled demolition website, is "by far the trickiest type of explosive project," which "only a handful of blasting companies in the world . . . possess enough experience . . . to perform."[47] Mark Loizeaux, the president of the aforementioned demolition firm, Controlled Demolition, Inc., has explained why: "[T]o bring [a building] down . . . so . . . no other structure is harmed," the demolition must be "completely planned," using "the right explosive [and] the right pattern of laying the charges."[48]

Would it not be a miracle if a fire-induced collapse, based on scattered fires on a few of WTC 7's floors, had produced a collapse that perfectly imitated the kind of planned, controlled demolition that can be carried out by only a few companies in the world?

Chris Hayes suggested that the 9/11 Truth Movement, by doubting the government's account of 9/11, exemplifies a resurgence of the "paranoid style" in American politics. But in accepting the government's account, as defended by the pseudo-scientific *Popular Mechanics*, he illustrated the other target of his article, the "credulous style," which, he pointed out, is generally exemplified by the American media.[49] Surely, however, his credulity does not extend to the acceptance of miracles.

3. WTC 7's Descent in Absolute Free Fall

Even if some readers question whether the two previously discussed features of the collapse of WTC 7, when understood within the framework of NIST's fire theory, imply miracles, there can be no doubt about a third feature: the now-accepted (albeit generally unpublicized) fact that WTC 7 came down in absolute free fall for over two seconds.

Although scientists in the 9/11 Truth Movement had long been pointing out that this building descended at the same rate as a free-falling object, or at least virtually so, NIST had long denied this. As late as August 2008, when NIST issued its report on WTC 7 in the form of a Draft for Public Comment, it claimed that the time it took for the upper floors—the only floors that are visible on the videos—to come down "was approximately 40 percent longer than the computed free fall time and was consistent with physical principles."[50]

As this statement implied, any assertion that the building *did* come down in free fall, assuming a non-engineered collapse, would *not* be consistent with physical principles—meaning basic laws of Newtonian physics. Explaining why not during a "WTC 7 Technical Briefing" on August 26, 2008, NIST's Shyam Sunder said:

> [A] free fall time would be [the fall time of] an object that has no structural components below it. . . . [T]he . . . time that it took . . . for those 17 floors to disappear [was roughly 40 percent longer than free fall]. And that is not at all unusual, because there was structural resistance that was provided in this particular case. And you had a sequence of structural failures that had to take place. Everything was not instantaneous.[51]

In saying this, Sunder was presupposing NIST's theory that the building was brought down by fire, which, if it could have produced a collapse of any type, could have produced only a *progressive* collapse.

In response, high-school physics teacher David Chandler, who was allowed to submit a question to this briefing, challenged Sunder's denial of free fall, stating that Sunder's "40 percent longer" claim contradicted "a publicly visible, easily measurable quantity."[52] Chandler then placed a video on the Internet showing that, by measuring this publicly visible quantity, anyone understanding elementary physics could see that "for about two and a half seconds. . . , the acceleration of the building is indistinguishable from freefall."[53] (This is, of course, free fall through the air, not through a vacuum.)

In its final report on WTC 7, which came out in November 2008,

NIST—rather amazingly—admitted free fall. Dividing the building's descent into three stages, NIST described the second phase as "a freefall descent over approximately eight stories at gravitational acceleration for approximately 2.25 s[econds]."[54] NIST thereby accepted Chandler's case—except for maintaining that the building was in absolute free fall for only 2.25, not 2.5, seconds (a trivial difference). NIST thereby affirmed a miracle, meaning a violation of one or more laws of physics.

Why this would be a miracle was explained by Chandler, who said: "Free fall can only be achieved if there is zero resistance to the motion."[55] In other words, the upper portion of Building 7 could have come down in free fall only if something had suddenly removed all the steel and concrete in the lower part of the building, which would have otherwise provided resistance (to make a considerable under-statment). If everything had not been removed and the upper floors had come down in free fall anyway, even if for only a fraction of a second, this would have been a miracle—meaning a violation of physical principles. Explaining one of the physical principles involved, Chandler said:

> Anything at an elevated height has gravitational potential energy. If it falls, and none of the energy is used for other things along the way, all of that energy is converted into kinetic energy—the energy of motion, and we call it 'free fall.' If any of the energy is used for other purposes, there will be less kinetic energy, so the fall will be slower. In the case of a falling building, the only way it can go into free fall is if an external force removes the supporting structure. None of the gravitational potential energy of the building is available for this purpose, or it would slow the fall of the building.[56]

That was what Sunder himself had explained, on NIST's behalf, the previous August, saying that a free-falling object would be one "that has no structural components below it" to offer resistance. But NIST then in November, while still under Sunder's leadership and still defending its fire theory of WTC 7's collapse, agreed that, as an empirical fact, free fall happened. For a period of 2.25 seconds, NIST admitted, the descent of WTC 7 was characterized by "gravitational acceleration (free fall)."[57]

Besides pointing out that the free fall descent of WTC 7 implied that the building had been professionally demolished, Chandler observed that this conclusion is reinforced by two features of the collapse mentioned above:

[P]articularly striking is the suddenness of onset of free fall. Acceleration doesn't build up gradually. . . . The building went from full support to zero support, instantly. . . . One moment, the building is holding; the next moment it lets go and is in complete free fall. . . . The onset of free fall was not only sudden; it extended across the whole width of the building. . . . The fact that the roof stayed level shows the building was in free fall across the entire width. The collapse we see cannot be due to a column failure, or a few column failures, or a sequence of column failures. All 24 interior columns and 58 perimeter columns had to have been removed . . . simultaneously, within a small fraction of a second.[58]

For its part, NIST, knowing that it had affirmed a miracle by agreeing that WTC 7 had entered into free fall, no longer claimed that its analysis was consistent with the laws of physics. Back in its August draft, in which it was still claiming that the collapse occurred 40 percent slower than free fall, NIST had said—in a claim made three times—that its analysis was "consistent with physical principles."[59] In the final report, however, every instance of this phrase was removed. NIST thereby almost explicitly admitted that its report on WTC 7, by affirming absolute free fall while continuing to deny that either incendiaries or explosives had been employed, is *not* consistent with basic principles of physics.

Accordingly, now that it is established that WTC 7 came down in absolute free fall for over two seconds, one cannot accept the official theory, according to which this building was not professionally demolished, without implying that at least one miracle happened on 9/11.

George Monbiot, as we saw, described members of this movement as "morons" who "believe that [the Bush regime] is capable of magic."[60] Unless Monbiot, upon becoming aware of NIST's admission of free fall, changes his stance, he will imply that al-Qaeda is capable of magic.

Matthew Rothschild said he was "amazed" at how many people hold the "profoundly irrational and unscientific" belief that "Building 7 . . . came down by planted explosives." Given the fact that progressive members of the 9/11 Truth Movement "so revere science on such issues as tobacco, stem cells, evolution, and global warming," Rothschild continued, it is "more than passing strange that [they] are so willing to abandon science and give in to fantasy on the subject of 9/11."[61]

NIST's report on WTC 7, however, provided the final proof that the 9/11 Truth Movement had been right all along—that those progressives who credulously accept the Bush-Cheney administration's explanation for WTC 7's collapse are the ones who "abandon science and give in to fantasy on the subject of 9/11."

4. The Twin Towers: Descending in Virtual Free Fall

Miracles are implied not only by the official account of WTC 7's collapse but also by the official account of the destruction of the Twin Towers. According to this account, the North Tower (WTC 1) and the South Tower (WTC 2) came down because of three and only three causes: (i) the airplane impacts, which caused structural damage; (ii) the ensuing fires, which were initially fed and spread by jet fuel from the planes; and (iii) gravity. Neither explosives nor incendiaries helped bring the buildings down. Internationally known architect David A. Johnson has written:

> [A]s a professional city planner in New York, I knew those buildings and their design. . . . So I was well aware of the strength of the core with its steel columns. . . . When I saw the rapid collapse of the towers, I knew that they could not come down the way they did without explosives and the severing of core columns at the base. . . . Moreover, the symmetrical collapse is strong evidence of a controlled demolition. A building falling from asymmetrical structural failure would not collapse so neatly, nor so rapidly. . . . [T]he official explanation doesn't hold water.[62]

Johnson was saying, in short, that the official story required miracles.

One of the miracles implicit in this account is that, although each building had 287 steel support columns—240 perimeter columns and 47 massive core columns—and although neither explosives nor incendiaries were used to destroy these columns, each building came down, as NIST itself put it, "essentially in free fall."[63] How would that have been possible?

According to NIST, each airliner took out several perimeter and core columns at its area of impact and also created huge fires, which began weakening the steel. After a period of time (56 minutes for the South Tower, 102 minutes for the North Tower), "the massive top section of [each] building at and above the fire and impact floors" fell down on the lower section, which "could not resist the tremendous energy released by [the top section's] downward movement."[64] Accordingly, NIST's report said:

Since the stories below the level of collapse initiation provided little resistance to the tremendous energy released by the falling building mass, the building section above came down essentially in free fall, as seen in videos.[65]

Trying to describe more fully its theory of how this happened, NIST wrote:

The potential energy released by the downward movement of the large building mass far exceeded the capacity of the intact structure below to absorb that energy through energy of deformation. . . . As the stories below sequentially failed, the falling mass increased, further increasing the demand on the floors below, which were unable to arrest the moving mass. In other words, the momentum [of the top stories] falling on the supporting structure below . . . so greatly exceeded the strength capacity of the structure below that [the latter] was unable to stop or even to slow the falling mass.[66]

Even before we think about any specific law of physics violated by this account (assuming that no explosives or incendiaries were used to remove the steel columns), we can see intuitively that this explanation implies a miracle: As NIST critic Jim Hoffman has pointed out, it "requires us to believe that the massive steel frames of the [lower structure of the] towers provided no more resistance to falling rubble than [would] air."[67]

As to why physics rules out NIST's account, William Rice, who has both practiced and taught structural engineering, pointed out that NIST's account "violates Newton's Law of Conservation of Momentum," which requires that, "as the stationary inertia of each floor is overcome by being hit," the speed of descent must decrease.[68] A paper by physicists and engineers published in an engineering journal agreed, stating:

NIST evidently neglects a fundamental law of physics in glibly treating the remarkable 'free fall' collapse of each Tower, namely, the Law of Conservation of Momentum. This law of physics means that the hundreds of thousands of tons of material in the way must slow the upper part of the building because of its mass.[69]

A letter to NIST signed by physicist Steven Jones, chemist Kevin Ryan, and architect Richard Gage, among others, made a similar point, saying:

> Basic principles of engineering (for example, the conservation of momentum principle) would dictate that the undamaged steel structure below the collapse initiation zone would, at the very least, resist and slow the downward movement of the stories above. There is, indeed, a good chance that the structural strength of the steelwork below would arrest the downward movement of the stories above.[70]

NIST, as we saw above, claimed that the lower portion would not retard—let alone arrest—the downward movement of the upper part, because the "tremendous energy" of the upper part's downward momentum would be irresistible. Let us examine this claim with regard to the North Tower. It was struck at the 95th floor, so the upper portion consisted of only 16 floors. Also, the structure at this height had relatively little weight to bear, compared with the structure lower down, so the steel columns in the upper part, above the area of impact, were much thinner than those in the lower part. This means that the upper 16 floors probably constituted less than 15 percent of the building's total weight. Also, the top portion would have fallen only a story or two before hitting the lower portion, so it would not have acquired much velocity before striking the lower portion. For these reasons, the top portion would have not had much momentum, so its energy would not have been so "tremendous," it would seem, as to be irresistible by the lower part, with its millions of pounds of interconnected steel.

This conclusion, based on a purely commonsense analysis, was confirmed by a technical analysis of the North Tower collapse by mechanical engineer Gordon Ross. Far from failing to retard the downward movement of the building's upper portion, his analysis showed, the lower portion would have quickly and completely stopped the top portion's descent. Having made the necessary calculations (which NIST failed to do), Ross concluded that the "vertical movement of the falling section would [have been] arrested . . . within 0.02 seconds after impact. A collapse driven only by gravity would not continue to progress beyond that point."[71]

If Ross's calculations are even close to accurate, then NIST's account—according to which the Twin Towers came down "essentially in free fall," even though they were not professionally demolished— implied two enormous miracles (one for each building).

Another element in NIST's account, to be sure, is the claim that the fires in the buildings weakened the steel, so that it provided less resistance than normal. "[W]hen bare steel reaches temperatures of 1,000 degrees Celsius," NIST wrote, "it softens and its strength reduces to roughly 10 percent of its room temperature value."[72] NIST thereby, without actually saying it, implied that the steel columns had been heated up to the point where they lost 90 percent of their strength.

NIST was in this way able to mislead some nonscientific journalists into thinking that fire could have caused the Twin Towers to collapse. Alexander Cockburn, stating that the collapses did not require preplaced explosives, said: "High grade steel can bend disastrously under extreme heat." Chris Hayes, stating that the 9/11 Truth Movement's claims about the Twin Towers are without merit, wrote (in a passage quoted earlier): "[S]teel might not melt at 1,500 degrees [Fahrenheit], the temperature at which jet fuel burns, but it does begin to lose a lot of its strength, enough to cause the support beams to fail."[73]

However, the idea that steel heated up by fire could account for the collapses of the Twin Towers is wrong for at least two reasons. In the first place, even if the steel had indeed lost 90 percent of its strength, it would still have offered *some* resistance, because the law of conservation of momentum would not have taken a holiday. So a collapse "essentially in free fall" would have been impossible.

In the second place, there is no empirical basis for claiming that either tower's steel had lost *any* strength, let alone 90 percent of it. On the one hand, as MIT engineering professor Thomas Eagar has pointed out, structural steel only "begins to soften around 425°C [797°F]."[74] On the other hand, scientific studies on 16 *perimeter* columns carried out by NIST scientists found that "only three [of these perimeter] columns had evidence that the steel reached temperatures above 250°C [482°F]." These NIST scientists also found no evidence that even this temperature (250°C [482°F]) had been reached by any of the *core* columns.[75]

Accordingly, far from having evidence that any of the steel in the columns reached the temperature (1,000°C [1,832°F]) at which it would have lost 90 percent of its strength, NIST had no evidence that any of the columns *would have lost even five percent* of their strength. If neither explosives nor incendiaries were used to remove the 287 steel support columns, therefore, the top portion of the building came down through the lower portion as if it were not there, even though the steel in that portion was cool and hence at virtually full strength.

In claiming, therefore, that both of the Twin Towers came down essentially in free fall without the aid of either incendiaries or explosives, NIST implied *enormous* violations of the physical principle known as the conservation of momentum. Although Rothschild accused the 9/11 Truth Movement of being "irrational and unscientific," this characterization applies instead to NIST's report on the Twin Towers and anyone who accepts it.

5. THE SOUTH TOWER'S MID-AIR MIRACLES

Having illustrated the previous miracle primarily in terms of the North Tower, I turn now to a miracle unique to the South Tower. It was struck at the 80th floor, so that its upper portion consisted of a 30-floor block. As videos of the beginning of this building's collapse show, this block began tipping toward the corner that had been most damaged by the airplane's impact. According to the law of the conservation of angular momentum, this section should have fallen to the ground far outside the building's footprint. "However," Jim Hoffman and fellow 9/11 researcher Don Paul have observed,

> as the top then began to fall, the rotation decelerated. Then it reversed direction [even though the] law of conservation of angular momentum states that a solid object in rotation will continue to rotate at the same speed unless acted on by a torque.[76]

And then, as if this were not miraculous enough:

> We observe [wrote physicist Steven Jones] that approximately 30 upper floors begin to rotate as a block, to the south and east. They begin to topple over, not fall straight down. The torque due to gravity on this block is enormous, as is its angular momentum. But then—and this I'm still puzzling over—this block turned mostly to powder *in mid-air*! How can we understand this strange behavior, without explosives?[77]

If someone were to ask how even explosives could explain this behavior, we could turn to a statement by Mark Loizeaux, the president of Controlled Demolition, Inc. In response to an interviewer's question as to how he made "doomed structures dance or walk," Loizeaux said:

> [B]y differentially controlling the velocity of failure in different parts of the structure, you can make it walk, you can make it spin, you can make it dance. We've taken it and moved it, then dropped it or

moved it, twisted it and moved it down further—and then stopped it and moved it again. We've dropped structures 15 storeys, stopped them and then laid them sideways. We'll have structures start facing north and end up going to the north-west.[78]

If we suppose that explosives were used, therefore, we can understand the mid-air dance performed by the upper portion of the South Tower.

If we refuse to posit explosives, however, we are stuck with a major miracle: Although the upper block was rotating and tipping in such a way that its angular momentum should have caused it to fall down to the side, it somehow righted itself by disintegrating.

This disintegration, incidentally, further undermines the official theory, according to which the "tremendous energy" of this block's downward momentum caused the lower part of the South Tower to collapse. This theory requires that the upper part smashed down, as a solid block, on the lower part. Videos show, however, that it did not. As Gage, Jones, Ryan, and other colleagues pointed out to NIST:

> [T]he upper portion of WTC 2 did not fall as a block upon the lower undamaged portion, but instead disintegrated as it fell. Thus, there would be no single large impact from a falling block . . . [but only] a series of small impacts as the fragments of the disintegrating upper portion arrived.[79]

6. Horizontal Ejections from the Twin Towers

Dwain Deets, former director of the research engineering division at NASA's Dryden Flight Research Center, has written that the "massive structural members being hurled horizontally" from the Twin Towers "leave no doubt" in his mind that "explosives were involved."[80]

Deets was referring to the fact that the disintegration of each of the Twin Towers began with a massive explosion near the top, during which huge sections of perimeter columns were ejected out horizontally so powerfully that some of them traveled 500 to 600 feet. Although this feature of the destructions was not mentioned in NIST's (2005) report on the Twin Towers, there could be no doubt about it, because some of these sections of steel implanted themselves in neighboring buildings, as can be seen in videos and photographs.[81]

These ejections are now, in any case, part of the official account, because NIST, apparently finding them necessary to explain how fires got started in WTC 7, mentioned them in its report on this building.

In Shyam Sunder's opening statement at the August 2008 press briefing to announce the release of NIST's draft report on WTC 7, he said: "The debris from Tower 1 . . . started fires on at least 10 floors of the building."[82] NIST's WTC 7 report said: "The fires in WTC 7 were ignited as a result of the impact of debris from the collapse of WTC 1, which was approximately 110 m[eters] (350 ft) to the south."[83]

NIST thereby admitted that debris had been thrown out horizontally from the North Tower at least 350 feet.[84] NIST's report also stated:

> When WTC 1 collapsed at 10:28:22 AM, . . . some fragments [of debris] were forcibly ejected and traveled distances up to hundreds of meters. Pieces of WTC 1 hit WTC 7, severing six columns on Floors 7 through 17 on the south face and one column on the west face near the southwest corner. The debris also caused structural damage between Floor 44 and the roof.[85]

Debris that caused such extensive damage, including the severing of seven steel columns, had to be quite heavy. NIST seemed to be granting, therefore, that sections of steel columns had been hurled at least 650 feet (because "hundreds of meters" would mean at least 200 meters, which would be about 650 feet). Enormous force would be needed to eject large sections of steel that far out.

What could have produced this force? According to NIST, as we saw earlier, there were only three causal factors in the collapse of the Twin Towers: the airplane impacts, the fires, and gravitational attraction. The airplane impacts had occurred 56 minutes (South Tower) and 102 minutes (North Tower) earlier, and gravitational attraction pulls things straight downward. Fire could, to be sure, produce horizontal ejections by causing jet fuel to explode, but the jet fuel had, NIST pointed out, burned up within "a few minutes."[86] Therefore, although NIST admitted that these horizontal ejections occurred, it suggested no energy source to explain them.

These ejections could be explained by explosives. According to NIST, however, explosives did not contribute to the destruction of the Twin Towers. Those who accept NIST's account must, therefore, regard these horizontal ejections as constituting yet another miracle.

7. Metal-Melting Fires

In light of the above-discussed unprecedented effects produced by the fires in the WTC buildings (according to the official account), it would seem that these fires must have had miraculous powers. This conclusion is reinforced by an examination of still more extraordinary effects.

Swiss-Cheese Steel: Within a few months of 9/11, three professors from Worcester Polytechnic Institute (WPI) had issued a brief report about a piece of steel recovered from the WTC 7 debris, stating that it had undergone "microstructural changes," including "intergranular melting."[87] A greatly expanded version of this report, which contained a description of a similarly eroded piece of steel from one of the Twin Towers, was included as an appendix to the first official report on the destruction of the World Trade Center, which was issued by FEMA in 2002.[88]

A *New York Times* story, noting that parts of these pieces of steel had "melted away," even though "no fire in any of the buildings was believed to be hot enough to melt steel outright," said that these discoveries constituted "[p]erhaps the deepest mystery uncovered in the investigation."[89] Describing these mysterious pieces of steel more fully, an article in WPI's magazine, entitled "The 'Deep Mystery' of Melted Steel," said:

> [S]teel—which has a melting point of 2,800 degrees Fahrenheit—may weaken and bend, but does not melt during an ordinary office fire. Yet . . . [a] one-inch column has been reduced to half-inch thickness. Its edges—which are curled like a paper scroll—have been thinned to almost razor sharpness. Gaping holes—some larger than a silver dollar—let light shine through a formerly solid steel flange. This Swiss cheese appearance shocked all of the fire-wise professors, who expected to see distortion and bending—but not holes.[90]

One of the three WPI professors, Jonathan Barnett, was quoted by the *Times* as saying that the steel "appear[ed] to have been partly evaporated in extraordinarily high temperatures."[91]

That the steel had actually evaporated—not merely melted—was also reported in another *New York Times* story. Professor Abolhassan Astaneh-Asl of the University of California at Berkeley, speaking of a horizontal I-beam from WTC 7, reportedly said: "Parts of the flat top of the I, once five-eighths of an inch thick, had vaporized."[92]

Why do these phenomena involve miracles? Because the fires could not possibly, even under the most ideal conditions (which did not obtain), have been hotter than 1,800 degrees Fahrenheit (the maximum possible temperature for hydrocarbon-based building fires, which these fires were said to be), whereas the melting and boiling points of steel are only slightly lower than those of iron, which are 2,800°F and 5,182°F, respectively.[93] So if one accepts the official account, according to which all the heat was produced by the building fires, then one must believe that these fires had miraculous powers.

NIST, which took over from FEMA the task of writing the official reports on the WTC, avoided this issue by simply not mentioning any of these pieces of steel, even though two of them had been discussed in a FEMA report appendix. NIST even claimed that no recovered steel from WTC 7 could be identified, because the steel used in this building, unlike that used in the Twin Towers, "did not contain . . . identifying characteristics."[94]

In making this claim, however, NIST was clearly not being truthful. For one thing, it had previously published a document in which it had referred to steel recovered from WTC 7—including the piece discussed by the WPI professors.[95] Also, NIST's claim about not identifying any WTC 7 steel was made in August 2008, shortly after the airing in July 2008 of a BBC program on WTC 7, in which one of those WPI professors, Jonathan Barnett, had discussed an "eroded and deformed" piece of steel from WTC 7, which he and his colleagues had studied in 2001. These professors knew "its pedigree," Barnett explained, because "this particular kind of steel" had been used only in WTC 7, not in the Twin Towers.[96]

So, although it called the collapse of WTC 7 "the first known instance of fire causing the total collapse of a tall building,"[97] NIST had demonstrated its awareness of a recovered piece of steel from this building that only a very miraculous fire could have produced. NIST was surely also aware of the similarly eroded piece of steel from one of the Twin Towers, which had likewise been reported by the WPI professors in their paper included as an appendix to the 2002 FEMA report.

If the fires in WTC 7 and the Twin Towers had miraculous powers, we would expect still more miraculous effects to have been discovered, and this was indeed the case.

Melted Iron: The RJ Lee Group, a scientific research firm, was hired by Deutsche Bank, which had a building close to the World Trade Center, to prove that the dust contaminating its building after 9/11 was not ordinary building dust, as its insurance company claimed, but had resulted from the destruction of the World Trade Center. The RJ Lee Group's reports showed that the dust in the bank's building shared the unique chemical signature of the WTC dust, part of which was "[s]pherical iron . . . particles."[98] The spherical shape shows that melting has occurred: The shape is produced by surface tension as the drops fly through the air.

There was, moreover, an enormous number of these particles: Whereas iron particles constitute only 0.04 percent of normal building dust, they constituted (a whopping) 5.87 percent of the WTC dust.[99] The existence of these particles, the RJ Lee Group said, proved that iron had "melted during the WTC Event."[100] The scientists conducting the EPA's WTC dust signature study, incidentally, had at one time considered including "iron spheres" among the components to be mentioned; it would be interesting to learn why this idea was dropped.[101]

In any case, the identification of iron spheres by both the EPA and the RJ Lee Group was another miraculous discovery, for the reason given above: The melting point of iron is 2,800°F, whereas the WTC fires could not possibly have gotten above 1,800°F.[102]

Melted Molybdenum: Scientists at the US Geological Survey, in a study intended to aid the "identification of WTC dust components," discovered an even more miraculous effect of the fires. Besides finding the spherical iron-rich particles, these scientists found that molybdenum, the melting point of which is 4,753°F (2,623°C), had also melted. Although these USGS scientists failed to mention this discovery in their published report,[103] another group of scientists, having obtained the USGS team's data through a FOIA (Freedom of Information Act) request, reported evidence showing that the USGS scientists had devoted serious study to "a molybdenum-rich spherule."[104]

8. INEXTINGUISHABLE FIRES

Besides having the power to produce the extraordinary effects already reported, the World Trade Center fires were also miraculously inextinguishable. The fact that fires continued burning in the Ground Zero rubble for many months, in spite of every attempt to put them out, was widely reported. The title of a *New York Times* story in the middle of November, two months after the attacks, referred to the "Most Stubborn Fire." A *New Scientist* article in December was entitled "Ground

Zero's Fires Still Burning." Very hot fires continued to burn in the Ground Zero debris piles, these stories reported, even though heavy rains came down, millions of additional gallons of water were sprayed onto the piles, and a chemical suppressant was pumped into them.[105]

According to Greg Fuchek, vice president of a company that supplied computer equipment to identify human remains at the site, the working conditions at Ground Zero remained "hellish" for six months, because the ground temperature ranged from 600 to 1,500 degrees Fahrenheit.[106]

These inextinguishable fires were a mystery. Assuming the truth of the official account of the destruction of the World Trade Center, there would have been nothing in the debris pile other than ordinary building materials, and these can burn only in the presence of oxygen. There would have been little oxygen available in the densely packed debris piles, and wherever it was available, the fires should have been easily suppressed by the enormous amounts of water and chemical suppressants pumped into the piles. The fires' seemingly miraculous power to keep burning could not be explained by the airplanes' jet fuel (which is essentially kerosene), because it would have all burned out, as mentioned above, within a few minutes.

A non-miraculous explanation is suggested by the discovery of a large amount of nanothermite residue in the WTC dust, which was reported in a peer-reviewed scientific journal in 2009. Nanothermite— "which can be tailored to behave as an incendiary (like ordinary thermite) or as an explosive"[107]—is one among several types of "energetic nanocomposites," which were described by an article in *The Environmentalist* as "chemical energetic materials, which provide their own fuel and oxidant and are not deterred by water, dust or chemical suppressants."[108] The discovery of nanothermite residue in the dust provided, therefore, an empirical basis for a non-miraculous explanation of the long-lasting fires at Ground Zero.

According to the official account, however, the buildings were all brought down without the aid of any incendiaries or explosives. WTC 7 was said by NIST, as we saw above, to have been brought down by fire alone, and this fire, NIST added, was "an ordinary building contents fire."[109] As for the Twin Towers, they were brought down through the combined effects of the airplane impacts and the ensuing fires: NIST explicitly rejected "alternative hypotheses suggesting that the WTC towers were brought down by controlled demolition using explosives."[110]

For anyone who accepts the official account, therefore, the inextinguishable underground fires at Ground Zero provide still another demonstration of miraculous powers that must have been possessed by the World Trade Center fires.

9. Supernatural Sulfur

In the seventh section, I discussed the two Swiss-cheese-appearing pieces of steel that had been recovered from the World Trade Center rubble—one from WTC 7, the other from one of the Twin Towers. In that discussion, however, I ignored one of the critical features of these pieces of steel, which was central to the reason they were said by the *New York Times* to constitute "the deepest mystery."

This was the fact that the thinning of the steel had resulted, according to the three WPI professors' report, from sulfidation, but there was no explanation for the source of the sulfur or the mechanism through which it entered into the steel. According to a preliminary analysis reported by the professors, said the *New York Times* article, "sulfur released during the fires—no one knows from where—may have combined with atoms in the steel to form compounds that melt at lower temperatures."[111]

This phenomenon was discussed more fully in the article, "The 'Deep Mystery' of Melted Steel," in WPI's magazine, which attributed the holes and the thinning to "a eutectic reaction" that "occurred at the surface, causing intergranular melting capable of turning a solid steel girder into Swiss cheese."[112]

In summarizing their findings in the paper included in the FEMA report, the three professors wrote:

1. The thinning of the steel occurred by a high-temperature corrosion due to a combination of oxidation and sulfidation.

2. Heating of the steel into a hot corrosive environment approaching 1,000°C (1,832°F) results in the formation of a eutectic mixture of iron, oxygen, and sulfur that liquefied the steel.

3. The sulfidation attack of steel grain boundaries accelerated the corrosion and erosion of the steel.[113]

Then, having mentioned sulfidation in each of these three points, the professors added: "The severe corrosion and subsequent erosion of Samples 1 and 2 are a very unusual event. No clear explanation for the source of the sulfur has been identified. . . . A detailed study into the mechanisms of this phenomenon is needed."[114]

However, although Arden Bement, who was the director of NIST when it took over the WTC project from FEMA, said that NIST's report would address "all major recommendations contained in the [FEMA] report,"[115] NIST ignored this recommendation. Indeed, as we saw earlier, it did not even mention these Swiss-cheese pieces of steel.

Also, when NIST was later asked about the sulfidation, it tried to maintain that the source of the sulfur was not actually a mystery, saying that "sulfur is present in the gypsum wallboard that was prevalent in the interior partitions."[116]

But there are three problems with this explanation. First, gypsum is calcium sulfate, so if all the sulfur discovered had been from gypsum wallboard, it would have been matched by about the same percentage of calcium. That, however, was not the case.[117]

Second, the WPI professors reported not merely that there was sulfur in the debris, but that the steel had been *sulfidized*. This means that sulfur had entered into the *intergranular structure* of the steel (which the *New York Times* article had indicated by saying that sulfur had "combined with atoms in the steel"). As chemist Kevin Ryan has said, the question NIST would need to answer is: "[H]ow did sulfates, from wallboard, tunnel into the intergranular microstructure of the steel and then form sulfides within?"[118] Physicist Steven Jones added:

> [I]f NIST claims that sulfur is present in the steel from gypsum, they should do an (easy) experiment to heat steel to about 1000°C in the presence of gypsum and then test whether sulfur has entered the steel. . . . [T]hey will find that sulfur does *not* enter steel under such circumstances.[119]

Chemistry professor Niels Harrit has explained why it would not: Although gypsum contains sulfur, this is not elemental sulfur, which can react with iron, but sulfur in the form of calcium sulfate, which cannot.[120]

The official account of the destruction of the World Trade Center, therefore, implies that the sulfidized steel had been produced by a twofold miracle: Besides the fact that the fires, as we saw earlier, could have melted steel only if they had possessed miraculous powers, the sulfur in the wallboard could have entered into this melted steel only by virtue of supernatural powers.

Once again, a non-miraculous explanation is available: We need only suppose that thermate, a well-known incendiary, had been employed. As Steven Jones has written:

> The thermate reaction proceeds rapidly and is in general faster than basic thermite in cutting through steel due to the presence of sulfur. (Elemental sulfur forms a low-melting-temperature eutectic with iron.)[121]

Besides providing an explanation for the eutectic reaction, thermate could also, Jones pointed out, explain the melting, oxidation, and sulfidation of the steel:

> When you put sulfur into thermite it makes the steel melt at a much lower temperature, so instead of melting at about 1,538°C [2,800°F] it melts at approximately 988°C [1,820°F], and you get sulfidation and oxidation in the attacked steel.[122]

NIST, however, insists that no incendiaries were employed: WTC 7 was brought down by fire alone; the Twin Towers by the fires combined with damage from the airplane impacts. Those who endorse the official account, therefore, are stuck with yet another miracle.

III WHICH 9/11 CONSPIRACY THEORY IS TRULY DISCREDITING AND DISTRACTING?

In light of the above facts, I ask Terry Allen, David Corn, Noam Chomsky, Alexander Cockburn, Chris Hayes, George Monbiot, Matthew Rothschild, and Matt Taibbi: Are you still comfortable with endorsing the official account of the destruction of the World Trade Center?

A symposium on "State Crimes against Democracy" in one of our major social science journals, *American Behavioral Scientist*,[123] has recently addressed this issue. Likening Orwell's "secret doctrine" that 2 + 2 = 4, which intellectuals must safeguard in dark times, to unquestioned laws of physics, one of the symposium's authors criticized "the awesome intellectual silence making permissible the blithe dismissal of more than one law of thermodynamics in the World Trade Center Towers' collapse."[124] Part of this silence has involved the failure of the academy to protest when "Professor Steven Jones found himself forced out of [a] tenured position for merely reminding the world that physical laws, about which *there is no dissent whatsoever*, contradict the official theory of the World Trade Center Towers' collapse."[125]

I wonder if you are still comfortable with giving your own consent to NIST's "blithe dismissal" of otherwise unquestioned physical principles—as did Cockburn, when he ridiculed the 9/11 Truth Movement for its "delirious litanies about . . . the collapse of the WTC buildings," and Taibbi, when he wrote dismissively of people who have tried to educate him "on the supposed anomalies of physics involved with the collapse of WTC-7."[126] I would think that, if there are good reasons to suspect that these physical principles have been dismissed in the interests of covering up a major state crime against democracy, you journalists would be especially uncomfortable with giving your consent to it.

Some of you have expressed fear, to be sure, that the left will be discredited insofar as it is seen as endorsing a 9/11 conspiracy theory. Having asked in 2007, "Why do I bother with these morons?" George Monbiot replied: "Because they are destroying the movements some of us have spent a long time trying to build."[127] In 2009, David Corn wrote: "[W]hen the 9/11 conspiracy theories were first emerging on the left, I wrote several pieces decrying them [for] fear . . . that this unsound idea would infect the left and other quarters—discrediting anyone who got close to it."[128]

Some of you, moreover, have objected to the 9/11 Truth Movement on the grounds that it has served as a distraction from truly important issues. The 9/11 conspiracy theories, Corn wrote in 2002, serve to "distract people from the real wrongdoing."[129] Cockburn, writing in 2006, agreed, saying: "The Conspiracy Nuts have combined to produce a huge distraction."[130] That same year, Chomsky said: "One of the major consequences of the 9/11 movement has been to draw enormous amounts of energy and effort away from activism directed to real and ongoing crimes of state."[131] And Monbiot, naming in 2007 some truly important issues from which, in his view, the 9/11 conspiracy theory has distracted us, mentioned "climate change, the Iraq war, nuclear proliferation, inequality, . . . [the fact] that corporate power stands too heavily on democracy, [and] that war criminals, cheats and liars are not being held to account."[132]

I will address these two fears—of being discredited and of being distracted—in order.

1. The Fear of Being Discredited

Left-leaning journalists are certainly right to fear that the left would be discredited by being aligned with a conspiracy theory that is scientifically unsupportable and even absurd. It is hard to imagine, however, what could discredit the left more than having many of its recognized leaders endorsing the Bush-Cheney administration's 9/11 conspiracy theory, especially at a time when more and more scientists and people in relevant professions are pointing out its absurdities.

Conspiracy Theories and the Official Account of 9/11: I realize, of course, that most of you do not like to acknowledge that the official account of 9/11 is itself a conspiracy theory, given the one-sided, propagandistic meaning with which this term is now commonly employed. As New Zealand philosopher Charles Pigden has pointed out in a superb essay entitled "Conspiracy Theories and the Conventional Wisdom":

> [T]o call someone 'a conspiracy theorist' is to suggest that he is irrational, paranoid or perverse. Often the suggestion seems to be that conspiracy theories are not just suspect, but utterly unbelievable, too silly to deserve the effort of a serious refutation.[133]

However, Pigden continues, using the term in this way is intellectually dishonest, because "a conspiracy theory is simply a theory that posits a conspiracy—a secret plan on the part of some group to influence events by partly secret means."[134] And, given this neutral, dictionary meaning of the term:

> [E]very politically and historically literate person is a big-time conspiracy theorist, since every such person subscribes to a vast range of conspiracy theories. . . . [T]here are many facts that admit of no non-conspiratorial explanation and many conspiracy theories that are sufficiently well-established to qualify as knowledge. It is difficult . . . to mount a coup [or an assassination] without conspiring. . . . Thus anyone who knows anything about the Ides of March or the assassinations of Archduke Franz Ferdinand or the Tsar Alexander II is bound to subscribe to a conspiracy theory, and hence to be a conspiracy theorist.[135]

In light of the neutral meaning of the term provided by Pigden, *everyone* is a conspiracy theorist about 9/11, not only people who believe that the US government was complicit. According to the government's theory, the 9/11 attacks resulted from a conspiracy between Osama bin Laden, other al-Qaeda leaders (such as Khalid

Sheikh Mohammed), and 19 young members of al-Qaeda who agreed to hijack airliners.[136]

Failure to recognize this point can lead to absurd consequences. For example, after an article about 9/11 by former Minnesota Governor Jesse Ventura, which had been posted at the Huffington Post, was quickly taken down, the HP editor gave this explanation:

> The Huffington Post's editorial policy . . . prohibits the promotion and promulgation of conspiracy theories—including those about 9/11. As such, we have removed this post.[137]

In response, I pointed out that this policy entails that the Huffington Post "cannot accept any posts that state, or imply, that al-Qaeda was responsible for the 9/11 attacks, for that is a conspiracy theory." This fact has been acknowledged, I added, by former Harvard law professor and current Obama administration member Cass Sunstein—who referred to the above-quoted article by Charles Pigden. I pointed out that this fact combined with the Huffington Post's policy would lead to a strange implication:

> [The Huffington Post] cannot allow President Obama to say that we are in Afghanistan to 'get the people who attacked us on 9/11,' because he's thereby endorsing the Bush-Cheney conspiracy theory about 9/11.[138]

But the Huffington Post, evidently not bothered by logical inconsistency, has not changed its policy.

In any case, once it is acknowledged that both of the major theories about 9/11 are conspiracy theories, the 9/11 Truth Movement's theory cannot rationally be rejected on the grounds that it is a conspiracy theory. Making a rational judgment requires comparing the two conspiracy theories to see which one is more plausible. And when the issue is posed in this way, the official theory does not fare well, whether viewed from a scientific or a merely prima facie perspective.

The Prima Facie Absurdity of the Official Conspiracy Theory: Even when viewed only superficially (prima facie), the central elements in the official story, if evaluated in abstraction from the fact that it *is* the official story, is certainly implausible—it probably would even have been too implausible to pass muster as the plot for a bad Hollywood movie. Matt Taibbi has made such a statement about the story implicit in the various claims made by the 9/11 Truth Movement, saying that if you combine those claims into a coherent script, "you get the dumbest story since Roman Polanski's *Pirates*."[139] However, aside from the fact that Taibbi failed to support this claim, he simply ignored the absurdity of the official story, which, boiled down to a one-sentence summary, says:

> Inexperienced Muslim hijackers, armed only with knives and box-cutters, took control of four airliners, then outfoxed the world's most sophisticated air defense system, then used two of these airliners to bring three skyscrapers down (indeed, straight down, in virtual free fall),[140] and then, almost an hour later—when the US air defense system would have been on highest alert—flew a third one, undetected, from the midwest back to Washington, DC, where—thanks to heroic piloting by a man who had never before flown an airliner and who was, according to the *New York Times*, known as a "terrible pilot," incapable of safely flying even a tiny plane—this third airliner went through an extremely difficult trajectory (even too difficult for themselves, said some experienced airline pilots) in order to strike the first floor of the Pentagon—surely the most well-protected building on the planet—without scraping the Pentagon lawn.

What could discredit "the left" more than the fact that you, some of its leading spokespersons, have endorsed such nonsense?

The Scientific Status of the Two Conspiracy Theories: Actually, there is one thing that would be even more discrediting: If, after having it pointed out to you that at least nine miracles are implied by this story, you fail to renounce your former acceptance of it.

Also, it is not only the miracles implicit in the official account that undermine your apparent assumption that good science supports the official account rather than that of the 9/11 Truth Movement. Although that assumption was less obviously unreasonable a few years ago, at least by people who either could not or would not look at the evidence for themselves, that assumption is now completely and obviously unreasonable, due to developments that have occurred in the past few years.

In 2006, as we saw above, Chomsky suggested that there would be two decisive tests for the physical evidence touted by the 9/11 Truth Movement: (i) "submit it to specialists [with] the requisite background in civil-mechanical engineering, materials science, [and] building construction," (ii) "submit it to a serious journal for peer review and publication."

To begin with the second test: A few months before December 2006, when Chomsky made this suggestion, physicist Steven Jones and some other scientists started a new online outlet, the *Journal of 9/11 Studies*. By 2011, it has published dozens of peer-reviewed papers, five of which were cited earlier: "Why Indeed Did the WTC Buildings Completely Collapse?" and "Revisiting 9/11/2001: Applying the Scientific Method" (by Jones himself); "Extremely High Temperatures during the World Trade Center Destruction" (by Jones and seven other scientists); "9/11: Acceleration Study Proves Explosive Demolition" (by Frank Legge); and "Momentum Transfer Analysis of the Collapse of the Upper Storeys of WTC 1" (by Gordon Ross).

Of course, people who are skeptical of the 9/11 Truth Movement's claims may assume—albeit wrongly, from what I have learned—that this journal, being favorable to such claims, may have a less than rigorous peer-review process. And what Chomsky had suggested, in any case, was that 9/11 Truth Movement scientists should submit articles to mainstream science journals, to see if they could pass their peer-review processes.

Jones and other physical scientists, deciding to take up Chomsky's challenge, started working on papers to submit, and since 2008, at least six papers disputing the official account of the WTC have been published in mainstream journals:

- "Fourteen Points of Agreement with Official Government Reports on the World Trade Center Destruction," by Steven E. Jones, Frank M. Legge, Kevin R. Ryan, Anthony F. Szamboti, and James R. Gourley, published in 2008 in the *Open Civil Engineering Journal*.[141]

- "Environmental Anomalies at the World Trade Center: Evidence for Energetic Materials," by Kevin R. Ryan, James R. Gourley, and Steven E. Jones, published in 2009 in *The Environmentalist*.[142]

- "Active Thermitic Material Observed in Dust from the 9/11 World Trade Center Catastrophe," by University of Copenhagen chemistry professor Niels Harrit and eight colleagues (including Jones, Ryan, Legge, and Gourley), published in 2009 in *The Open Chemical Physics Journal*.[143]

- "Discussion of 'Progressive Collapse of the World Trade Center: A Simple Analysis' by K.A. Seffen," by physicist Crockett Grabbe, published in 2010 in the *Journal of Engineering Mechanics*, which is published by the American Society of Civil Engineers (ASCE).[144]

- "Discussion of 'Mechanics of Progressive Collapse: Learning from World Trade Center and Building Demolitions' by Zdenek P. Bazant and Mathieu Verdure," by chemical engineer James R. Gourley, published in 2010 in the ASCE's *Journal of Engineering Mechanics*.[145]

- "Discussion of 'What Did and Did Not Cause Collapse of World Trade Center Twin Towers in New York?' by Zdenek P. Bazant, Jia-Liang Le, Frank R. Greening, and David B. Benson," by Anders Björkman, published in 2010 in the ASCE's *Journal of Engineering Mechanics*.[146]

Given the time it takes to write scientific papers and get them through the peer-review process, combined with the relatively small number of scientists writing about these issues, this is an impressive achievement. It would seem that this part of Chomsky's test has been met.

These publications demonstrate, moreover, that many of the same scientists who had been publishing in the *Journal of 9/11 Studies* have now written papers that have gotten through the peer-review process of mainstream science journals. There is no empirical basis, accordingly, for the assumption that the *Journal of 9/11 Studies'* peer-review process is any less critical. We can, therefore, add the 25 scientific papers about the WTC collapses in the *Journal of 9/11 Studies* to the six recent papers in mainstream journals, giving us a total of over 30 peer-reviewed scientific articles challenging the official theory about the destruction of the WTC that have appeared since 2006.

I turn now to Chomsky's other suggested way for members of the Truth Movement to test physical evidence that they see as disproving the official story: "submit it to specialists [with] the requisite background in civil-mechanical engineering, materials science, [and] building construction." This has now been done and, as a result, the movement has large and continually growing numbers of physical scientists, engineers, and architects.

Some scientists (beyond those already mentioned) who have recently formed an organization called Scientists for 9/11 Truth include:

- Dr. A. K. Dewdney, professor emeritus of mathematics and physics, University of Western Ontario.

- Dr. Timothy E. Eastman, Consultant, Plasmas International, Silver Spring, Maryland.

- Dr. Mark F. Fitzsimmons, senior lecturer in organic chemistry, University of Plymouth.

- Dr. David L. Griscom, former research physicist at the Naval Research Laboratory; principal author of 100 papers in scientific journals; fellow of the American Physical Society and of the American Association for the Advancement of Science.

- Dr. Jan Kjellman, research scientist in nuclear physics and nanotechnology, École Polytechnique Federale, Lausanne.

- Dr. Herbert G. Lebherz, professor emeritus, Department of Chemistry, San Diego State University.

- Dr. Eric Leichtnam, professor of mathematics and physics, University of Paris.

- Dr. Terry Morrone, professor emeritus, Department of Physics, Adelphi University.

- Dr. John D. Wyndham, former research fellow, California Institute of Technology.[147]

With regard to architects and engineers: In December 2006, when Chomsky issued his suggestion, there were few if any architects and engineers who had publicly questioned the official account of the destruction of the World Trade Center. But in January, 2007, architect Richard Gage, a member of the American Institute of Architects (AIA), founded Architects and Engineers for 9/11 Truth, and by 2011 its membership had grown to include over 1,500 professional architects and engineers. Here are a few of the architects:

- Daniel B. Barnum, AIA fellow; founder of the Houston AIA Residential Architecture Committee.

- Bertie McKinney Bonner, M. Arch; AIA member; licensed architect in Pennsylvania.

- David Paul Helpern, AIA fellow; founder of Helpern Architects.

- Cynthia Howard, M. Arch; licensed architect in Maine and Massachusetts; past president, AIA's New England Chapter.

- Dr. David A. Johnson, internationally known architect and city planner; chaired the planning departments at Syracuse and Ball State universities; former president of the Fulbright Association of the United States.

- Kevin A. Kelly, AIA fellow; author of *Problem Seeking: An Architectural Programming Primer*, which has become a standard textbook.

- Anne Lee, M. Arch, AIA member; licensed architect in Massachusetts.

- Dr. David Leifer, coordinator of the Graduate Program in Facilities Management, University of Sydney; former professor at Mackintosh School of Architecture, Glasgow.

- Paul Stevenson Oles, fellow of the AIA, which in 1989 called him "the dean of architectural illustrators in America"; co-founder of the American Society of Architectural Perspectivists.

- David A. Techau, B. Arch., MS; AIA member; licensed architect in Hawaii.[148]

Here are a few of the engineers:

- Dr. John Edward Anderson, professor emeritus, Mechanical Engineering, University of Minnesota; licensed Professional Engineer (PE).

- Dr. Robert Bowman, former head, Department of Aeronautical Engineering, US Air Force Institute of Technology; director of Advanced Space Programs Development ("Star Wars") under Presidents Ford and Carter.

- Ronald H. Brookman, MS Eng; licensed Professional Civil and Structural Engineer in California

- Dwain Deets, former Director for Research Engineering and Aerospace Projects, NASA Dryden Flight Research Center, which awarded him the NASA Exceptional Service Award.

- Dr. Joel Hirschhorn, former professor, Metallurgical Engineering, University of Wisconsin, Madison; former staff member, Congressional Office of Technology Assessment.

- Richard F. Humenn, licensed PE (retired); senior Project Design Engineer, World Trade Center electrical systems.

- Dr. Fadhil Al-Kazily, licensed Professional Civil Engineer.

- Dr. Jack Keller, professor emeritus, Civil Engineering, Utah State University; member, National Academy of Engineering; named one of the world's 50 leading contributors to science and technology benefiting society by *Scientific American*.

- Dr. Heikki Kurttila, Safety Engineer and Accident Analyst for Finland's National Safety Technology Authority.

- Dr. Ali Mojahid, Civil and Architectural Engineering; licensed PE.

- Edward Munyak, Mechanical and Fire Protection Engineer; former Fire Protection Engineer for California and the US Departments of Energy and Defense.

- Kamal S. Obeid, MS, licensed Professional Structural and Civil Engineer.[149]

In addition to Scientists for 9/11 Truth and Architects and Engineers for 9/11 Truth, many other 9/11 organizations of professionals with relevant types of expertise have been formed, including Firefighters for 9/11 Truth, Intelligence Officers for 9/11 Truth, Medical Professionals for 9/11 Truth, Military Officers for 9/11 Truth, Pilots for 9/11 Truth, and Veterans for 9/11 Truth.[150]

Less obviously relevant, but surely not entirely irrelevant, are some other professional organizations, including Actors and Artists for 9/11 Truth, Journalists and Other Media Professionals for 9/11 Truth, Lawyers for 9/11 Truth, Political Leaders for 9/11 Truth, Religious Leaders for 9/11 Truth (the organization to which I belong), and Scholars for 9/11 Truth and Justice.[151] If we combine the membership of these organizations with those in the previous paragraph, we can see that several thousand professional people have publicly announced their alignment with the 9/11 Truth Movement.

In light of the above-mentioned developments, could any fair-minded person deny that the 9/11 Truth Movement's evidence has passed Chomsky's twofold test with flying colors?

Given the make-up of the 9/11 Truth Movement, could any such person agree with the claims about this movement quoted in the first part of this chapter, according to which its members are "conspiracy nuts," "idiots," and "morons," who, being devoid of "any conception of evidence," are "willing to abandon science" in favor of "magic"? In one of his 2009 essays, David Corn expressed concern about "9/11 conspiracy silliness."[152] But it is hard to imagine anything sillier, and hence more self-discrediting, than making such claims about the scientists, architects, engineers, intelligence officers, lawyers, medical professionals, political leaders, and other professionals who have publicly aligned themselves with the 9/11 Truth Movement.

As I stated on a lecture tour in early 2009:

> Among scientists and professionals in the relevant fields who have studied the evidence, the weight of scientific and professional opinion is now overwhelmingly on the side of the 9/11 Truth Movement. Whereas well over 1,000 such people have publicly supported the stance of this movement, there are virtually no scientists or professionals in the relevant fields who have gone on record in defense of the official story—except for people whose livelihood would be threatened if they refused to support it. This caveat is important, because, as Upton Sinclair famously observed: "It is difficult to get a man to understand something when his salary depends upon his *not* understanding it."[153] Except for such people, virtually everyone who has expertise in a relevant field, and who has

seriously studied the evidence, rejects the official conspiracy theory. It is time, therefore, for journalists and everyone else to take a second look.[154]

A More General Problem with the Official Conspiracy Theory: In addition, the twofold fact that the official conspiracy theory's account of the WTC destruction implies miracles and has been increasingly rejected by informed and independent people in relevant professions, this theory is rendered unworthy of belief by a more general problem: when its various details are subjected to critical scrutiny, the entire story falls apart—as I showed in my 2008 book, *The New Pearl Harbor Revisited*[154] (which, incidentally, was a *Publishers Weekly* "Pick of the Week" in November 2008,[155] an honor not normally bestowed on books written by morons and idiots).

One of the things that falls apart, as we will see in Chapter 5, is the idea that the existence of al-Qaeda hijackers on the airliners was shown by the reported phone calls from the airliners. All of you have evidently accepted these calls as genuine.

For example, Matthew Rothschild, defending the government's account of what happened on United Flight 93, wrote: "we know from cell phone conversations that passengers on board that plane planned on confronting the hijackers."[156] As pointed out in Chapter 5, however, the cell phone technology at that time did not allow cell phone calls to be made from airliners flying at high altitudes.

Chris Hayes faulted the Truth Movement for focusing on what he called "physical minutiae," such as "the altitude in Pennsylvania at which cellphones on Flight 93 should have stopped working."[157] It would appear, however, that the FBI took such "minutiae" seriously. As pointed out in Chapter 5, the FBI in its 2006 report to the Moussaoui trial stated that of all the reported phone calls from the four flights, only two of them were calls from Flight 93 when it, about to crash, was at a low altitude. This meant that the reported calls from Tom Burnett had to be recategorized as onboard calls, even though Deena Burnett told the FBI that she knew her husband had used his cell phone, because she recognized his cell phone number on her phone's Caller ID.[158]

By denying that either the Burnett call or any of the other calls from United 93 when it was flying above 35,000 feet were made on cell phones, the FBI got rid of the problem of technologically impossible (miraculous) phone calls. But if Tom Burnett had really called his wife using a seatback phone, as the FBI now claims, and yet his cell phone number showed up on Deena Burnett's Caller ID, this would have to count as a miracle.

I have also raised questions, as I point out in Chapter 5, about the alleged phone calls from CNN correspondent Barbara Olson. As one of several of my views that Rothschild treated with derision, he said: "Griffin casts doubt on whether the phone calls actually happened."[159] But in the FBI's 2006 report on phone calls, as I show in Chapter 5, the FBI did not support the claim that the calls from Barbara Olson "actually happened." Although Ted Olson said he had received two lengthy calls from his wife, the FBI says that Barbara Olson attempted *one* call, which was "unconnected," so that it (of course) lasted "0 seconds."[160] Is Rothschild so certain that the reported calls from Barbara Olson "actually happened" that he now regards the FBI with derision?

The reported calls from Barbara Olson were very important: They provided the first evidence given to the public that the planes had been hijacked; they were instrumental in getting the American public ready to strike back at Muslims in a "war on terror"; and they were also the only source for a piece of information that everyone "knows"— that the hijackers had box-cutters. One would think, therefore, that it would be of more than passing interest to people concerned about the direction of US foreign policy since 9/11 that an FBI report in 2006 indicates that these calls never happened.

This is the same FBI that—in spite of Rothschild's confident claim that there is no doubt of Osama bin Laden's responsibility for the attacks, because he (allegedly) claimed responsibility for them in a video (allegedly) found in Afghanistan by the US military—does not list him as wanted for 9/11. Why? Because, an FBI spokesman explained, "the FBI has no hard evidence connecting Bin Laden to 9/11."[161] The FBI must be less certain than Rothschild about the evidentiary value of that so-called confessional video—and for good reason, as I have shown elsewhere.[162]

Accordingly, insofar as you left-leaning detractors of the 9/11 Truth Movement have been concerned not to discredit yourselves by endorsing an unsupported, implausible, irrational, and even scientifically impossible conspiracy theory, that is precisely what you are doing so long as you stand by your endorsements of the Bush administration's—and now the Obama administration's—9/11 conspiracy theory.

2. THE FEAR OF BEING DISTRACTED

The second fear—that the focus on a false conspiracy theory has been distracting many people from more important matters—is equally valid. But this fear has been directed toward the wrong conspiracy theory. Nothing has distracted the United States and its allies from issues such as global apartheid, the ecological crisis, nuclear proliferation, and corporate power more than the "war on terror"—with its huge operations in Afghanistan and Iraq, its incessant terror alerts and stories of attacks prevented, and its depletion of our national treasury. Lying at the root of this so-called war on terror, both historically and as present justification, is the official account of 9/11. So this official account is, as I wrote in response to Cockburn in Le Monde Diplomatique four years ago, "The Truly Distracting 9/11 Conspiracy Theory."[163]

Had the falsity of this account been exposed within weeks—as it certainly could and should have been—the war in Afghanistan, which has now been consuming the country's time, talent, treasury, and young lives for a decade, could have been avoided altogether. If the falsity of the Bush-Cheney 9/11 conspiracy theory had at least been exposed within a year, the fiasco in Iraq could have been avoided. If the truth had been exposed within three years, those wars could have been closed down long ago and the Bush-Cheney administration dismissed before it had a second term. If so, the next administration, not distracted by two major wars and exaggerated fears about terrorist attacks on the "homeland," might have focused on the fact that many environmental regulations needed to be strengthened. One consequence might have been that the Gulf oil blowout (not "spill"), which was very destructive to our planet's ecosystem, might never have occurred. The fact that the official conspiracy theory about 9/11 has distracted the United States and its allies from the ecological crisis— especially global climate change—is no trivial matter, and this is merely one of many illustrations that could be given.

That the 9/11 Truth Movement, by contrast, cannot be rationally considered a distraction from more important matters was persuasively expressed in August 2006 by former CIA official Bill Christison, who by the end of his 28-year career had risen to the position of Director of the CIA's Office of Regional and Political Analysis (and who, sadly, died in 2010).[164] In an article entitled "Stop Belittling the Theories About September 11," Christison wrote:

After spending the better part of the last five years treating these theories with utmost skepticism, I have devoted serious time to actually studying them [and] have come to believe that significant parts of the 9/11 theories are true, and that therefore significant parts of the 'official story' put out by the U.S. government and the 9/11 Commission are false.

Then, after listing nine judgments that had led him to this conclusion—one of which was that the "North and South Towers of the World Trade Center almost certainly did not collapse and fall to earth because hijacked aircraft hit them"—he added:

If [these] judgments . . . are correct, they . . . strongly suggest that some unnamed persons or groups either inside or with ties to the government were actively creating a 'Pearl Harbor' event, most likely to gain public support for the aggressive foreign policies that followed—policies that would, first, 'transform' the entire Middle East, and second, expand U.S. global domination.

Finally, explaining why the evidence for this conclusion cannot reasonably be dismissed as a distraction from more important matters, Christison wrote:

A manageable volume of carefully collected and analyzed evidence is already at hand . . . that elements within the Bush administration, as well as possibly other groups foreign or domestic, were involved in a massive fraud against the American people, a fraud that has led to many thousands of deaths. This charge of fraud, if proven, involves a much greater crime against the American people and people of the world than any other charges of fraud connected to the run-up to the invasion of Iraq in March 2003. It is a charge that we should not sweep under the rug because what is happening in Lebanon, Gaza, Iraq, Syria, and Iran seems more pressing and overwhelming. It is a charge that is more important because it is related to all of the areas just mentioned—after all, the events of 9/11 have been used by the administration to justify every single aspect of U.S. foreign policy in the Middle East since September 11. It is a charge that is more important also because it affects the very core of our entire political system. If proven, it is a conspiracy, so far successful, not only against the people of the United States, but against the entire world.[165]

In this passage, Christison expressed this charge of fraud conditionally, saying "if proven." He later made clear, however, that he had personally found the evidence convincing, referring to the 9/11 attacks as "an inside job."[166]

In any case, besides saying that 9/11 is more important than America's crimes in the Middle East because "the events of 9/11 have been used by the administration to justify every single aspect of U.S. foreign policy in the Middle East since September 11," Christison also, in saying that the 9/11 fraud "affects the very core of our entire political system," anticipated the above-cited symposium in the *American Behavioral Scientist*, which treated 9/11 as a probable instance of its topic: State Crimes against Democracy. Christison's implicit message to Chomsky, therefore, was: Given your concern with "real and ongoing crimes of state," I would respectfully suggest that you do what I finally did: Actually examine the evidence that 9/11 was one of these crimes.

As for the concern to prosecute war criminals, what bigger war criminals could there be than people within our own government who engineered these attacks, then used them as a pretext for the wars in Afghanistan and Iraq, which have killed millions?[167]

As for the hope of stopping these horribly deadly and terribly expensive wars, what better means could be had than proof—which scientists, architects, engineers, firefighters, and pilots in the 9/11 Truth Movement have provided—that the official account of 9/11 is a lie and that the attacks had to be, at least in part, an inside job?

CONCLUDING STATEMENT

In a 15-city tour in 2010, I presented as a lecture what became the first chapter of this book, asking whether the war in Afghanistan was justified by 9/11. My hope was that, by providing clear evidence that it is not justified—because the official account of 9/11 is false from beginning to end—"the 9/11 Truth Movement and more traditional Peace and Anti-War groups [would] be able to combine forces to oppose this illegal and immoral war."[168] The present book as a whole is in part animated by this hope. But if this hope is to be fulfilled, erstwhile left-leaning detractors of the 9/11 Truth Movement will need to prove that the charges about this movement's members leveled by Cockburn—"They're immune to any reality check"—and Corn—they "are not open to persuasion"[169]—are not instead true of themselves.

If the anti-war community in general becomes willing, as did Bill Christison in particular, to look at the evidence, it will quickly realize that 9/11 was a false-flag operation, intended to enable the US military machine to attack Muslim countries without much examination of the grounds for those attacks. The anti-war coalition will then be able to add to the already well-rehearsed arguments against these wars the fact that the US government, with its Pentagon, murdered almost three thousand people in order to launch an anti-Muslim "war on terror." The strongest proof of the false-flag nature of these attacks is that the government's story could be true only if many miracles happened that day. And surely, one hopes, left-leaning journalists are not willing to accept such miracles.

3. WHY HAVE BILL MOYERS AND ROBERT PARRY IN PARTICULAR ENDORSED MIRACLES?

As we saw in the previous chapter, the 9/11 Truth Movement argued from the outset that 9/11 was a false-flag attack, designed to allow the Bush-Cheney administration and its Pentagon to attack Afghanistan and Iraq, but that most of the traditional anti-war journalists did not endorse the 9/11 Truth Movement. Most of them, in fact, attacked it.

In the first years, to be sure, the Movement did not have a very impressive membership: It had few professionals in relevant disciplines. But in recent years, a dozen professional organizations have been formed, including Architects and Engineers for 9/11 Truth, Firefighters for 9/11 Truth, and Scientists for 9/11 Truth. The 9/11 Truth Movement is now very impressive in both size and professional leadership.

Nevertheless, the traditional anti-war leadership has continued to distance itself from the 9/11 Movement. There have been a few notable exceptions—including Richard Falk and former CIA analysts Bill Christison and Ray McGovern. But most of the anti-war leaders have maintained the stance they took in the first years after 9/11, in spite of all the changes in the 9/11 Truth Movement in the intervening years. For example, when I was interviewed on *Democracy Now!* in 2004, the main argument against my position was that I could not name "one structural engineering expert who said it is not feasible that the planes caused the towers to go down."[1] The movement's lack of architects and engineers at that stage constituted a persuasive argument. But now that there are 1,500 professional members of Architects and Engineers for 9/11 Truth, who say "it is not feasible that the planes caused the towers to go down," one would suppose that *Democracy Now!* would have reassessed its position. But it has not.

Progressive journalists in general have not availed themselves of the evidence provided by the 9/11 Truth Movement to argue against the legitimacy of the so-called "war on terror." If any major journalist could have been expected to do so, it would have been Bill Moyers.

Moyers began his public life by working for President Lyndon Johnson, ending up as the White House press secretary. But having become increasingly opposed to Johnson's war in Vietnam, Moyers resigned in 1966. Next becoming the publisher of *Newsday*, Moyers turned this conservative paper into a progressive organ, which in five years won over 30 awards for journalism, including two Pulitzer Prizes. Then after a brief stint at CBS, Moyers spent most of the rest of his professional life at PBS producing and writing the *Bill Moyers Journal*.

In these programs, Moyers argued that democracy cannot co-exist with a permanent war state. His 2007 program on "The Secret Government" exposed ways in which presidents have deceived the people to promote war, and another 2007 program, "Buying the War,"[2] showed that the media, instead of exposing truths that could have prevented the war in Iraq, served as cheerleaders.

However, while driving home the fact that the media failed to expose Saddam Hussein's lack of weapons of mass destruction, Moyers failed to expose Osama bin Laden's lack of responsibility for the 9/11 attacks. And then in 2011, he attacked the 9/11 Truth Movement. After criticizing Rush Limbaugh and Fox News for providing disinformation that undermines the truths needed for democratic self-government, Moyers added:

> Disinformation is not unique to the right. . . . Like other journalists, I have been the object of malevolent assaults from the '9/11 truthers' for not reporting their airtight case proving that the Bush administration conspired to bring about the attacks on the World Trade Center.[3]

In referring to this "airtight case," Moyers spoke sarcastically, considering this case anything but airtight. In fact, he said that "the truthers," having no real evidence, simply "'cherry-picked' a few supposed 'anomalies' to build an 'inside-job' story line."[4]

II ROBERT PARRY

In criticizing this case, Moyers was paraphrasing a statement by independent journalist Robert Parry, who said: "Lacking any real evidence . . . , the 'truthers' have built their case on alleged anomalies in the collapse of the buildings."[5] In drawing on Parry, Moyers was aligning himself with one of the best of the independent journalists. Having helped to reveal the Iran-Contra affair and having been the first journalist to report Oliver North's involvement, Parry received the George Polk award for journalism in 1984 and was a finalist for a Pulitzer the following year. In 1995, having resigned from both the Associated Press and *Newsweek* because they put brakes on stories he wanted to report, he created Consortiumnews.com, the first online magazine of investigative journalism. "What distinguishes Parry's project from the mass media's cyber-ventures," Norman Solomon wrote, "is his passionate belief that journalism has a responsibility to follow the trail of the truth, wherever it leads."[6] In 2004, explaining the motivation behind Consortiumnews, Parry wrote:

> [T]he Consortiumnews.com Web site . . . was meant to be a home for important, well-reported stories that weren't welcome in the . . . conventional-wisdom-driven national news media . . . . I was distressed by the silliness . . . that had pervaded American journalism by the mid-1990s. I feared, too, that the decline of the U.S. press corps foreshadowed disasters that would come when journalists failed to alert the public about impending dangers.

In concluding that 2004 essay, Parry said: "[T]he fight for honest information is a battle for the future of American democracy."[7] Given Parry's commitments, we would have expected him to explore some of the contradictions in the official 9/11 story.

There is still another reason why we would have expected Parry to expose obvious lies in the official 9/11 narrative. After Parry had won awards for his reporting about the Iran-Contra affair, he delved more deeply into this story, finding evidence to support the theory that the Reagan-Bush administration's contact with the Iranian government of Ayatollah Khomeini had begun years earlier, during the 1980 presidential campaign. President Jimmy Carter was trying to negotiate the release of US citizens being held as hostages by the Iranian government. The Republicans reportedly feared that Carter would arrange an "October Surprise"—a last-minute release of the hostages, which would guarantee Carter's reelection.

But Parry moved toward the theory that the Reagan-Bush campaign had worked out a different "October Surprise"—according to which the Iranians, in exchange for weapons for their war with Iraq, would hold the hostages until after the election, thereby virtually guaranteeing victory by the Republicans. This theory had been argued in a

1989 book, entitled *October Surprise*, by Barbara Honegger[8] (who had worked in the Reagan White House until she resigned for reasons of conscience in 1983). But Parry publicly endorsed this view only after he had investigated the claims himself, uncovering additional evidence.

Having left *Newsweek* in 1990 after it insisted that Parry quit reporting about Iran-Contra, he was approached by PBS's *Frontline* to do a special about the October Surprise allegations. Parry knew his career would be improved if he joined other journalists in debunking the charge that the Reagan-Bush ticket had won the election by means of a dirty trick. However, finding multiple testimonies that George Bush, then the Republican vice-presidential candidate, and Bill Casey, the Republican campaign chairman, met with Iranians in Madrid and Paris in 1980, he reported these events in a 1991 *Frontline* program. This program, appearing the same week as a *New York Times* op-ed by Iranian expert Gary Sick, led to a congressional investigation. But these allegations were widely denounced in the press, and Democratic congressman Lee Hamilton, who headed the congressional task force, declared that the theory of a secret deal had "no credible evidence."

In reality, there was a lot of credible evidence. Jamshid Hashemi, the brother of Iranian banker Cyrus Hashemi, said that he and his brother had met with Casey in Madrid on July 27 and 28, 1980. And testimony that Bush and Casey had met with Iranian officials was provided by former Iranian President Bani-Sadr, by Russian intelligence, and by the biographer of France's chief of intelligence. However, Hamilton and his chief counsel, Lawrence Barcella, hid some of this evidence and disputed the rest of it by means of false claims and ludicrous alibis.[9]

One task force member, Democratic Representative Merv Dymally, recognized the absurdity of the alibis and planned to dissent. But Hamilton used threats to get him to remain silent, so the task force's report was accepted without dissent. Hamilton then wrote a *New York Times* op-ed entitled "Case Closed" (January 24, 1993), in which he stated that the task force's findings "should put the controversy to rest once and for all." Consequently, Parry wrote, "Washington's 'conventional wisdom' quickly solidified around the judgment that the October Surprise story was a loony conspiracy theory."[10]

However, in spite of this conventional wisdom, Parry did not recant. Indeed, he founded Consortiumnews.com in large part because of new documents "that put the history of the 1980s in a new . . .

light,"[11] especially showing that the Reagan-Bush team had won the presidency in 1980 by virtue of a dirty trick that bordered on treason. But the press continued to hold, Parry wrote, that "the October Surprise story was a bogus conspiracy theory, despite the fact that many of the same Reagan figures had been caught lying about the secret Iran-Contra guns-for-hostages negotiations in 1985-86."[12]

Parry's continuing insistence on the truth and importance of the October Surprise, wrote a sympathetic journalist in 1996, has "made him persona non grata" in the media establishment.[13] Parry himself said: "It used to be that you were admired if you took on a tough story. Now you're portrayed as a nut."[14]

Given Parry's commitment to truthful journalism, combined with his awareness that the October Surprise became relegated to the status of a "bogus conspiracy theory" only because of lying politicians and careless and dishonest journalists, we would have expected him to engage in meticulous reporting about independent (from the government) intellectuals, including scientists, who have expressed dissent from the official account of the 9/11 attacks. We would have expected him to be suspicious of the official account because it was provided by the Bush-Cheney administration, which is now known to have lied about Iraq. And we would have expected Parry to be even more suspicious about the official story of 9/11 because the chief of the lying politicians in the October Surprise case, Lee Hamilton, served as the Democratic co-chair of the 9/11 Commission.[15]

Moreover, Parry could have learned from a book entitled *The Commission*, by *New York Times* writer Philip Shenon, that Hamilton's duplicitous ways continued in his new role.[16] Hamilton, together with the Republican co-chair Thomas Kean, appointed Philip Zelikow to be the commission's executive director, even though he was essentially a member of the Bush White House.[17] Hamilton also, with Kean, concealed from the staff the fact that Zelikow had written a detailed outline of the Commission's final report, complete with "chapter headings, subheadings, and sub-subheadings," before the staff had its first meeting.[18]

III MOYERS AND PARRY VS. 9/11 TRUTH

For all of these reasons, we should have expected Parry, as well as Moyers, to have done good reporting about the 9/11 attacks. They instead used bad reporting to attack the 9/11 Truth Movement's claim that 9/11 was an inside job.

Both Moyers and Parry, as we saw earlier, said that "truthers" had rejected the official account of 9/11 on the basis of *alleged* or *supposed* anomalies. "Anomalies," coming from the word *nomos*, refers to occurrences that are exceptions to norms, rules, or regularities. In saying that the 9/11 Truth Movement speaks of *supposed*, or *alleged*, anomalies in the collapse of the World Trade Center buildings, Moyers and Parry were saying that the official account, according to which the buildings were brought down by the airliners and the resulting fires, contained no *real* anomalies—no exceptions to the regularities of physics and chemistry, no miracles.

1. WORLD TRADE CENTER MIRACLES

In truth, the official account of the destruction of the World Trade Center contains many anomalies, and some of them so obviously and violently violate laws of science, as we saw in the previous chapter, that they must be called "miracles." Insofar as Moyers and Parry endorse the official account of the destruction of the World Trade Center, they accept all of these miracles. I will focus on six of the miracles discussed in the previous chapter.

WTC 7 As Brought Down By Fire: When people talk about the World Trade Center, they usually have in mind the Twin Towers. But a third building came down: World Trade Center 7, a 47-story building two blocks from the Twin Towers, which came down at 5:21 in the afternoon.

It came to be widely accepted that the collapse of the Twin Towers was understandable, because they were struck by airliners, which caused damage, and the planes' jet fuel led to big fires. But WTC 7 was not hit by a plane, so its collapse seemed to be unprecedented, being the first steel-framed building to collapse because of fire. And this building's fires, moreover, were neither very big nor very long-lasting, compared with earlier building fires—such as the 1991 fire in Philadelphia's One Meridian Plaza, which raged for 18 hours.[19]

New York Times writer James Glanz referred to the collapse of this building as a "mystery."[20] The obvious solution to this mystery would be to say that WTC 7 was brought down by explosives—and there was much evidence for this conclusion. But the Bush administration and

NIST—an agency of the federal government—insisted that no explosives were used.

From the perspective of the official account, therefore, the collapse of WTC 7 was definitely an anomaly. If Moyers and Parry endorse the official view of this building, do they not therefore endorse a miracle?

Imitation of a Controlled Implosion: As we saw in the previous chapter, Building 7 collapsed *symmetrically*, coming down with an almost perfectly horizontal roofline—which means that all 82 of the steel columns supporting the building had to fail *simultaneously*. Even if we leave aside the fact that fires could not have caused a steel-framed building to collapse, the pattern of fires in WTC 7 was very asymmetrical, and a symmetrical effect could not be caused by a very asymmetrical pattern of causes. Also, rather than starting to sag, as the fires gradually heated up, the collapse had a *sudden onset*, changing in a split second from complete immobility to coming down in free fall.

These two characteristics of Building 7's collapse—the symmetrical pattern and the sudden onset—are characteristics of a controlled *implosion*, in which incendiaries and explosives are used to slice the building's steel support columns so as to cause the building to come straight down. And engineering an implosion, as we saw, is "by far the trickiest type of explosive project," which "only a handful of blasting companies in the world . . . possess enough experience . . . to perform."[21]

If Moyers and Parry hold that Building 7 came down without the aid of explosions, then they imply that scattered fires in this building produced a collapse that perfectly imitated the kind of controlled implosion that could be performed by only a few companies in the world. Moyers and Parry would be stuck, therefore, with a miracle.

WTC 7's Descent in Absolute Free Fall: If Moyers and Parry believe that WTC 7 was brought down by fire, they imply that a third miracle is constituted by the fact that WTC 7 came down in free fall for over two seconds.

As we have seen, Shyam Sunder, who was in charge of NIST's World Trade Center reports, pointed out that WTC 7, assuming that it was brought down by fire, could not have come down in free fall, "because there was structural resistance."[22] Later, however, NIST came to agree with physicist David Chandler that the building came down in free fall for over two seconds. NIST had rightly said that this would be impossible in a fire-induced collapse. But NIST, continuing to insist that no explosives were used, continued to presuppose a fire-induced collapse.

If Moyers and Parry accept the official account, therefore, they would imply that the free-fall descent of WTC 7 was a miracle.[23]

The Twin Towers: Descending in Virtual Free Fall: The Twin Towers came down, in NIST's words, "essentially in free fall."[24] In trying to explain this fact while denying that explosives were used, NIST said, as we saw in the previous chapter, that "the massive top section of [each] building" fell down on the lower section, which "was unable to stop or even to slow the falling mass."[25]

As we further saw, however, this idea violates one of the fundamental principles of physics and (hence) engineering, called "the conservation of momentum." By this principle, the "undamaged steel structure" of the lower part would necessarily retard the descent of the upper part and perhaps even completely arrest it.

In claiming, therefore, that each of the Twin Towers came down essentially in free fall without the aid of explosives, NIST implied *enormous* violations of the conservation of momentum. If Moyers and Parry endorse the official view of the destruction of the Twin Towers, therefore, they would imply the occurrence of two more miracles.[26]

Horizontal Ejections from the Twin Towers: As we also saw, the collapse of each tower began with a massive explosion near the top, during which huge sections of perimeter columns were ejected out 500 to 600 feet. Enormous force would have been needed to eject such large sections of steel that far out. But these ejections could not have been produced by any of the three causal factors allowed by NIST: airplane impacts, fires, and gravity. NIST would not allow that these horizontal ejections were produced by explosives. If Moyers and Parry really mean to endorse the official account, therefore, they imply that these horizontal ejections were miracles.

Metal-Melting Fires: Moyers and Parry probably did not think of the fires in the World Trade Center as having had miraculous powers. But NIST's account, as we saw in the previous chapter, implies they did. According to professors at Worcester Polytechnic Institute and the

University of California, steel in the Twin Towers and WTC 7 melted and even evaporated—a process requiring a temperature almost three times that of an ordinary building fire. Equally extraordinary was evidence by the US Geological Survey that something in the World Trade Center melted molybdenum, the melting point of which is over two and a half times the temperature that the building fires could have produced.[27]

So if Moyers and Parry reaffirm the official account, they would imply that the World Trade Center fires had miraculous powers.

2. Trying to Explain Moyers and Parry

Moyers and Parry have not, of course, explicitly endorsed miracles. In fact, they would surely deny that the destruction of the World Trade Center involved any miracles. But insofar as they accept the official account, their views of the six phenomena I have discussed violate principles of physics, so these phenomena would have to be classified as miracles.

Wrong Answers: Why would Moyers and Parry accept the official account, even though it implies miracles? One answer might be that they, like many other journalists, have accepted the official view out of fear for their reputations. But Moyers and Parry have repeatedly shown that they have the courage to stand up for truth as they see it, regardless of the consequences.

So why did Parry, who was wrongly charged with making "baseless accusations" about an October Surprise,[28] wrongly charge "truthers" with making "unsubstantiated and bizarre claims about 'controlled demolitions'"?[29] As we have seen, there is nothing unsubstantiated about the claims that the Twin Towers and Building 7 were brought down by means of explosives. Parry claims that "scientists and engineers have provided plausible explanations" for the official view.[30] But only a handful of scientists and engineers have stated in print that they see nothing wrong with the official view, and most of them have been dependent upon the government. (Remember Upton Sinclair's famous statement: "It is difficult to get a man to understand something, when his salary depends upon his *not* understanding it!"[31]) By contrast, thousands of professionals have publicly stated that the official view cannot be true, and these professionals include scientists, firefighters, intelligence officers, military officers, and over 1,500 architects and engineers.[32]

Parry has unfairly been called a "nut" because of his persistence in laying out the evidence for the October Surprise. So why did he, on the basis of inadequate study, turn around and say: "To label the 'truther' version of the 9/11 events nutty would seem an understatement."[33]

Moyers has also treated 9/11 poorly. Observing that "America seems more and more unable to deal with reality," Moyers rightly said in his 2011 lecture that "many people inhabit a closed belief system on whose door they have hung the 'Do Not Disturb' sign."[34] But Moyers' own belief system has evidently made him unable to deal with the reality revealed by the 9/11 Truth Movement.

Moyers' Bias Against Truthers: Moyers' bias against 9/11 Truth was manifested, it seems, three years before his 2011 statement. On February 1, 2008, in preparation for the presidential election, the *Bill Moyers Journal* asked viewers: "What one book do you want your next president to read?" The next week, Moyers named the three books receiving the most votes, while adding: "We detected only one organized campaign behind a certain book, and we disqualified it as a result."[35] The book in question, viewers learned the following week, was my book 2007 book, *Debunking 9/11 Debunking*—which was the book that actually received the most votes.[36]

Was the alleged "organized campaign" the real reason why this book was disqualified? It would seem not, for three reasons. First, Moyers had not, in explaining the contest, said anything about disallowing organized campaigns.

In the second place, the so-called organized campaign consisted entirely of one person writing a statement on 9/11 Blogger. Saying that he suspected most members of the 9/11 Truth Movement would be recommending one of my 9/11 books, he suggested that they agree on one of them, and he suggested the most recent, *Debunking 9/11 Debunking*. I myself played no role in this "campaign." Indeed, I did not even know about the contest until it was over.

In the third place, one of the book authors, Kim Michaels, organized a campaign on behalf of his own book, *The Art of Non-War*. On his website, he wrote: "Bill Moyers is asking viewers to recommend the one book that the next president of the United States should take to the White House. If you feel so inclined, please recommend *The Art of Non-War*."[37] As a result, Michaels' book came in third, a fact that the book's publisher used to promote the book.[38] However, the *Bill Moyers Journal* did not eliminate Michaels' book from the competition in spite of his self-organized campaign. In justifying the exclusion of my book because of "signs of an orchestrated campaign," Moyers said: "I wouldn't call it a conspiracy, but I wouldn't call it fair, either."[39] But if unfairness was the reason why my book was excluded, the Michaels book—the campaign for which could have easily been detected—should also have been excluded.[40]

It would seem, accordingly, that my book was excluded because Bill Moyers did not want to announce that his program had recommended my book, with its claim that 9/11 was an inside job.

By taking together Moyers' treatment of my book with his 2011 attack on "truthers," we can see that he, like Parry, has expressed hostility to the 9/11 Truth Movement that is not justified by the empirical evidence.

The Esteemed Friends Who Are Truthers: I have yet another question for Moyers and Parry. Given their negative characterization of people they call "truthers"—such as Moyers' statement that they employ "sophistry" and Parry's charge that they have "preposterous" ideas— one would assume that none of their esteemed friends would have anything good to say about such people. But one of Moyers' most esteemed friends was William Sloane Coffin, who after leaving the CIA became famous as a preacher, an anti-Vietnam-war activist, and a leader of the civil-rights movement. Moyers interviewed Coffin in 2004 and then spoke at his funeral in 2006.[41] Shortly before his death, Coffin wrote:

> All Americans who love their country enough to dig into the facts of these critical times will be well rewarded by examining Professor Griffin's books. 9/11 truth is a very important issue with the power to bring lasting change to our country.

Another of Moyers' esteemed friends whom he interviewed is Joseph Hough, who at the time was the president of Union Theological Seminary.[42] Hough wrote a blurb for my first 9/11 book, saying that it "ought to be read by any American who values our democracy."

One of Parry's esteemed friends is Ray McGovern, who as a CIA analyst prepared the President's Daily Brief for three presidents and more recently founded Veteran Intelligence Professionals for Sanity. McGovern has published many articles in Consortiumnews.com, and he and Parry have lectured together. And yet McGovern wrote endorsements for two of my 9/11 books, saying in one of them that he hoped readers did not "prefer the comfort of acquiescing to the official version of 9/11 and the imperial wars it facilitated."

How would Moyers and Parry reconcile the comments by these esteemed friends with their negative treatment of "truthers"? I do not know.

The Big Lie: But can we at least understand why Moyers and Parry developed such hostility to the 9/11 Truth Movement? Might the explanation be that the spin machine has been so effective in presenting the 9/11 Truth Movement as "kooky" that Moyers and Parry simply accepted this view and never seriously looked at the best evidence? I suspect that this is part of the answer. Although Parry charged "truthers" with being guilty of "anti-empiricism,"[43] it is Parry and Moyers who have violated the need for empiricism about 9/11— for which I called, incidentally, in the lecture I gave in Seattle in 2007, "9/11: Let's Get Empirical."[44]

However, whereas Moyers' and Parry's anti-empiricism about 9/11 is probably due in part to the spin machine, this surely cannot be the whole answer. Parry and Moyers both know how effective the spin machine can be with regard to any charge that would put the government in a bad light, so they would know the need to get behind the spin by examining the best evidence for the issue at hand.

So why did they not do this with regard to 9/11? For many journalists and other people, the answer would be what I have called "nationalist faith"—the mythical belief that the American government would never deliberately do anything terribly evil. But Parry and Moyers have both reported stories that contradict this myth.

We can distinguish, however, between the kinds of evils they have reported and the type of enormous evil to which Hitler alluded in his discussion of "the Big Lie," in which he said:

> [Ordinary people] more readily fall victims to the big lie than the small lie, since they themselves often tell small lies in little matters but would be ashamed to resort to large-scale falsehoods. It would never come into their heads to fabricate colossal untruths, and they would not believe that others could have the impudence to distort the truth so infamously.[45]

I suspect that, although Moyers and Parry have been more willing than most American journalists to expose ugly truths about American political and military leaders, they drew the line at 9/11. For American political leaders to have planned 9/11, they felt, would have been *so* evil, and the resulting lie would have been *so* colossal, that they could not believe that any American politicians—even Bush and Cheney—would have done it.

The very idea that 9/11 could have been an inside job, Parry said, is "preposterous." Any right thinking person would know this, he seemed to think, and so one could know the claims of the "truthers" to be false without delving into their arguments.[46] One can know a priori, for example, the falsity of their claim that explosives brought down the Twin Towers and Building 7. One does not need to know why the buildings came down to know that they were not brought down by explosives, because explosives would mean that it was an inside job, and this idea is preposterous.

The "truthers" are so obviously wrong that it is not necessary to study their writings. The truth about 9/11 is provided by the NIST reports and the *Popular Mechanics* book, both of which Parry recommended.[47] Perhaps David Ray Griffin wrote a book criticizing *Popular Mechanics* and the NIST report on the Twin Towers and another entire book on Building 7. But Moyers and Parry could know, without reading them, that these books could safely be ignored. And if Parry and Moyers are now aware that the 9/11 Truth Movement contains thousands of professional people—including architects, engineers, lawyers, pilots, medical professionals, scientists, and religious and political leaders—they think that the very fact that these people have become "truthers" shows that something is wrong with their thought processes.

This is my answer to the question, Why do Bill Moyers and Robert Parry endorse the official 9/11 story, even though this story implies that massive miracles occurred on 9/11? Moyers and Parry have fallen for the Big Lie. Whereas they would usually, as Norman Solomon said about Parry, "follow the trail of the truth, wherever it leads," Moyers and Parry did not follow the trail of truth laid down by the independent scientists and other intellectuals who inform the 9/11 Truth Movement.

Whereas Parry said that journalists should not accept "patently absurd reasoning," he and Moyers accepted NIST's patently absurd claims about the Twin Towers and Building 7. Parry said that time spent on 9/11 "means that real crimes . . . get neglected."[48] But 9/11 was the biggest crime in American history. Parry started Consortiumnews.com because he feared that "the decline of the U.S. press corps foreshadowed disasters that would come when journalists failed to alert the public about impending dangers." But the failure to expose the 9/11 crime is the supreme example of the decline of the American press. Parry rightly said that "the fight for honest information is a battle for the future of American democracy,"[49] and Moyers said that he and Bill Coffin agreed that democracy had reached a fork in the road, one fork of which "leads to an America where military power serves empire rather than freedom." Yet nothing has promoted American imperialism and distorted American democracy more than the Big Lie about 9/11.

One example of this Big Lie at work, I have suggested, is that even Bill Moyers and Robert Parry, two of our best journalists, fell for it. One of the next steps for the 9/11 Truth Movement, I propose, is to focus on the relatively small number of journalists who are both honest and courageous as well as intelligent, trying to help them, starting with Moyers and Parry themselves, to see that the 9/11 Big Lie is indeed a lie.

4. Building *What*? How State Crimes against Democracy Can Be Hidden in Plain Sight

At 5:21 PM on 9/11, Building 7 of the World Trade Center collapsed, even though it had not been hit by a plane. This fact is important, as we saw in Chapter 2, because of the widespread acceptance of the idea, in spite of its scientific absurdity, that the Twin Towers collapsed because of the combined effect of the impact of the airliners plus the ensuing jet-fuel-fed fires. Even if the government's account of the Twin Towers is accepted (in spite of its scientific impossibility), the collapse of Building 7 undermines the official account of the destruction of the World Trade Center, according to which it was accomplished by al-Qaeda hijackers. This fact—that the official explanation of the World Trade Center, based on the Twin Towers, is radically changed by taking into account WTC 7—was emphasized in the title of a review of my 2009 book, *The Mysterious Collapse of World Trade Center 7*,[1] by National Medal of Science-winner Lynn Margulis: "Two Hit, Three Down—The Biggest Lie."[2]

I Why the Collapse of WTC 7 Created an Extraordinary Problem

The collapse of WTC 7 created an extraordinary problem for the official account of 9/11 for several reasons.

1. An Unprecedented Occurrence

One reason is that, because of the collapse of WTC 7, the official account of 9/11 includes, as pointed out in Chapter 2, the dubious claim that, for the first time, a steel-framed high-rise building was brought down by fire, and science looks askance at claims of unprecedented occurrences regarding physical phenomena. After *New York Times* writer James Glanz, who himself has a Ph.D in physics, made his previously quoted statement—"that experts said no building like it, a modern, steel-reinforced high-rise, had ever collapsed because of an uncontrolled fire"—Glanz quoted a structural engineer as saying: "[W]ithin the structural engineering community, [WTC 7] is considered to be much more important to understand [than the Twin Towers]," because engineers had no answer to the question, "why did 7 come down?"[3]

2. VISUAL EVIDENCE OF IMPLOSION

Equally remarkable, besides the mere fact that this building came down, was the way it collapsed: straight down, in virtual free fall, making it appear to be an example of the type of controlled demolition known as "implosion," in which explosives and/or incendiaries are used to slice the building's steel support columns in such a way as to cause the building to collapse into its own footprint. CBS anchor Dan Rather, not one to let a remarkable fact go unremarked, said:

> [I]t's reminiscent of those pictures we've all seen . . . on television . . . , where a building was deliberately destroyed by well-placed dynamite to knock it down.[4]

Dan Rather, moreover, was not the only reporter to make such a comment. Al Jones, a reporter for WINS NYC News Radio, said: "I turned in time to see what looked like a skyscraper implosion—looked like it had been done by a demolition crew."[5]

Moreover, whereas Jones and Rather, being laymen in these matters, merely said that the collapse of Building 7 *looked like* a controlled demolition, experts, upon seeing the video, could tell immediately that it *actually was* a controlled demolition.

In 2006, for example, a Dutch filmmaker asked Danny Jowenko, the owner of a controlled demolition company in the Netherlands, to comment on a video of the collapse of WTC 7, without telling him what it was. (Jowenko had been unaware that a third building had collapsed on 9/11.) After viewing the video, Jowenko said: "They simply blew up columns, and the rest caved in afterwards. . . . This is controlled demolition." When asked if he was certain, he replied: "Absolutely, it's been imploded. This was a hired job. A team of experts did this."[6]

3. TESTIMONIES ABOUT EXPLOSIONS

Besides the obviousness from the very appearance of the collapse of Building 7 that it had been brought down by explosives, there were testimonies about explosions in this building.

One of these was provided by Michael Hess, New York City's corporation counsel and a close friend of Mayor Rudy Giuliani. While on his way back to City Hall, Hess was stopped for an interview at 11:57 that morning, during which he said:

> I was up in the emergency management center on the twenty-third floor [of WTC 7], and when all the power went out in the building, another gentleman and I walked down to the eighth floor [sic] where there was an explosion and we were trapped on the eighth floor with smoke, thick smoke, all around us, for about an hour and a half. But the New York Fire Department . . . just came and got us out.[7]

Hess thereby reported a mid-morning explosion in WTC 7.

The other gentleman, Barry Jennings of the New York City Housing Authority, reported the same thing during another on-the-street interview, reporting that he and "Mr. Hess" had been walking down the stairs when they became trapped by a "big explosion."[8] Jennings, in fact, said that explosions continued going off while they were waiting to be rescued.[9]

There were also reports of explosions in the late afternoon, just as WTC 7 started coming down. Reporter Peter Demarco of the *New York Daily News* said:

> [T]here was a rumble. The building's top row of windows popped out. Then all the windows on the thirty-ninth floor popped out. Then the thirty-eighth floor. Pop! Pop! Pop! was all you heard until the building sunk into a rising cloud of gray.[10]

NYPD officer Craig Bartmer gave the following report:

> I was real close to Building 7 when it fell down. . . . That didn't sound like just a building falling down to me . . . . There's a lot of eyewitness testimony down there of hearing explosions. . . . [A]ll of a sudden. . . I looked up, and . . . [t]he thing started pealing in on itself. . . . I started running . . . and the whole time you're hearing "boom, boom, boom, boom, boom."[11]

A New York University medical student, who had been serving as an emergency medical worker that day, gave this report:

> [W]e heard this sound that sounded like a clap of thunder. . . . [T]urned around—we were shocked. . . . [I]t looked like there was a shockwave ripping through the building and the windows all busted out. . . . [A]bout a second later the bottom floor caved out and the building followed after that.[12]

4. Physical Evidence

In addition to the visual and testimonial evidence, there was clear physical evidence that WTC 7 was brought down by explosives. As pointed out in Chapter 2, professors from Worcester Polytechnic Institute reported discovering a piece of steel from Building 7 with holes in it, giving it a Swiss-cheese appearance. The steel had melted, they said, and evidently even partly vaporized.[13] And Professor Abolhassan Astaneh-Asl of the University of California at Berkeley also stated, according to New York Times reporter Kenneth Change, that parts of a beam from this building had vaporized.[14]

These reports clearly showed that something other than fire had been making things happen in the buildings, because the fires could not possibly have been higher than 1800 degrees Fahrenheit, while the boiling point of steel is roughly the same as that of iron, which is 5182°F.[15] But even if the steel had simply melted, that by itself would have proved the point, because the melting point of steel is only a little less than that of iron, which is 2800°F.[16]

5. Evidence in Plain Sight

Therefore, clear evidence against the official account of Building 7, according to which it was brought down by fire, existed in plain sight in the form of videos of its collapse, published testimonies about explosions in the building, and physical evidence reported in the New York Times. The reasonable inference to draw from this evidence—namely, that the official account is false, because explosives were used—was reinforced by the first official report on this building's collapse, which was issued in 2002 by FEMA. Besides including as an appendix the report by the three professors on the Swiss-cheese appearing piece of steel, the scientists who wrote the report for FEMA admitted that their "best hypothesis" about why WTC 7 collapsed had "only a low probability of occurrence"[17]—which was science-speak for: "It would not happen in a million years."

6. Failure to Become Well Known

In addition to all these facts, WTC 7 was a very big building, being 47 stories high and having a base about the size of a football field. Although it was dwarfed by the 110-story Twin Towers, it would have been the tallest building in half of the states in the nation. For all of these reasons, the collapse of this building should have become one of the best-known facts about 9/11. But it did not.

A Zogby poll in May 2006 found that 43 percent of the American people were unaware that WTC 7 had collapsed.[18] That same year, as we saw earlier, Danny Jowenko of the Netherlands still did not know about this building's collapse, even though controlled demolition was his field.

1. BUILDING *WHAT?*

A dramatic example of the fact that this building's collapse has not been prominent in the public consciousness was provided in a New York City courtroom in September 2009. Judge Edward Lehner was hearing arguments about a petition, sponsored by NYC CAN (NYC Coalition for Accountability), to allow residents to vote on whether New York City should have its own investigation of the World Trade Center attacks. After Judge Lehner had remarked that the 9/11 Commission had carried out an investigation and issued a report, Dennis McMahon, a lawyer for NYC CAN, said that this report left many unanswered questions. "One of the biggest questions," he added, "is why did Building 7 come down"—at which point Judge Lehner asked: "Building what?" McMahon replied: "World Trade Center Seven. There were three buildings that came down." When the judge, continuing to illustrate his ignorance about this building, asked if it was owned by the Port Authority, McMahon replied that it was owned by Larry Silverstein.[19]

Judge Lehner, it should be emphasized, was not simply an ordinary American citizen. Besides being a judge presiding in New York City, he had been assigned to a case involving the 9/11 attacks in this city. So his ignorance about this building was surprising. And yet it was typical. With his "Building what?" query in 2009, he expressed the same ignorance that had been manifested in 2006 by controlled demolition expert Danny Jowenko and by almost half of the American people. How can we account for this ignorance?

2. ABNORMAL CIRCUMSTANCES

In a *New York Times* story in November 2001, James Glanz wrote that the collapse of WTC 7 was "a mystery that under normal circumstances would probably have captured the attention of the city and the world."[20] Clearly these were not normal circumstances.

Part of the abnormality was the fact that Building 7, while huge, was overshadowed by the Twin Towers, which were over twice as tall. This fact by itself, however, would not account for the enormous ignorance about this third building's collapse. Knowledgeable people had said right away, as Glanz pointed out, that there was a sense in which the collapse of Building 7 should have been the bigger story. Why was it not?

3. DELIBERATE SUPPRESSION

The answer seems to be that it was a deliberately suppressed story. This conclusion is supported by the following facts:

- First, after 9/11 itself, our television networks played videos of the Twin Towers being hit by planes, then coming down, over and over, but the collapse of Building 7 was seldom, if ever, shown.

- Second, when The 9/11 Commission Report was issued in 2004, it did not even mention that Building 7 came down.

- Third, after NIST—the National Institute for Standards and Technology—took over from FEMA the task of explaining the destruction of the World Trade Center, it repeatedly delayed its report on WTC 7. In 2003, NIST said that this report would be issued along with its report on the Twin Towers, the draft of which was to appear in September 2004.[21] However, even though NIST's report on the Twin Towers did not actually appear until 2005, the promised report on WTC 7 was not included: NIST said that it would appear in 2006. But when August of 2006 came, NIST said: "It is anticipated that a draft report [on WTC 7] will be released by early 2007."[22] But it was not released in 2007—either early or late. Instead, NIST in December 2007 "projected" that it would release draft reports on July 8, 2008, followed by final reports August 8, 2008.[23] Instead, the draft report did not appear until August, and the final report not until November of that year—when the Bush-Cheney administration was about to leave office.

To expand on this third point: When in 2008 NIST was accused of having deliberately delayed its report on WTC 7 (which the 9/11 Truth Movement had long considered the "Achilles' Heel" or "Smoking

Gun" of the official account of 9/11[24]), NIST lied, saying that it had worked on this report only since 2005 and hence for only three years—the same length of time it had worked on its Twin Towers report. However, NIST had filed progress reports on WTC 7 in December 2002 and May 2003;[25] in June 2004, it published an *Interim Report on WTC 7*;[26] and in April 2005, NIST released another preliminary report on WTC 7.[27] Then, after ceasing work on this building until after the report on the Twin Towers was issued in October 2005, NIST reported, "the investigation of the WTC 7 collapse resumed."[28] In truth, therefore, NIST had worked on its report on WTC 7 for almost six years, not merely three. So there was good reason to suspect that this report had been deliberately delayed for as long as possible.

III NIST's Draft for Public Comment: Mystery Solved?

In any case, when the Draft for Public Comment did finally appear in August 2008, it was announced at a press conference with much bravado. Shyam Sunder, NIST's lead investigator for its World Trade Center projects, said:

> Our take-home message today is that the reason for the collapse of World Trade Center 7 is no longer a mystery. WTC 7 collapsed because of fires fueled by office furnishings. It did not collapse from explosives.[29]

The mainstream media for the most part simply repeated Sunder's claims. For example, an Associated Press story entitled "Report: Fire, Not Bombs, Leveled WTC 7 Building," began by saying: "Federal investigators said Thursday they have solved a mystery of the Sept. 11, 2001, attacks: the collapse of World Trade Center building 7, a source of long-running conspiracy theories." Then, after reinforcing this message by quoting Sunder's assurance that "the reason for the collapse of World Trade Center 7 is no longer a mystery," this story concluded by quoting Sunder's claim that the science behind NIST's findings is "incredibly conclusive," so that "[t]he public should really recognize that science is really behind what we have said."[30]

Reporters, however, could easily have discovered that this was not so. They could have seen, in fact, that NIST's WTC 7 report committed scientific fraud in the technical sense, as defined by the National Science Foundation.

IV NIST FALSIFICATION OF EVIDENCE

One type of fraud is falsification, which includes "omitting data."[31] While claiming that it "found no evidence of a . . . controlled demolition event,"[32] NIST simply omitted an enormous amount of evidence that explosions had brought WTC 7 down.

1. OMITTING TESTIMONIAL EVIDENCE

NIST failed, for one thing, to mention any of the testimonial evidence for explosions. Besides claiming that the event described as a mid-morning explosion by Michael Hess and Barry Jennings was simply the impact of debris from the collapse of the North Tower— which occurred at 10:28 and hence about an hour later than the explosion they had described—NIST failed to mention any of the reports of explosions just as the building started to come down.

2. OMITTING PHYSICAL EVIDENCE

NIST's report on this building also omitted various types of physical evidence, such as the piece of Swiss-cheese steel reported by the three professors in the appendix to the 2002 FEMA report.

The Swiss-Cheese Steel: After describing this piece of steel, the professors said: "A detailed study into the mechanisms of this phenomenon is needed."[33] When NIST took over from FEMA the responsibility of issuing the official reports on the World Trade Center, NIST's director promised that its reports would address "all major recommendations contained in the [FEMA] report."[34] However, when NIST's report on Building 7 appeared in 2008, it did not even mention this mysterious piece of steel, let alone explain how it had been produced. NIST even claimed that no recovered steel from this building had been identified.[35]

Melted Iron and Molybdenum: As we saw in Chapter 2, the RJ Lee research organization reported that steel was melted during "the WTC Event." This report by the RJ Lee Group was made known in an article published in January 2008 by a team of scientists led by physicist Steven Jones,[36] but these reports were simply ignored by NIST.

Scientists at the US Geological Survey, besides also finding evidence that steel had melted, found that molybdenum,[37] with its extremely high melting point (4,753°F),[38] had melted. NIST failed to mention this discovery by another federal agency, although the Steven Jones group had reported it ten months before NIST's final report on WTC 7.

Nanothermite: A report by Jones and several other scientists, including University of Copenhagen chemist Niels Harrit, showed that the WTC dust contained unreacted nanothermite. Nanothermite, Harrit has said, can be tailored to behave as an incendiary (like ordinary thermite), and as an explosive.[39] This report, which was published in a peer-reviewed science journal,[40] was not published until after NIST's final report on WTC 7 appeared. But NIST should have tested the WTC dust for signs of incendiaries, such as ordinary thermite, and explosives, such as nanothermite. But in spite of guidelines mandating examinations to ascertain whether such substances were used,[41] NIST evidently did not do so: When NIST was asked whether it had carried out such tests, NIST said that it had not.[42] When a reporter asked NIST spokesman Michael Newman why not, he replied: "[B]ecause there was no evidence of that." When the reporter asked, "[H]ow can you know there's no evidence if you don't look for it first?" Newman replied: "If you're looking for something that isn't there, you're wasting your time . . . and the taxpayers' money."[43]

V NIST's Fabrication of Evidence

Besides omitting and otherwise falsifying evidence, NIST also committed the type of scientific fraud called fabrication, which means simply "making up results."[44]

1. No Girder Shear Studs

For example, in offering its explanation as to how fire caused Building 7 to collapse, NIST said that the culprit was thermal expansion, meaning that the fire heated up the steel, thereby causing it to expand. Expanding steel beams on the 13th floor, NIST claims, caused a steel girder connecting columns 44 and 79 to break loose. Having lost its support, column 79 failed, starting a chain reaction in which the other 81 columns all failed.[45]

Leaving aside the question of whether this is even remotely possible, let us simply ask: Why did that girder fail? NIST's answer was that it was not connected to the floor slab with shear studs. NIST wrote: "In WTC 7, no studs were installed on the girders."[46] In another passage, NIST said: "Floor beams . . . had shear studs, but the girders that supported the floor beams did not have shear studs."[47]

However, NIST's *Interim Report on WTC 7*, which it published in 2004 before it had developed its girder-failure theory, said shear studs were used to anchor "[m]ost of the beams and girders," including the girder in question.[48]

2. A Raging 12th Floor Fire at 5:00

Although in its 2004 *Interim Report on WTC 7*, NIST said that by 4:45 PM, "the fire on Floor 12 was burned out,"[49] it claimed in its 2008 report that at 5:00, just 21 minutes before the building collapsed, the fire on this floor was still going strong.[50]

VI NIST's Final Report: Affirming a Miracle

As we saw in Chapter 2, NIST denied in its next-to-final report on WTC 7—the Draft for Public Comment—that this building had come down in free fall or even close to it. Shyam Sunder, who headed up NIST's reports on the World Trade Center, even stated that free fall would have been impossible. Speaking in August of 2008, he explained:

> [A] free fall time would be [the fall time of] an object that has no structural components below it. . . . [But] there was structural resistance . . . . And you had a sequence of structural failures that had to take place. Everything was not instantaneous.[51]

But in its final report on WTC 7, which came out in November 2008, NIST admitted that free fall did occur for over two seconds, reporting "a freefall descent over approximately eight stories at gravitational acceleration for approximately 2.25 s[econds]."[52]

While making this admission, NIST did not revise its explanation as to why the building came down: It still claimed that WTC 7 was brought down by fire. And yet Sunder had explained only three months earlier (in the previous indented statement) that a fire-induced collapse (which was what he was defending) could not possibly have come down in free fall.

Physicist David Chandler, who provoked NIST to admit free fall, had explained why a fire-induced collapse could not come down in free fall: "Free fall can only be achieved if there is zero resistance to the motion."[53] In other words, a fire-induced collapse of a steel-framed building—assuming for the sake of argument that this might be possible—could not enter free fall, because even if the top floor came down, its descent would encounter resistance. The top floor of Building 7 could have come down in free fall only if something had suddenly removed all the steel and concrete in the lower part of the building, so that there would be zero resistance.

This removal could only have been produced—assuming that there was no divine intervention—by explosives. And yet NIST, continuing to insist that explosives were not used, implied that a violation of laws of physics occurred. Knowing full well that it had violated laws of physics, NIST—as we saw in Chapter 2—removed every instance of the phrase, stated in the preliminary report, that its report on WTC 7 is "consistent with physical principles."[54]

VII EXPLAINING THE IGNORANCE ABOUT WTC 7

NIST's admission that WTC 7 came down in free fall for over two seconds—an admission that implies either explosives or a miracle—should have been front-page news. Given the fact that the collapse of WTC 7 had been declared a mystery from the outset, the world should have been waiting with baited breath for every new clue as to why this 47-story building had come down. Upon hearing Building 7 mentioned, nobody in the world with access to CNN should have replied, "Building what?" How do we explain the fact that five and even ten years after the mysterious collapse of this building, ignorance about it was still widespread?

To begin answering this question, let us return to James Glanz's statement that the collapse of WTC 7 was "a mystery that *under normal circumstances* would probably have captured the attention of the city and the world."[55] As I stated before, the abnormality seems to have been such that the fact of this building's collapse, and especially videos of this collapse, were deliberately suppressed. What was this abnormality?

1. SCADs

As mentioned in Chapter 2, an issue of *American Behavioral Scientist*, a leading social science journal, had a symposium on State Crimes against Democracy, which is abbreviated SCADs.[56] The authors of this symposium argue that this is an increasingly important type of criminality, so that social scientists need to develop a scientific approach to studying it. SCADs are understood as "concerted actions . . . by government insiders intended to manipulate democratic processes and undermine popular sovereignty." Having the "potential to subvert political institutions and entire governments," SCADs are "high crimes that attack democracy itself."[57]

There are two types of SCADs. On the one hand, there are *officially proven* SCADs, such as "the Watergate break-ins and cover-up . . . , the secret wars in Laos and Cambodia . . . , the illegal arms sales and covert operations in Iran-Contra . . . , and the effort to discredit Joseph Wilson by revealing his wife's status as an intelligence agent."

On the other hand, there are *suspected* SCADs for which there is good evidence. The symposium authors included in this category

> the fabricated attacks on U.S. ships in the Gulf of Tonkin in 1964 . . . , the "October Surprises" in the presidential elections of 1968 . . . and 1980 . . . , the assassinations of John Kennedy and Robert Kennedy . . . , the election breakdowns in 2000 and 2004 . . . , the numerous defense failures on September 11, 2001 . . . , and the misrepresentation of intelligence to justify the invasion and occupation of Iraq.[58]

As this list of illustrations shows, the symposium authors discuss as merely *suspected* SCADs some events that are widely considered *proven*, such as the Gulf of Tonkin hoax and the false claim that Saddam Hussein's Iraq had weapons of mass destruction.

In any case, besides regarding the 9/11 attacks as one of the suspected SCADs for which there is good evidence, this symposium treated it as its *primary* example. The abstract for the introductory essay began thus: "The ellipses of due diligence riddling the official account of the 9/11 incidents continue being ignored by scholars of policy and public administration."[59]

The symposium's final essay, criticizing the majority of the academic world for its "blithe dismissal of more than one law of thermodynamics" that is violated by the official theory of the World Trade Center collapses,[60] also criticized the academy for its failure to protest when "Professor Steven Jones found himself forced out of a tenured position for merely reminding the world that physical laws, about which *there is no dissent whatsoever*, contradict the official theory of the World Trade Center Towers' collapse."[61]

2. Hiding the Most Obvious Evidence that 9/11 Was a SCAD

Now, if 9/11 was a SCAD, we would understand the full extent to which the destruction of the World Trade Center occurred under "abnormal" circumstances, and we would thereby be in a position to understand why the collapse of Building 7, which "under normal circumstances would probably have captured the attention of the city and the world," did not do so.

The fact is that it was not allowed to become well known, for reasons mentioned earlier: Unlike the Twin Towers, it was not hit by a plane; because of this, there was no jet fuel to spread big fires to many floors; and its collapse, unlike that of each of the Twin Towers, looked exactly like a classic implosion, in which the collapse begins from the bottom and the building folds in upon itself, ending up almost entirely in its own footprint. That Building 7 was brought down by explosives was, therefore, much more obvious than the fact that the Twin Towers were explosively demolished.

This greater obviousness is illustrated not only by Danny Jowenko's response, but also by the many engineers and scientists who joined the 9/11 Truth Movement only after seeing a video of this building's collapse. For example, Daniel Hofnung, an engineer in Paris, wrote:

> In the years after the 9/11 events, I thought that all I read in professional reviews and French newspapers was true. The first time I understood that it was impossible was when I saw a film about the collapse of WTC 7.[62]

Likewise, civil engineer Chester Gearhart wrote:

> I have watched the construction of many large buildings and also have personally witnessed 5 controlled demolitions in Kansas City. When I saw the towers fall on 9/11, I knew something was wrong and my first instinct was that it was impossible. When I saw building 7 fall, I *knew* it was a controlled demolition.[63]

This video was also decisive for University of Copenhagen chemist Niels Harrit, who later became the first author of the nanothermite paper. When asked how he became involved with these issues, he replied:

It all started when I saw the collapse of Building 7, the third skyscraper. It collapsed seven hours after the Twin Towers. And there were only two airplanes. When you see a 47-storey building, 186 meters tall, collapse in 6.5 seconds, and you are a scientist, you think "What?" I had to watch it again. . . and again. I hit the button ten times, and my jaw dropped lower and lower. Firstly, I had never heard of that building before. And there was no visible reason why it should collapse in that way, straight down, in 6.5 seconds. I have had no rest since that day.[64]

Given these reactions, it is obvious that, if 9/11 was a State Crime against Democracy, the fact of Building 7's collapse, and especially the video of this collapse, had to be suppressed as much as possible. In order to prevent awareness that this building came down in virtual free fall, the cover-up artists prevented videos of WTC 7's "collapse" from being shown on television. And in order to forestall as long as possible widespread awareness that this third building even came down, these cover-up artists prevented this fact from being mentioned in *The 9/11 Commission Report.*

3. WTC 7 as a Dud

Having made this point, I need to respond to an obvious objection: If those who were responsible for bringing down Building 7 were going to need to suppress the video of its collapse, why did they not bring this building down until late in the afternoon, when the air was clean and cameras would be trained on the building—with the consequence that we have perfectly clear videos of the collapse of WTC 7 from various angles, each one showing its straight-down, virtual free-fall, descent? Why did they not bring it down in the morning, shortly after one of the Twin Towers had collapsed, when the resulting dust cloud would have made any images impossible? After the collapse of the North Tower at 10:28, for example, visibility did not return sufficiently for film crews to come back to the area, NIST reported, until 11:00.[65] Had Building 7 been imploded at, say, 10:45, we would not have these videos clearly showing it coming straight down in virtual free fall.

There are many reasons, as I showed in an appendix to *The Mysterious Collapse of World Trade Center 7*, to believe that this had indeed been the plan—that is, to bring it down at about 10:45 AM— but that this building was, as one researcher put it, "a dud"[66]—meaning that "the demolition system in WTC 7 simply did not respond as intended and the building defiantly remained intact."[67] If this is what happened, then it would make sense that agents would have been sent into the building to set fires, so that the cover-story could be that fires had brought the building down. This hypothesis would explain why, although the fires in Building 7 were supposedly started by flaming debris from the North Tower's collapse at 10:28, no flames were visible in this building, NIST admitted, until after noon, and on some floors there is no photographic evidence of fire until 3:40, 4:00, and 5:00 PM.[68]

In any case, had the demolition system worked as intended, this building's collapse would still have been a big mystery, but there would have been no videos showing that it had come straight down and, for over two seconds, in absolute free fall.

I have emphasized this likelihood—that the destruction of WTC 7 was a botched operation—because if true it provides the clearest possible illustration of the theme of this chapter, namely, that SCADs can be hidden in plain sight. There are literally dozens of contradictions in the official account of 9/11 that show it to have been an inside operation. But the clearest proof of this is provided by the video of this enormous building coming straight down in free fall—virtual free fall for the entire period, which was about seven seconds, and absolute free fall for 2.25 seconds of that period. And yet even though this proof has existed in plain sight for all these years, the fact that 9/11 was an inside job, and hence a State Crime against Democracy, has remained a hidden fact, at least in the sense that it is not part of the public conversation. If the destruction of WTC 7 was a botched operation, then the hiding of the fact that 9/11 was a SCAD is even more impressive. How was this hiding achieved?

4. Hiding SCADs: The Role of the Mainstream Media

Peter Dale Scott, discussing the erosion of the US constitution in recent times, suggests that "this erosion has been achieved in part through a series of important deep events in [post-World-War-II] American history—events aspects of which . . . will be ignored or suppressed in the mainstream media."[69] Indeed, Scott adds:

> [T]he mainstream U.S. media . . . have become so implicated in past protective lies . . . that they, as well as the government, have now a demonstrated interest in preventing the truth about *any* of these events from coming out. This means that the current threat to

constitutional rights does not derive from the deep state alone. . . .
[T]he problem is a global dominance *mindset* that prevails not only
inside the Washington Beltway but also in the mainstream media . . .
, one which has come to accept recent inroads on constitutional
liberties, and stigmatizes, or at least responds with silence to, those
who are alarmed by them. . . . [A]cceptance of this mindset's notions
of decorum has increasingly become a condition for participation in
mainstream public life.[70]

Referring thereby to events such as the JFK assassination, the
Tonkin Gulf hoax, and 9/11, Scott by "deep events" means the same
types of events called SCADs by the authors of the symposium on that
topic. Indeed, one of those authors cited Scott's writings, treating his
"deep events" as examples of SCADs and quoting his statements about
the complicity of the mainstream media in covering up the truth about
these events.[71]

These authors also make the same point themselves, remarking
that "the U.S. government's account of 9/11 [is] parroted by the
mainstream media"[72] and commenting on "the profound disavowal of
still burning, molten questions originating at 9/11 Ground Zero gone
begging by the American media."[73]

Besides parroting the government's account of 9/11 and
stigmatizing those who provide alternative accounts with the
discrediting label "conspiracy theorist," how has America's mainstream
media kept the truth about WTC 7 hidden from the majority of the
American people? Through various means:

- First, by never replaying the statements by Dan Rather and
  other reporters about how the collapse of WTC 7 looked just
  like a controlled demolition.

- Second, by seldom, if ever, replaying the video of this
  building's collapse.

- Third, by never mentioning credible critiques of the official
  account. For example, my 2009 book, *The Mysterious Collapse
  of World Trade Center 7: Why the Final Official Report about
  9/11 is Unscientific and False*, which has been endorsed by
  prestigious scientists and engineers, has never been reviewed
  in the mainstream media, even though my previous 9/11 book,
  The New Pearl Harbor Revisited, was a *Publishers Weekly* "Pick
  of the Week" in 2008.[7]

- Fourth, by never mentioning, except for one story that apparently slipped through,[75] the existence of an organization called Architects and Engineers for 9/11 Truth, which by now has over 1,500 licensed and/or degreed members calling for a new investigation of WTC 7 as well as the Twin Towers.[76]

- Fifth, by never reporting scientific evidence contradicting the official account of these buildings' destruction, such as the reported discovery of nanothermite in the WTC dust.

- Sixth, by overlooking the fact that NIST's report on WTC 7 omitted an enormous amount of evidence showing that explosives must have been used. For example, although the *New York Times* in 2002 called the piece of Swiss-cheese steel recovered from this building "the deepest mystery uncovered in the investigation," it did not issue a peep when NIST's 2008 report on this building failed to mention this piece of steel and even claimed that no steel from this building had been identified. The *Times* knew better but said nothing.

- Seventh, by reporting NIST's press briefing of August 2008 announcing the Draft for Public Comment, in which Shyam Sunder announced with great bravado that the "the reason for the collapse of World Trade Center 7 is no longer a mystery" and that "science is really behind what we have said," but then *not* reporting on NIST's final report in November, in which it almost explicitly admitted that science does *not* stand behind, but *contradicts*, its theory of this building's collapse (by admitting that it came down in absolute free fall for over two seconds, even though Sunder had pointed out that free fall would, in a fire-induced collapse, have been impossible).

CONCLUSION

Through these and related means, the truth about the collapse of Building 7 has been effectively hidden, even though it has existed in plain sight all these years. Even the bare fact of the collapse itself has been so effectively hidden that over 40 percent of the American public in 2006 did not know that WTC 7 had come down on 9/11, and in 2009 a judge in New York City, upon hearing a reference to Building 7, could ask: "Building what?"

I offer this chapter as a case study in the power of the forces behind SCADs to hide things that exist in plain sight, because if they can hide the straight-down free-fall collapse of a 47-story building captured on video in broad daylight, they can hide almost anything.

POSTSCRIPT

When I delivered the lecture on which this chapter is based in 2010, I said that I made the closing point—that "they can hide almost anything"—not to instill despair but to point to the seriousness of the problem, and also to pave the way for making a proposal: Recognizing the high correlation between those who know about the collapse of WTC 7 and those who believe that a new—or rather real—9/11 investigation is needed, I proposed that the international 9/11 Truth Movement should initiate, starting in September 2010, a year-long Building 7 campaign. This would involve expanding the Building What? campaign that had already been launched in New York by the NYC Coalition for Accountability (NYC CAN). This campaign would seek to increase greatly, by the tenth anniversary of 9/11, the level of awareness worldwide of what happened to World Trade Center 7.

The campaign became quite successful. In August 2010, a 30-second "Building What?" video ad was made by a first-rate filmmaker.[77] Through small donations, $100,000 was raised to purchase commercial time on cable television in the NYC area.

On November 13, Geraldo Rivera of Fox News, having seen the ad, arranged a segment about Building 7 with engineer Tony Szamboti, a member of Architects and Engineers for 9/11 Truth, and Bob McIlvaine, who lost his son in the 9/11 attacks. "What caught my eye," Rivera said, was the fact that over 1,300 architects and engineers disagreed with NIST's conclusion about WTC 7. At the end of this segment, Rivera, who had previously derided "Truthers" (telling them to "get a life"), said: "I certainly am much more open minded about it than I was, because of the involvement of the 9/11 families, and all these engineers and architects—clearly they know more than I do."[78]

On November 19, 2010, Rivera was interviewed by Judge Andrew Napolitano, Fox's legal analyst, on his Fox Business show *Freedom Watch*. In light of Rivera's acknowledgement that over 1,300 architects and engineers disagree with NIST's conclusion, Napolitano asked Rivera whether *he* doubts the official conclusion. Rivera said:

> I think that it is highly unlikely that the government would do any-
> thing nefarious on a scale of this epic nature. However, the building
> does appear to come down in a way that is reminiscent of a
> controlled demolition.

Rivera even said that, if the building was indeed brought down by explosives, then "the most obnoxious protestors in recent years are right."[79]

The following week, Judge Napolitano said: "It's hard for me to believe that it came down by itself. . . . It couldn't possibly have been done the way the government told us."[80]

In March 2011, the campaign, having changed its name to "Remember Building 7," created a video ad of that name. Pointing out that the government claimed that, in Sunder's words, the building collapsed "primarily due to fires," an engineer states: "I along with 1,400 other architects and engineers have found the government's conclusion to be physically impossible."[81] Another $100,000 was raised to inform still more people.

Simultaneously with releasing this new ad in June, the Remember Building 7 campaign released the results of a new poll. Among other things, this poll revealed that, although people in NYC surely are much more aware than people in the rest of the country, 33 percent of New Yorkers were still unaware that a third building had come down. And only 14 percent could name this building. So if the goal was to keep people ignorant about WTC 7, the perpetrators should be pleased.

But even more important, given Remember Building 7's effort to overcome this ignorance, is this information: Of those who were aware that Building 7 came down, 24 percent of them believed it was a controlled demolition (while 49 percent believed it to be caused by fire). When people were informed that 1,500 architects and engineers dispute the government's explanation of WTC 7's collapse, the percentage who believe it was a controlled demolition rises from 24 to 36 percent. Assuming that the government has "encouraged" the press not to report about the existence of professional 9/11 organizations, such as Architects and Engineers for 9/11 Truth, this finding by the poll would confirm the government's wisdom in seeking to keep the public uninformed.

Likewise, these same poll results show the wisdom of Remember Building 7's twofold approach: Informing people that not only the Twin Towers, but also Building 7 came down, and also that a growing number of architects and engineers say that the government's explanation is physically impossible.

5. PHONE CALLS FROM THE 9/11 PLANES: HOW THEY FOOLED AMERICA

The public has been led to believe that passengers and flight attendants on the 9/11 airplanes made telephone calls to people on the ground, telling them what was happening on the planes. According to these messages, the airplanes were hijacked. The reported phone calls fooled America, with even well-educated people believing that the reported calls were real. As we saw in Chapter 2, Matthew Rothschild, the editor of *The Progressive*, said in a 2006 essay defending the official account of 9/11: "we know from cell phone conversations that passengers on board that plane planned on confronting the hijackers."

Besides convincing people that the 9/11 planes had been hijacked, some of the reported calls were more specific, saying that the planes were taken over by "Middle Eastern-looking men." One caller, reporting having gotten a close look at one of the hijackers, described him as having "an Islamic look."[1]

These reported phone calls have been of utmost importance to the official story about 9/11. They provided the main basis for the twofold belief that (1) the planes had been hijacked and that (2) the hijackers were from the Middle East. The authorities quickly identified the alleged hijackers as members of al-Qaeda.

There is a multi-faceted argument against the official account of 9/11 (according to which the 9/11 attacks were carried out by Muslim members of al-Qaeda). Part of this argument is that the "phone calls from the planes" were not authentic. The present essay provides various types of evidence that the calls were, indeed, faked.

I THE ALLEGED HIJACKERS: NO EVIDENCE THEY EXISTED, EVIDENCE THEY DID *NOT* EXIST

The final section of Chapter 1 dealt primarily with evidence that was provided by US authorities for the claim that there were hijackers on four flights: AA 11 and 77 and UA 175 and 93. This evidence included incriminating evidence said to have been found in Mohamed Atta's luggage; al-Qaeda operatives captured on airport security videos; the voice of a member of al-Qaeda, generally thought to be Atta, on a radio transmission; al-Qaeda passports at crash sites; an al-Qaeda headband at a crash site; and passenger manifests generally thought to contain the names of the men identified as the hijackers. As we saw in Chapter 1, however, all of this proffered evidence, when examined, disintegrates.

In addition to this negative evidence—that there is no evidence for the claim that al-Qaeda operatives hijacked the planes—there is also, as we saw, evidence for a stronger conclusion: that there simply were no al-Qaeda hijackers. This conclusion is grounded in three types of evidence: (1) That there were no authentic passenger manifests with the names of the alleged hijackers (in fact, with any Arab names whatsoever). (2) That the autopsies for the attack on the Pentagon contained no names of any of the alleged hijackers (indeed, no Arab names whatsoever). (3) That not a single one of the eight pilots squawked the hijack code. These facts count heavily—indeed decisively—against the idea that there were Arab-Muslim hijackers on the planes. And if there were no Arab-Muslim hijackers, then there would have been no phone calls from the planes in which passengers and flight attendants described such hijackers.

II EVIDENCE FOR FAKED PHONE CALLS: THE BURNETT CALLS

Some people may argue, nonetheless, that the presence of hijackers on the planes was proved by phone calls from passengers and flight attendants on the 9/11 flights—phone calls in which the existence of hijackers was reported. If authentic, these calls would provide strong evidence for the existence of hijackers.

However, as I have pointed out (along with others[2]), there is strong evidence that these calls were faked. To support this conclusion, one does not need to show that all, or even a large number, of the purported calls were faked. It is sufficient, logically, to show that one of the purported calls was faked. A century ago, philosopher William James pointed out that it takes only one white crow to prove that not all crows are black. Likewise, it takes only one faked call to prove that not all of the reported calls from the 9/11 airliners were authentic.

But at this point, the parallel with James' white crow example breaks down. Spotting a white crow does not provide evidence that all, most, or even several crows are white. But realizing that one of the purported calls was faked does suggest that all of the purported phone calls were faked. Why? Because if some group or agency within the US government (including the US military) made a phone call that was supposed to be from one of the 9/11 planes, this could have come about only with considerable advance planning. This planning would disprove the official account of 9/11, according to which the planes were taken over in a surprise operation. And if the official account is false on this point, then it must be supposed that all of the purported calls were faked.

But while one example would suffice, I will discuss several purported phone calls from the 9/11 planes, showing that it would be very difficult to escape from the conclusion that they were faked. In the present section, I discuss the case of Deena Burnett, who reportedly received calls from her husband.

1. The Calls Received by Deena Burnett

Deena Burnett reported that while her husband, Tom Burnett, was on UA 93, she received "three to five cellular phone calls" from him.[3] This is important, because it would have been impossible—see the next section—for these calls to have been made using a cell phone. And yet it seems equally impossible to doubt her report about the calls she received.

With regard to some reports about people saying they had been called by a friend or relative using a cell phone, we can suspect that the person receiving the call misunderstood the caller, or that a reporter got the facts wrong. But such explanations would not work in relation to Deena Burnett, because she had recognized, she said, her husband's cell phone number on her phone's caller ID. She, in fact, told this to the FBI. The FBI's summary of the interview said:

> [Deena] Burnett was able to determine that her husband was using his own cellular telephone because the caller identification showed his number, 925 980-3360. Only one of the calls did not show on the caller identification as she was on the line with another call.[4]

We might, of course, assume that by the time Deena Burnett was interviewed, her memory had become confused. But this interview with the FBI occurred on 9/11 itself, only hours after she received the phone calls.

It seems, therefore, that one could explain away Deena Burnett's testimony—that her caller ID indicated that she was called from Tom Burnett's cell phone—only by arguing that she must have lied. However, besides the absence of evidence that Deena Burnett lied, there also appears to be no plausible hypothesis as to *why* she would have lied. Moreover, any suspicion that she is the type of person who might have lied would surely be dissolved by reading a 2006 interview.[5] We must conclude, therefore, that Deena Burnett's caller ID indicated that *she was called from Tom Burnett's cell phone*. Given this conclusion, would there be any way to deny that these calls must have somehow been faked?

2. REASON TO BELIEVE THAT THE BURNETT CALLS HAD BEEN FAKED

At the times when Tom Burnett supposedly made his calls from UA 93, this plane would have been flying at an altitude of between 34,300 and 40,700 feet.[6] Scientific studies have shown that the calls reported by Deena Burnett could not have come from Tom Burnett using his cell phone aboard UA 93. The most rigorous evidence of this kind has been provided by Canadian mathematician and scientist A. K. Dewdney, who for many years wrote a column for *Scientific American*. In 2003, he carried out experiments, using all the kinds of cell phones that were available in 2001 that he could find.[7] In my 2008 book, *The New Pearl Harbor Revisited*, I wrote this about him:

> [Dewdney] conducted some experiments with single- and double-engine airplanes to test the likelihood of successful cell phone calls from high altitudes. He found that in a single-engine plane, successful calls could be counted on only under 2,000 feet. Above that altitude, they became increasingly unlikely. At 20,000 feet, Dewdney concluded, "the chance of a typical cellphone call making it to ground and engaging a cellsite there is less than one in a hundred." . . . In later experiments using a twin-engine plane, which has greater mass and hence provides greater insulation from electronic signals than a single-engine plane, Dewdney found that the success rate decayed to 0 percent at 7,000 feet.[8] A large airliner, having much greater mass, would provide far greater insulation.[9]

I also wrote:

> [A] cell phone had to complete a 'handshake' with a cellsite, and this took several seconds, so cell phones in high-speed planes would

have had trouble staying connected to a cellsite long enough to complete a call.[10]

Therefore, cell phone calls in airliners flying over 30,000 feet, especially calls that lasted long enough to have conversations, would have been out of the question.

A researcher named Erik Larson has dismissed Dewdney's work as "not relevant" to the 9/11 flights on the grounds that "it was done in Canada, and no evidence was provided that conditions were similar."[11] However, Dewdney wrote:

> [N]ot only is the cellphone technological base in Canada identical to its US counterpart, but Canadian communication technology is second to none, Canada being a world-leader in research and development.[12]

Given the fact that Dewdney, as a scientist, would have known that the relevant conditions needed to be similar, it was up to Larson, if he wanted to dismiss Dewdney's findings, to provide evidence that the conditions were *not* similar.

Larson's dismissal of Dewdney's work appears in the midst of an essay entitled "Critique of David Ray Griffin's Fake Calls Theory." Disputing my argument against the authenticity of the 9/11 phone calls, Larson claims that "there's no actual evidence any of the phone calls were faked," even the Burnett calls.[13]

Larson refers the reader to "myriad credible sources" that "indicate cell phone calls from airplanes were possible prior to 2001." But the issue is not whether cell phone calls could have been made from planes. The issue is whether *cell phone calls that lasted long enough for people to have conversations could have been made from high-altitude, fast-moving airliners*. With regard to this issue, Larson, in spite of his dismissal of Dewdney's work, said:

> Cell phone calls from planes were possible before 2001, but it's obvious that reception quality and the ability to connect and maintain a quality connection would decrease at higher altitudes and speeds. Some of the reported cell phone calls did take place at lower altitudes, but other reported calls, including Tom Burnett's, were at higher altitudes.[14]

Given that recognition, there are only three options for dealing with the Burnett calls: First, one could claim that, in spite of Deena Burnett's testimony that her husband used a cell phone, he actually used an onboard phone; this was the FBI's approach. Second, one could claim that the calls were produced by fakery; that is my approach. Third, one could suggest that Tom Burnett's cell phone received an electronic boost as part of a different type of fakery; this is Larson's approach (although he has not referred to it is a type of fakery). I will look first at the FBI's approach.

3. THE CONFLICT WITH THE FBI's REPORT
TO THE MOUSSAOUI TRIAL

The FBI's report on its interview with Deena Burnett on September 11, 2001, as we have seen, said she stated that her husband used his cell phone to call her, and that she knew this because she saw its number on her caller ID. Nevertheless, when the FBI issued its report on phone calls from the planes—which it made public in 2006 for the trial of Zacarias Moussaoui[15]—it said that all of Tom Burnett's calls were made from a passenger-seat phone. (The report even indicated the rows from which the calls were supposedly made, saying that one call was made from Row 25 and two of them from Row 24.)[16]

Why, in light of the fact that Deena Burnett had clearly told the FBI in 2001 that her husband had used his cell phone to call her, did the FBI in 2006 state that Tom Burnett had used passenger-seat phones?

The answer seems to be that the FBI decided to make all of the reports of phone calls from the 9/11 airliners consistent with the evidence that cell phones available in 2001 would not work, at least reliably, from airliners at high altitudes. Dewdney's work may have helped convince the FBI that it could not present a formal report that made claims thought to be impossible.

It had widely been reported that roughly 15 phone calls from the four 9/11 flights had been made from cell phones—some of which were, of course, the Burnett calls. But in its 2006 report, the FBI described all but two of these calls as having come from onboard phones.[17] The only two calls listed as cell phone calls were from UA 93, and they both were said to have occurred at 9:58 AM. This was when the plane had reportedly descended to 5,000 feet,[18] which was an altitude at which cell phone calls might seem plausible (even if Dewdney considered such calls quite unlikely above 1,000 feet). All of the other phone calls were said to have been made from onboard phones.

Is it not surprising that so many calls that for several years were considered cell phone calls are now designated onboard phone calls by the FBI? Is it really plausible that all of these calls had been made from onboard phones, in spite of the fact that news stories at the time reported that they had been made on cell phones? Does it not appear that the FBI simply changed their reports to prevent the stories about phone calls from being discredited by the evidence that high-altitude cell phone calls would have been impossible?

In the FBI's defense, there are reasons to believe that many of the 15 reported calls in question had actually been described as onboard calls in some news stories from the beginning. For example, a *Newsweek* story about UA 93, published in September 2001, said: "Elizabeth [Honor] Wainio, 27, was speaking to her stepmother in Maryland. Another passenger, she explains, had loaned her a cell phone and told her to call her family."[19] Although that story clearly indicated that Wainio had used a borrowed cell phone, a *Pittsburgh Post-Gazette* story, published only a month later, said that the phone she borrowed was an "Airphone."[20] With this and many other cases, we cannot say that the calls were consistently reported as having been made by cell phones.

There was also ambiguity with the case of flight attendant Amy Sweeney. In previous writings, I had taken as definitive an FBI affidavit about her testimony, in which FBI agent James Lechner stated that the American Airlines employee with whom Sweeney had a long discussion, Michael Woodward, said that Sweeney had been "using a cellular telephone."[21] However, an FBI agent named Craig Ring reported having interviewed Woodward on that day, according to an FBI report dated September 11, 2001, and that he said Woodward "talked to flight attendant Amy Sweeney via air phone."[22] Also, a recording reportedly discovered in 2004 by the FBI said that Sweeney had used a passenger-seat phone thanks to "an AirFone card, given to her by another flight attendant."[23] So the evidence for the Sweeney call is ambiguous.

But with regard to Deena Burnett, as we have seen, there is no ambiguity, because there can be no reasonable way to deny her statement that her husband had called her from his cell phone, because her caller ID showed its number. And there is no reasonable way to deny, we have also seen, that her caller ID did indeed indicate that she had been called from his cell phone.

However, it is virtually impossible that Tom Burnett could have actually used his cell phone to call from UA 93, because this plane was reportedly flying at over 40,000 feet, and in 2001 it would have been impossible for Tom Burnett to have had three cell phone conversations with his wife while flying at that altitude.

Even Deena Burnett, who had been a flight attendant, found this puzzling. After writing in her 2006 book that she "looked at the caller ID and indeed it was Tom's cell phone number," she added: "I didn't understand how he could be calling me on his cell phone from the air."[24]

Most important, the FBI, when writing its report on phone calls from the 9/11 planes—made public in 2006 in relation to the trial of Zacarias Moussaoui—evidently concluded that Tom Burnett could not have called his wife using his cell phone. So, although Deena Burnett had clearly said that her caller ID showed that she had been called from her husband's cell phone, the FBI said in its report for the Moussaoui trial that Tom Burnett's calls had been made from onboard phones.

4. WHY WOULD THE FBI HAVE ALTERED DEENA BURNETT'S REPORT?

There are good reasons to believe that the FBI altered the report about the calls to Deena Burnett to avoid having this report contain a claim—that Tom Burnett made cell phone calls while Flight 93 was over 40,000 feet in the air—that was technologically impossible. This is strongly suggested by the fact that the FBI treated Deena Burnett's testimony differently from the way it treated the testimony of Lorne Lyles, the husband of CeeCee Lyles, a flight attendant on UA 93.

The FBI interviewed Lyles about a phone call from CeeCee Lyles to him that was said to have occurred at 9:58 AM, when her plane had descended to 5,000 feet. The 9:58 call from her was one of the two reported cell phone calls that were accepted by the FBI as having truly been made from cell phones. In the FBI's summary of its interview with Lorne Lyles about the call from his wife, it said:

> At 9:58 AM, Lorne Lyles received a call at home from her celular [sic] telephone. . . . Lyles commented that CeCe [sic] Lyles' telephone number 941-823-2355 was the number on the caller ID.[25]

The FBI's telephone report for the Moussaoui trial shows that the FBI accepted Lorne Lyles's testimony, based on information derived from his caller ID, that his spouse had used a cell phone. But even though Deena Burnett provided the same type of evidence—that her spouse's cell phone number had appeared on her phone's caller ID[26]—the FBI's report did not reflect her testimony. It instead said that her husband had used a seat-back phone. The difference in treatment seems to reflect the fact that the Burnett calls occurred when UA 93 was over 35,000 feet in the air, whereas the Lyles call occurred when the plane was only 5,000 feet in the air, where cell phone calls would at least be possible. This contrast provides strong evidence that the FBI's report was tailored to avoid affirming any high-altitude cell phone calls.

The Burnett case, therefore, provides evidence for two conclusions: On the one hand, this case indicates that the phone calls to Deena Burnett had been faked, because the evidence shows that she was called from Tom Burnett's cell phone, even though he could not possibly have carried on cell phone conversations from UA 93 while it was over 35,000 feet in the air. On the other hand, the FBI's treatment of Tom Burnett's reported calls—its claim that he had made the calls from onboard phones, even though his wife had clearly said that he had used his cell phone—strongly suggests an attempt to cover up faked calls.

III Fakery By Means of Voice Morphing

The FBI illustrated, as we have seen, one of the ways of dealing with the Burnett calls: simply deny that they were cell phone calls. Considering that a dishonest way of dealing with the Burnett calls, I have argued that these calls must have been faked. In previous writings,[27] I have argued that this fakery could have been achieved by means of the technology of voice morphing. Later in this essay, I will discuss another way in which the fakery might have been achieved. For the present, however, I will discuss voice morphing.

I have argued, in agreement with others,[28] that voice morphing had been sufficiently developed by September 2001 to provide a way in which the calls to Deena Burnett might have been made. According to this hypothesis, although Deena Burnett was convinced that the calls were made by her husband, they were actually produced by means of voice morphing.

Voice-morphing technology was already quite advanced by early 1999, when an article entitled "When Seeing and Hearing Isn't

Believing" was published by *Washington Post* journalist William Arkin. "By taking just a 10-minute digital recording of [anyone's] voice," wrote Arkin, voice morphing experts at the Los Alamos National Laboratory in New Mexico can "clone speech patterns and develop an accurate facsimile," causing people to appear to have said things that they "would never otherwise have said."[29]

To illustrate, Arkin described a demonstration in which the voice of General Carl Steiner, former commander-in-chief of the US Special Operations Command, said: "Gentlemen! We have called you together to inform you that we are going to overthrow the United States government." The voice "sounds amazingly like [Steiner]," wrote Arkin.

"To refine their method," Arkin continued, the members of the voice-morphing team—which was headed by scientist George Papcun—"took various high quality recordings of generals and experimented with creating fake statements." One of the generals spoofed by this team was Colin Powell, whose voice was heard to say: "I am being treated well by my captors."[30]

People are quite familiar with photo and video morphing, as illustrated by the 1994 film *Forest Gump*, in which Tom Hanks, in the title role, was seen to shake hands with President Kennedy. But voice morphing has been equally well developed. And, as Arkin points out, these types of morphing can be used not only by Hollywood but also by military and intelligence agencies: "For Hollywood, it is special effects. For covert operators in the U.S. military and intelligence agencies, it is a weapon of the future."

One agency interested in this "weapon of the future," Arkin reported, was "the Information Operations department of the National Defense University in Washington, the military's school for information warfare." Adding that video and photo manipulation had already "raised profound questions of authenticity for the journalistic world," teaching it that "seeing isn't necessarily believing," Arkin pointed out that the addition of voice morphing means that "hearing isn't either." He meant, of course, that hearing *shouldn't* necessarily be believing, because one now needs to be aware that voices can be morphed.

Morphed voices can be convincing, thanks to an array of techniques. As Dewdney said, the operator assigned to a particular call would have a voice changer, which has been adjusted to reproduce the timbre, pitch, and other characteristics of the voice of the person being simulated. The operator would also have various types of information about the person. If a call is supposed to be to the person's spouse, for example, the operator would be supplied with the married couple's pet names for each other and also "commonplace items such as references to 'the kids.'" Moreover, audio engineers for 9/11 calls would have tapes that "portray mumbled conferences among passengers or muffled struggles, replete with shouts and curses."

The voice morphing hypothesis can explain why Deena Burnett was convinced that her husband used his cell phone to call her from UA 93 in the air, even though that would have been impossible.

Erik Larson belittled this notion, referring to "easily exposed flaws in the voice morphing theory."[31] Those who have seriously studied voice morphing, however, know that it cannot be so easily dismissed.[32]

Larson belittled voice-morphing techniques by appealing to George Papcun himself, saying that Papcun "has commented that voice-morphing a conversation in near real time would be more complex than fabricating a simple recorded statement, and would require an extensive recording as a sample." But according to Arkin's article, the capacity to morph voices in "near real time" using a ten-second voice sample had already been developed by early 1999, more than two years before the 9/11 attacks. And surely there would have been no great difficulty in getting sufficiently extensive recordings of the people in question. As researcher Aidan Monaghan has written:

> Advance booking of 9/11 flight reservations by 9/11 flight passengers would make surveillance of them and recordings of their pre-9/11 cell phone or other phone conversations possible. In 2006, the FBI 'hacked' into cell phone accounts of known organized crime figures to record their voices.[33]

In a statement entitled "Voice Morphing and the Alleged 9/11 Government Conspiracy,"[34] Papcun made other arguments against the idea that morphing might have been used in the 9/11 calls. And this is not surprising: Papcun would naturally be inclined to minimize the possibility that his creation was instrumental in the 9/11 attacks, in which almost 3,000 people were killed.

In any case, the important question is not Papcun's motivation, but the persuasiveness of his arguments. And his arguments are problematic. For example, Papcun stated: "[T]he conspiracy theory purveyors have needed to claim that someone (namely, me) created the voices of the passengers in those phone calls." I know of no one, however, who has suggested that Papcun himself created the voices for the phone calls.

Also, in Papcun's arguments against what he calls "wild-eyed theories" that voice morphing was used in the 9/11 calls, he stated:

[I]n this situation it would be necessary to know what someone would say to his or her loved ones under such circumstances. What pet names would be used?

But I think anyone reading the summaries of the statements made by alleged passengers—such as those purportedly made by Tom Burnett, as reported by Deena Burnett—would find statements that could have been made by operators who had studied the targeted passengers. Dewdney, having quoted passages from many of the reconstructed conversations, wrote that "all the conversations are consistent with [a voice-morphing] operation, along with a sprinkling of tantalizing clues that are more consistent with the operation than actual in-flight calls."[35]

Papcun also asked, rhetorically: "What references would be made to children and other loved ones?" As we have seen, however, operators making the calls would normally be supplied with phrases for children, such as "the kids," and if having conversations with "the kids" would be uncomfortable for the operators, they could easily be avoided (as with the case at the end of the final call by "Tom Burnett," treated later in this chapter).

Larson, building on Papcun's statements, has said:

It would be [especially] difficult to fool the subject's family members, who, in addition to being familiar with the person's voice, would be familiar with their unique communication style and intimate details of their lives.[36]

Unfortunately for this argument, however, Papcun published a letter he had received, in which a woman wrote to him:

I came across an article called "When Seeing and Hearing is not believing," where your name was mentioned as the inventor of a technology in which human voice can be cloned in real time without the voice owner saying all the things in a recording. I am writing to seek your assistance. . . . The reason I am asking this is that my husband heard a fake voice of me with another man and he is now suspecting me. My marriage is becoming a hell. . . . I swore to him and told him the voice was not me, but he actually doesn't believe that such a technology exists. Can you please help me show him that such a thing is possible and I am not lying to him?[37]

Papcun "declined to become involved." But without entering into the question as to whether he could have said something helpful without becoming "involved," we can draw the most important conclusion: Just as voice morphing is good enough to fool friends of military generals, it is also good enough to fool spouses.

Given the voice morphing technology that was available in 1999, Arkin pointed out that hearing "should not necessarily be believing." But this lesson has not been widely appreciated. Individuals who received phone calls on 9/11 from people who identified themselves as friends or relatives, as well as people who heard recordings of flight attendants from the 9/11 flights, have evidently accepted the phone calls as authentic. Even journalists have evidently accepted the authenticity of the calls without question. The point of Arkin's 1999 article, however, was that people should understand that "hearing is not necessarily believing," at least when there are reasons to doubt the authenticity of the calls.

And with the 9/11 calls, there are objective bases for questioning the authenticity of some of them. Insofar as people had been told that the calls they received were made from cell phones, they clearly had bases for doubting their authenticity. Former flight attendant Deena Burnett herself knew that there was good reason to wonder about the purported calls from her husband, because, as we saw earlier, she said: "I didn't understand how he could be calling me on his cell phone from the air."[38] Likewise, Lorne Lyles, the husband of flight attendant CeeCee Lyles, reported that he said something similar after hearing the tape-recording of the previously-discussed 9:58 AM call from her:

> I looked at the caller ID [said Lyles], and noticed that . . . it was from her cell phone. And I'm like, OK, *wait a minute. How can she call me from on the plane from a cell phone, because cell phones don't work on a plane?* That's what I'm thinking.[39]

As pointed out earlier, her plane, UA 93, was reportedly at 5,000 feet, and that is an altitude at which cell phone calls might have been possible. Nevertheless, Dewdney said, cell phone calls above 2,000 feet would have been "unlikely."[40]

Moreover, even if cell phone usage might be made possible because of a plane's altitude, it might be rendered impossible by the "handshake" problem, if the plane is still flying at the normal cruising speed—approximately 500 mph. The problem is that the plane, Dewdney says, would not be over the cellsite long enough to complete the electronic 'handshake' (which takes several seconds to complete) before arriving over the next cellsite, when the call has to be handed off from the first cellsite to the next one.[41]

UA 93 was reportedly flying at a very high speed: 580 mph. Therefore, even the two reported cell phone calls that were allowed by the FBI, both of which would have been at 9:58 AM when UA 93 was at 5,000 feet, would have to be rated as very unlikely.

In any case, as we have seen, the calls received by Deena Burnett provide very clear examples of faked calls.

IV FURTHER EVIDENCE FOR FAKED CALLS ON 9/11

There are other objective reasons for doubting the authenticity of many of the 9/11 calls, beyond the calls to Deena Burnett, as the following sections will show.

1. "TOM BURNETT" DECLINES CHANCE TO TALK TO CHILDREN

The Burnett case, as we have seen, provides seemingly incontrovertible evidence that the phone calls received by Deena Burnett must have been faked, because her caller ID indicated that the calls came from Tom Burnett's cell phone, even though Tom could not possibly have called her on his cell phone while his plane was 40,000 feet in the air.[42]

There is, however, another reason to doubt that the Burnett calls were really made by Tom Burnett while he was in an airplane hijacked by foreign terrorists. In the final call received by Deena Burnett, she told him (in her retelling of the conversation) that their "kids" had been asking to talk to him. Tom, however, replied: "Tell them I'll talk to them later."[43]

It is most unlikely, assuming that the events had developed in the purported way, that Tom Burnett would have responded this way. The reported response by Tom occurred after he told his wife he had realized that the hijackers were on a suicide mission, planning to "crash this plane into the ground," so that he and others had decided to try to gain control of the plane as soon as it was "over a rural area." And the hijackers had already killed one person. So Tom would have known there was a good chance that he would die in the next few minutes. And yet, rather than taking this probably last opportunity to speak to his children, he told his wife to say that he would "talk to them later."[44] It is difficult to believe that the real Tom Burnett, dealing with a real situation, would have responded in this way.

However, if someone, using voice morphing, had been pretending to be Tom, we could well imagine why he would not want to talk to the children. For example, he might not have been told their names—in Deena's accounts, the caller referred to the children only as "the kids." Even if he had been told their names, he might not have wanted to admit that he did not know much about them, or that he could not distinguish their voices.

In addition to these two facts about the Burnett calls, there are additional facts about the "phone calls from the planes" that cast doubt on their authenticity.

2. THE CEECEE LYLES CALL: "YOU DID GREAT"
The most direct evidence of fakery is provided by the previously-discussed call to Lorne Lyles, the husband of flight attendant CeeCee Lyles, which he later heard on his answering machine. In the message, which his machine indicates was received on Tuesday at 9:47 AM, the CeeCee Lyles voice said:

> Hi Baby. I'm . . . . Baby, you have to listen to me carefully. I'm on a plane that's been hijacked. I'm on the plane. I'm calling from the plane. I wanna tell you I love you. Please tell my children that I love them very much. And I'm so sorry, babe. Un, I don't know what to say. There's three guys, they've hijacked the plane. I'm trying to be calm. We're turned around and I've heard there's planes that's been, been flown into the World Trade Center. I hope to be able to see your face again, baby. I love you. Goodbye.[45]

After these words have been said, but before the recorded message comes to an end, a voice can be heard to whisper: "You did great." How could anyone not take this whispered comment as clear evidence that the "CeeCee Lyles" message was a fake?

To call it a "fake" means that the message was not what it purported to be. It could have been a fake produced by voice morphing. Or it could have been CeeCee Lyles reading a script she was forced to read—in which case, the whispered message might have been by a person coaching her. But in either case, the message was not authentic.

It is important to realize that the whispered statement occurs in the official recording of the call—the one included in the computer presentation of the 9/11 phone calls given as evidence for the 2006

Moussaoui trial.[46] Otherwise, we could suspect that the whispered message had been added by someone later, perhaps as a hoax. How and why the whispered comment got included on the official recording of this call will likely remain a mystery. In any case, this whispered comment undermines the official story about 9/11.

3. THE LACK OF NOISE AND EMOTION

Assuming that foreign terrorists had really hijacked the four 9/11 planes, and that some of the passengers and flight attendants had been able to use telephones to convey to people on the ground what was happening on board, we would not assume that the cabin would be quiet and that the passengers and flight attendants would be calm. And yet that is what was reported in numerous accounts.[47]

Flight Attendants: I will begin with flight attendants whose calls from the planes were reportedly characterized by surprising calmness. Sandy Bradshaw, a flight attendant on UA 93, was described by a United Airlines manager as "shockingly calm."[48] Calmness by her or any of the other flight attendants would indeed have been "shocking," given what people on UA 93 supposedly experienced. According to *The 9/11 Commission Report:*

> [Passengers and crew members who made phone calls] understood the plane had been hijacked. They said the hijackers wielded knives and claimed to have a bomb. . . . Callers reported that a passenger had been stabbed and that two people were lying on the floor of the cabin, injured or dead—possibly the captain and first officer. One caller reported that a flight attendant had been killed.[49]

The flight attendants on AA 11 should also have been very frightened. *The 9/11 Commission Report* said that "a man in first class had his throat slashed; two flight attendants had been stabbed . . . ; the flight attendants were unable to contact the cockpit; and there was a bomb in the cockpit."[50] And yet Amy Sweeney, a flight attendant on AA 11, was said to have spoken "very, very calmly" while giving information about the hijackers.

Betty Ong was another flight attendant on American 11. Besides observing all the events witnessed by Sweeney, Ong was reportedly subjected to Mace, making it very difficult for her and others to breathe.[51] Moreover, she reported:

Our No. 1 (flight attendant) got stabbed. Our purser is stabbed. Nobody knows who stabbed who. We can't even get up to business class right now, because nobody can breathe. Uh, our No. 1 is stabbed right now. Our No. 5, our first class passenger, er, our first class galley flight attendant and our purser have been stabbed. And we can't get into the cockpit. The door won't open.[52]

Nevertheless Ong, like Sweeney, reportedly remained very calm. Fellow American Airlines employee Nydia Gonzalez said of her: "Betty was calm, professional, and in control throughout the call."[53] When Ong's family heard the recording of her call, said an ABC reporter, they "couldn't believe the calm in Betty's voice."[54] An Associated Press story about her said: "[She] seemed calm and professional beyond reason as she reported a ghastly scenario during a 23-minute telephone call."[55]

Individual Passengers: The same calmness was reported about passengers. For example, Tom Burnett's wife, Deena, said of him: "It was as if he was at Thoratec [the company for which he worked], sitting at his desk, and we were having a regular conversation. It was the strangest thing because he was using the same tone of voice I had heard a thousand times."[56]

Jack Grandcolas, referring to a call from his wife, Lauren Grandcolas, said: "She sounded calm."[57] *New York Times* reporter Jere Longman said: "It sounded to Jack as if [his wife] were driving home from the grocery store or ordering a pizza."[58]

Lyz Glick, speaking about calls from her husband, Jeremy Glick, said: "He was so calm, the plane sounded so calm, that if I hadn't seen what was going on on the TV, I wouldn't have believed it."[59]

Kathy Hoglan, the aunt of passenger Mark Bingham on UA 93, said that he sounded "calm, matter-of-fact." Bingham's mother, Alice Hoglan, said: "His voice was calm. He seemed very much composed."[60]

Esther Heymann, discussing a conversation she had had with her stepdaughter, Honor Elizabeth Wainio, said that her stepdaughter remained "remarkably calm throughout our whole conversation."[61]

Todd Beamer, the passenger on UA 93 who became immortalized as the person who (reportedly) said "Let's roll" before he and others took on the hijackers, was also described as calm. Lisa Jefferson, a supervising customer service operator for GTE-Verizon who reportedly received a long telephone call from Beamer, said that he "stayed calm through the entire conversation."[62] Indeed, Jefferson later wrote, "his voice was . . . so tranquil it made me begin to doubt the authenticity and urgency of his call."[63]

The Passengers as a Whole: Not only these individuals, but also the passengers in general, seem to have been calm and quiet. For example, Jack Grandcolas, the husband of UA 93 passenger Lauren Grandcolas, commented: "It was really quiet in the background. There wasn't screaming."[64]

Lyz Glick, also speaking about UA 93, said: "I was surprised by how calm it seemed in the background. I didn't hear any screaming. I didn't hear any noises. I didn't hear any commotion."[65]

According to *New York Times* reporter Jere Longman, Esther Heymann, while listening to a call from her stepdaughter, Honor Elizabeth Wainio, "could not hear another person. She could not hear any conversation or crying or yelling or whimpering. Nothing."[66]

Vanessa Minter, an American Airlines employee who listened to Ong's call, commented: "You didn't hear hysteria in the background. You didn't hear people screaming."[67]

Mark Bingham's mother, Alice Hoglan, said that a discussion between passengers about taking back the plane from the hijackers, which she overheard while talking with Mark, sounded like a "calm boardroom meeting."[68]

If the reported calls by these flight attendants and passengers were truly made from the four 9/11 flights, then such calmness would border on the miraculous. But if the calls were made elsewhere, then we have not supernatural calmness but merely poor acting.

4. The Mysterious Betty Ong Call

The call by flight attendant Betty Ong, which was mentioned above, was surprising partly because of the extraordinary calmness of this call. But it was also surprising because "Betty Ong" did not contact either of the places that we would have expected an experienced flight attendant to contact: American Airlines in Boston, from which her flight had departed, or American Airlines headquarters in Dallas-Fort Worth, Texas.

The Call to Cary, North Carolina: Rather, "Betty Ong" called the airline's tiny reservations office in Cary, North Carolina. Betty Ong was, as we saw, praised for being "calm, professional, and in control." If so, why did she not call a security office in Boston or Dallas, rather than a reservations office in Cary?

Also surprising is the fact that her phone call lasted for 27 minutes. American Airlines officials in Dallas-Fort Worth were eventually notified, but this was only because one of the employees in North Carolina alerted them. If Betty Ong was "calm and professional," why did she use her telephone to go on and on with reservations workers in Cary, North Carolina, rather than contacting people who could have done something useful with her information?

If we assume that the "Betty Ong" phone call was actually made by the flight attendant named Betty Ong (who according to reports was indeed an excellent flight attendant), and that this call was made in the midst of a genuine hijacking, the phone call to Cary, North Carolina, is a complete mystery.

A Possible Solution to the Call to Cary: However, if one supposes that the Betty Ong call was produced by voice morphing, then one can formulate a plausible hypothesis as to why this call went to the reservations office in Cary, North Carolina. Rowland Morgan wrote:

> A clue about why the Ong voice chose to call such a remote part of the American Airlines organisation might come from the following supposition. Plotters might have known that American's reservations office in Cary, N.C., had just installed new recording equipment that recorded the first four minutes of any reservations call, for call-screening and archiving purposes. . . . Calling the Cary office ensured that the Ong voice would be recorded, not for the whole duration of the call, but just for a handy four-minute snippet, long enough to frighten the daylights out of the U.S. public, but not long enough for any blunders by the teleoperator to be exposed for all to hear (although the recorded Ong voice did at first misidentify the flight as Flight 12 on the recording).[69]

And indeed, the four-minute call by "Betty Ong" proved very useful. Although it was not heard by the public until 2004, this call was heard immediately by American Airlines supervisor Nydia Gonzalez and also a manager in Fort Worth—this being the first message about hijacking received by authorities. This message was also available to be played in 2004, when the 9/11 Commission was reporting its findings.[70]

In any case, there are good reasons to take the "Betty Ong call" as inauthentic.

5. Telephone Calls Lasting After the Crashes

Another reason for taking the phone calls from the 9/11 planes to be fakes is that, according to the records, two of the telephones stayed connected after the crash of the airplane on which they supposedly were located.

The Jeremy Glick Call: Lyzbeth Glick, while visiting her parents (Richard and JoAnne Makely), received a call that they all assumed to be from Lyzbeth's husband, Jeremy Glick, onboard UA 93. After a conversation with "Jeremy," she agreed with him that he should join a group of men who were going to try to wrest control of the plane from the hijackers. According to the FBI's report of its interview the next day with Lyzbeth Glick:

> Jeremy told Lyzbeth that he loved her and asked her not to hang-up the telephone. Lyzbeth remained on the phone for a few minutes and then handed the telephone to her father, Richard Makely.[71]

In a book she wrote, she said: "I handed the receiver to my dad, ran into the bathroom, and gagged over the sink."[72] The FBI's summary of its interview with her father said:

> When Makely got the telephone from Lyzbeth, he only heard silence on the telephone, then three, four, or five minutes went by, and there were high pitched screaming noises coming over the telephone . . . . There was then several minutes of silence on the telephone. Then Makely heard a series of high pitched screaming sounds again, followed by a noise which he described as 'wind sounds.' The 'wind sounds' were followed by noises that sounded as though the airplane telephone was hitting a hard surface several times or banging around. Then there was silence on the telephone. During the screaming and other sounds that Makely heard, a telephone operator from Horizon broke into the telephone call and relayed the information to police officers. . . . Makely and the telephone operator stayed on the telephone for approximately 1 1/2 hours, until approximately 10:45 AM, but never heard any further noises on the telephone.[73]

UA 93 crashed at 10:03, according to the 9/11 Commission[74]—or at 10:06, according to the seismology report and local reporters.[75] In either case, Makely and the operator remained on the line long after UA 93 crashed. According to the FBI's report on phone calls from the planes, indeed, the phone remained connected for 7,565 seconds (two hours and six minutes).[76] Did a voice-morpher forget to hang-up?

The Long-Lasting Todd Beamer Call: Verizon employee Lisa Jefferson, as mentioned above, had a long conversation with a man who described himself as Todd Beamer, a passenger on UA 93. Beamer became the most celebrated of the "heroes" of UA 93, thanks to his being credited with saying, as a group of passengers started their counter-attack on the hijackers, "Let's roll."

Various problems with the "Todd Beamer" call will be discussed in the following section. For now, I focus only on the length of the call. Although Lisa Jefferson apparently showed, in a 2006 book she co-authored,[77] that she accepted the authenticity of the "Todd Beamer call," she elsewhere made clear that the telephone of the man with whom she had been speaking remained connected after UA 93 crashed:

> After he said, "Let's roll," he left the phone, and I would assume that's at the point that they went to charge the cockpit. And I was still on the line and the plane took a dive, and by then, it just went silent. I held on until after the plane crashed—probably about 15 minutes longer and I never heard a crash—it just went silent because—I can't explain it. We didn't lose a connection because there's a different sound that you use. It's a squealing sound when you lose a connection. I never lost connection, but it just went silent.[78]

As with the Jeremy Glick call, telephone company information indicating that the telephone line remained open was accepted by the FBI. According to that information, the Todd Beamer call lasted for 3,925 seconds, slightly over 65 minutes. So rather than ending at 10:03 or 10:06 AM, when the plane crashed, the phone stayed connected until 10:49.[79]

Interpretation: The Jeremy Glick call, as we saw, lasted even longer: for 7,565 seconds, or two hours and six minutes.

What do we make of these long-lasting calls? It is hard to explain how these calls happened. What seems clear, however, is that these calls were not made from phones in an airplane that crashed a few minutes after 10:00 AM, because the crash would certainly have caused the calls to be disconnected. The calls, therefore, could not have been from UA 93 (assuming, of course, that a flight designated "UA 93" actually crashed).

6. The Todd Beamer Call

As we have seen, Todd Beamer became celebrated as a hero of UA 93. Larry Ellison, who headed the company for which Beamer worked, wrote of him: "He helped prevent the airplane from reaching its target - our nation's Capitol. . . Todd's brave actions saved countless lives on the ground."[80] The phrase "Let's roll," which Beamer supposedly uttered at the end of his call, became "the Pentagon's recruitment slogan," as Rowland Morgan put it,[81] for the US-led "war on terror." (This so-called war on terror has, of course, been aimed at Muslim countries.) By early 2002, the phrase "Let's roll" had not only been "[e]mbraced and promoted by President Bush as a patriotic battle cry," wrote the *Washington Post,* but this phrase was also "emblazoned on Air Force fighter planes, city firetrucks, school athletic jerseys, and countless T-shirts, baseball caps and souvenir buttons."[82] There are problems, however, with the idea of Beamer as hero.

One problem is the evidence that in her first account of Todd Beamer's final words, Lisa Jefferson did not attribute the "Let's Roll" phrase to Beamer. Jefferson claimed later that she heard Beamer say, as he put down the phone to her, "Are you guys ready? Let's roll!"[83] But in an interview shortly after 9/11, Jefferson reportedly quoted Beamer as having said only, "Are you ready? OK." *Pittsburgh Post-Gazette* reporter Jim McKinnon wrote:

> He [Beamer] addressed his cohorts, still calm, saying, "Are you ready? OK," Jefferson said. She did not complete the phrase that [Todd Beamer's wife] Lisa Beamer relayed in an earlier interview with the *Pittsburgh Post-Gazette* in which she quoted her husband using a family catch phrase: "Are you guys ready? Let's roll!"[84]

However, although McKinnon's suggestion that Todd Beamer did not actually use this catch phrase on 9/11 is of historical interest, it does not provide a reason to doubt the authenticity of the "Todd Beamer phone call." But a reason to doubt this has been provided by the fact that the call continued long after UA 93 crashed. And there are, we will see next, some additional reasons.

"Todd Beamer" Passes Up Chance to Call Wife: Much more important is the fact that the self-identified Todd Beamer talking to Lisa Jefferson did not call Lisa Beamer—Todd Beamer's wife—even though he had ample opportunity to do so. Rather, he talked the entire period to

GTE/Verizon Airfone operators, whom he had never met. After spending the first few minutes of his call talking with an Airfone operator named Phyllis Johnson, he spent the remainder of it talking with Lisa Jefferson.[85]

At first, as we saw earlier, "Todd Beamer" seemed calm. But as it seemed that the passengers on UA 93 were going to die, he expressed fear. He told Jefferson: "I know we're not going to make it out of here."[86] He cried out: "Oh my God, we're going down! We're going down! Jesus help us." A little later, having asked Lisa Jefferson to say the Lord's Prayer with him, he said:

> Jesus help me. . . . I just wanted to talk to someone, and if I don't make it through this, will you . . . tell my wife and family how much I love them?[87]

However, we must wonder: Why did he not call his wife and two children and tell them himself, or ask to be connected to them? There could have been no problem in reaching his wife, given the fact that he was talking with an Airfone supervisor. In fact, Jefferson volunteered: "Would you like me to try to reach your wife and patch her call through?" In response, however, "Todd" replied:

> No, no. I don't want to upset her unnecessarily. She's expecting our third child in January, and if I don't have to upset her with any bad news, then I'd rather not.[88]

If this were the real Todd Beamer, and if he believed that he was probably going to die in the next few minutes, would he not have realized that his wife would be "upset with [some] bad news" when she learned he was killed? Would he not suspect she would be especially upset if she learned that he had passed up the opportunity to talk to her one last time? Can we, in any case, believe that he would have passed up this last chance to speak to his wife and children? As Rowland Morgan says: "The contrast between a young man facing his end and his refusal to speak to his wife is implausible."[89] The refusal of (the real) Todd Beamer to speak to his wife would have been as strange as (the real) Tom Burnett not speaking to his children.

However, if the man on the line was not really Todd Beamer, but merely someone who knew some facts about him, we can perfectly understand why he would not have wanted to talk to Todd Beamer's wife.

Was the Conversation Not Taped? One more difficult-to-believe feature of this story involves Lisa Jefferson's claim that she did not tape her telephone conversation with Todd Beamer. Her explanation: "I had not had time to press the switch in my office that initiates the taping of a conversation." But given the high-tech office in which she worked and given the fact that she had been an Airfone supervising operator for 17 years, her statement that the call was not recorded is, as Rowland Morgan says, implausible.[90]

In fact, a *Pittsburgh Post-Gazette* story published eight days after 9/11 said: "[B]ecause [the Beamer call] was to an operator, [it] was tape-recorded."[91] This report contradicts what was asserted by Airfone and the government. If there was indeed a tape of the phone call that has been concealed from the public, we can only wonder why. The recorded conversation might have shown, we could suspect, that the phrase "Let's Roll" was missing—just as it was evidently missing from Lisa Jefferson's first account of the call. Worse yet, we might suspect, the caller's voice might not have sounded sufficiently like Todd Beamer's to convince people who knew him.

In any case, the concealment of the tape recording would be yet another reason to believe the "Todd Beamer phone call" was inauthentic.

To Summarize: We have at least three reasons to consider the "Todd Beamer call" inauthentic:

- The call remained connected long after UA 93 crashed.

- The man making the call passed up the opportunity to call Todd Beamer's wife and sons.

- Lisa Jefferson and the authorities claimed, implausibly, that no tape of the call was made.

7. The Barbara Olson Calls

Barbara Olson was a well-known commentator on CNN and the wife of US Solicitor General Theodore "Ted" Olson. On 9/11, Ted Olson told CNN and the FBI that his wife had called him twice from AA 77, with the first call lasting "about one (1) minute,"[92] and the second one "two or three or four minutes."[93] His wife told him, he reported, that "all passengers and flight personnel, including the pilots, were herded to the back of the plane" by hijackers, who were armed with "knives and cardboard cutters."[94]

An Implausible Story: One problem with this story was that the alleged hijackers were rather small men. "The so-called muscle hijackers," the 9/11 Commission pointed out, "were not physically imposing, as the majority of them were between 5'5" and 5'7" in height and slender in build."[95] If these small men were armed only with knives and box-cutters, they surely could not have held off 60 passengers and crew members, who included pilot Charles "Chic" Burlingame, a former Navy pilot who was a weightlifter and a boxer, who was described as "really tough" by one of his erstwhile opponents.[96]

Moreover, even aside from the question of the size of the "muscle hijackers," the story is implausible because of its claim that the pilots "were herded to the back of the plane." Pilots do not give up their planes easily. Chic Burlingame's brother Mark, in fact, said: "I don't know what happened in that cockpit, but I'm sure that they would have had to incapacitate him or kill him because he would have done anything to prevent the kind of tragedy that befell that airplane."[97] The historians at the Pentagon expressed this view, saying that "the attackers either incapacitated or murdered the two pilots."[98]

Cell Phone Calls Ruled Out: A second problem was whether a passenger on AA 77 could have made calls, from either a cell phone or an on-board phone. The summary of the FBI's interview with Ted Olson said: "[Mr. Olson] doesn't know if the calls were made from [Barbara Olson's] cell phone or the telephone on the plane." But Ted Olson seemed to lean towards the cell phone view, saying: "She always has her cell phone with her."[99] And this was what Ted Olson told CNN, saying that his wife had "called him twice on a cell phone."[100] He later surmised on *Hannity & Colmes* that she must have been using the "airplane phone."[101] But that same day, he suggested to Larry King that she used her cell phone.[102]

Thanks to the first report on CNN plus this Larry King appearance, most Americans accepted the idea that Barbara Olson had used a cell phone to call her husband. In statements made in later months, however, Ted Olson said that she had used a seatback phone.[103] But these statements evidently had little influence in America: On the first anniversary of 9/11, CNN was still reporting that Barbara Olson had used a cell phone.[104]

However, Barbara Olson could not have used her cell phone to call from AA 77. Her first call, according to the 9/11 Commission, occurred "between 9:16 and 9:26 AM," when Flight 77, the official report said, would have been at an altitude of between 25,000 and 14,000 feet.[105] This would have been far too high for someone flying in an airliner in 2001 to have made cell phone calls lasting a minute or longer.

In any case, an FBI report ruled out this possibility in 2004, saying: "All of the calls from Flight 77 were made via the onboard airphone system."[106]

Evidence There Were No Functioning Seatback Phones: Unfortunately for the claim that onboard calls were made from AA 77, there is strong evidence that this plane did not have a functioning onboard phone system. In 2004, Ian Henshall and Rowland Morgan had come to suspect that the Boeing 757s used by American Airlines did not have onboard telephones. Accordingly, they asked American Airlines whether its "757s [are] fitted with phones that passengers can use." An AA spokesperson replied: "American Airlines 757s do not have onboard phones for passenger use." Then, to check on the possibility that Barbara Olson might have borrowed a phone intended for crew use, they asked: "[A]re there any onboard phones at all on AA 757s, i.e., that could be used either by passengers or cabin crew?" The response was: "AA 757s do not have any onboard phones, either for passenger or crew use. Crew have other means of communication available."[107]

Then in 2006, a person on a German Internet forum reported that he had asked American Airlines this same question:

> "On your website [he wrote], there is mentioned that there are no seatback satellite phones on a Boeing 757. Is that info correct? Were there any such seatback satellite phones on any Boeing 757 before or on September 11, 2001 and if so, when were these phones ripped out?"

An AA representative named Chad Kinder responded thus:

"That is correct; we do not have phones on our Boeing 757. The passengers on flight 77 used their own personal cellular phones to make out calls during the terrorist attack."[108]

Captain Ralph Kolstad has also provided testimony on this point. After serving for 20 years in the US Navy—he was a fighter pilot and an air combat instructor at the US Navy Fighter Weapons School, where he was twice designated Top Gun—he served as an airline pilot for 27 years, during 13 of which he flew Boeing 757s and 767s for American Airlines. He wrote:

> [T]he "air phones," as they were called, were . . . deactivated in early or mid 2001. They had been deactivated for quite some time prior to Sep 2001. . . . I have no proof, but I am absolutely certain that the phones were disconnected on the 757 long before Sep 2001. They were still physically installed in the aircraft, but they were not operational.[109]

The same testimony has been given by a former American Airlines flight attendant, Ginger Gainer, who wrote: "I am sure the 757's on which I flew during that time frame either had the phones totally removed, or they were in place in the seat backs, but disabled."[110]

The FBI's 2006 Report: In any case, the evidence that Barbara Olson could not have made calls from either a cell phone or an onboard phone is no longer needed to contradict the belief that she called her husband twice on the morning of 9/11, because the FBI has now stated that she made no calls. As we saw earlier, Ted Olson said he received two telephone calls from his wife that morning, the first of which, he told the FBI, "lasted about one (1) minute."[111] A few minutes later, he said, he received the second call, during which, he later told CNN's Larry King, they "spoke for another two or three or four minutes."[112]

But the FBI's report to the Moussaoui trial said that Barbara Olson attempted one call, and it was "unconnected" and (therefore) lasted "0 seconds."[113] This report contradicted Ted Olson's statement that he talked to his wife twice while she was on AA 77.

This report does not, to be sure, deny that there were calls to Ted Olson's office that appeared to be from Barbara Olson. That such calls occurred was well supported.[114]

The FBI's Moussaoui trial report also does not deny that Barbara Olson called her husband and talked to him. The telephone information indicated only that *there were no calls to Ted Olson's office by Barbara Olson using phones aboard AA 77.*

What really happened is, to be sure, mysterious. I am reporting only what the evidence indicates. This is one of many issues on which people in the 9/11 Truth Movement cannot be expected to figure out "what really happened." But the new Department of Justice, given all the resources it has, could surely answer this question, if only it would try, by conducting a new and unrestrained investigation into the 9/11 attacks.

A Last-Ditch Attempt to Salvage the Olson Story: In spite of the fact that the FBI report said unambiguously in 2006 that there were no calls from Barbara Olson on AA 77 to her husband, some people, including Larson, have sought to reaffirm that those calls took place. These attempts are based on the fact that the FBI's report to the 9/11 Commission in 2004 and to the Moussaoui trial in 2006 said that, in addition to the unconnected call from Barbara Olson, there were five calls from this flight for which the details were unknown. They were, in fact, doubly unknown: Each call was made by an "unknown caller," and each call went to an "unknown number." Four of these five calls were, however, listed as "connected."[115]

The most obviously desperate attempt to salvage the Olson story was provided by the 9/11 Commission. With no mention of American Airlines' evidence that Barbara Olson only attempted one call, which lasted "0 seconds," the Commission suggested that all four of the "connected calls to unknown numbers" were calls from Barbara Olson to her husband. It wrote:

> The records available for the phone calls from American 77 do not allow for a determination of which of [these four calls] represent the two between Barbara and Ted Olson, although the FBI and DOJ believe that all four represent communications between Barbara Olson and her husband's office.[116]

This was, I wrote in 2007:

> [A] very strange conclusion: If Ted Olson reported receiving only two calls, why would the Commission conclude that the DOJ had received *four* connected calls from his wife?"[117]

Larson agreed, writing:

> It is puzzling the DOJ/FBI reached this conclusion, given that Solicitor General Ted Olson, his Special Assistant Helen Voss, and his Secretary Lori Keyton all told the FBI there had been two calls from Barbara Olson.[118]

Larson added, however: "It would have been reasonable for the FBI to conclude that there were two connected calls from Barbara Olson to Ted Olson."[119]

But would it? The most likely of the two unknown calls to be considered calls from Barbara Olson would be the first two.[120] The first one started at 9:15:34 and lasted for one minute and 42 seconds; the second began at 9:20:15 and lasted for four minutes and 34 seconds.[121]

But there are several problems with this two-call hypothesis.

For one thing, the first of the connected unknown calls started precisely at 9:15:34, whereas the first of the calls from Barbara Olson was said to be "between 9:16 and 9:26 AM."[122] According to these records, therefore, the first of the unknown but connected calls started 26 seconds earlier than the first of the calls from Barbara Olson.

Raising a second problem, one commentator pointed out:

[I]t is very strange that the FBI did not have any confirmed calls from Barbara Olson to Ted Olson. There were 4 connected calls with unconfirmed numbers and unconfirmed callers. That is odd. If they were able to confirm a call by Barbara Olson that was unconnected to the DOJ and lasted zero seconds, why not calls that were actually connected and lasted several minutes long?[123]

Discussing this "very strange" set of ideas, I wrote:

[It] appears to be so bizarre as to be completely implausible. If the FBI was able to identify the number dialed for a call that failed to connect—so that it did not endure for even a hundredth of a second—could anyone give a plausible explanation as to why the FBI could not identify the number reached by two calls that, besides connecting, endured for over 1.5 and 4.5 minutes, respectively?[124]

Third, I added:

This problem becomes even more severe when we focus on the hypothesis that two of the connected calls to unknown numbers were from Barbara Olson to the Department of Justice, which was also reportedly the number reached by an attempted call from her that failed to connect. If the FBI was able to determine that Barbara Olson had at 9:18:58 unsuccessfully attempted to reach the Department of Justice, why would it have been unable to determine that the calls that she—according to the two-call hypothesis—made at 9:15:34 and 9:20:15 had reached that same Department of Justice?[125]

A New Analysis of Primary Telephone Records: A recent analysis of evidence from newly discovered primary telephone records confirms the FBI's conclusion that Barbara Olson did not attempt any calls to her husband's office from AA 77.[126] This is important: The FBI's report, according to which Barbara Olson attempted a call from AA 77 (even if it was an unconnected call, which lasted "0 seconds"), still provided support for the claim that she was on AA 77 and it was still aloft. The full importance of this evidence will be made clear in Chapter 7.

Conclusion: On the one hand, a combination of evidence shows that Barbara Olson did not make two successful calls to her husband's office from AA 77.[127] On the other hand, it seems impossible to deny that Ted Olson's office received two calls that seemed to be from Barbara Olson. When taking these two points together, we must conclude that the Barbara Olson calls were in some sense faked.

8. The Small Number of Passengers Who Made Calls
Another reason for doubting the authenticity of the 9/11 phone calls is the very small number of passengers who, according to the official story, took advantage of the opportunities to make phone calls. The number of passengers who did so was significant in only one of the four airplanes.

AA 11: With regard to AA 11, we were told that although two flight attendants—Betty Ong and Amy Sweeney—made calls, no passenger did so. Rowland Morgan has written:

> There were about 76 passengers sitting unsupervised in business and coach while the alleged hijackers were locked away. . . . All of them sat facing seatback phones. [A] voice over the public address system ostensibly had announced "If you try to make any moves you'll endanger yourself and the airplane. Just stay quiet."

In spite of this announcement, Morgan was emphasizing, these men and women, being unsupervised and having phones right in front of them, could have made calls easily and with little fear of being detected by the hijackers. And yet, Morgan asked rhetorically, "no passenger called 9-1-1?"

Given the fact that AA 11 was the first of the airplanes to be involved, the passengers would not have known that it was to be crashed into a building. We might assume, therefore, that they thought that the hijackers simply planned, like most hijackers, to use them to extort money or some agreement from the authorities, and that if they simply sat quietly, no harm would come to them. As we saw earlier, however, the hijackers reportedly killed one passenger, stabbed two flight attendants, and sprayed Mace. The passengers would have known that developments were not promising. Surely some of them would have tried to call a relative, a friend, or 9-1-1. "The official account of Flight 11," according to which not a single person placed a call, "is implausible," Morgan wrote.[128]

United 175: What about United 175? According to the official account, there were 51 passengers on this flight, but only three of them placed calls.[129] It might be thought that this account is at least more plausible than that of AA 11, because three of 51 passengers on United 175 made calls, whereas none of the 76 passengers on AA 11 made calls.

But the official account of this flight is even more implausible. One can imagine that, because no passengers on AA 11 were making calls, they all may have assumed that there must have been some good reason why no one was using a phone. But once three passengers on United 175 proved that calls could be made successfully, many of the other passengers would surely have followed their lead. (The first successful call from United 175 reportedly occurred at 8:52 AM, so there would have been 11 more minutes in which calls could have been made.) We cannot believe that phone calls would have been made by three, and only three, of 51 passengers on this flight.

AA 77: According to the FBI's 2006 account of AA 77, only one of this plane's 57 passengers and flight attendants used a phone to reach someone, this being flight attendant Renee May.[130] If Renee May had made a successful call, while standing or sitting near to other flight attendants and passengers, it is hard to believe that none of the other flight attendants and passengers would have made their own calls. It is, in fact, unthinkable that, if calls were possible, only one person on this flight made calls.

UA 93: We might think the official account of UA 93 is more credible, because it tells us that 11 of its 38 passengers made calls. Rowland Morgan wrote:

> It is commonly thought that, while most passengers inexplicably did not call from the three earlier doomed flights, those aboard Flight 93 had longer to decide, and were influenced by the news of the 9/11 events received by those who had called, so lots of them called.[131]

However, Morgan pointed out:

> [C]allers were still an inexplicably small minority of those aboard. . . . [A]ccording to the Moussaoui evidence only about 11 of [the 38 passengers] called the ground. . . . That is to say: 33 passengers aboard Flight 93 flew for some 35 minutes, ostensibly knowing that their plane had been hijacked by a murderous gang, without calling home, office or police on one of the phones that were installed opposite their

faces. Calling required only a credit card. . . . But . . . three-quarters of the passengers, . . . passing around news that indicated their plane might be doomed as well as hijacked, nevertheless did not call anyone.

When looked at from this perspective, the story about UA 93 is no more plausible than that of the other three flights. Given the position implied in the official account, that everyone on this flight knew that hijackers were planning to fly the plane into a building, it is hard to believe that only 11 of 38 passengers would have called someone— that is, that 27 of them would not. Could people watch Todd Beamer talk on the phone for 20 minutes while not calling someone to talk for a minute or two? Could someone near Tom Burnett watch him call his wife three times while not making a single call?

To the evidence cited in the previous sections, therefore, we must add this consideration: that the numbers of passengers on the 9/11 flights who supposedly made phone calls—from 11 passengers on UA 93 to 0 passengers on AA 11—are implausible. These implausible figures count strongly against the view that the reported phone calls from the 9/11 flights were authentic.

V COULD 9/11 CALLS HAVE BEEN FAKED IN ANOTHER WAY?

Because I, like some others, have tended to equate phone fakery with voice morphing, the two ideas have widely come to be equated. However, the idea that the calls to Deena Burnett, along with other 9/11 calls, were faked should not be simply equated with the idea that these calls were produced by voice morphing. Rather, that is only one way in which they might have been faked. I referred to this point in some writings.

In my 2010 book, *Cognitive Infiltration*, I wrote:

> It would appear . . . that the reported calls from Tom Burnett, along with all of the other reported high-altitude cell phone calls, had *somehow* been faked.[132]

In that book, I also wrote:

> If Tom Burnett had actually used a seat-back phone, as the FBI's report now says, why did Deena Burnett see his cell phone number on her Caller ID? The official defenders of the government's

conspiracy theory have offered no answer to this question. And for good reason: There is no possible answer except to admit that these calls had been *faked, in one way or another.*[133]

As these statements indicate, there could be more than one way in which phone calls could be faked. We must, in other words, distinguish clearly between fact and hypothesis. We have seen, I believe, sufficient evidence to consider it beyond reasonable doubt that at least some of the 9/11 phone calls were faked.[134] Voice morphing is merely a hypothesis about a way in which these calls could have been faked. We need to remain open to the possibility that the calls might have been faked in a different way.

1. THE "REPEATER" HYPOTHESIS

In fact, a different way in which the 9/11 calls could have been faked was suggested by Erik Larson—although he has not portrayed it as a type of fakery. Larson based his suggestion on the following statement by scientist and 9/11 researcher Jim Hoffman:

> [A repeater] is sufficiently powerful to establish reliable connections with ground stations for several minutes at a time, and forwards all the communications between the cell phones aboard the plane and ground stations.[135]

Building on Hoffman's hypothesis, Larson said that "cell phone repeaters could have been placed on the 9/11 flights." These repeaters would have made it possible for cell phones to work at altitudes at which they normally would not. Therefore, Deena Burnett and other people who received calls would have learned what was going on in the planes.

Larson's idea is evidently that there were real hijackers on the planes, who would be allowed to carry out their activities, but that everything was ultimately under the control of US operatives who had arranged physical processes that would destroy the World Trade Center and damage the Pentagon. Because passengers and flight attendants would see the plane being taken over by Middle Eastern terrorists, their messages to loved ones and colleagues would be filled with the types of genuine emotion needed to get the American public ready for the planned "war on terror." In Larson's words:

> It could easily have been anticipated by insiders arranging for planes to be successfully hijacked and hit their targets on 9/11, that

passengers, once aware of the hijackings, would attempt to use their cell phones and report hijackings by Middle-Eastern-looking men. It would have been obvious that news reports of these calls would be emotionally-charged, and could be used to convince the public that Islamic radicals were responsible for 9/11, as well as channel the public's fear and anger into support for a "war on terror."[136]

As shown by the first sentence of this passage—"It could easily have been anticipated by insiders arranging for planes to be successfully hijacked and hit their targets"—we have here a version of phone call fakery that would not have involved voice morphing.

In this scenario, real passengers and flight attendants would have made the calls. But they would not have been doing so in the context presented by the official account of 9/11, according to which the planes were hijacked in an operation that surprised our national political and military leaders. Rather, the people who made the phone calls would be under the control of the US perpetrators of the 9/11 attacks. This point is made clear in the following statement by Hoffman, in which he explained an advantage of this hypothesis:

> [T]his method would have afforded the attack planners great benefits with little risk of exposure. Genuine reports of the theatrics of the red-bandanna-wearing bomb-displaying Arabic-looking patsies aboard Flight 93 could be allowed to get through as long as the operatives wanted, adding realism to the hijackings so central to the official account. But the same operatives could "cut the feed" at the moment events took a turn threatening to evince something other than that account.

According to this scenario, there would be Arab-looking patsies on the planes, but the calls would be "allowed to get through [only] as long as the operatives wanted," and the operatives "could 'cut the feed' at the moment events took a turn threatening to evince something other than [the official] account." Within this framework, the so-called "hijackers" would not have really hijacked the planes. They would have believed that this was what they were doing, but they would have simply been employed, unbeknownst to them, to play roles in apparent hijackings.

So, although Larson presented the "repeater hypothesis" as an *alternative* to the view that "the phone calls were faked," this is really another version of phone call fakery. Once this is seen, the next question is whether this version is better than the one employing voice morphing.

2. Is the "Repeater" Fakery Better?

Larson claimed that if repeaters had been carried onto UA 93, this would explain the Burnett calls. He admitted that "no direct evidence has surfaced [that repeaters were involved]." Also, this hypothesis has evidently not even been tested. I asked Jim Hoffman, who originated this idea, whether there have been "any demonstrations that repeaters would allow conversations of a few minutes at (say) 35,000 feet."[137] Hoffman replied: "I'm not aware of specific tests relating to portable repeaters used to relay cellular calls from jets at 35K feet."[138]

Larson criticized A.K. Dewdney's ideas about the functioning of cell phones in airplanes, although these ideas were based on empirical tests. And Larson criticized voice morphing, even though this technology had been publicly demonstrated in 1999. And yet Larson proposed that the Burnett calls worked because repeaters had been placed on UA 93—even though he admittedly has no evidence that they were actually involved, and even though Hoffman admittedly does not know of any tests to determine whether repeaters would have enabled cell phones in 2001 to call home while cruising at 35,000 feet. It seems that Larson is excessively critical of Dewdney's ideas and excessively uncritical of the repeater hypothesis, as I will suggest next.

3. Why Repeater Fakery Cannot Explain Most of the Inauthentic Phone Calls

In any case, even if repeater-boosted cell phones could have successfully made calls to the ground, the idea that repeaters accounted for some of the 9/11 calls seems unlikely. I will briefly explain why.

Tom Burnett's Refusal to Speak to 'the Kids': If the man with whom Deena Burnett was talking were not really her husband, but only seemed to be him thanks to voice morphing, we could understand why that man would not have spoken to "the kids." But if the real Tom Burnett had been speaking to his wife on his cell phone aided by repeaters (about which he would not have known), there would have been no reason, when his wife told him that the children wanted to talk to him, for him to decline. It is very hard, in fact, to believe that he would have passed up probably the last chance to speak to his children. So, even if the repeater hypothesis could explain how the Burnett calls could have been connected, it would not give a credible account of these calls as a whole.

The Lack of Noise and Emotion: If the "phone calls from the planes" were fabricated using voice morphing, we could readily understand how the passengers and flight attendants could have been so calm and the cabins so quiet. But if repeaters had allowed Tom Burnett and other passengers to make cell phone calls from UA 93 when the plane had been taken over by foreign hijackers, some people had been killed, and the passengers had learned that the hijackers planned to fly the plane into a building, we would have no explanation of the calm and quiet behavior of the passengers and flight attendants.

It is interesting that Hoffman said that this plan—having repeater-magnified phone calls reporting hijackings carried out by Arab-looking men—would help the 9/11 operation by "adding realism to the hijackings,"[139] and Larson said that "news reports of these calls [were] emotionally-charged." The idea seems to be that the reports were emotionally charged because the phone calls themselves had been emotionally charged. As we have seen, however, the phone calls were notable for the calmness and lack of emotion of most of the passengers and flight attendants. It is true, to be sure, that if the phone calls were actually reporting the kinds of events described, we would expect the calls to have been very emotionally charged. The fact that they were generally not charged with the level of emotion we would expect counts against the application of the repeater hypothesis to 9/11.

The Small Number of Passengers Who Made Calls: As we have seen, Larson has said that once passengers became aware of hijackings, some of them would try to use their cell phones to report them, and if the calls went through—thanks to repeaters—many others would surely have used cell phones to make calls. So we would have expected most of the passengers on UA 93 to have made cell phone calls.

According to the FBI report made available to the Moussaoui trial in 2006, however, there were only two cell phone calls—the 9:58 AM calls made by passenger Ed Felt and flight attendant CeeCee Lyles.

It seems that Larson disagreed with the FBI's report with regard to—and perhaps only with regard to—the Burnett calls: Whereas the FBI said that Tom Burnett had used a seatback phone, Larson said that Burnett, thanks to repeaters, had used his cell phone. But Larson's account disconfirms his expectation "that passengers, once aware of the hijackings, would attempt to use their cell phones and report hijackings by Middle-Eastern-looking men." Three repeater-assisted cell phone calls by Tom Burnett would be a much smaller number of calls than could have reasonably been expected from 38 passengers on UA 93.

Also, if repeaters were put on Flight 93, they would also presumably have been placed on Flights 11, 175, and 77. But any expectation that repeaters on those planes would have led to the widespread use of cell phones would not have been fulfilled. According to the FBI, there were no cell phone calls by passengers on any of those three flights. But even if Larson said, in opposition to the FBI's stance, that all of the calls on these three flights described by the FBI as onboard calls were actually cell phone calls, there still would have been very few cell phone calls.

Again, Larson is certainly right to suggest that, if passengers on 9/11 flights had become aware of hijackers on their planes and had discovered that cell phones would work, they would probably have made numerous phone calls, many of which would have been cell phone calls. Therefore, the very low number of cell phone calls on the 9/11 flights, even UA 93, serves to disconfirm the repeater hypothesis.

4. STILL ANOTHER WAY TO FAKE CALLS?

However, the failure of the repeater hypothesis does not necessarily mean that the voice-morphing hypothesis is correct. There may still be another way in which the phone calls from the planes could have been faked. And this is important. Those who believe, for some reason, that the calls could not have been morphed should not, for that reason, conclude that the calls were not faked. We need to keep a clear distinction between the evidence for a phenomenon that needs to be explained (called by philosophers of science the *explanandum*) and the explanation for that phenomenon (the *explanans*). We might reject all the available explanations. But that rejection will not do away with the *explanandum*, which in this case is the evidence that reported phone calls from the planes were faked. This chapter has focused primarily on this evidence. A secondary purpose is to show that voice morphing provides a possible explanation for these faked calls. But there might be a better explanation, which is presently unknown—except perhaps to the perpetrators.

It was the "phone calls from the 9/11 planes" that first convinced the public that America had been attacked by al-Qaeda, and until the public comes to see that these calls were faked, the United States will probably never shake free from the myth of "the al-Qaeda attack on America."

Those who speak and write about 9/11 should, of course, take an evidence-based approach. And the evidence that the "calls from the planes" were faked is strong. The evidence against the authenticity of the phone calls from the planes is especially strong when we remember all the types of evidence summarized in the first section of this chapter. Some of this evidence shows there is no credible proof that the alleged hijackers were on the planes, and some of it supports an even stronger point: that the alleged hijackers *simply were not* on the planes. Obviously, if there were no hijackers on the planes, then purported descriptions of such hijackers by passengers and hijackers cannot be authentic.

Accordingly, there are two ways of showing that all of the "phone calls from the planes" were faked. One of those has just been stated: If there were no hijackers on the planes, then there could have been no phone calls from the planes reporting their activities. The second way of showing that all of the purported calls were inauthentic begins with a few of these calls—such as the Tom Burnett, the CeeCee Lyles, the Betty Ong, the Todd Beamer, and the Barbara Olson calls—which were rather obviously faked. We then move to the point that, if some of the calls were faked, then all of them must have been inauthentic, because if the official account—according to which the planes were hijacked in a surprise operation—were true, then no one would have been prepared to fake any calls.

In any case, the reported "phones from the planes" were central to the processes through which the perpetrators of the 9/11 attacks convinced Americans that these attacks were planned and carried out by Muslims. These reported phone calls were, therefore, a central element of the 9/11 SCAD, or state crime against democracy—this plan "by government insiders intended to manipulate democratic processes and undermine popular sovereignty."

Unfortunately, this plan succeeded brilliantly, allowing the Bush-Cheney administration to pass the so-called PATRIOT Act, through which the US Constitution was subverted; to increase military spending enormously; and to launch attacks on Afghanistan and Iraq, even though these attacks did not work out well for the United States—except to further increase military spending.

6. Cheney's *Meet the Press* Interview: Why Did the 9/11 Commission Contradict It?

On September 16, 2001, just five days after the 9/11 attacks, Vice President Dick Cheney was interviewed at Camp David for a special edition of NBC's *Meet the Press*.[1] Cheney was interviewed by Tim Russert, the long-time moderator of that program, who died seven years later, on June 13, 2008. During an interview with NBC's Matt Lauer the morning after Russert died, Cheney referred to the Camp David interview, saying:

> I always, when I think of Tim and think of *Meet the Press*, that's the show that always comes to mind. . . . It was a remarkable moment in American history.[2]

Lauer, commenting that he himself "remember[ed] that interview vividly," asked: "Anything stand out from that interview?" In his reply, Cheney said: "We went back and reminisced to some extent about what had actually happened on the morning of 9/11. So it was—it was a remarkable moment in my career."[3]

The Cheney-Russert interview itself was "a remarkable moment in American history." One thing that made it remarkable was the fact that, in reminiscing about his movements that morning, Cheney contradicted a claim that the 9/11 Commission would later make.

Alluding to Russert's reputation for being a rigorous, well-prepared interviewer, Cheney said to Lauer: "He would ask you tough questions, he would remind you of quotes you made previously in other settings or on earlier shows, so you never got away with anything going up vis-à-vis Tim."[4] We should apply Russert's method to Cheney's interview with him at Camp David, reminding ourselves of exactly what Cheney said about his movements that morning, then comparing his statement with what the 9/11 Commission said.

After discussing with Cheney the US response to the 9/11 attacks, Russert turned to September 11 itself, asking Cheney where he was when he learned of the first attack on the World Trade Center. Replying that he was in his White House office, Cheney said that, after seeing the second attack on television, he convened a meeting in his office with Condoleezza Rice and others, then talked by telephone to President Bush (who was in Florida), discussing the public statement the latter might make. (This call would have needed to take place shortly after Bush left the classroom, which was reportedly at about 9:12,[5] if it was to help him prepare his address to the nation, which was to be given at 9:30. The *New York Times* wrote: "[A]t 9:12, [Bush] abruptly retreated [from the classroom], speaking to Mr. Cheney and New York officials."[6]) Cheney then said:

> While I was there, over the next several minutes, watching developments on the television and as we started to get organized to figure out what to do, my Secret Service agents came in and, under these circumstances, they just move. They don't say "sir" or ask politely. They came in and said, "Sir, we have to leave immediately," and grabbed me and. . . .[7]

Russert asked: "Literally grabbed you and moved you?" Cheney replied:

> Yeah. And, you know, your feet touch the floor periodically. But they're bigger than I am, and they hoisted me up and moved me very rapidly down the hallway, down some stairs, through some doors and down some more stairs into an underground facility under the White House, and, as a matter of fact, it's a corridor, locked at both ends, and they did that because they had received a report that an airplane was headed for the White House.

After confirming Russert's supposition that this was Flight 77, Cheney continued:

> And when it entered the danger zone and looked like it was headed for the White House was when they grabbed me and evacuated me to the basement. . . . [O]nce I got down into the shelter, the first thing I did—there's a secure phone there. First thing I did was pick up the telephone and call the president again, who was still down in Florida, at that point, and strongly urged him to delay his return.

After discussing that advice in terms of the need to secure "presidential succession," Cheney continued the narrative about his own movements that day, saying:

> Once I left that immediate shelter, after I talked to the president, urged him to stay away for now, well, I went down into what's called PEOC,[8] the Presidential Emergency Operations Center, and there, I had Norm Mineta . . . . I had Condi Rice with me and several of my key staff people. We had access, secured communications with Air Force One, with the Secretary of Defense over in the Pentagon. We had also the secure videoconference that ties together the White House, CIA, State, Justice, Defense.

After giving still more details, Cheney said: "I was in a position to be able to see all the stuff coming in, receive reports and then make decisions in terms of acting with it." Cheney made clear, in other words, that he had everyone and everything he needed in the PEOC to take charge. He then added: "But when I arrived there within a short order, we had word the Pentagon's been hit.

II SUMMARY OF CHENEY'S ACCOUNT TO RUSSERT

According to what Vice President Cheney told Tim Russert, only five days after 9/11, the sequence of events went like this:

1. The Secret Service came into Cheney's office to take him downstairs after they "received a report that an airplane was headed for the White House." Although it turned out that the plane "turned away and . . . flew a circle" (after which the plane "came back in and then hit the Pentagon"), it was "when it entered the danger zone and looked like it was headed for the White House," Cheney said, that "they grabbed me and evacuated me to the basement." (This was shortly after his 9:12 phone call with the president, perhaps at about 9:15.)

2. The Secret Service agents hustled Cheney down to the underground corridor (which he also called the "immediate shelter," evidently meaning the part of the bomb shelter that one reaches first).

3. While in this corridor, Cheney used the secure phone available in the corridor to talk to the president again, this time urging him to delay his return to Washington.

4. Cheney then went from this corridor to the Presidential Emergency Operations Center, or PEOC (which is also called the "shelter conference room").

5. After he arrived in the PEOC (which is under the East Wing of the White House), Cheney learned that the Pentagon had been hit. Cheney's statement here—"[W]hen I arrived there within a short order, we had word the Pentagon's been hit"—is ambiguous. Did "within a short order" mean that Cheney arrived in the PEOC soon? Or did it mean that, soon after arriving there, he learned that the Pentagon had been hit? The latter seems more likely. The main point, in any case, is clear: *Cheney learned about the Pentagon attack only after arriving in the PEOC. He did not learn about the Pentagon attack while he was still in the corridor.*

This is significant because it contradicts what the 9/11 Commission would state three years later.

III THE 9/11 COMMISSION'S ACCOUNT

According to *The 9/11 Commission Report*, the sequence of events was as follows:

1. At 9:33, the Secret Service learned that an unidentified aircraft was coming toward the White House. "No move was made to evacuate the Vice President at this time," because the Secret Service learned at 9:34, just before sounding the alarm, "that the aircraft was turning south." (So, whereas Cheney's account to Russert on *Meet the Press* indicated that he was taken down to the underground corridor at roughly 9:15, this account by the 9/11 Commission says that Cheney was still in his office at 9:33.)

2. Just before 9:36, the Secret Service, having learned that the plane had started circling back, "ordered the immediate evacuation of the Vice President." (This account by the 9/11 Commission has Cheney being taken downstairs 15 to 20 minutes later than Cheney's *Meet the Press* account suggested.)

3. After being hustled downstairs: "The Vice President entered the underground tunnel leading to the shelter at 9:37. Once inside, Vice President Cheney and the agents paused in an area of the tunnel that had a secure phone, a bench, and television."

4. While there, "The Vice President [telephoned Florida] and asked to speak to the President, but it took time for the call to be connected." (Cheney's *Meet the Press* account did not include the unbelievable claim that it took some time for Cheney on this secure phone to reach the president—a claim evidently included to kill some time.)

5. "He [Cheney] learned in the tunnel that the Pentagon had been hit, and he saw television coverage of the smoke coming from the building." (Whereas this account by the 9/11 Commission claimed that Cheney learned about the Pentagon attack while he was still in the tunnel (corridor), Cheney had told *Meet the Press* in 2001 that he learned about the Pentagon attack only after he entered into the PEOC.)

6. Mrs. Cheney, having arrived at the White House at 9:52, "joined her husband in the tunnel."

7. "[A]t 9:55, the Vice President was still on the phone with the President, advising that three planes were missing and one had hit the Pentagon."

8. "After the call ended, Mrs. Cheney and the Vice President moved from the tunnel to the shelter conference room. . . . [T]he Vice president arrived in the room shortly before 10:00, perhaps at 9:58."[9]

As a comparison of these two timelines shows, the 9/11 Commission's account differs significantly from the account that Cheney gave to Russert.

IV CONTRADICTIONS BETWEEN THE TWO ACCOUNTS

The crucial difference is that, according to Cheney's *Meet the Press* interview, he arrived in the PEOC *before* he learned about the attack on the Pentagon. But according to the 9/11 Commission, Cheney entered the PEOC *after* he learned about this attack (and, in fact, about 20 minutes after the attack, assuming we accept the Commission's judgment that the attack occurred at 9:38 AM).

The two accounts appear, moreover, to contradict each other with regard to the time at which Cheney was taken downstairs to the underground corridor. According to what Cheney told Russert, this occurred as soon as the Secret Service agents heard that a plane was approaching the White House (they did not wait until the plane came in that direction a second time), and this seems to have been shortly after Cheney called the president about the latter's public statement—a call that, according to the *New York Times*, occurred at 9:12. If Cheney was taken downstairs approximately five minutes later, his account would be compatible with the testimony of Secretary of Transportation Norman Mineta, who told the 9/11 Commission during an open hearing in 2003 that Cheney was already in the PEOC when he got there at 9:20.[10]

If Cheney meant something close to this, his account would, however, strongly contradict *The 9/11 Commission Report*, according to which Cheney did not head downstairs until 9:36 and did not enter the corridor until 9:37.

Also, the natural interpretation of Cheney's statement about the Pentagon—"when I arrived there [in the PEOC] within a short order, we had word the Pentagon's been hit"—seems to be that the Pentagon attack occurred *after* Cheney was in the PEOC. Worded otherwise, Cheney was in the PEOC before the attack on the Pentagon.

One can point out, to be sure, that Cheney did not actually say this. Cheney said only that he *learned about* the Pentagon attack after he entered the PEOC—that is, that he was already in the PEOC when he learned about the Pentagon attack. One who wanted to support the 9/11 Commission's timeline might argue that, although the Pentagon was attacked at 9:38, Cheney did not *hear about* this attack until approximately 20 minutes later—after he, as the Commission says, entered the PEOC at 9:58. On that basis, one might argue, Cheney's account and that of the Commission could be reconciled.

However, besides being extremely implausible (by suggesting that Vice President Cheney, who was formerly the secretary of defense and on 9/11 was the person in charge at the White House, would not have been notified about such an attack for over 20 minutes), this attempted reconciliation would be ruled out by the Commission's timeline, which says that *Cheney learned about the Pentagon attack while he was still in the corridor, before he entered the PEOC*. Cheney told Russert that he learned about the Pentagon after he was in the PEOC.

It is impossible, therefore, to reconcile the two accounts. If the story that Cheney told Russert at Camp David, just five days after 9/11, was true, then the story told by the 9/11 Commission in July 2004—almost three years later—was false.

V THE UNIQUE SOURCE FOR THE 9/11 COMMISSION'S TIMELINE

On what did the 9/11 Commission base its timeline? It claimed that the 9:37 time for Cheney's entry into the corridor, from which the 9:58 estimate for his entry into the PEOC followed, was based on a timeline in a Secret Service report. By the Commission's own admission, however, the Secret Service said that "the 9:37 entry time in their timeline was based on alarm data, which is no longer retrievable."[11] There is no official documentation, in other words, for the claim that Cheney entered the corridor at 9:37.

Could the Commission cite journalistic accounts to support its timeline? It appears that there was one journalistic account, and only one, that supported this timeline: an MSNBC-*Newsweek* article by Evan Thomas, which was dated December 31, 2001, at MSNBC and appeared in the January 7, 2002, issue of *Newsweek*. This article said: "Shortly before 10 a.m., the Cheneys were led into the PEOC conference room. . . . [T]hey looked up at the TV screens. It was 9:58 a.m."[12]

In saying this, Thomas disagreed not only with what Norman Mineta would later tell the 9/11 Commission—namely, that Cheney was in the PEOC before 9:20, when Mineta arrived down there—but also with what Richard Clarke would say in *Against All Enemies*, which became a best-selling book in 2004 while the 9/11 Commission was holding hearings.

According to Clarke, shortly after the meeting that Cheney had with Condoleezza Rice following the second attack on the World Trade Center (which occurred at 9:03), the Secret Service wanted Rice as well as Cheney to go down to the PEOC. Rice, however, first went with Clarke to the White House's Video Teleconferencing Center (which is in the Situation Room, in the West Wing of the White House), where Clarke was to set up a video conference. This conference, Clarke's statements suggest, began at about 9:10.[13] After spending a few minutes there, Rice said, according to Clarke: "You're going to need some decisions quickly. I'm going to the PEOC to be with the Vice President. Tell us what you need." Clarke replied: "What I need is an open line to Cheney and you."[14] Some minutes later, evidently at about 9:15, Norman Mineta arrived and Clarke, after receiving him in the Situation Room, "suggested he join the Vice President."[15] Clarke thereby seemed to imply that Cheney was in the PEOC prior to 9:15.

An ABC News program narrated by Peter Jennings on the first anniversary of 9/11 agreed—in advance—with Norman Mineta's 2003 account, according to which Cheney was down in the PEOC before Mineta arrived. ABC's Charlie Gibson said: "In the bunker, the Vice President is joined by [Condoleezza] Rice and Transportation Secretary Norman Mineta."[16]

According to another ABC News program that same week, Cheney's own White House photographer, David Bohrer, also supported the early descent time. This program, having Bohrer describe the moment when the Secret Service agents said to Cheney, "Sir, you have to come with us," portrayed this event as happening "just after 9 AM." ABC presumably portrayed it thus because that is what Bohrer himself had said.[17]

The 9/11 Commission's timeline, according to which Cheney arrived much later, was based on a twofold claim: that Cheney did not enter the corridor until 9:37 AM, and that his phone call to the president then took about 20 minutes, so that he did not go into the PEOC until about 9:58 AM.

As we saw above, the alleged Secret Service claim that Cheney did not enter the corridor until 9:37 was, by the Commission's own admission, undocumented. Surely this undocumented claim cannot trump the combined testimony of Norman Mineta, Richard Clarke, David Bohrer (as described by ABC News), and even Dick Cheney himself (as given to Tim Russert five days after 9/11).

However, the claim that Cheney did not enter the corridor until 9:37 was mentioned by one journalistic account: the aforementioned MSNBC-*Newsweek* article by Evan Thomas. According to Thomas, it was 9:35 when the Secret Service entered Cheney's office (where the vice president was not in a take-charge mode but was simply "standing by his desk, looking at the TV in the corner"). This article also contains the other main elements later articulated in *The 9/11 Commission Report*: Cheney's time-consuming phone call to the president (who was "not easy to reach"); Cheney's being told about the Pentagon attack while he was still in the corridor; Lynne Cheney's arrival while the vice president was still on the phone; and then the conclusion: "Shortly before 10 a.m., the Cheneys were led into the PEOC conference room. . . . [T]hey looked up at the TV screens. It was 9:58 a.m."[18]

If the 9/11 Commission's timeline was derived from the Thomas article, the question becomes: Where did Thomas get the information on which he based his account?

The note provided by the 9/11 Commission (464 n. 211) for its conclusion—that the Cheneys arrived in the PEOC "shortly before 10:00, perhaps at 9:58"—mentions three transcripts, all of which are White House transcripts: "Lynne Cheney interview with *Newsweek*, Nov. 9, 2001"; "Vice President Cheney interview with *Newsweek*, Nov. 19, 2001"; and "Rice interview with Evan Thomas, Nov. 1, 2001."

Evidently, therefore, the Evan Thomas MSNBC-*Newsweek* article of December 31, 2001, was based significantly on interviews with Condoleezza Rice and the Cheneys.

It would appear, accordingly, that the account given by Cheney to *Newsweek* in the interview of November 19, 2001, differed significantly from what he had told Tim Russert on *Meet the Press* two months earlier. He told Russert that he learned about the Pentagon attack after he was already in the PEOC, thereby suggesting agreement with all the above-named witnesses who would later indicate that he was in the PEOC prior to the Pentagon attack. But according to the story that he (along with his wife and Rice) apparently told *Newsweek*, which was later accepted by the 9/11 Commission, Cheney did not enter the PEOC, where he took charge of matters, until about 20 minutes after the attack on the Pentagon had already occurred.

VI POSSIBLE MOTIVES FOR CHANGING THE TIMELINE

What possible motives would there have been for Cheney to change the timeline? What possible motives might the 9/11 Commission have had for accepting Evan Thomas's timeline, even though it was apparently the only journalistic account that depicted Cheney as not entering the PEOC until almost 10:00?

I mentioned above the fact that Secretary of Transportation Norman Mineta reported to the 9/11 Commission in 2003 that, when he arrived in the PEOC at about 9:20, Cheney was already there. Mineta then gave the following account of a conversation he witnessed:

> During the time that the airplane was coming in to the Pentagon, there was a young man who would come in and say to the Vice President, "The plane is 50 miles out." "The plane is 30 miles out." And when it got down to "the plane is 10 miles out," the young man also said to the Vice President, "Do the orders still stand?" And the Vice President turned and whipped his neck around and said, "Of course the orders still stand. Have you heard anything to the contrary?"[19]

When asked by Commissioner Timothy Roemer how long this conversation occurred after his arrival at 9:20, Mineta said, "Probably about five or six minutes." That, as Roemer pointed out, would have been "about 9:25 or 9:26."[20]

During an informal interview in Seattle in 2007, Mineta reaffirmed that Cheney was already there when he arrived in the PEOC, saying "absolutely." When Mineta was told by the interviewer that the Commission had said that Cheney did not arrive until 9:58, Mineta expressed surprise and said: "Oh no, no, no; I don't know how that came about." Although Mineta said he "might have been mistaken on the 9:25," he said that Cheney was definitely there before the Pentagon was struck, and "so was Mrs. Cheney."[21]

Mineta's 2003 testimony at the 9/11 Commission hearing created two problems for the official story of the day's events. For one thing, it indicated that Cheney—who, as he told Russert, was in contact with Secretary of Defense Rumsfeld—knew that an aircraft was approaching Washington several minutes before the Pentagon was struck. This implication directly contradicted the official claim, according to which Pentagon officials did not know that an aircraft was approaching their building. This claim was essential for explaining why the Pentagon had not been evacuated, with the result that 125 Pentagon employees were killed. For example, one Pentagon spokesperson, having been asked why this evacuation did not occur, said: "The Pentagon was simply not aware that this aircraft was coming our way."[22]

A second problem created by Mineta's story involved the nature of "the orders." Although Mineta assumed, he said, that they were orders to have the aircraft shot down, no aircraft approaching Washington was shot down. Mineta's interpretation also made the young man's question unintelligible. Given the fact that the airspace over the Pentagon is categorized as "forbidden," meaning that commercial aircraft are never permitted in it; the fact that two hijacked planes had already crashed into the Twin Towers; and the fact that still other hijacked planes had been reported, the expected orders, if an unidentified plane were approaching that airspace, would have been to shoot it down. Had Cheney given those orders, there would have been no reason for the young man to ask if the orders still stood. The young man's question made sense only if the orders were to do something unexpected: *not* to shoot it down. The most natural interpretation of Mineta's story, accordingly, was that he had inadvertently reported that he had heard Cheney confirm stand-down orders.

That Mineta's testimony was perceived as a dangerous threat to the official account is suggested by four steps taken by the 9/11 Commission.

The first step was the one on which we have focused: the claim, based on the White House-supplied MSNBC-*Newsweek* story, that Cheney only entered the PEOC after the Pentagon had been struck—at which time he went into his take-charge mode (prior to that, he was talking with the president and watching television).

A second step was to make no mention of this portion of Mineta's testimony in *The 9/11 Commission Report*.

A third step was to remove this portion of Mineta's testimony from the 9/11 Commission video archive.[23]

A fourth step was the creation of an alternative version of the story about an incoming aircraft. *The 9/11 Commission Report* wrote:

> At 10:02, the communicators in the shelter began receiving reports from the Secret Service of an inbound aircraft. . . . At some time between 10:10 and 10:15, a military aide told the Vice President and others that the aircraft was 80 miles out. Vice President Cheney was asked for authority to engage the aircraft. . . . The Vice President authorized fighter aircraft to engage the inbound plane. . . . The military aide returned a few minutes later, probably between 10:12 and 10:18, and said the aircraft was 60 miles out. He again asked for authorization to engage. The Vice President again said yes.[24]

Although this story by the 9/11 Commission had some elements in common with Mineta's story, it differed in two major respects. First, it portrayed Cheney as having issued a shoot-down, not a stand-down, order. Second, it indicated that Cheney's order came far too late to have had any relevance to the Pentagon attack.[25]

CONCLUSION

As we have seen, it would appear that the 9/11 Commission's time-line—which rules out the possibility that Cheney could have been responsible for the attack on the Pentagon—came from Cheney himself, via the account that he (along with Lynne Cheney and Condoleezza Rice) gave to *Newsweek*.

Very strong evidence against the 9/11 Commission's timeline is provided by the account that Cheney had given to Tim Russert on the September 16, 2001 edition of *Meet the Press*, because this account was given by Cheney himself, and it was given just five days after 9/11, when the events of that day were still fresh in his mind. This interview was very well known. Matt Lauer, for example, said: "I remember that interview vividly. . . . I was glued to that."[26]

In describing Russert's typical method on *Meet the Press*, Cheney said, as we saw earlier: "He [Russert] would ask you tough questions, he would remind you of quotes you made previously in other settings or on earlier shows, so you never got away with anything going up vis-à-vis Tim." But Cheney has thus far gotten away with the contradiction between what he told Russert and what he apparently told *Newsweek*, which became the position of *The 9/11 Commission Report*. Should journalists today not apply Russert's method to Cheney's own statements about his movements on 9/11, asking about the contradiction between what he told Russert and what the 9/11 Commission, evidently under his guidance, said?

Further evidence of the truth of the account given to Russert by Cheney has, moreover, been provided by a document obtained through a FOIA request. In 2010, Aidan Monaghan received a memorandum from the Secret Service, dated October 1, 2001, that rehearsed the movements of various people that morning. One item said: "SAIC [Special Agent in Charge] Anthony Lotto had telephoned. . . during the initial states to advise that Vice President Cheney had been relocated to the PEOC."[27]

In any case, the contradiction between Cheney's statement to Russert, according to which Cheney was in the PEOC before the Pentagon attack, and the 9/11 Commission's account—according to which Cheney did not enter the PEOC, where he took charge, until almost 10:00 AM, long after the Pentagon attack—provides us with an introduction to problems faced by the official story about the Pentagon attack, according to which it was struck by American 77 under the control of al-Qaeda.

7. The Pentagon:
A Consensus Approach

As we saw in the previous chapter, Dick Cheney and the 9/11 Commission went to great lengths to try to cover up the fact that Cheney was in the PEOC prior to the attack on the Pentagon. This attempted cover-up had become essential because Norman Mineta, in an unscripted moment during a televised public hearing of the 9/11 Commission, had revealed (apparently innocently) that Cheney had stated, in response to a question of what to do about a plane approaching Washington, that the previously given orders should stand—meaning that the plane should *not* be shot down.

As this episode illustrates, the attack on the Pentagon was an "inside job" as fully as was the destruction of the World Trade Center. As Chapters 2, 3, and 4 have shown, there is overwhelming evidence that the official story about the WTC attacks is a lie. There is likewise abundant evidence that the official story about the Pentagon, according to which *the Pentagon was attacked by American Airlines Flight 77 (AA 77) under the control of al-Qaeda*, is a lie. This is the most important point about the Pentagon attack, and it is a point about which all members of the 9/11 Truth Movement agree.

This consensus about the primary issue has been disguised by an ongoing debate about a quite secondary question: *What hit the Pentagon?* (Was there a strike by a large airliner, probably a 757, perhaps even AA 77? Or was it a strike by a smaller airplane or a missile? Or was there no strike at all, so that explosives accounted for all the damage? Or was the damage caused by a strike—whether by a large or small aircraft—combined with explosives?) Members of the 9/11 Movement have sometimes pointed out that, regardless of what position is held on this secondary question, there is ample evidence about the primary issue: the falsity of the claim that the Pentagon was attacked by Flight 77 under the control of al-Qaeda. Nevertheless, the question of whether a Boeing 757 struck the Pentagon has been discussed in such a way as to create the impression that this is the primary issue.

By contrast, the 9/11 Truth Movement in dealing with the World Trade Center has focused almost entirely on showing that the official story, according to which al-Qaeda destroyed the buildings by means of airplane strikes and resulting fires, is a lie. Members of the Truth Movement have marshaled arguments that the buildings could not have been brought down without explosives, combined with evidence—physical and testimonial—that explosives were indeed used to bring down the buildings. There has been, to be sure, some discussion about the secondary question of what hit the Twin Towers (AA 11 and UA 175; drones; or no aircraft whatsoever). Overwhelmingly, however, the discussion has focused on the primary point: The official story is shown to be false by evidence that the Twin Towers and Building 7 were brought down with explosives.

By analogy, the most important evidence to be lifting up about the Pentagon is simply the various types of evidence showing the falsity of the official story, according to which the Pentagon was attacked by AA 77 under the control of al-Qaeda. But if we were to focus primarily on evidence supportive of our personal views about what caused the Pentagon damage, we would imply that the main audience for our talks and writings consists of other members of the 9/11 Truth Movement. We need to remember that most of the press and the public, at least in the United States, still accept the official story, according to which al-Qaeda terrorists hijacked an airliner in order to attack the Pentagon. We need to focus, therefore, on various types of evidence against the official story about which all of us in the 9/11 Truth Movement agree, regardless of our position on the secondary question, What hit the Pentagon?

If we come to focus our efforts about the Pentagon on this primary point—rather than continuing to argue about a secondary issue—then the 9/11 Truth Movement could address the press and the public on the basis of a consensus about the Pentagon, as it already does for the most part with regard to the World Trade Center. Insofar as we are able to show that the 9/11 Truth Movement has achieved consensus with regard to the attacks in both Washington and New York, we will greatly increase our chances for success.

I myself played a role in the battle about what damaged the Pentagon, not fully realizing that this issue is not only of very secondary importance, but also that this issue, unless seen to be quite unimportant, can be very destructive.

With regard to the question of unimportance: Because the official story claimed, contrary to appearances, that the Pentagon was struck by a Boeing 757, the "no 757" position seemed a natural corollary of the rejection of the official story. It needs to be understood, however, that people can endorse the 757 view while fully rejecting the official story.

With regard to possible destructiveness: Because the evidence against the 757 claim has seemed far more convincing to most members of the 9/11 Truth Movement than any arguments to the contrary, a battle about it surely would not, I assumed, greatly damage the 9/11 Movement. I have now, however, come to see that a battle about this issue could easily become destructive—that is, if it is indeed a *battle* between the two positions, based on the assumption that the issue is quite important, rather than a *discussion*, based on the fact that the issue is relatively unimportant.

In order to emphasize the fact that we do have consensus on the most important point, I have called the approach in this chapter "A Consensus Approach." In the first part of this chapter, I explain why a serious dispute about whether a 757 hit the Pentagon is unnecessary, because this issue is quite unimportant. In the second part, I explain why a serious dispute about this issue might be (needlessly) destructive.

I The Question of What Struck the Pentagon as Quite Unimportant

Most members of the 9/11 Truth Movement have long associated defenders of the 757 claim with defenders of the official story about the Pentagon. People who identified with the 9/11 Truth Movement, while defending the 757 claim, have rather naturally, therefore, given rise to suspicions. In recent times, however, a number of scientists have articulated full-fledged rejections of the official story about the Pentagon while endorsing, or at least leaning toward, the 757 claim.[1]

This development shows that any serious dispute about what hit the Pentagon is unnecessary. That this issue should not divide the 9/11 Truth Movement is demonstrated most clearly by a set of facts showing that, regardless of what damaged the Pentagon, the attack was engineered not by al-Qaeda but by Cheney and cohorts—including his long-time colleague Donald Rumsfeld, who was then Secretary of Defense. I will mention 14 such facts.

1. The Pentagon Should Not Have Been Struck

The Pentagon was probably the best protected building in the world. Without some kind of stand-down order, it simply could not have been attacked by amateur hijackers. This point can be, and has been, articulated by people who hold, or at least lean towards, the view that the Pentagon was struck by a 757. It could even be held by people who affirm that this 757 was AA 77.

Scientist Frank Legge, in an article entitled "What Hit the Pentagon?" wrote: "[The Pentagon] should have been well defended. . . . There was ample time to send up fighters to intercept, as is the normal procedure."[2] Likewise, physicist David Chandler and engineer Jonathan Cole asked, rhetorically:

> How could the Pentagon, the hub of the US military, have been so poorly defended that it could be hit . . . . after the buildings in New York City had already been hit and other hijacked planes were known to still be in the air?[3]

Critics of the official story have often commented, in fact, that the failure of the US military, with its unprecedented intelligence and power, to protect its own headquarters stands as the most obvious evidence that the official story is false.

2. Cheney's Guilt

The previous chapter pointed out that Dick Cheney and the 9/11 Commission went to great lengths to claim, falsely, that he did not enter the PEOC until almost 10:00, and thereby to claim that he was not in the PEOC prior to the attack on the Pentagon. This claim was used to bury Norman Mineta's story about Cheney's discussion with a young man concerning whether the "orders" still stood. Because Cheney's response that they *did* stand could only be understood as orders for the military to "stand down," this episode leaves no question about who was behind the Pentagon attack.

Legge, calling Mineta's testimony "crucial," wrote: "There is little doubt that Cheney had it in his hand to block this attack [on the Pentagon]."[4] Chandler and Cole asked: "Why was Norman Mineta's testimony about Cheney's response to the approach of the aircraft discounted in the 9/11 Commission report?"[5]

3. Hani Hanjour's Incompetence

The official story is rendered especially dubious by its claim that the Pentagon was struck by a Boeing 757 flown by al-Qaeda's Hani Hanjour. As the title of a *New York Times* story revealed in 2002, Hanjour, who was taking lessons in a single-engine plane, was known as "a trainee noted for incompetence," about whom an instructor said: "He could not fly at all."[6] The 9/11 Commission later even reported that in 2001, just months before 9/11, a flight instructor, after going up with Hanjour, "declined a second request because of what he considered Hanjour's poor piloting skills."[7]

And yet on September 11, 2001, before Hanjour had been declared by authorities to have been the pilot of the plane that hit the Pentagon, a *Washington Post* story said:

> [J]ust as the plane seemed to be on a suicide mission into the White House, the unidentified pilot executed a pivot so tight that it reminded observers of a fighter jet maneuver. . . . Aviation sources said the plane was flown with extraordinary skill, making it highly likely that a trained pilot was at the helm.[8]

A *Post* story the following year stated: "[A]viation experts concluded that the final maneuvers of American Airlines Flight 77 . . . was the work of 'a great talent.'"[9] This was clearly impossible: A man who could not safely fly a single-engine plane could not possibly have flown a giant airliner with "extraordinary skill," like "a great talent."

Legge agrees that the claim that Hanjour flew a 757 into the Pentagon may be ruled out by his "poor flying skills."[10] Chandler and Cole ask, rhetorically: "How could an untrained pilot have performed the difficult maneuvers?"[11]

4. Wedge 1 Required Extraordinary Maneuver

Another disproof of the official story involves the extraordinary maneuver attributed to a 757 airliner hijacked by al-Qaeda. This maneuver would have been so difficult in a 757 that the impossibility of the official story could not have been avoided by simply choosing a less incompetent al-Qaeda trainee. Ralph Kolstad, who was a US Navy "top gun" pilot before becoming a commercial airline pilot, has said: "I have 6,000 hours of flight time in Boeing 757's and 767's and I could not have flown it the way the flight path was described."[12] If the maneuver could not have been executed in a 757 by one of America's top pilots, it could not have been executed by any of the alleged hijackers.

The extreme difficulty of this maneuver raises the question of why a pilot would have chosen this trajectory. The answer is that it was made necessary if the plane was to strike the first two floors of Wedge 1. This target required the pilot to execute a downward spiral. The Flight Data Recorder says that the plane descended about 8,000 feet in somewhat over three minutes. The plane then came in at 530 miles per hour, close to the ground, striking the building between the first and second floors.[13] This was the maneuver that even Kolstad could not have executed in a 757.

Legge has said that, even if al-Qaeda could not have flown this trajectory, this fact would say nothing against the 757 theory, given "the possibility that the plane was hijacked by an on-board device, pre-programmed to take over the autopilot."[14] Chandler and Cole have made the same suggestion, asking: "Was the plane flown by some kind of automatic controls and/or guided by a homing beacon?"[15]

5. Why Would al-Qaeda Not Have Crashed into the Roof?

If al-Qaeda masterminds had wanted to strike the Pentagon, they would not have targeted Wedge 1, thereby requiring an amateur pilot to fly a trajectory that even an expert professional probably could not have executed. The masterminds would have told the pilot simply to crash into the roof, thereby having a 29-acre target.[16]

Chandler and Cole have made this point, writing: "Why would the purported hijackers risk mission failure by choosing a difficult ground level approach when they could have simply dived into the building?"[17] Legge has asked: "Why did [the plane] not hit the relatively weak roof?"[18]

6. Wedge 1 Required Extra Time

Given the fact that the al-Qaeda hijackers would have been flying through the most restricted airspace in the United States, they should have feared that they would be intercepted by fighter jets and shot down. And yet executing the downward spiral required by targeting Wedge 1 meant that the hijacked plane needed to be aloft considerably longer than if it had simply flown straight to the Pentagon and crashed into its roof. Al-Qaeda masterminds would not have had the pilot take this extra risk, through which the whole mission might have failed.

7. Wedge 1 Alone Presented Obstacles

The only part of the Pentagon that presented an obstacle course for an attacking airplane was Wedge 1: There were elevated signs (because this part of the Pentagon was close to a highway); there was a control tower for the Pentagon's heliport; and there were many large objects on the lawn because of the renovation. (According to reports, in fact, the plane's wings struck a cyclone fence, a generator trailer, and a mobile home, among other things.) By contrast, any of the other wedges would have provided an obstacle-free approach path. Again, Wedge 1 would have been the least likely part of the Pentagon for al-Qaeda to have targeted.

8. Wedge 1 Guaranteed the Safety of Pentagon Leaders

If the official story, according to which the Pentagon attack was carried out by al-Qaeda operatives, were true, these operatives would surely have wanted to kill the top military officers and the secretary of defense. But the offices of these men are about as distant as possible from Wedge 1. Al-Qaeda terrorists would not have planned the attack at a location virtually guaranteeing the safety of the top brass and Secretary of Defense Donald Rumsfeld.

These facts evidently created some cognitive dissonance in the authors of two books supportive of the official narrative. Steve Vogel, while accepting in his history of the Pentagon every detail of the official account, remarked that "the plane had hit the building in the best possible place." Vogel explained:

> The hijackers had not hit the River or Mall sides, where the senior military leadership had been concentrated since 1942. Rumsfeld had been sitting in the same third-floor office above the River entrance as every secretary of defense since Louis Johnson in 1949, a location that had been a matter of public record all that time. The joint chiefs . . . were arrayed in various prime E-Ring offices on the River and Mall sides. . . . [T]he National Military Command Center could have been decimated . . . , a disaster that could have effectively shut down the Pentagon.[19]

In saying that the hijackers' plane hit the Pentagon "in the best possible place," Vogel meant: from the perspective of the Pentagon's leaders. But from the perspective of al-Qaeda, the plane had struck the Pentagon in *the worst possible place*. Assuming that al-Qaeda terrorists wanted to kill Rumsfeld, they could have killed these Pentagon leaders by the method mentioned above: simply crashing their plane into the roof above Rumsfeld's third-floor office. In *Firefight*, Patrick Creed and Rick Newman wrote:

> Had terrorists been targeting not just the Pentagon, but the senior government officials inside, there was plenty of information available to help them figure out exactly where to aim. . . . Yet the VIPs in the most prestigious part of the Pentagon were strangely immune.[20]

There would have been nothing strange about the Secretary of Defense's immunity, of course, if he did the targeting.

9. Wedge 1 Renovated

The Pentagon was being renovated (with steel-reinforced concrete, blast-resistant windows, fire-resistant Kevlar cloth, and a new sprinkler system) to make the Pentagon less vulnerable to terrorist attacks. Wedge 1 was the only part of the Pentagon in which this renovation had been carried out—a renovation that was virtually complete. Thanks to this renovation, the attack on Wedge 1 caused much less damage than would have an attack on any other section of the Pentagon. Al-Qaeda terrorists, wanting to inflict damage on America's chief symbol of military power, would not have chosen to hit the section where the least damage would be inflicted.

10. Wedge 1 Sparsely Occupied

The renovation was not quite completed. For this reason, Wedge 1 was only sparsely occupied. Accordingly, whereas a strike on any other part of the Pentagon would have caused hundreds of deaths, perhaps even thousands, the attack on Wedge 1 killed only 125 Pentagon employees. Al-Qaeda terrorists, wanting to kill Americans working at the Pentagon, would not have struck Wedge 1, where the attack would cause the smallest number of deaths.

Chandler and Cole, endorsing this point, along with point 8, wrote: "Why would the purported hijackers perform a difficult spiral descent to hit the face of the Pentagon that had the least number of people in it, and was opposite from the offices of the Pentagon high command?"

As points 3 through 10 show, the al-Qaeda "mastermind" behind the attack on the Pentagon would have been the stupidest mastermind conceivable: Besides selecting a completely incompetent pilot to attack the Pentagon, he ordered Hanjour to attack Wedge 1, thereby forcing him to fly an impossibly difficult trajectory, to get through an obstacle course, and to spend extra time for the approach, during which his plane could have been shot down. The choice of Wedge 1 also resulted in the least damage and the fewest deaths, including no deaths whatsoever among the Pentagon's leadership. This summary shows that, no matter what position is taken on what damaged the Pentagon—a Boeing 757, a smaller plane, simply explosives, or some combination—the fact that Wedge 1 was targeted demonstrates, by itself, that the Pentagon attack was not engineered by al-Qaeda.

11. Rumsfeld's Guilt

Whereas points 3 through 10 have provided evidence for the negative fact that the Pentagon attack was not an al-Qaeda operation, the remaining points enlarge the evidence for the positive fact stated in the first point, namely, that the Pentagon attack was an inside operation. Point 2's having already established Cheney's guilt, the present point documents Rumsfeld's.

Just as Cheney's guilt is shown by his false claim (endorsed by the 9/11 Commission) that he was not in the PEOC between 9:15 and almost 10:00 AM, Rumsfeld made the false claim (endorsed by the 9/11 Commission) that he was not in the Pentagon's video conference center, participating in Richard Clarke's White House video conference, in the period between the second attack on the World Trade Center (9:03) until shortly after the attack on the Pentagon.

Just as the official story about Cheney was contradicted by Clarke's book *Against All Enemies*—which appeared in 2004 while the 9/11 Commission was holding its hearings, and which *The 9/11 Commission Report* never once mentioned—the fact that Rumsfeld actually participated in Clarke's video conference was reported by Clarke in his book.

As Clarke entered the Video Center, he wrote, he "could see . . . Donald Rumsfeld" rushing into a studio.[21] After the attack on the Pentagon, Clarke said: "I can still see Rumsfeld on the screen."[22] Slightly later, Clarke wrote, "Rumsfeld said that smoke was getting into the Pentagon secure teleconferencing studio," after which Rumsfeld, in response to a suggestion by Franklin Miller that he should take a helicopter to the Department of Defense's alternative site, retorted: "I am too goddam old to go to an alternate site."[23]

Rumsfeld gave a very different account to the 9/11 Commission, saying he was in his office from before 9:03, when the second tower was hit, until "9:38, [when] the Pentagon shook with an explosion." Rumsfeld said he did not make it to the Executive Support Center, which houses the Pentagon's teleconferencing studio, until about 10:00.[24]

Rumsfeld's version was endorsed in *The 9/11 Commission Report*, which said that Rumsfeld had remained in his office until the Pentagon was struck, and that it was not until shortly after 10:00 when Rumsfeld went to the Executive Support Center, "where he participated in the White House video teleconference."[25]

The falsity of Rumsfeld's account of his actions, which was implied by Clarke's account, was confirmed by a former Green Beret who served as one of Rumsfeld's assistants. Robert Andrews, a CIA liaison to the White House and Department of Defense, was on 9/11 the acting assistant secretary of defense for special operations and low intensity conflict. After the second attack on the World Trade Center at 9:03, Andrews stated in a 2004 interview, Rumsfeld went across the hall from his office to the Executive Support Center (ESC), where he joined Clarke's teleconference.[26] Knowing that "Secretary Rumsfeld would need the most up-to-date information," he gathered up various kinds of data available at the Pentagon's counterterrorism center in order "to take it to him in the Executive Support Center."[27] Andrews added: "I was there in the [Executive] Support Center with the Secretary when he was talking to Clarke on the White House video-teleconference."[28]

Rumsfeld's false account shows that, regardless of what position is taken on what damaged the Pentagon, the attack was engineered by the Pentagon under the leadership of then-Secretary of Defense Donald Rumsfeld.

12. Myers' Guilt

The highest-ranking military officer on 9/11 was General Richard B. Myers, who was the acting chairman of the Joint Chiefs of Staff. As with Cheney and Rumsfeld, Myers gave an account of his own activities that differed radically from that by Richard Clarke.

Having indicated that the White House videoconference began at about 9:10, Clarke said: "Air Force four-star General Dick Myers was filling in for the Chairman of the Joint Chiefs, Hugh Shelton, who was over the Atlantic."[29] His first actual exchange with Myers, Clarke suggested, occurred shortly before 9:28, when he asked: "JCS [Joint Chiefs of Staff], JCS. I assume NORAD has scrambled fighters and AWACS. How many? Where?" Myers replied: "Not a pretty picture Dick. . . . Otis has launched two birds toward New York. Langley is trying to get two up now." Clarke then asked: "Okay, how long to CAP over D.C.?" Myers replied: "Fast as we can. Fifteen minutes?" While asking this question, Clarke stated, Myers was "looking at the generals and colonels around him."[30] After getting the report that a plane had hit the Pentagon, Clarke announced that he had received from Cheney (at roughly 9:50) the authority to shoot planes down, leading Myers to ask: "Okay, shoot down aircraft, but what are the ROE [Rules of Engagement]?"[31]

According to Myers, however, none of these conversations with Clarke took place. Rather than being in the Pentagon, participating in Clarke's videoconference—with "generals and colonels around him"—Myers between 8:40 and 9:40 was in the office of Senator Max Cleland, preparing for Myers' confirmation hearing to be chairman of the Joint Chiefs of Staff. Having learned from television, while waiting in Cleland's outer office, about the first strike on the World Trade Center, which Myers understood to be "a small plane," he and Cleland went ahead with their meeting. While they were talking, the second tower was struck, but: "Nobody informed us of that." Myers did not learn about this second attack until he came out of the office "right at [the] time somebody said the Pentagon has been hit." Myers then got a cell phone call from General Eberhart (the commander of NORAD in Colorado Springs), after which he "jumped in the car, ran back to the Pentagon."[32] The 9/11 Commission, endorsing Myers' account, wrote: "Myers was on Capitol Hill when the Pentagon was struck, . . . saw smoke as his car made its way back to the building,"[33] and returned to the Pentagon's National Military Command Center "shortly before 10:00."[34]

Even apart from contradicting Clarke's account, Myers' account is unbelievable because of implausibilities and contradictions.

With regard to implausibilities: After the first airplane strike on the World Trade Center, Myers, the acting chairman of the Joint Chiefs of Staff, simply went ahead with a scheduled meeting without checking to see what had really happened. After the second strike, which everyone reportedly took as evidence that the country was under attack, Myers was not told about this strike by Cleland's secretary or anyone from the Pentagon. Even after the Pentagon itself was attacked, no one from this building called him to ask his advice. Indeed, Myers, according to this account, was not contacted by anyone until General Eberhard called from Colorado Springs. (Eberhard had evidently not considered the second attack on the World Trade Center to be important enough to bother Myers.)

With regard to contradictions: In his confirmation hearing of September 13, 2001, Myers said: "I spoke, after the second tower was hit, I spoke to the commander of NORAD, General Eberhart."[35] But in his interview of October 17, 2001, which was cited above, Myers said that no one told him about the attack on the second tower and that Eberhart did not call him until after the Pentagon strike.[36] In testimony to the 9/11 Commission in 2004, Myers gave still another version, saying that he was already driving from Cleland's office toward the Pentagon when he got a call from Eberhart, after which the Pentagon was hit.[37]

In light of these implausibilities and contradictions, combined with the fact that Myers' account is contradicted by that of Clarke—which has proved to be accurate with regard to both Cheney and Rumsfeld—we can safely say that Myers' account, according to which he was not at the Pentagon when the attacks on the Twin Towers and the Pentagon occurred, is a lie. And because of Myers' lying, we can say, independently of what struck the Pentagon, that the US military—in the person of the highest-ranking military officer in the Pentagon—directed the attack on the Pentagon.

13. Pentagon's Claim of Ignorance

Those who planned the Pentagon attack clearly wanted some people in the Pentagon to die. As we saw in the previous chapter, Cheney knew several minutes before the Pentagon attack that an unidentified aircraft was approaching Washington. A Rumsfeld spokesman, in explaining why the Pentagon had not evacuated, said: "The Pentagon was simply not aware that this aircraft was coming our way."[38] But this excuse is contradicted by several facts.

First, an E-4B, which CNN's John King rightly called a "state-of-the-art flying command post," was flying over the area at the time. The E-4Bs belong to an Air Force Unit with the motto *Videmus Omnia*—"We See All." Thanks to the E-4B over the area, the military leaders would have been able to monitor all aircraft in the vicinity.[39] The claim that the Pentagon "was simply not aware" that an aircraft was coming in its direction was, therefore, a lie—a lie that would explain why the Pentagon told another lie, claiming that the white plane seen over Washington that morning was not a military plane, even though proof to the contrary was presented on CNN's *Anderson Cooper 360°*.[40]

Second, Dr. Thomas Mayer, chair of the Department of Emergency Medicine and medical director for Fairfax County Fire and Rescue, was notified by air traffic control that a hijacked aircraft was missing. He said (in a statement quoted in *Pentagon 9/11*): "We knew that something was headed towards the national capital area. We didn't know where. But we knew we needed to get ready. So we immediately went on disaster planning mode."[41] If Mayer "knew that something was headed towards the national capital area," it is impossible to believe that the Pentagon "was simply not aware."

Third, a United States Park Police helicopter, which was a Huey and was seen flying around the Pentagon and even landing on the helipad (near where the Pentagon was to be hit),[42] had been instructed, according to Navy historian John Darrell Sherwood, to "try to distract the plane" that was coming toward the Pentagon—to "try to do something to, you know, prevent the plane from going into the Pentagon."[43] The official story claims that this Huey, along with another one, took off only after the Pentagon had been hit.[44] But Sherwood's claim, according to which at least one of the Hueys was launched prior to the attack on the Pentagon, has been supported by Stephanie Hughes, a nurse at Johns Hopkins Hospital, who was dating one of the helicopter pilots, Keith Bohn. She was supposed to meet Bohn at the aviation unit that morning, but when she arrived, she found a note from Bohn saying: "Got called into the air, there is another plane headed this way, go home and wait for me to call."[45] Further evidence that the official story was a lie is shown by the fact that Bohn and the other Huey pilot, Ronald Alan Galey, both gave contradictory accounts in their attempts to claim that they had not been told to launch their crafts until after the Pentagon was struck.[46]

The information about the E-4B, Thomas Mayer's statement, and the cover-up of the time of the Huey launching reinforces what was made clear by Norman Mineta's report about Cheney in the PEOC: that the Pentagon knew that an aircraft was coming its way several minutes in advance, so there would have been time to have evacuated at least some of the Pentagon—certainly the ground floor, where 92 of the 125 Pentagon deaths occurred.[47]

In spite of what Mineta himself may have believed, as we have seen, his story about "orders" can only be understood as Cheney's confirmation of previously given stand-down orders. According to Charles Lewis, who had worked on security systems at Los Angeles International Airport (LAX), the fact that such orders had been given was discussed by some law-enforcement officers at LAX. Receiving information on walkie-talkies, these officers were at first upset because the FAA had failed to notify NORAD. But these officers were soon even more upset, because they learned that the FAA *had* notified NORAD, but that it did not respond because it had been "ordered to stand down." Asking who had issued this stand-down order, the officers were told that it had come "from the highest level of the White House"[48]—which, given the fact that the president was in Florida, would have meant Cheney.

14. Wedge 1's Ground Floor Targeted

When people ask why the Pentagon, as well as the World Trade Center, was attacked, we can say that the attack on the Pentagon supported the purpose of 9/11 as a false-flag attack. Americans readily accepted the idea that radical Muslims would have wanted to attack not only the World Trade Center, as the chief symbol of America's economic power, but also the Pentagon, as the chief symbol of America's military might. But to get a more realistic understanding, we must ask not merely why the Pentagon was attacked, but why a particular part of the Pentagon was targeted.

As indicated earlier, Cheney and the Pentagon leaders could have simply had the "terrorists" fly into the roof. This would have been the sensible thing, if their goal was to accuse al-Qaeda of attacking the Pentagon, and to make the accusation credible. But they strained credulity by targeting Wedge 1, because it would have been very difficult for an amateur pilot to strike Wedge 1. For such a pilot to have hit Wedge 1's ground floor would have been impossible. And yet that was the target, as shown by the fact that 92 of the 125 Pentagon deaths occurred on the ground floor.[49] There must have been an overwhelming reason, therefore, for the perpetrators to target the ground floor of Wedge 1.

A possible clue to the reason has been provided by the report that the Pentagon was missing $2.3 trillion dollars—a report that was released the day before 9/11, with the result that the story disappeared.[50] (Chandler and Cole raised this issue, asking: "Why was the target the newly reinforced west face of the building, occupied primarily by accountants that were tracing down what happened to the missing trillions of dollars announced just a few days earlier?"[51]) This supposition fits with the fact that the area with the greatest damage included the Army's financial management/audit area, where many of those killed were accountants, bookkeepers, and budget analysts.[52] Michael Gleason, a civilian auditor who worked in the Operations Office of the Army's Financial Management Branch—who survived because he was out of the office at the time of the attack— replied affirmatively to a question whether his office might have been targeted because of the missing money. The records, he added, were destroyed.[53]

Some people argue against an "inside job" conception of the Pentagon attack, incidentally, on the grounds that military officers would not have organized a self-inflicted attack. But the US Air Force, under General Myers, did not attack its own people: No Air Force personnel were killed. All the victims were either in, or worked for, the Army or the Navy.[54]

In any case, there likely would have been another motive, as suggested by the fact that, whereas a high percentage of the victims were in the Army's financial management/audit area, an even higher percentage—over half of the victims—"were in the Navy Command Center,"[55] where 43 of the 44 people present that morning died.[56] That is an extremely high percentage, implying that this office was the target of a highly specific and deadly attack. Author E.P. Heidner concluded that the perpetrators targeted agents of the Office of Naval Intelligence, in order to cover up financial crimes they had been investigating.[57]

In any case, people seeking to understand 9/11 can, regardless of their view about what hit the Pentagon, understand a portrait of Donald Rumsfeld, Richard Myers, and Dick Cheney—who was Secretary of Defense long before he became Vice President—as having engineered attacks on the Pentagon, as well as the World Trade Center. And we can understand attacks as having had particular goals, as well as the general goal of initiating a "war on terror" directed at Muslim nations.

If it is not realized that the question of what hit the Pentagon is relatively unimportant, compared with all the points that unite the 9/11 Truth Movement in its rejection of the official view of the Pentagon attack, then a focus on this issue could be quite divisive. As Frank Legge says: "The evidence regarding what hit the Pentagon is contradictory."[58] Because of this, reaching agreement will be difficult, perhaps impossible.

Some people, being impressed by evidence supporting the 757 view, will tend to suggest that evidence for the "no 757" view can be easily explained away. Other people, being impressed with the evidence for the "no 757" view, will tend to believe that the evidence supporting the 757 view can be easily explained away. My experience in dealing with this issue has led me to conclude that, because different people are impressed by different types of evidence, few people on one side of the issue or the other will be persuaded to change their minds.

In the first section, I will report various types of evidence that have been cited on behalf of the view that the Pentagon was struck by a Boeing 757. In the second section, I will explain reasons why many people do not find this evidence persuasive. In the third section, I will summarize my main argument—that the question of what damaged the Pentagon is relatively unimportant, in comparison with the 9/11 Truth Movement's consensus on the above points. If we continue to discuss the question of what hit the Pentagon, we should keep in mind that this is a question of only secondary importance, no more important than the question of what aircraft hit the Twin Towers.

1. Evidence that a 757 Struck the Pentagon

The 757 as the Default View

Scientists who believe that a 757, perhaps AA 77, hit the Pentagon tend to hold this view as the default position, holding that this view should be accepted unless it can be disproved. Frank Legge has stated this explicitly, saying: "I think it is perfectly valid to say that the default position should be the official explanation that AA77 hit the Pentagon."[59]

Witness Testimony

Legge does not mean, however, that no evidence is needed. The main evidence consists of witness testimony. "Think of all the people who saw [the impact]," Legge says. "Why would anyone even begin to doubt it?"[60] David Chandler and Jonathan Cole have written:

> The nearly unanimous testimony of over a hundred eyewitnesses, is that a large aircraft, consistent with a 757, flew very low at very high speed, clipped several light poles, and crashed into the face of the Pentagon at ground level. . . . The eyewitness testimony is consistent with the pattern of damage both inside and outside of the Pentagon.[61]

Jim Hoffman, who has dealt with the evidence at length, says:

> Anyone who reads the collections of Pentagon witness accounts such as Eric Bart's is likely to be impressed by the broad agreement among witnesses on aspects of the event—the low-angle approach of a large jetliner followed by a huge explosion and billowing smoke.[62]

The 757 View as Not Disproved by Physical Evidence

Finding the witness testimony to constitute overwhelming evidence of the 757 view, the holders of the 757 theory say that the main point to be shown with regard to physical evidence is that it cannot disprove the claim that the Pentagon was hit by a 757. Legge has said that "it cannot be conclusively proved that no 757 hit the Pentagon."[63] David Chandler and Jonathan Cole made essentially the same statement, while specifying that what is not ruled out is the possibility that it was "American Airlines Flight 77" that struck the Pentagon.[64] Drawing especially on Jim Hoffman, who has done the most work on evidence for the 757 view, we can see that there is a long list of physical facts that are taken to support, or at least not contradict, the 757 view.

Debris: Although critics of the 757 view have written about a debris deficit, Legge says:

> [There is] a massive amount [of debris] inside the Pentagon and ample outside for the light parts, as seen in videos immediately after the impact, and no evidence whatsoever for truck loads of this material being carted to the site.[65]

Hoffman, arguing that the debris is "consistent with a jetliner crash," says that seeing this requires understanding several points. First, although very little debris was visible from outside, "the vast majority of debris ended up inside of the building." Second, although "no photographs show large pieces of aircraft, it is not reasonable to expect large pieces to have survived intact given the nature of the crash." Third, "there are relatively few public photographs of the interior of the Pentagon after the crash." Fourth, "seats, passengers, and luggage would [not] have survived the over 500-mph crash and subsequent fires in a form yielding to easy identification in photographs," and any photographs taken "would [not] have been made public."[66]

Specific Debris Matches: Hoffman states that, although most of the debris shown in photographs is too small to be identifiable, there were a few identifiable pieces, and all of these "plausibly match parts of a 757." These include a rotor that matches "several of the high-pressure rotors in a 757 engine," and a scrap, photographed by Mark Faram on the lawn, with a silver, white, and red color scheme matching that of an AA jet. Although it has been alleged that "[o]nly one engine was found," we "have no way of knowing how many or what engine pieces were found."[67]

The Damage to the Façade: Legge says that "the size of the hole in the wall [is] more than large enough for all the heavy parts of the plane," and also that the "damage to the wall [is] in the outline of a plane, right to the wing tips."[68] According to Hoffman, the façade damage fits what a 757 would do, as there was a hole of at least 96 feet, and probably 105 feet, on the first floor, so most of a 757 would have been admitted. And there is no reason, contrary to the expectation of many observers, that the impact of a 757 should have left a clear imprint of its profile on the façade's very thick limestone facing.

With regard to the widespread view that the vertical stabilizer should have damaged the façade at the second floor level above the central impact region: There is no proof, Hoffman says, that the stabilizer would cause such damage. And the trajectory of the vertical tail section could have been altered in any one of various ways, including a "bomb in the luggage hold exploded just as the front of the fuselage was beginning to impact the façade," or a "surface-to-air missile exploded on the aft starboard side of the jetliner just as the nose was beginning to impact the façade."[69] (These possibilities make very clear that Hoffman sees the Pentagon attack as an inside operation.)

Interior Damage: Damage to the Pentagon's interior, Hoffman argues, is consistent with a 757 crash. The floor space from the façade to the C Ring was mainly unobstructed, so the fuselage debris "could have produced the punch-out hole."[70]

Damage to Surroundings: The damage to the surroundings also, Hoffman argues, fits what a 757 crash would have caused. In the first place, the five lamp poles that were downed had to be hit by an aircraft with a wingspan of at least 100 but not more than 130 feet, and a 757's wingspan is 125 feet. (Hoffman knows that some people claim that the lamp poles "were pulled out or toppled the wrong way," but he has "yet to find a single coherent exposition of it.") Hoffman also finds the positions of the cable spools to be consistent with a 757 crash; those who think otherwise, Hoffman says, have not realized how far the photographs were taken from the façade.[71]

The Attack Plane's Approach: Although a 757 is normally not flown in the manner taken by the downward spiral, this maneuver is not beyond a 757's capabilities. Although the plane's final 1,000 yards, flying quite low (albeit not "inches from the ground"), would have been impossible for Hani Hanjour, especially given ground effect turbulence, it would have been "an easy task for a 757's autopilot."[72]

The Flight Data Recorder File: Legge adds another point: "The FDR file [is] an exquisite compilation of data, indicating the plane descended smoothly, pulled up safely, passed through the light poles, and hit the Pentagon, accurate to within a couple of feet of the impact mark."[73] Although Legge knows that there is no proof that this file actually reflects the flight of AA 77 and that one must be suspicious—he has written about "known falsehoods in other crucial 9/11 documents[74]"— Legge believes that it is authentic, revealing the actual trajectory of AA 77.[75]

Conclusion: Whereas the physical evidence "comports with the crash of a Boeing 757," Hoffman says, "the evidence does not conclusively prove that the aircraft was a 757, much less that it was Flight 77." Both

Hoffman and Legge believe, however, that the physical evidence, especially when taken together with the testimonial evidence, provides very strong evidence that the Pentagon was struck by a 757, likely AA 77.

2. Reasons to Doubt that a 757 Struck the Pentagon
The above summary seems to provide impressive evidence for the 757 theory. However, if the attack was *not* what it was claimed to be by Pentagon and FBI officials, that is just what we would expect: lots of witnesses to support the 757 claim and lots of physical evidence to back up this testimony.

I can understand why some members of the 9/11 Truth Movement say that, even though the government's claims about the World Trade Center are almost entirely false, the official theory about the Pentagon attack contains more truth. They add, to be sure, that the official theory is ultimately false, because al-Qaeda hijackers did not fly AA 77 into the Pentagon. But the physical and testimonial evidence, they say, supports the view that the Pentagon was struck by a 757, perhaps even AA 77.

However, while I can understand this view, I am more impressed by the places where the evidence for the official story falls down, including places where there are signs of fraud.

Given the fact that the defenders of the 757 view rest their case primarily on eyewitness testimony, I will begin with a discussion of this.

Eyewitness Testimony: What Does It Say?
Among those who claim that the Pentagon was hit by a Boeing 757, it has been common to suggest, as we have seen, that the issue is largely settled by witness testimony, because the witnesses supporting the official theory are too numerous to doubt. For example, Matt Taibbi, in a debate with me, suggested that my position required "that thousands of witnesses who saw a plane [meaning a large airliner] hit the Pentagon were wrong."[76] *Popular Mechanics* more modestly claimed only that "hundreds of witnesses saw a Boeing 757 hit the building."[77] But that is still much too high. The best-known list of witnesses to the Pentagon attack, and the primary one appealed to by Jim Hoffman, is the list compiled by Eric Bart. His list contains 152 people who were regarded as "witnesses" in some sense,[78] but only some of them claimed to have seen an airliner hit the Pentagon.

Some of the other people gave quite different reports, with six of them speaking of a small or mid-sized aircraft, perhaps a commuter jet or even a missile.[79] Still others believed that the damage had been caused by one or more bombs.[80] Only 66 of the 152 people claimed to have seen an airliner *headed toward* the Pentagon. And Dr. Jerry Russell, focusing on those who "provide *explicit, realistic and detailed claims* that a 757 crashed into the Pentagon after executing a high velocity, low altitude approach," found that there were only 31 such individuals.[81]

The 31 Explicit Witnesses: An examination of those 31 "explicit" witnesses, moreover, raises doubts about the authenticity of at least some of them. Russell—who earned advanced degrees in both engineering and psychology—discovered that of these 31 witnesses, 13 of them fit his category of "elite insiders," meaning "highly placed military officers, government officials, media officials, or employees of the Pentagon renovation team and security staff," and that 24 of these 31 people "worked for either the Federal Government or the mainstream media."[82] We can be more specific, furthermore, about the seven mainstream media journalists: five of these seven worked for Gannett (primarily *USA Today*), and another for the Armed Forces Information Service. So six of the seven journalists worked for organizations known to support the government's position on military-related matters.[83]

The fact that almost half of the 31 explicit witnesses were "elite insiders," combined with the fact that a great majority (77 percent) of the 31 witnesses worked for either the government or a Gannett news organization, should give pause. There were very few individuals who could be considered neutral, in the sense of not occupationally biased in favor of the government's account of events. We cannot, therefore, simply assume them to be disinterested, and thereby trustworthy, witnesses.

Criteria of Trustworthiness: In judging the trustworthiness of witnesses, there is a principle commonly used by historians in evaluating conflicting testimonies of people who belong to a movement or institution. Let's say that two strong political supporters of John Smith give different accounts of some event in his life. One account makes him seem noble and heroic, while the other account reflects poorly on him. All other things being equal, we would give more credence to the critical account, because such an account from a John Smith supporter would be surprising, suggesting that party loyalty has been trumped by honesty.

Likewise, if a member of an organization has given testimony about an issue that contradicts the position of that organization, we should take that testimony more seriously than we take testimonies that reflect the organization's party line.

There is, however, a principle that is neutral with regard to a person's membership in an organization: We rightly regard with skepticism any testimony that includes claims that seem impossible or at least extremely improbable.

Bias, Impossibility, Implausibility: Applying these principles to the testimony of reporters for the corporate press—which has been completely supportive of the official account of 9/11—we are rightly skeptical of claims that reflect the government's position about the Pentagon attack, if those claims conflict with physical evidence or are otherwise extremely implausible, or if these claims reflect the government's claims while being challenged by other journalists or by people outside the government.

An example of conflict with physical evidence is provided by the testimony of Steve Anderson of *USA Today*, who said that he watched as a plane "banked slightly to the left, drug its wing along the ground and slammed into the west wall of the Pentagon."[84] Given the fact that photographs of the Pentagon lawn immediately after that attack showed no sign of the enormous scar that would have been caused by a wing dragging along the ground, Anderson's testimony must be considered untrustworthy.

Likewise, retired Army officer Frank Probst, supporting the idea that an American airliner came towards the Pentagon very close to the ground, claimed that it was flying so low that he dove to the ground for fear of being hit.[85] Probst, in fact, claimed that one of the plane's engines passed by him "about six feet away."[86] But Dave McGowan, with reference to the wind turbulence created by large airliners, noted that if a Boeing 757 going over 500 miles an hour had come this close to Probst, he would have been a victim, not a witness.[87]

Choosing between Mainstream Reporters: With regard to conflict between various reporters within the mainstream media, seven reporters on Eric Bart's list, as we have seen, claimed to have watched an airliner hit the Pentagon. But two highly respected reporters gave accounts that made it difficult to understand how a large airliner could have hit the Pentagon. CNN's Jamie McIntyre, describing what he saw outside the Pentagon after inspecting the area near the "strike zone" shortly following the attack, said:

> [I saw only] very small pieces of the plane. . . . The biggest piece I saw was about three feet long. [All the pieces] are small enough that you can pick up in your hand. There are no large tail sections, wing sections, fuselage, nothing like that anywhere around.[88]

ABC's John McWethy, who was able to get *inside* the Pentagon, said: "I got in very close, got a look early on at the bad stuff. I could not, however, see any plane wreckage." Then, perhaps repeating an explanation that he had received from the Pentagon official who took him inside, added that the plane "had been, basically, vaporized."[89]

As this example shows, it is not simply a matter of accepting or rejecting testimony from the mainstream press. One has to decide which testimonies have greater credibility (all other things being equal).

Choosing between Pentagon Employees: The same principle can be applied with regard to Pentagon personnel. They provided nine of the most graphic accounts of an airliner hitting the Pentagon. But other witnesses gave testimonies that make it difficult to understand how a large airliner could have hit the Pentagon.

Karen Kwiatkowski, who was then an Air Force Lieutenant Colonel employed at the Pentagon, wrote: "There was a strange lack of visible debris on the Pentagon lawn, where I stood only moments after the impact. . . . I saw . . . no airplane metal or cargo debris."[90]

Sgt. Reginald Powell said: "I was . . . impressed . . . with how the building stood up, after they told me the size of the plane. And then I was in awe that I saw no plane, nothing left from the plane. It was like it disintegrated as it went into the building."[91]

Naval Officer Sheryl Alleger, having gone past the crash site that afternoon in an ambulance, said: "[Y]ou couldn't see any bits of the airplane, that was the thing that got me. . . . I expected to see the tail sticking out. . . . But—nothing. It was like the building swallowed the plane."[92]

Registered Nurse Eileen Murphy said:

> I knew it was a crash site before we got there, and I didn't know what it was going to look like. I couldn't imagine because the building is like rock solid. I expected to see the airplane, so I guess my initial

impression was, "Where's the plane? How come there's not a plane?" I would have thought the building would have stopped it and somehow we would have seen something like part of, or half of the plane, or the lower part, or the back of the plane. So it was just a real surprise that the plane wasn't there.[93]

Research analyst Will Jarvis, having hoped to see the plane, said: "There was just nothing left. It was incinerated. We couldn't see a tail or a wing or anything."[94]

April Gallop, a US Army executive administrative assistant with top security clearance, had just returned to work on the morning of September 11 after a two-month maternity leave. Although she planned to take her baby son to the day-care center, she was told that she needed to take care of some work on her computer immediately, so she took her baby to her work station. As soon as Gallop pushed the button to start her computer, she said, she heard a huge "boom," which "sounded like a bomb." The ceiling caved in, injuring her and her son.[95] After regaining consciousness and locating her son, she took him outside through the "impact hole," but she saw no evidence that a plane had hit the Pentagon.

> I had no jet fuel on me. . . . I didn't see any airplane seats. I didn't see any plane parts. . . . I didn't see anything that would give me any idea that there was a plane.[96]

Later, knowing that she had had a traumatic experience, Gallop checked with other people who had been there, but "they did not see anything of this nature as well."[97] Asked if she saw any fire, Gallop said: "Coming out of the computers. There were flames coming out of . . . the computers." (Another woman in the D Ring named Tracy Webb reported that her "computer burst into flames."[98]) But there was no fire, Gallop was certain, on the floor: Having lost one of her shoes, her foot did not feel anything hot.[99] This account is difficult to reconcile with the view that an airliner with thousands of gallons of jet fuel crashed into the Pentagon and exploded.[100]

Substantial Errors and Contradictions: In explaining grounds for doubting the testimonies that an airliner hit the Pentagon, Russell also stated that many of these testimonies contain "substantial errors or contradictions."[101] Here are some examples.

In addition to *USA Today*'s Steve Anderson, quoted earlier, three other people claiming to have seen a plane hitting the Pentagon said that it hit the ground first. Mary Ann Owens, who like Anderson worked for Gannett, said "the left wing dipped and scraped the helicopter area." David Marra reportedly said that after the wing touched the helicopter pad, the plane "cartwheeled" into the Pentagon. Self-described pilot Tim Timmerman, who told CNN that the Pentagon was "hit by an American Airlines Boeing 757," said that "it hit right in front of . . . the building; most of the energy was dissipated in hitting the ground."[102] These testimonies are disproved by the available photographic evidence, as it shows that the lawn was not marred by an airliner.[103]

Other sets of testimonies are discredited by being mutually contradictory. For example, Major Lincoln Leibner, saying that the plane "completely entered the building," added: "The plane went into the building like a toy into a birthday cake." Whereas *USA Today* reporter Narayanan Vin said: "The hijacked jet slammed into the Pentagon at a ferocious speed. But the Pentagon's wall held up like a champ. It barely budged."[104]

Insiders and Skepticism: Emphasizing that most of the 31 people who claimed to have seen an airliner hit the Pentagon worked for the US government or a government-supportive news organization; that almost half of these 31 witnesses were "elite insiders," meaning "highly placed military officers, government officials, media officials, or employees of the Pentagon renovation team and security staff"; and that 24 of these 31 people "worked for either the Federal Government or the mainstream media," we need to remember that Americans supported the unprovoked war in Iraq on the basis of demonstrably false statements made by members of the mainstream press and the military, including General Colin Powell.

> So why should we be surprised [asked Jerry Russell] if "eyewitness" sources strongly linked to the US corporate and media elite might also provide false testimony about the events of September 11? . . . If all the perpetrators need to do is produce sufficient lying eyewitnesses on behalf of any sort of nonsense, what hope is there for the truth?[105]

Still More Witnesses: Firefighters: Another relevant principle is that, if there are members of an organization who could be considered neutral, or who might even be inclined to support the official story, members of this organization should be taken with special seriousness if they have given accounts contrary to the official account. This principle is exemplified by some firefighters.

Brian Ladd, a firefighter from Fort Myers, reported that, although he had expected to see pieces of the airplane's wings or fuselage, he instead saw "millions of tiny pieces" of debris spread "everywhere."[106]

When Captain Dennis Gilroy—the acting commander of the Fort Myers fire department—arrived, "he wondered why he saw no aircraft parts."[107]

Still another firefighter, Captain John Durrer—also quoted (like Ladd and Gilroy) in *Pentagon 9/11*—"had expected to see large parts of the plane and thought, 'Well where's the airplane, you know, where's the parts to it? You would think there'd be something.'"[108]

The most interesting firefighter in this respect is county fire chief Ed Plaugher, who had been in charge of putting out the fire. At a Pentagon briefing the day after the attack, Plaugher was asked whether anything was left of the airplane. He replied that there were "some small pieces . . . but not large sections . . . . [T]here's no fuselage sections and that sort of thing."[109]

Eight months later, Plaugher was much more supportive of the official story. Having arrived at the scene 35 to 40 minutes after the attack, he said, he saw "pieces of the fuselage, the wings, the landing gear, pieces of the engine, seats." He added: "I can swear to you, it was a plane."[110] However, when someone has given earlier and later statements, one of which contradicts the other, we generally assume the earlier statement to have been closer to the truth, as long as there is no reason to suspect the person to have lied. This is especially the case if there was pressure on the person to change his or her statement—which could reasonably be suspected to have occurred in this case.

Pilots: Major Dean Eckmann, one of the F-16 pilots who were sent to Washington from Langley Air Force Base, was asked, according to a book published in 2003, by NEADS to fly over the Pentagon and report on the extent of the damage. He reported that he suspected that the damage had been caused by "a big fuel tanker truck because of the amount of smoke and flames coming up and . . . there was no airplane wreckage off to the side."[111] The previous year, Eckmann said, according to a 2002 Associated Press story: "My initial thought was that it was a truck bomb. . . . [W]e didn't actually find out it was an airliner until the next day."[112]

As stated earlier, Keith Bohn, a Huey pilot for the Park Police, who was flying near the Pentagon prior to the attack, had to claim that he had not been sent to the Pentagon until after the attack. But Bohn, in an interview at the US Naval Historical Center in November 2001, did not fully support the official story, saying:

> When I landed on the scene, there was actually a particular slit into the side of the Pentagon, which is hard to believe that an aircraft made it, but it's that small of a slit. A large portion of the Pentagon is gone now. But when I got there, there was a slit that I couldn't believe an aircraft had actually penetrated. I could not see any aviation parts. I couldn't see an engine or a wing. There was just rubble, pieces, small pieces.[113]

A second Huey pilot for the Park Police who flew to the Pentagon that morning was Ronald Alan Galey. In his interview with the Naval Historical Center, he said, having arrived "easily within four minutes of the impact":

> My first, all of our impressions [he means the impressions of himself and the helicopter's other crew members] were it couldn't possibly have been a 757. The building had not collapsed at that point and there was spot fires everywhere. In fact the most fire that I saw was the crash truck, foam truck on fire. That was creating the greatest amount of fire at the particular point and it was a relatively small hole in the side of the building. I'm going, "This couldn't possibly have been a 757." There's absolutely nothing that you could identify as an aircraft part anywhere around there. Nothing. Just couldn't have been. We saw what appeared to us to have been the flight path of the aircraft with the lights being knocked down and such, but that was only supposition on our part at that point. I just, I just can't emphasize enough, the initial damage, looking at it, it just didn't look like a 757 hit that building. . . . [T]he building started, it collapsed and I'm going, "Oh, Oh, Not good." But even with the collapse it still didn't look like a 757 hit it.[114]

Besides reinforcing the position of Bohn and others that the damage did not seem commensurate with an airplane the size of a 757, Galey made two other points of interest: First, he said, like April Gallop, that shortly after the attack there was not a big fire. Second, even having seen the building's collapse and "the lights being knocked down," he still thought "it didn't look like a 757 hit it."

Others: Judy Rothschadl, a documentary producer, was—like ABC's John McWethy—able to get inside the Pentagon. She reported: "There weren't seats or luggage or things you find in a plane."[115]

Engineer Steve DeChiaro, the president of a technology firm, said: "[W]hen I looked at the site, my brain could not resolve the fact that it was a plane because it only seemed like a small hole in the building. No tail. No wings. No nothing."[116]

Scott Cook and his boss, Ray, were in the conference room of the Portals building in Washington. This room had a wide window looking directly at the Pentagon, with Reagan Airport to the left. Having learned about the attacks in New York and thinking that Washington might be attacked next, they kept their eyes on the landscape as well as the TV set. Suddenly they saw that the Pentagon had been struck. Cook later wrote:

> We didn't know what kind of plane had hit the Pentagon. . . . Later, we were told that it was a 757 out of Dulles, which had come up the river in back of our building, turned sharply over the Capitol, ran past the White House and the Washington Monument, up the river to Rosslyn, then dropped to treetop level and ran down Washington Boulevard to the Pentagon. I cannot fathom why neither myself nor Ray, a former Air Force officer, [saw] a big 757, going 400 miles an hour, as it crossed in front of our window in its last 10 seconds of flight.[117]

Witnesses to Bombs and Cordite: April Gallop's conviction that one or more bombs had gone off in the Pentagon was shared by other people.

Army Lt. Colonel Victor Correa said: "We thought it was some kind of explosion. That somehow someone got in here and planted bombs because we saw these holes."[118]

When Lt. Nancy McKeown heard an explosion and saw ceiling tiles coming down, reported *Pentagon 9/11*, she yelled "Bomb!"[119]

Military reporter Steve Vogel, while supporting the official view, wrote that there was much confusion: "Some thought a bomb had exploded; almost no one understood the building had been hit by a plane."[120]

Michael J. Nielsen, who was a civilian auditor for the Department of the Army on temporary assignment at the Pentagon, reported that, after he heard an explosion and felt the building shake, hundreds of panicked Pentagon personnel ran down the corridor outside his office towards the south entrance yelling "Bombs!" and "A bomb went off!"[121]

The conclusion that the explosions really were caused by bombs is supported by the fact that some witnesses said they smelled cordite, a substance used in bombs that has a very distinctive smell, completely different from that of jet fuel.

Don Perkal, the deputy general counsel for the secretary of defense, wrote:

> People shouted in the corridor outside [my office] that a bomb had gone off. . . . Even before stepping outside I could smell the cordite. Then I knew explosives had been set off somewhere.[122]

Gilah Goldsmith, an attorney at the Pentagon, reported that, after hearing an "incredible whomp noise," she saw a "huge black cloud of smoke," adding that it smelled like cordite or gun smoke.[123]

Death and Destruction in A and B Rings: The conclusion that bombs went off is also supported by reports of death and destruction in the B and A Rings—which were further inside the building than the C Ring, beyond which the airliner reportedly did not go. The day after the event, a *Washington Post* story said:

> The attack destroyed at least four of the five "rings" that spiral around the massive office building. . . . A 38-year-old Marine major . . . said he and dozens of his colleagues rushed to the area in the Pentagon that appeared most heavily damaged—the B ring between the 4th and 5th corridors.[124]

If all the damage was due to an airliner, which crashed into the E Ring and did not travel past the C Ring, why would the B Ring have suffered severe damage?

Moreover, there should not have been deaths in the A Ring. But Robert Andrews—the acting assistant secretary of defense who had gone to the Pentagon's counterterrorism center to gather up materials for Rumsfeld—reported that after he and his aide had felt the effects of some kind of explosive, they were rushing to get to the other side of the Pentagon to join Rumsfeld. Entering the corridor on the A Ring, he reported, they "had to walk over dead bodies."[125] In a notarized statement, swearing that she was giving a true summary of what she was told by Andrews, Barbara Honegger said she asked Andrews "if he really meant that he'd had to step over dead bodies in the innermost A ring. He said yes the inner ring."[126]

Conclusion to Section on Witnesses: The moral of this discussion is that, contrary to the view that witness testimony provides overwhelming support for the 757 theory, it does not, for two reasons: First, although many people did indeed claim to see a 757 hit the Pentagon, most of these were employees of the government or of news organizations known to support military views, and many of these employees were "elite insiders," so their testimony, insofar as it is challenged by other points of view, should be regarded with skepticism. In the second place, the 757 claim has been challenged by other witnesses at the Pentagon—by people who witnessed the attack but gave different accounts, and by people who witnessed the Pentagon after the attack and saw no signs of a 757, whether inside or outside the Pentagon.

Therefore, the witness testimony cannot be said to supply overwhelming evidence for the 757 view. Whether it does provide *some* positive support will surely be a matter of perspective.

Physical Evidence: What Can Be Drawn from It?

The eyewitness evidence shows that, if the 757 view were to be advocated, the advocates cannot remain content with stating that the 757 view is not contradicted by the physical evidence. They would need to point to physical evidence that provides unambiguously positive support for this view. But the available evidence is ambiguous. Although there is much to support the 757 view (as shown above), there is much evidence that counts against it.

False Claims Supporting the 757 Theory

I will begin with three cases in which the government provided false evidence to support its claim that the Pentagon was struck by AA 77, beginning with a video supposedly showing the Pentagon being struck by a 757.

Videos Purportedly Showing 757 Hitting Pentagon: In 2002, five frames of a video from a Pentagon parking lot were released by the Department of Defense.[127] Analyses of these frames raised many problems. These frames purportedly show an airliner flying across the Pentagon lawn and striking the building, causing a big explosion with a bright red flame. However, the first frame shows only what appears, on its right-hand side, to be a white trail of smoke; and ahead of the smoke, it might be argued, a tail can be seen. In any case, a cement column hides whatever it is that causes the trail of smoke. The next frame simply shows an explosion (because, the Department of Defense presumably would have explained, the plane, due to its speed, would have hit the Pentagon). The rest of the video shows the smoke billowing up.[128]

In 2004, Judicial Watch made a FOIA request for all videos relevant to the question of what hit the Pentagon. The DOD refused, saying that videos could not be released while the trial of Zacarias Moussaoui was continuing.

Finally, in 2006, the DOD said that, because the trial of Moussaoui was over, "we are able to . . . provide the video."[129] The DOD actually released two videos, one of which contained the five frames released in 2002, which we can call the video from Camera 1.

Whereas Camera 1 is stationed behind a cement post, which partially obscures its view of the "flight path," Camera 2 is situated in front of this column and hence has a clear field of view.

The Camera 2 video shows nothing for the first minute, after which a police car drives through the line of vision. After another 10 seconds, we get an unobstructed view of what we had seen in the 2002 video, with this difference: Rather than seeing a plane followed by a white trail of smoke just before the explosion, we see only what appears to be the nose of a plane appearing in the right-hand corner.[130]

The video from Camera 1 has action from the beginning, with the police car appearing after only a couple of seconds, then ten seconds later the white trail of smoke followed by the explosion.

However, a new analysis of these videos has been provided by award-winning Italian film-maker Massimo Mazzucco.[131] Though the available footage from the Camera 2 video starts and ends before the Camera 1 video, Mazzucco shows that the videos overlap in the middle sections of the footage, where they are identical and perfectly synchronized—due to being controlled by a single recording system—except for Frame 23, which is where the plane presumably flies across the lawn. The key to understanding these videos lies in this pair of frames.

Having watched the Camera 1 video, for which our vision (in Frame 23) of whatever was leaving a trail of smoke was blocked, we would expect the Camera 2 video, which has an unblocked shot of the lawn, to show what is in front of the trail of smoke. However, instead of seeing that, we see the nose of an airplane just coming into view on the right. It is further from the Pentagon than is the trail of smoke in

Camera 1's Frame 23. This means that the plane's "tail" is in front of its "nose."

Since the appearance of these videos in 2006, students of the videos and digital experts had been unable to provide a technical explanation of the discrepancy. But, explains Mazzucco, Italian digital expert Pier Paolo Murru,[132] using "Boolean subtraction," was able to identify an area of pixelation that was identical in both frames. "What is said to be the nose of the airplane in Camera 2 is also present as part of the smoke trail in Camera 1."

"As this is obviously impossible in the physical world," Mazzucco added, "we are forced to conclude that at least one of the two frames is the result of an intentional alteration—doctoring."

As to the nature of the doctoring, Mazzucco said: "It looks as if someone has partially covered the trail of smoke in Camera 1, through cut-and-paste means, leaving the end of the smoke trail visible, to make it look like the nose of the plane in Camera 2."[133]

Mazzucco's film confirms what students of these videos have long suspected: that the idea that the videos show an airliner moving across the Pentagon lawn involves deception. This fact suggests that the Department of Defense, even though its cameras were pointed at the Pentagon, had nothing to show that the Pentagon was struck by a Boeing 757.

Phone Calls from Barbara Olson: In the first years after the 9/11 attacks, it was believed that Barbara Olson had made two calls to her husband, Theodore "Ted" Olson, from aboard AA 77. This belief was very important to the official story, because the FAA had lost track of this flight at 8:56 AM, never again to receive any signal from its transponder. In fact, the FAA came to believe that this flight had crashed. *USA Today* reported: "Another jet disappears from radar and might have crashed in Kentucky. The reports are so serious that [FAA head Jane] Garvey notifies the White House that there has been another crash. Only later does she learn the reports are erroneous."[134]

The evidence that these reports were "erroneous" evidently consisted of two supposed facts: the "fact" that Barbara Olson had called her husband at his office in the Justice Department—he was the US solicitor general—from AA 77 shortly before the Pentagon was hit, and the "fact" that AA 77 had hit the Pentagon.

With regard to the Pentagon being hit by AA 77, this "fact" was from the beginning not obvious. Fox, NBC, and MSNBC all reported that an explosion took place at the Pentagon.[135] An AP story reported that "an aircraft crashed on a helicopter landing pad near the Pentagon."[136] Fox TV reported that the Pentagon had been hit by a US Air Force flight.[137] What would become the official story began to emerge with a report from the American Forces Press Service, which said: "Authorities confirmed that a commercial airliner, possibly hijacked, had crashed into the building."[138] And then that afternoon, the *Los Angeles Times* reported that some military officials, speaking on condition of anonymity, said that the Pentagon had been struck by AA 77.[139] As these stories show, the notion that the Pentagon was struck by AA 77 was not based on visible evidence. The press came to believe it simply because it was stated by sources within the military.

For that claim to be plausible, however, there had to be reason to believe that AA 77 had not crashed in the Midwest. This reason was provided by the report, supplied by the government's solicitor general, that Barbara Olson had made calls from AA 77 shortly before it crashed.

But in 2006, as we saw in Chapter 5, the FBI failed to support that story. Ted Olson had said that his wife had made two phone calls to him, the first of which lasted "about one minute,"[140] the second of which lasted "two, three, or four minutes."[141] Having indicated that she could not have used a cell phone, because "[a]ll of the calls from Flight 77 were made via the onboard airphone system,"[142] the FBI said that there was only one seatback phone call from Barbara Olson, and it was an "unconnected call," which (obviously) lasted "0 seconds."[143] Moreover, although the FBI's report supported the idea that Barbara Olson at least attempted a call from this flight, it provided no evidence for this claim: Whereas the FBI's reports on the (claimed) calls from United 93 and United 175 specify the rows from which the calls were supposedly made, the FBI's AA 77 report gives no information about the alleged attempted call by Barbara Olson. It merely states her assigned seat number.

Given the fact that the alleged Olson calls were evidently faked, they cannot provide a basis for saying that Flight 77 was still aloft after it disappeared from the FAA radar at 8:56.

To be sure, the official story still has flight attendant Renee May as having made a call. But as I argued in Chapter 5, it is "unthinkable that, if calls were possible, only one person on this flight made calls."

So, besides there being no evidence that AA 77, and hence a 757, hit the Pentagon, there is not even any evidence that AA 77 was aloft after it disappeared from the FAA's radar at 8:56. Accordingly, there is no reason to think of the aircraft that made the three-plus-minute downward spiral as a Boeing 757, especially given the fact that air traffic controller Danielle O'Brien, who followed the blip on radar, said: "The speed, the maneuverability, the way that he turned, we all thought in the radar room, all of us experienced air traffic controllers, that that was a military plane." To be sure, she added: "You don't fly a 757 in that manner. It's unsafe." The fact remains that, according to her testimony, she and the other controllers thought at the time that it was a military plane.[144]

The C Ring Hole: There was a round hole, about 9 feet in diameter, in the Pentagon's C ring in Wedge 2, about 310 feet from the "impact zone." This hole was in line with the official trajectory for AA 77.

The original explanation for the hole, called the "exit hole," was that it was created by AA 77's nose. (Although the strike zone was in Wedge 1 of the Pentagon, the reported trajectory of "AA 77" was such that, by the time it reached the C ring, it would have been in Wedge 2.) Two days after 9/11, Donald Rumsfeld, appearing on ABC's *Good Morning America*, said:

> [The plane] came in . . . between about the first and second floor . . . .
> And it went in through three rings. I'm told the nose is—is still in
> there, very close to the inner courtyard, about one ring away.[145]

Two days later, Lee Evey, the program manager for the Pentagon Renovation Project, said at a Pentagon news briefing:

> The plane actually penetrated through the . . . E ring, D ring,
> C ring. . . . The nose of the plane just barely broke through the inside
> of the C ring, so it was extending into A-E Drive a little bit.[146]

However, the nose of a 757 is very fragile. It could not have gone through the outer (E ring) wall, with its steel-reinforced concrete, and then punched out a large hole in the C-ring wall, with its steel mesh and eight inches of brick. French critic Thierry Meyssan wrote:

> The nose of a plane . . . contains the electronic navigation system.
> In order to allow passage of the waves emitted by the apparatuses, it
> is not made of metal, but of carbon fibers. [It is] thus extremely fragile
> [and] would be crushed rather than piercing through.[147]

And as a matter of fact, no official document endorsed the Rumsfeld-Evey claim.

The *Arlington County After-Action Report* stated that "Flight #77 penetrated the outer wall of the Pentagon's E Ring" and that "the damage extended all the way through the inner wall of the C Ring," but it did *not* say that any part of Flight 77 continued to the C Ring.[148]

The *Pentagon Building Performance Report*, prepared by the American Society of Civil Engineers, was more explicitly critical, saying that the "data suggest that the front of the aircraft disintegrated essentially upon impact."[149]

The Rumsfeld-Evey position was even rejected in the *Popular Mechanics* book of 2006, which said that "the hole was not made by. . . the nose of Flight 77 pushing through the building's interior."[150]

In his book on the history of the Pentagon, *Washington Post* writer Steve Vogel said that "the nose came to an almost immediate stop."[151]

Even the book *Pentagon 9/11*, written in 2007 by historians employed by the Office of the Secretary of Defense, did not support the story told by their former boss. Just before mentioning "the so-called 'punch out hole' in the C Ring wall," they said that, when the plane struck the building, "the front part of the relatively weak fuselage disintegrated."[152]

Summary: We must wonder: If the Pentagon was actually hit by AA 77, why were lies told—about two videos of an apparent plane, about Barbara Olson, and about the C Ring—to support that claim?

Physical Evidence That Suggests the Falsity of the 757 Claim

Some scientists, in support of the 757 theory, have stated very modest requirements for supporting this theory. Frank Legge, as we have seen, has said that "it cannot be conclusively proved that no 757 hit the Pentagon."[153] Perhaps not, but the evidence certainly suggests that it is unlikely.

Incidentally, the physical evidence surveyed here does not include all the evidence that contradicts the entirety of the official theory, according to which *the Pentagon was hit by AA 77 under the control of al-Qaeda*, with perhaps Hani Hanjour at the controls. The present discussion is with people who agree that the al-Qaeda theory is absurd, but who nevertheless believe that the Pentagon was struck by a Boeing 757, perhaps AA 77, being guided automatically by the US military.

Given the nature of this discussion, I have not included several points that would be relevant only against the view of the attack as directed by al-Qaeda. I have not, for example, included the fact that the lawn was not scarred, because it seems at least conceivable that a 757 being guided automatically might have been able to strike the ground floor of the Pentagon without hitting the lawn.

Debris Deficit: In response to the claim that there is "too little debris," Legge said: "There are photographs which show ample small fragments scattered over a wide area."[154] But the question is whether the debris, both inside and outside, could have possibly added up to the weight of a Boeing 757. As former airline pilot Russ Wittenberg pointed out: "It's roughly a 100 ton airplane. An airplane that weighs 100 tons all assembled is still going to have 100 tons of disassembled trash and parts after it hits a building."[155] Dave McGowan, doubting that the trash and parts would have come anywhere close to 100 tons, wrote: "Even if all of the photos did actually depict debris from a 757, . . . then a few hundred pounds of Flight 77 has been accounted for."[156] McGowan probably underestimated. But can anyone point to photos suggesting even 20 or 30 thousand pounds of trash and parts, let alone 80 or 90 tons?

Videos: If a Boeing 757 had really hit the Pentagon, that would have been easy for authorities to prove. A FOIA request to release the relevant videos led the Department of Justice to admit that it has 85 videos that were confiscated from cameras on or near the Pentagon. The DOJ denied the request, however, saying that these videos were "exempt from disclosure."[157] The 9/11 Commission, far from using its subpoena power to obtain these videos, did not even mention their existence. Brief segments of a few videos have been released, but they have shown nothing definitive.[158] Is it believable that of the 85 videos, none would give a clearer idea of what did and did not hit the Pentagon than the few frames that have been released? Can we believe that the government would not release them if they supported its story?

Some people, to be sure, say yes: The government likely has videos that would prove that the Pentagon was struck by AA 77, which it is saving to unleash at an opportune moment. Legge wrote:

> Evidence that proves that a 757 did hit the Pentagon would function as [the authorities'] insurance policy. If they feel endangered by the

progress of public opinion toward demanding a new investigation, and realizing that this will likely lead to criminal charges and convictions, they will produce this evidence.[159]

Yes, there is a (remote) possibility that the authorities have evidence that the Pentagon was hit by a 757. But there is also a remote possibility that the authorities have an explosives-free explanation of the collapse of World Trade Center 7. Should that possibility prevent Legge and other scientists from declaring that this building was almost certainly brought down with explosives? Of course not. Imaginings of remote possibilities should not be allowed to dissuade us from our judgments based on the best evidence we have.

And the possibility that the videos would prove the truth of the government's claim—that the Pentagon was hit by AA 77—is *very* remote. The majority of the 9/11 Truth Movement is right to assume that the reason the government has not released the videos is that they would prove its claim to be a lie.

Time-Change Parts: There would have been an even more definitive way for the government to prove that AA 77 hit the Pentagon, if it really did. Retired Air Force Colonel George Nelson, who had specialized in the investigation of aircraft mishaps, has pointed out that every plane has many "time-change parts," which must be changed periodically because they are crucial for flight safety. Each time-change part has a distinctive serial number. These parts, moreover, are virtually indestructible, so an ordinary fire resulting from an airplane crash could not possibly "destroy or obliterate all of those critical time-change parts or their serial numbers."[160] By identifying some of those numbers, investigators can determine the make, model, and registration number of a crashed aircraft. Accordingly, if Flight 77 did indeed hit the Pentagon, the FBI, which took charge of the investigation, could have proven this to the press within hours.

Legge, however, believes that the government may have these parts with their serial numbers, along with the videos, and is waiting to release them at an opportune moment. And, Legge worries: "As many members of the 9/11 truth movement believe that no 757 hit the Pentagon, this evidence will throw the movement into disarray and create crippling loss of credibility."[161] However, in the extremely unlikely event that the government releases proof that AA 77 really did hit the Pentagon, this would cause us no loss of credibility. We could simply ask—along with a majority of the American public: Why did the government sit on this evidence all this time? It would be the government's credibility, not ours, that would suffer.

Flight Data Recorder: In any case, one more sure-fire way for authorities to have proven that AA 77 struck the Pentagon, if it did, would have been to show the press the serial number of the plane's flight data recorder (FDR), which Pentagon authorities claimed to have found in the wreckage. As Aidan Monaghan has shown with extensive documentation: When the NTSB (National Transportation Safety Board) issues a report on a crashed airplane, it almost always lists the serial number of the FDR.[162] Indeed, the only exceptions between 1991 and 2006—excluding planes with no FDRs—have evidently been the reports about the four planes that allegedly crashed on 9/11.[163] How can we avoid suspecting that the NTSB's report on AA 77's FDR does not mention its serial number because no FDR with the serial number for that flight was found at the Pentagon?

In 2007, Monaghan sent a FOIA request to the FBI for "documentation pertaining to any formally and positively identified debris by the FBI, from all four civilian commercial aircraft used in the terrorist attacks of September 11, 2001." The FBI replied (in August 2008) that "any potentially responsive records were located in a pending file of an ongoing investigation, and [are] therefore . . . exempt from disclosure."[164]

Monaghan then asked the FBI for "documentation revealing the process by which wreckage recovered by defendant [the FBI] . . . was positively identified by defendant (with the aid of the National Transportation Safety Board), . . . presumably through the use of unique serial number identifying information." The FBI responded with a truly incredible claim: that no such documentation existed because "the identity of the three [sic] hijacked aircraft has never been in question by the FBI, NTSB or FAA."[165] I asked Monaghan if he knew "of any similar report." He replied: "To my knowledge there is not another example of the feds withholding identifying information of a crashed commercial jet because everyone supposedly knew what the plane was."

In any case, the FBI itself admits that it has no documentation to prove that the aircraft that hit the Pentagon was AA 77.[166]

There is another problem with the alleged flight data recorder for AA 77. The Pentagon's file on this FDR, based on information downloaded from it, was created over four hours before this FDR was reportedly found. That is, according to a widely published report, the FDR from Flight 77 was found Friday, September 14, 2001, at 4:00 in the morning. *USA Today*, for example, wrote:

> Searchers on Friday found the flight data and cockpit voice recorders from the hijacked plane that flew into the Pentagon and exploded, Department of Defense officials said. The two "black boxes," crucial to uncovering details about the doomed flight's last moments, were recovered at about 4 a.m., said Army Lt. Col. George Rhynedance, a Pentagon spokesman. Rhynedance said the recorders were in the possession of the FBI, and that officials from the National Transportation Safety Board were providing technical assistance in reading any data they contain.[167]

This story also reported that despite some damage to the boxes, "the FBI still was confident the data can be recovered from both."[168] *Newsweek* had a similar story.[169]

However, according to a file released by the NTSB (in response to a FOIA request from Aidan Monaghan), the flight data file for AA 77, which was based on this FDR, was created at 11:45 PM on Thursday, September 13.[170] The presence of this problem—that the flight data file was created before the FDR itself was found—suggests that the story about the discovery was invented.

There is yet another problem: According to the *USA Today* story just quoted, the FDR was found "right where the plane came into the building." The *Newsweek* story likewise stated that the FDR was discovered "near the impact site."[171] But according to the *Pentagon Building Performance Report*, the FDR was found "nearly 300 ft into the structure."[172] This view was made well known by *Popular Mechanics*, which said that that the FDR "was found almost 300 feet inside the building."[173]

Given these problems, it is difficult to take seriously the claim that AA 77's flight data recorder was found in the debris at the Pentagon.

Fires: As we saw earlier, April Gallop stated that there was no evidence of fire on the first floor where she walked from her office to the "entrance hole." Sgt. Ronald Alan Galey, having gotten to the Pentagon within a few minutes, said that there was nothing but "spot fires" and that "the most fire that [he] saw was the crash truck . . . on fire."

These testimonies lift up one of the problems with the 757 theory: that the crash of a plane carrying several thousand gallons of fuel should have immediately ignited fires similar to the jet-fuel-fed fires that occurred in the first ten minutes after the strikes on the Twin Towers. There was, to be sure, an initial fireball, but it was very localized and lasted only a few seconds.

A video by freelance videographer Bob Pugh, which began only a few minutes after the attack,[174] shows what Galey said: that there were only spot fires and that the greatest amount of fire, producing most of the smoke, was from a truck on fire. Ralph Omholt, on the basis of photographs, says:

> There are no firemen with shiny aluminized protective hoods donned, prepared to penetrate a jet fuel fire, in a rescue attempt. . . . There is no suggestion of an aircraft crash and the expected fuel fire. . . . An aircraft full of fuel, crashing at 300 Knots will *not* experience a delay in the full burning of its fuel . . . [T]he fire—what little there is—comes from the second-floor windows. What happened to all that fuel which is supposed to be spilled on the ground floor?[175]

There is again a disconnect between the official theory and the empirical evidence.

Seismic Evidence: Seismologist Won-Young Kim, of Columbia University's Lamont-Doherty Earth Observatory, and Gerald R. Baum, of the Maryland Geological Survey, were asked by the Army to determine the exact time of the four 9/11 flights. They found that the signal for the Pentagon attack—alone of the four attacks—was too weak to produce a detectable signal (above the "noise"). They wrote:

> We analyzed seismic records from five stations in the northeastern United States, ranging from 63 to 350 km from the Pentagon. Despite detailed analysis of the data, we could not find a clear seismic signal. Even the closest station . . . did not record the impact. We concluded that the plane impact to the Pentagon generated relatively weak seismic signals.[176]

Having made this point in a previous book, I asked:

> If United 93, also a Boeing 757, created a detectable signal by crashing into the soft soil in Pennsylvania, how could a detectable signal not be created by a Boeing 757 crashing into the Pentagon's steel-reinforced outer wall at several hundred miles per hour?[177]

This seemed to me strong evidence that the Pentagon had not been struck by a Boeing 757.

However, well-respected seismologist Terry Wallace, who also could find no signal at the Pentagon (above the noise), calculated the magnitude of a 757 strike on this building to be only 0.8. He calculated this relatively low magnitude on the basis of the fact that the impact would have been "on the wall," rather than being a vertical crash, striking the ground, and the noise at all the stations was above 0.8.[178] It has been suggested that this could explain why neither he nor the Kim-Baum team could detect any signal for the Pentagon attack.

According to *ScienceDaily*, however:

> On September 11, seismographs operated by Columbia University's Lamont-Doherty Earth Observatory in Palisades, New York, recorded seismic signals produced by the impacts of the two aircraft hitting the Twin Towers of the World Trade Center and the subsequent collapse of the 110 story towers.[179]

If a Boeing 767 striking one of the Twin Towers produced a detectable seismic signal, then a Boeing 757 striking the Pentagon should likewise produce a detectable seismic signal. The Pentagon, especially at Wedge 1, with its reinforcement, was much more rigid than the Twin Towers. This fact should compensate for the fact that the Boeing 767s, which hit the towers, were larger than the 757, which reportedly hit the Pentagon. Accordingly, if all three buildings were hit by airliners, as reported, then all three should have produced seismic signals.

Bodies from the Plane: One of the "proofs" that AA 77 hit the Pentagon was that the bodies sent to be autopsied apparently included people killed in the airplane as well as the 125 people who were in the Pentagon. However, there is no proof that the bodies were all from the Pentagon.

The reason for uncertainty began when the FBI immediately took complete control of the Pentagon crash site. Dr. Marcella Fierro, the chief medical examiner of Virginia, pointed out that it was her office's responsibility to carry out the autopsies. But the FBI insisted that the autopsies be carried out by the Armed Forces Institute of Pathology at Dover Air Force Base. Also, when the bodies arrived at the Dover Institute, they were brought by the Army and accompanied by the FBI.[180] Therefore, although the remains of reportedly 189 bodies were evidently delivered to the Dover Institute with word that they had all come from the Pentagon, there is no independent evidence that all of them were actually brought from that site.

The victims of the Pentagon attack were taken to a temporary morgue in the Pentagon's north parking lot loading dock. They were then trucked to Davison Army Airfield at Fort Belvoir, then flown by helicopter to Dover. "FBI agents rode in the trucks, participated in the escort, and accompanied the remains during the flight to preserve the chain of custody."[181] For all we know, however, human remains from two different sites could have been combined by FBI and military personnel before they were brought to Dover.[182]

The Dover Institute's radiology report said that "specimens ranging from relatively intact bodies to small body-part fragments were received from the Pentagon site."[183] But remains from the Pentagon site could have been mixed at Davison with remains of bodies from elsewhere. And we certainly cannot simply assume that the military would not do such a thing, given its tampering and deceit with regard to the video purportedly showing a 757 hitting the Pentagon.

The Five Lamp Poles: In the above section on "Damage to Surroundings," in evidence supportive of the 757 theory, the most important element was the fact that five lamp poles were downed. Frank Legge, writing with Warren Stutt, said:

> [I]mpact with five light poles not only establishes the track through the damaged area, but also provides evidence that the wingspan of the plane, if it was a plane, is consistent with that of a Boeing 757, 124 feet 10 inches.[184]

But this is sometimes mentioned as if serious doubts had not been raised about it. Critics have made the following points:

- If lamp poles had been torn out of the ground by an airliner going close to 500 mph, these poles, which were quite heavy—weighing 180 to 300 pounds—would surely have skidded over the lawn, creating gouges in it. But photographs show none.[185]

- Could the airliner not have been caused to go off course, or even crash, by hitting these lamp poles?

- Do not the lamp poles appear to be cut at the base, rather than having the jagged edge of a pole that was knocked down by a plane's wing?

Summary: Although the available physical evidence cannot strictly prove that a Boeing 757 did not hit the Pentagon, some of the evidence fails to suggest the 757 hypothesis, and some of the evidence even counts against the truth of this hypothesis.

Additional Reason for Skepticism about Secondary Matters:
Attack at 9:31

Having said that there is a growing consensus in the 9/11 Truth Movement about a primary matter—namely, that the Pentagon was not struck by AA 77 under the control of al-Qaeda—I have given reasons to be skeptical about secondary matters. Although at first glance there appears to be overwhelming witness testimony supporting the view that a 757 hit the Pentagon, a critical examination supports a skeptical attitude toward this testimony. And although the physical evidence has long seemed to contradict the 757 view, some scientists have endorsed the 757 view in recent years. So there seems to be evidence on both sides.

There is an additional reason for skepticism about the Pentagon attack. On the one hand, virtually everyone has agreed that the attack occurred at only a few seconds before 9:38. On the other hand, there is powerful evidence that the attack on the Pentagon occurred almost seven minutes earlier, between 9:30 and 9:32.

In the first place, early stories by Reuters, *USA Today*, and the *New York Times* reported that the Pentagon attack occurred at "about 9:30" and the *U.S. News and World Report* said that it occurred "shortly after 9:30."

In the second place, an FAA Timeline document, "Executive Summary: Chronology of a Multiple Hijacking Crisis, September 11, 2001," stated that at 9:32 Air Traffic Control reported "aircraft crashes into west side of Pentagon."

In the third place, and most important, several time-pieces in the Pentagon stopped between 9:30 and 9:32.

- The US Navy website, with a note saying "clock frozen at the time of impact," shows a photograph of a clock with the hands at 9:31:40.[186]

- The electric clock that hung on the wall of the Pentagon Heliport, which is now in the national 9/11 exhibit at the Smithsonian Institution, shows its hands as having stopped at 9:31:30.[187]

- April Gallop, who was knocked unconscious by the attack, has kept her watch, the hands of which stopped shortly after 9:30.[188]

- Assistant Secretary of Defense Robert Andrews reported that, while he was in the Counterterrorism Center, an explosive event occurred at about 9:32. (Although his watch actually said 9:35, he reported, he kept it a few minutes fast in order to get to meetings on time.)[189]

- Denmark's soon-to-be Foreign Minister Per Stig Møller, who was in Washington, DC, reported that, having immediately looked at his wrist watch upon hearing an explosion and seeing smoke rise from the Pentagon, saw the time to be 9:32.

III EMPHASIZING CONSENSUS

In the first part of this essay, we saw that there is consensus within the 9/11 Truth Movement on the most important issue regarding the attack on the Pentagon: that the official story, according to which the Pentagon was attacked by AA 77 under the control of al-Qaeda, is a lie.

Unfortunately, this consensus has often been overshadowed by battles on secondary matters, especially the question of what hit the Pentagon. This battle allows the press to portray the 9/11 Movement as absurd, with members being more concerned with their battles against other "truthers" than with their differences from the government's account.

It is important, therefore, to realize that the question of what hit the Pentagon is really a very secondary matter. The passionate concern with this issue is a hangover from the 9/11 Truth Movement's battle with the government's position. In that battle, rejecting the government's position was widely regarded as rejecting the idea that the Pentagon was struck by a 757, which might have been AA 77. But it is now recognized that there is no necessary connection between these ideas: Some people who believe that the Pentagon was struck by a 757, perhaps even by AA 77, completely reject the idea that Pentagon was *struck by AA 77 under the control of al-Qaeda.*

Given the consensus on this point—that whatever hit the Pentagon was controlled not by al-Qaeda hijackers but by the Pentagon's leadership—the issue of what hit the Pentagon loses most of its importance.

The recognition that this consensus on the essential point exists is important, the second part of this chapter argued, because a battle about the secondary question of what hit the Pentagon would likely be endless. Most people who are convinced by the arguments on behalf of the 757 view are not likely to be dissuaded from it by the arguments I presented against it. And most people who reject the 757 view are not likely to be persuaded to change their mind by the arguments on behalf of the 757 view.

It might be thought that this is defeatism, that scientists should be able to provide sufficiently persuasive arguments for one view or the other, so that consensus on the question of what hit the Pentagon could be attained. As many commentators have pointed out, however, the government, by keeping so many facts hidden, has prevented the Truth Movement from achieving consensus on this point.

But—and this is the most important point—consensus on this secondary point is not essential. The only consensus that is essential is that which we already have: that regardless of what hit the Pentagon, the Pentagon was not struck by AA 77 under the control of al-Qaeda. And given this consensus, the 9/11 Truth Movement now has the same kind of agreement with regard to the Pentagon that we have with regard to the World Trade Center.

8. NATIONALIST FAITH: HOW IT BLINDS AMERICA TO THE TRUTH ABOUT 9/11[1]

I t is often said that Christian faith is the dominant form of faith in America. It is also often said that faith is a bad thing, which prevents religious people from determining the answers to various vital questions on the basis of the relevant evidence. Faith, in other words, is regarded as not simply blind, but blinding.

The truth about America, however, is more complex. Another kind of faith, radically different from Christian faith, is actually the dominant faith in our country. Even within the church, Christian faith tends to be subordinate to this other form of faith. With regard to certain truths, moreover, this other form of faith is blinding, while Christian faith at its best is illuminating.

One of these truths is the truth about 9/11. "The evidence that 9/11 was an inside job," I said at the outset of my book 2007 book, *Debunking 9/11 Debunking*, "is overwhelming. Most people who examine this evidence with an open mind find it convincing."[2] The only real problem is to get people to examine this evidence, at least with, in Richard Falk's phrase, "even just a 30-percent open mind."[3]

Why is it so difficult for many people, including journalists—as we saw in Chapters 2 and 3—to seriously examine the evidence? There are many reasons, especially when we are talking about journalists. But one of those reasons, probably the main one, I will suggest, is the blinding power of the dominant faith of Americans.

I will then suggest that Christian faith at its best opens us to the truth about 9/11 by allowing us to look at the evidence without flinching. (I could equally well talk about Jewish faith, or Islamic faith, or other types of theistic faith. But I am focusing on Christian faith because it is my own religious tradition and also because it is the dominant theistic tradition in the United States.) Christian faith is not necessary, of course: Many members of the 9/11 Truth Movement are not Christians. But Christian faith can help, partly because it contains warnings against the kind of faith that makes it difficult for many Americans, and especially for America as such, to see the truth about 9/11.

I THE TRUTH ABOUT 9/11: A FALSE-FLAG ATTACK

What is this truth? It is, as I already suggested, that 9/11 was an inside operation, orchestrated by forces within our own government. It was a false-flag attack, with evidence planted to make it appear to have been planned and carried out by Arab Muslims. The expression "false-flag attack" originally referred to operations in which the attackers, perhaps in ships, literally showed the flag of an enemy country, so that it would be blamed. But the expression has come to be used for any attack made to appear to be the work of some country or group other than that to which the attackers themselves belong.

1. HISTORY OF FALSE-FLAG ATTACKS

Imperial powers have regularly staged such attacks when they wanted a pretext to go to war.

When Japan's army in 1931 decided to take over Manchuria, it blew up the tracks of its own railway near the Chinese military base in Mukden, blamed Chinese solders, then proceeded to slaughter hundreds of thousands of Chinese. This "Mukden incident" began the Pacific part of World War II.[4]

In Germany in 1933, the Nazis, wanting a pretext to arrest leftists, shut down unfriendly newspapers, and annul civil rights, started a fire in the German Reichstag and blamed it on Communists. Their proof that Communists were responsible was the presence at the site of a feeble-minded left-wing radical, who had been brought there by the Nazis themselves.[5]

In 1939, when Hitler wanted a pretext to attack Poland, he had Germans dressed as Poles stage raids on German outposts on the Polish-German border. In some cases, a dead German convict dressed as a Pole was left at the scene. The next day, Hitler, referring to these "border incidents," attacked Poland in "self-defense," thereby starting the European part of World War II.[6]

We Americans, viewing our country as the "exceptional nation," like to believe that our wars have not originated in such deceit. But an examination of the historical evidence reveals otherwise—for example, the Mexican-American war, with its false claim that Mexico had "shed American blood on the American soil,"[7] the Spanish-American war, with its "Remember the Maine" hoax,[8] the war in the Philippines, with its false claim that the Filipinos fired first,[9] and the Vietnam war, with its Tonkin Gulf hoax.[10]

After World War II, moreover, the United States organized false-flag terrorist attacks in European countries, such as Italy, France, and Belgium, to discredit Communists and other leftists, to prevent them from coming to power through the ballot box. NATO, guided by the CIA and the Pentagon and working with right-wing organizations, orchestrated terrorist attacks that killed innocent civilians and then, by having evidence planted, got the attacks blamed on leftists.[11]

Would the US military do this if it involved killing US citizens? In 1962, shortly after Fidel Castro had overthrown the pro-American dictator Batista, the Joint Chiefs of Staff prepared a plan, known as Operation Northwoods, that contained "pretexts which would provide justification for US military intervention in Cuba." American citizens would have been killed in some of the scenarios, such as a "Remember the Maine" incident, in which: "We could blow up a U.S. ship in Guantánamo Bay and blame Cuba."[12] Only President Kennedy's veto prevented these plans from becoming operational.

Were there reasons why the Bush-Cheney administration and its Pentagon would have staged the 9/11 attacks to make them appear to have been orchestrated by Muslim terrorists from the Middle East? This administration, wanting to control the oil from the Caspian Sea area, had made plans to go to war in Afghanistan several months before 9/11.[13] It also, as is now well known, had an attack on Iraq at the top of its agenda when it came into office.[14] Finally, General Wesley Clark has revealed, the Pentagon under this administration was planning on attacking six more predominantly Muslim countries: Syria, Lebanon, Libya, Somalia, Sudan, and Iran.[15]

2. Evidence that 9/11 Was a False-Flag Attack

Accordingly, the idea that 9/11 was an inside job, with evidence planted to make it appear to be the work of Middle Eastern Muslims, should not have been ruled out a priori. Indeed, those with the responsibility to discover what really happened, including our major media, should have been alert from the first day for evidence that 9/11 was a false-flag operation. And that evidence is now abundant.

NIST and the Destruction of the World Trade Center: As we saw in earlier chapters, the official account of the World Trade Center cannot be true. This official account was given by NIST, the National Institute for Standards and Technology. NIST is an agency of the Commerce

Department and it was, thereby, an agency of the Bush-Cheney administration. A document signed by over 11,000 scientists, including 52 Nobel Laureates and 63 recipients of the National Medal of Science, said that the Bush administration repeatedly "distort[ed] scientific knowledge for partisan political ends."[16] Such distortion runs throughout the NIST reports on the Twin Towers and WTC 7. A former NIST scientist stated that this agency had become extremely politicized by 2001:

> [E]veryone in NIST leadership had been trained to pay close heed to political pressures. There was no chance that NIST people "investigating" the 911 situation could have been acting in the true spirit of scientific independence, nor could they have operated at all without careful consideration of political impact. Everything that came from the hired guns was by then routinely filtered through the front office, and assessed for political implications before release.[17]

Part of NIST's distortion was the way it ignored the existence of at least 200 people, including over 100 members of the Fire Department of New York, reporting evidence of explosions in the towers. For example, Fire Department Captain Dennis Tardio said: "I hear an explosion and I look up. It is as if the building is being imploded, from the top floor down, one after another, *boom, boom, boom.*"[18] *Wall Street Journal* reporter John Bussey said: "I . . . looked up out of the [WSJ] office window to see what seemed like perfectly synchronized explosions coming from each floor. . . . One after the other, from top to bottom, with a fraction of a second between, the floors blew to pieces."[19] There are dozens of such testimonies. But NIST simply ignored them.

As shown by the way in which NIST dealt with evidence, the official reports about the World Trade Center were not simply wrong. They were lies.

Hijackers and the Pentagon Attack: This conclusion is strengthened by problems in the official story of the attack on the Pentagon. I will provide only one example.

According to the official story, the Pentagon was struck by AA 77 under the control of al-Qaeda hijacker Hani Hanjour. Numerous reports had indicated, however, that Hanjour was a terrible pilot, who could not even safely fly a single-engine plane. As one flight instructor quoted by the *New York Times* put it: "He could not fly at all."[20] And yet the plane that hit the Pentagon, according to the official story, was flown with military precision. After completing a 330-degree downward spiral, it came in at ground level to hit the Pentagon between the first and second floors, and it did this without even scratching the Pentagon lawn. The *Washington Post* wrote: "Aviation sources said the plane was flown with extraordinary skill, making it highly likely that a trained pilot was at the helm."[21]

Hani Hanjour, who could barely fly a Cessna, could not have done this in a Boeing 757. As Ralph Omholt, a former 757 pilot, has said: "The idea that an *unskilled* pilot could have flown this trajectory is simply too ridiculous to consider."[22] If one checks Pilots for 9/11 Truth, one can see that many other pilots agree.

II BLINDING NATIONALIST FAITH

The facts provided in this and the previous chapters should be sufficient, for those with eyes to see, that the official story is false. Not everyone, however, has eyes to see. Many Americans have a kind of faith that blinds them to the truth about 9/11. This faith also prevents this evidence from being discussed in the mainstream media. What is this faith?

1. NATIONALIST FAITH

I am drawing here from an essay by Christian theologian John Cobb. Pointing out that people generally presuppose "the vision of reality" of the society in which they grow up, Cobb said: "We may call [this] largely unconscious underlying and overarching view of the world, as well as the more conscious beliefs in which it is expressed, 'a faith.'" "For a thousand years prior to the Renaissance," Cobb added, "the 'faith' of the great majority of Europeans was Christian." In the modern world, however,

> one's loyalty and one's identity [came to be] defined by geography rather than religion. . . . Virtue was redefined as patriotism. . . Saints were replaced by national heroes. The stories of one's nation took over from the Christian story in education and in public functions. . . . [B]eing a Christian became optional. Public debates pro and con Christianity are fully acceptable. But . . . [t]here is no public debate about national loyalty. In short the dominant "faith" of most people in the modern world has been nationalist.[23]

What is the American form of this nationalist faith? It is that "the United States is a fundamentally virtuous nation." This faith does not mean that there can be no criticism of America's actions. "But the criticism is [only] that the nation's actions are not in its true interests or do not accord with its true character." These criticisms hence express the nationalist faith, which is that our country is essentially good, never deliberately doing anything terribly evil.

From the point of view of this faith, the claim that 9/11 was an inside job simply cannot be true. After pointing out several facts that make the official story extremely implausible, Cobb wrote:

> The response of most Americans [to a recitation of such facts] shows how powerful is the hold upon them of their nationalistic "faith." They do not want to hear that members of their government may have deceived them on a matter of such importance. They do not want to examine the evidence. They "know" in advance that the questioner is out of line. They "know" this because the alternative does not fit with their "faith."[24]

But surely, we may respond, Americans by now know that the Bush-Cheney administration lied us into the war in Iraq. Why would most Americans continue to accept this administration's astounding story about 9/11? "The answer," Cobb suggests,

> may be that deception about matters of who has what weapons can be tolerated. We can understand that the real motives for fighting a war are often different from the announced reason. But to believe that high officials in an American administration . . . would organize a massive attack killing thousands of American citizens would deeply wound the American sense of the basic goodness of the nation, a conviction which belongs to the depths of our national faith.[25]

2. Conspiracy Theory

Given the pervasiveness of this faith in our country—and especially in the public sphere, controlled by the mass media—it is easy to marginalize those of us who question the official story about 9/11. The chief method, other than simply ignoring us, is to label us "conspiracy theorists." This label lets people know that we are irrational, that our claims are simply products of fevered minds, so that even examining our claims to refute them would be a waste of time.

From a purely rational-empirical point of view, the effectiveness of this label is remarkable. A *conspiracy*, according to my dictionary, is simply "an agreement to perform together an illegal, treacherous, or evil act."[26] To hold a conspiracy theory about some event, accordingly, is simply to believe that it resulted from such an agreement. We accept new conspiracy theories every day, insofar as we believe news reports about cigarette companies conspiring to conceal the dangers of smoking, oil companies conspiring to deny the reality of human-caused global warming, and corporations conspiring to defraud customers. We are all conspiracy theorists.

Everyone is, in fact, a conspiracy theorist about 9/11, because the official theory is itself a conspiracy theory. It says that 9/11 resulted from a secret agreement between Osama bin Ladin and various members of al-Qaeda.

Nevertheless, the term "conspiracy theorist" is used only for people who reject the official conspiracy theory in favor of the alternative theory, according to which 9/11 was an inside job. For example, Jim Dwyer wrote a *New York Times* story entitled "2 U.S. Reports Seek to Counter Conspiracy Theories About 9/11."[27] A more accurate title would have been: "2 U.S. Reports Say Government's Conspiracy Theory Is Better than Alternative Conspiracy Theory." But the *Times* would never have used any such headline.

This one-sided use of the term does not occur only in the main-stream media. It is just as prevalent on the left. For example, Salim Muwakkil, a senior editor of *In These Times*, wrote in 2005:

> The [9/11] movement caught my attention when I saw Dr. David Ray Griffin speaking at the University of Wisconsin at Madison on C-SPAN earlier this year. . . . Griffin . . . has written several well-regarded books on religion and spirituality. . . and is considered one of the nation's foremost theologians. I . . . regard him as a wise writer on the role of spirituality in society.
>
> So, it was shocking to see him pushing a radical conspiracy theory about 9/11 on C-SPAN. . . . What could have transformed this sober, reflective scholar into a conspiracy theorist?28

I, of course, had been a conspiracy theorist all along. The only thing that changed in 2003 was that I rejected the official conspiracy theory in favor of the alternative theory.

From the point of view of *In These Times*, however, that was when I first became a conspiracy theorist, leading the magazine to ask, "what happened to Griffin?" Another writer for the magazine, Terry Allen, answered: "I think part of it is that he's a theologian who operates on faith."[29] My own answer—that I finally looked at the evidence—was evidently ruled out a priori, because there could be no good evidence for a conspiracy theory. These two writers also seemed to be completely devoid of any suspicion that their rejection of my position was itself based on faith—the nationalist faith that our leaders would not do such a thing.

These two examples, in any case, show how the term "conspiracy theory" is used in this discussion. It is not used in the generic sense, to mean any secret agreement to do something illegal. It is used for a theory alleging that our own government did something illegal—in this case, something so terrible as to contradict our faith in our nation's goodness.

The fact that such theories, according to which our own government did something horrible, are not to be seriously entertained in public discourse was made clear by President Bush in his address to the United Nations two months after 9/11. He said: "Let us never tolerate outrageous conspiracy theories concerning the attacks of 11 September—malicious lies that attempt to shift the blame away from the terrorists."[30] What would an *outrageous* conspiracy theory be?

If we were operating in a philosophy-of-science context, it would be clear. A good theory is one that can explain, in a coherent way, all or at least most of the relevant facts and is not contradicted by any of them. A bad theory is one that is contradicted by some of the relevant facts. An *outrageous* theory would be one that is contradicted by virtually *all* of the relevant facts. By this criterion, the official conspiracy theory is clearly the outrageous one.

However the public discussion of 9/11 occurs not in a philosophy-of-science context but in a *political* context, and in this context, the alternative theory is the outrageous one, because it says that members of the Bush Administration ordered it, not Osama bin Laden. That claim makes it outrageous by definition. Evidence has nothing to do with it.

3. THE MEDIA'S NON-TOLERATION OF MY BOOKS

In warning people not to *tolerate* outrageous conspiracy theories, Bush was reminding people, especially people who control the mainstream media, that anyone saying that 9/11 was an inside job was not to be given a sympathetic or even neutral hearing.

This injunction has been obeyed. Since I know my own case the best, I will use myself as an example.

My 9/11 Books: My first book, *The New Pearl Harbor*, has sold about 150,000 copies in English and been translated into several other languages. *Debunking 9/11 Debunking* received a Bronze Medal in the 2008 Independent Publisher Book Awards. My 2008 book, *The New Pearl Harbor Revisited*, was chosen by Publishers Weekly as a "Pick of the Week." And then in 2009, the *New Statesman* named me one of "The 50 People Who Matter Today." One would think that at least some of my nine books would have been reviewed in mainstream newspapers and magazines, and that I would have been interviewed in mainstream radio and television programs.

One would especially think this given the fact that, prior to beginning to write about 9/11, I was a fairly well-respected philosopher of religion and theologian, who had written over 20 books. The fact that such a person was now writing books accusing members of the Bush administration of orchestrating the 9/11 attacks, one would think, would be just the thing newspapers and magazines would headline in order to increase readership and that radio and television programs would interview me to increase ratings. Contrary to widespread opinion, however, there is something more important than sales and ratings: never publicly contradicting the national faith.

Jonathan Kay's Book about "Truthers": Mainstream newspapers, magazines, and television shows are not, to be sure, uninterested in books about 9/11. It is that they review only the right kinds of books. To illustrate: Whereas the *New York Times* has never reviewed any of my books, including the one named "Pick of the Week" by *Publishers Weekly*, the *Times* did review the pseudo-sociological study, *Among the Truthers*, by first-time author Jonathan Kay (who is a columnist for a very conservative Canadian newspaper). Calling this a "remarkable book," which describes Truthers "superbly," the reviewer, Jacob Heilbrunn,[31] does not seem bothered by the fact that Kay never offers any evidence to support his description of Truthers as "cranks."

The *Wall Street Journal*, which likewise thought Kay's book worthy of lengthy discussion, entitled its review "Beyond the Lunatic Fringe" and referred to Truthers as "nutters." But the reviewer, Sonny Bunch, while saying that Kay "wants to understand where conspiracy theories come from,"[32] does not point out that Kay systematically ignores the evidence that members of the 9/11 Truth Movement give for their positions. Writing condescendingly about the man who founded

Architects and Engineers for 9/11 Truth,[33] Bunch described Kay as "patiently listen[ing] to Richard Gage, a San Francisco-based architect who claims that explosives brought down the World Trade Center." But Bunch, like Kay, seemed uncurious about why over 1,500 architects and engineers have joined Gage's organization.

To find illuminating reviews of Kay's book, one needs to look behind the mainstream newspapers. For example, Dr. Anthony J. Hall, Professor of Globalization Studies at the University of Lethbridge, points out that in a 2008 article, Kay admitted that he had smeared a Truther without doing any research to back up his attack, but added:

> [T]he truth is I . . . never bothered with schooling myself on the minutiae of 9/11-ology. . . . I never felt the need to because, on a purely instinctual level, I always felt the Truthers case was complete nonsense.[34]

This explains why, even though I gave Kay several hours of my time, his book contains not a word about the reasons why I consider the official story about 9/11 a lie from beginning to end. A book reflecting Kay's attitude is evidently deemed worthy of respectful reviews in the *New York Times* and the *Wall Street Journal*, as long as the book mouths the correct assessment: the members of the 9/11 Truth Movement, regardless of their credentials, are cranks and nutters.

Tucker Carlson on Sin and Blasphemy: Although I was almost completely excluded from mainstream media, I did appear in 2006 on the MSNBC program hosted by Tucker Carlson. But this was not a normal interview, in which I was allowed to present my ideas in a sympathetic or even neutral atmosphere. Rather, Carlson denounced me, even calling my statements "blasphemous" and "sinful"[35]—thereby perfectly illustrating that his faith in American goodness is a *religious* faith. From a Christian, Jewish, or Islamic perspective, this would be an *idolatrous* faith—as pointed out by a viewer, who made this response to Carlson:

> Regarding your comment: "I'm merely saying it is wrong, blasphemous, and sinful for you to suggest, imply, or help other people come to the conclusion that the U.S. government killed 3,000 of its own citizens." I would like to suggest keeping things in perspective; we are not talking about God here. We are talking of a government, an institution consisting of people and as history bears out, no government and in particular no individual is immune to corruption. Profit,

greed, and hunger for power can corrupt any individual and in turn corrupt institutions. The framers of our Constitution understood this, and as strong as it is, it is not foolproof.

In any case, I have been interviewed calmly on television shows in Canada and some European countries, including England. But never in the United States. In the public sphere, where our national faith rules, the alternative conspiracy theory is not to be tolerated.

III Christian Faith and 9/11

In the church, however, things should be different. Here, one would presume, the dominant faith would be Christian faith, and Christian faith at its best would allow people to look at the evidence that 9/11 was an inside job. Why?

1. Christian Faith At Its Best

Christian faith is first of all faith in God, and faith is best understood as fidelity or loyalty. The Greek term for faith in the New Testament, *pistis,* is often best translated "fidelity." The issue, as Richard Horsley explains in *Jesus and Empire*, is whether one was loyal to God or the Roman emperor.[36] In speaking of God, one is speaking of the creator and lover of all peoples.

Christian faith also teaches that God is truth, so that to be loyal to God is to be committed to knowing and proclaiming the truth. From the point of view of Christian faith, therefore, it would be idolatrous to regard our nation as worthy of ultimate allegiance. Christians can, of course, be patriots, loving and serving their country. But they cannot, without forsaking their Christian faith, give *ultimate* loyalty to their nation, so as to blind themselves to, or hide from others, ugly truths about their own nation.

Another relevant feature of Christian faith is its doctrine of original sin. Although this doctrine has often been expressed in mythological and even horrible ways, its basic point is that the tendency to sin is universal. No party, no religion, no country can be assumed to be free from the tendency to sin. What is this tendency to sin?

On the one hand, our unique capacities as human beings allow us, unlike other creatures, to understand that we are simply one among others: All people are children of God, hence all people should have equal rights, equal opportunities, including equal access to the world's resources. We know that we should love our neighbors as ourselves and hence do unto others as we would have them do unto us. (We can even know, as the Dalai Lama puts it, that we should care more for others than we do for ourselves: there are so many more of them.)

And yet we generally do not. We generally use our unique capacities, as Reinhold Niebuhr pointed out, not to treat ourselves as simply one among others, but to gain advantages for ourselves and those to whom we are close, even when this means harming, perhaps killing, others. This tendency especially comes out in people who gain political power. This point was expressed most famously in Lord Acton's dictum: "Power tends to corrupt, and absolute power corrupts absolutely."[37]

Christians should, therefore, be especially suspicious of political and military leaders who show signs of seeking absolute power. Andrew Bacevich, a Christian who is a political science professor and a former military officer, has said that the US military has been attempting "to achieve something approaching omnipotence."[38] The Bush-Cheney administration, dominated by neoconservatives, was seeking a "unipolar" world, in which the United States would lay down the rules.[39] Christians should suspect, therefore, the presence of absolute corruption—corruption sufficient, at least, to orchestrate 9/11.

2. CHRISTIAN FAITH OFTEN SUBORDINATE TO NATIONALIST

Unfortunately, the fact that a majority of people in America identify as Christians does not mean that their Christian faith trumps their American faith. They often seem to take the latter with greater seriousness. I have never had a lecture in a church cancelled because someone took exception to my christology or doctrine of God, but more than one church has cancelled lectures I was scheduled to give about 9/11, and many more churches have refused to allow their buildings be used—even to be rented out—for this purpose in the first place. The leaders of these churches are unwilling to expose their people to, or be seen as supporting, such heresy.

I have, to be sure, spoken in a few churches. And the petition at Religious Leaders for 9/11 Truth has been signed by over a hundred Christian leaders, including some prominent theologians, such as John Cobb, Rosemary Ruether, Joe Hough (while he was the president of Union Theological Seminary), and the late William Sloane Coffin.

But I have been attacked by others.

Ian Markham: For example, after my first book, *The New Pearl Harbor*, was published, Christian ethicist Ian Markham, while he was the Dean of Hartford Seminary, published a critique of it in a Christian magazine. He said: "There need to be limits to the range of possibilities considered; and I want to suggest that Griffin is outside them." Explaining this statement, he said:

> When a book argues that the American President deliberately and knowingly was "involved" in the slaughter of 3000 US citizens, then this is irresponsible.[40]

In a letter of response, I suggested to Markham that "our difference on 9/11 has to do primarily with a priori assumptions as to what the US government, and the Bush administration and its Pentagon in particular, would and would not do." Markham confirmed this judgment, saying: "Yes, I am operating with an a priori assumption that Bush would not kill 3000 citizens for the sake of a political justification to invade the Middle East for oil."[41]

David Heim: My third book, *Christian Faith and the Truth behind 9/11: A Call to Reflection and Action*, was reviewed in the *Christian Century* magazine, which has long been a voice for liberal, socially-concerned Christian faith. However, editor David Heim, who took it upon himself to write the review, said not a word about my chapters on Jesus and empire, demonic evil, or my call to churches to reflect about 9/11. Rather, he devoted his review entirely to discouraging such reflection by ridiculing my claim that 9/11 was an inside job.

Using the same technique as secular critics, he gave his review a belittling title, "Whodunit? A 9/11 Conspiracy Theory." He then made clear the heretical nature of the book in the first sentence:

> According to theologian David Ray Griffin, the attacks of 9/11 were not the work of jihadist suicidal terrorists but were orchestrated by the Bush administration to provide the pretext for its military adventures and its quest for global dominance.[42]

Calling my argument "loopy," he suggested that I had departed from the truth because I had "drunk deeply from the murky well of the '9/11 truth' forums on the Internet." Then, demonstrating that my arguments are easily refuted, he wrote:

[Griffin] notes that though the hijackers are alleged to have been devout Muslims, during their time in the U.S. they drank alcoholic beverages and visited strip clubs. The 9/11 commission never admitted or resolved this contradiction, Griffin says, apparently scoring his first point against the official explanation. Griffin ignores the many reports showing that some hijackers . . . exhibited exactly this psychological profile: they were alternately attracted and repelled by the moral laxity of the West; their sense of its allure spurred their sense of repulsion. Such modest nuances of reflection seem too much for Griffin.[43]

By thus demonstrating his own superior capacity for nuance, at least to his own satisfaction, he implied that he had taken care of all the questions about the hijackers.

With regard to the World Trade Center, Heim answered all questions by appealing to the report put out by NIST, the National Institute for Standards and Technology. As mentioned earlier, NIST is an agency of the Commerce Department and hence of the Bush administration when the report was issued—an administration that, the Union of Concerned Scientists said, had repeatedly "distort[ed] scientific knowledge for partisan political ends."[44]

But this fact did not trouble Heim. His implicit argument seemed to be: We can know a priori that the Bush administration was not responsible, so we can trust the report put out by NIST, because NIST would have had no motive to lie.

After using such circular arguments to deal with other questions, Heim said:

The war on terrorism has been invoked to sponsor a foolish military adventure. The disastrous overreach in Iraq was fueled by imperialist delusions about remaking the Middle East. But tying that critique of U.S. policy to an outlandish theory about U.S. complicity in 9/11 can only invite ridicule.

Heim provides a perfect illustration of nationalist faith. The invasion of Iraq was foolish, based on delusions, not evil, based on a lie. To suggest otherwise was outlandish and would invite ridicule.

Heim closed his review by asking: "Why did a Presbyterian publishing house sign up this corrosive and monomaniacal book?"[45]

Mark Tooley: Heim was not alone in criticizing Westminster John Knox for publishing my book. The Institute for Religion and Democracy (IRD) put out a press release headed: "IRD:

Presbyterian-Published 9/11 Conspiracy Book is Absurd." The IRD's Mark Tooley said: "That senior mainline church officials would publish this kind of absurd revisionist history is a scandal."[46]

Conservative Presbyterians: Especially severe criticism of Westminster John Knox came from conservative factions within the Presbyterian church. John H. Adams, the editor of the *Presbyterian Layman*, said that it is not the Presbyterian Church's place to publish a conspiracy theory, and that for Westminster John Knox to do so is tantamount to saying the denomination agrees with the view that 9/11 was orchestrated by forces within our own government. Although Adams admitted that he had not actually read my book, he felt free to describe the book's thesis as "a hare-brained idea" and to criticize the press for moving into "the pulp category of theology."[47] Just knowing the book's claim about the Bush administration was obviously sufficient to make such charges.

Toby Brown, a Presbyterian pastor in Texas, who also had not read the book, said: "Why, out of all the things they could be publishing, would the church choose this? What business does the church have getting involved in theories about 9/11? It makes it look like our church might be endorsing the book's ideas." Many Presbyterians, he added, were planning to boycott the publisher.[48]

James Berkley, the director of Presbyterian Action for Faith and Freedom, called WJK's decision to publish my book "laughable," "pathetic," and "kooky"[49] and said that it had damaged the image of Presbyterians.[50]

The Rev. Joan Gray, the moderator of the Presbyterian Church of America, said: "To me personally, and I am sure for the great majority of Presbyterians, the idea that the United States government engineered the 9/11 attacks is too over the top to be taken seriously."[51]

Westminster's President Defends the Book: Such attacks led Davis Perkins, the president and publisher of Westminster John Knox, to issue a defense, saying:

> In his preface to the controversial *Christian Faith and the Truth behind 9/11* . . . , David Ray Griffin writes "One of our main tasks as theologians is to deal with current events in light of the fact that our first allegiance must be to God, who created and loves all people—indeed all forms of life. If we believe that our political and military leaders are acting on the basis of policies that are

diametrically opposed to divine purposes, it is incumbent upon us to say so." At Westminster John Knox Press we share Griffin's primary allegiance and seek to encourage sustained, informed, and respectful dialogue about the most pressing issues of our times. Professor Griffin's thorough research and intellectually rigorous arguments have persuaded us that this book should have a place in that conversation, regardless of the conclusions readers come to accept.

Perkins thereby clearly said that for Westminster John Knox Press, allegiance to God must take priority over our allegiance to our political and military leaders.

Kenneth Godshall Responds to Pressure: But the Presbyterian Publishing Corporation's board of directors, in the face of mounting criticism from within the denomination, would not support Perkins. In an official statement, Kenneth Godshall, the chair of this board of directors, said:

> David Ray Griffin is a distinguished theologian who has published a number of books with PPC. This particular volume is not up to WJK editorial standards and not representative of the PPC publishing program.

What was wrong with this book?

> The book makes the extraordinary claim that the terrorist attacks on September 11, 2001 were orchestrated by the federal government and made to appear to be the work of al-Qaeda. . . . Griffin's theological reflections are helpful and timely. The Board believes the conspiracy theory is spurious and based on questionable research.[52]

So, the reason this book is "not up to WJK editorial standards" has nothing to do with its theology. The problem is only the book's claim that contradicts our nationalist faith. Godshall did not, of course, put it that way. He said that the board had concluded that the book was based on "questionable research."

But as I told the *Louisville Courier-Journal*, which contacted me about this:

> This [issue] is something I've worked on almost daily for years. . . . I doubt any of the . . . members of the board have spent nearly the time on it I have. They were really not in the position to make such a statement.

How did Godshall defend his charge? According to the *Courier-Journal*, he said "that Griffin failed to take into account rebuttals of his theories, such as one published by Popular Mechanics."[53]

But that was false. In 2005, *Popular Mechanics* magazine had published an article entitled "9/11: Debunking the Myths."[54] In my chapter on the destruction of the World Trade Center, I had stated:

> *Popular Mechanics* . . . completely ignores the suddenness, verticality, rapidity, and totality of the collapses as well as failing to mention the testimonies about molten steel, demolition rings, and the sounds of explosions.[55]

If you cannot explain why the buildings came straight down in virtually free fall, and you have to ignore part of the relevant evidence, you have not explained the collapses. Also, referring to the article by *Popular Mechanics* as "a spectacularly bad article," I pointed out some absurd claims this article made, after which I referred readers to two critiques in which it had been "effectively debunked."[56]

Accordingly, Godshall's claim that "Griffin failed to take into account rebuttals of his theories, such as one published by Popular Mechanics," was simply false.

Furthermore, at the time Godshall made his statement, I was writing *Debunking 9/11 Debunking*, the subtitle of which is: *An Answer to* Popular Mechanics *and Other Defenders of the Official Conspiracy Theory*. Had Godshall really wanted to know my response to the claims made by *Popular Mechanics*, I could have sent him my written response to its book, *Debunking 9/11 Myths*, which had come out a few months earlier. My response shows that not a single one if its main claims stands up to scrutiny. There are, of course, no reviews of my book in the mainstream press where one can see if reviewers have concurred. But if one reads the customer reviews of the *Popular Mechanics* book on Amazon.com, one will see that virtually all reviewers who have read both that book and mine say that I have thoroughly debunked it.

I have spent some time on this because the only support Godshall gave for his charge—that my book contained a "spurious" conspiracy theory based on "questionable research"—was his claim that I had not responded to the counterclaims of *Popular Mechanics*. The fact that Godshall had made no effort to determine the truth of this allegation suggests that his real reason for censuring my book was to placate members of his denomination—members who objected to Westminster John Knox's publication of my book solely because of its violation of their faith in America's goodness.

Godshall Removed Publishers: Godshall, moreover, did not merely censure my book and Westminster John Knox for publishing it. The two men at the press who made the decision to publish it were soon to depart.

According to the story in the *Louisville Courier-Journal*, "Godshall said no one would be disciplined for approving the book" and that "the board would continue to defend the editorial independence of the corporation."[57]

In fact, however, Godshall began micromanaging, so Davis Perkins, who was already angry at Godshall for having apologized for the publication of my book, resigned as president and publisher of Westminster John Knox to take another position. The very next week, Jack Keller, the vice president for publication, was fired.

What is the message? While Jack Keller was vice president for publishing at WJK, it had published several books by me. One of them, *God, Power, and Evil*, rejects the traditional doctrine of omnipotence. It even specifically criticizes this doctrine as held by John Calvin, the founding theologian of the Presbyterian Church. Another book explicitly denies that God can interrupt the world's normal causal relations, which means that there can be no miracles as traditionally understood and no infallibly inspired scriptures. But no one was fired for publishing these books. No one screamed that by publishing these books, the press was implying that the Presbyterian Church accepted these ideas.

The message to publishers at church presses is that they can publish books that are highly critical of traditional Christian doctrines without losing their jobs. But they had better not publish anything that challenges the idea that America is fundamentally good, the exceptional nation, because this is the one religious belief that cannot be challenged.[58]

Do we not here have a clear illustration of the fact that all too often, Christian faith is less important to Christians in America than their American faith? The evidence that 9/11 was an inside job, I have argued, is overwhelming to anyone with eyes to see, and Christian faith at its best serves to open people's eyes to this evidence. When Christian faith is subordinated to faith in American goodness, however, it becomes a blinding faith, producing Christians with eyes wide shut.

In working so long to expose the truth about 9/11, one of my central hopes has been that this exposure will lead American Christians to repent of this idolatrous subordination. And once Christians in our country see 9/11 for what it was—a pretext to extend the American empire in predominantly Muslim countries—I hope that they will realize that to be loyal to Jesus, who preached an anti-imperial gospel,[59] they will need to oppose American imperialism as strongly as they had opposed Nazi and Soviet imperialism.

9. WHEN STATE CRIMES AGAINST DEMOCRACY SUCCEED

As we saw in Chapter 4, a 2010 symposium in a leading social science journal argued that SCADs—State Crimes against Democracy—constitute a very important type of criminality. They are exceedingly important because SCADs, being "high crimes that attack democracy itself," have the "potential to subvert political institutions and entire governments."[1]

This recognition is important to the present book because these social scientists suggested that 9/11 was a SCAD. Indeed, they portrayed 9/11 as the most important contemporary instance of a suspected SCAD—with the adjective "suspected" meaning that there is good evidence for the belief that 9/11 was a state crime, although the state's involvement has thus far not been officially acknowledged (putting 9/11 in the same category as, for example, the Watergate break-in before the Nixon administration's involvement was confirmed by the US Senate).

I EVIDENCE FOR 9/11 AS A FALSE-FLAG ATTACK

With regard to the notion that there is "good evidence" for thinking of 9/11 as a SCAD, I have in this book summarized a portion of the evidence that points to 9/11 as having been a false-flag attack.

- Chapter 1 showed that Osama bin Laden was never indicted for 9/11 by the US Department of Justice, because the FBI had "no hard evidence connecting Bin Laden to 9/11."

- The FBI did try to prove that al-Qaeda hijacked the four 9/11 airliners, but all of the purported evidence, I argued, falls apart upon examination. Having dealt with most of this purported evidence in the first chapter, I devoted Chapter 5 to showing that the so-called "phone calls from the planes" were fabricated—as demonstrated most clearly in the calls to Deena Burnett.

- Chapters 2 through 4 showed that the official accounts of the "collapse" of the Twin Towers and WTC 7 imply several miracles, in the sense of violations of long-established laws of science.

- The sixth chapter showed that the 9/11 Commission—based on an interview of Cheney for a *Newsweek* article that appeared at the end of December 2001—contradicted what Cheney had acknowledged in his *Meet the Press* interview five days after 9/11: that he was already in the PEOC when he learned about the Pentagon attack. This chapter explained why, after Norman Mineta reported an interchange in the PEOC implying that Cheney had issued a stand-down order, the 9/11 Commission had to bury that story.

- Chapter 7 pointed out that, in addition to the Mineta-Cheney story, there is a long list of facts that show the official account of the Pentagon attack to be false. This list includes the fact that no al-Qaeda pilot, most emphatically Hani Hanjour, could have flown a 757 through the trajectory described by the AA 77 Flight Data Recorder, and also the fact that an al-Qaeda mastermind would not, for a number of reasons, have targeted Wedge 1.

There are, moreover, many reasons to consider the official account of 9/11 false that were not covered in the present book, such as:

- Just seven weeks before 9/11, the control of the World Trade Center was transferred from the Port Authority to Silverstein Properties. The arrangements stipulated that, in the event of a terrorist attack, Silverstein Properties, controlled by Larry Silverstein, would collect billions of dollars and also be freed from obligations.[2]

- Most of the steel that had supported the World Trade Center buildings was removed from Ground Zero before it could be studied, even though *Fire Engineering* said: "The destruction and removal of evidence must stop immediately."[3]

- The White House did everything it could to prevent an investigation into 9/11.[4]

- When such an investigation could be delayed no longer, the White House on November 27, 2002, appointed Henry Kissinger, arguably the worst possible choice for a truth-seeking commission, to be the chairman.[5] A *New York Times* editorial, in fact, suggested that the choice was "a clever maneuver by the White House to contain an investigation it has long opposed."[6]

- When the appointment of Kissinger did not work out—he refused to name his corporate clients as required[7]—the White House replaced him with former New Jersey Republican governor Thomas Kean, who knew absolutely nothing about Washington and national politics,[8] and Lee Hamilton, who had previously served as a Democratic "fixer" for Republican illegal operations (as reported in Chapter 3, above).

- The White House then managed to get the all-important position of the 9/11 Commission's executive director filled by Philip Zelikow, who was no better, for the hope of having an honest investigation, than Kissinger: He was virtually a member of the Bush administration, and he had written *National Security Strategy 2002*—which articulated the "Bush doctrine," according to which the United States was able to attack Iraq, although there was no evidence (as required by international law) that it was intending to attack the United States.[9]

- The White House then provided ridiculously inadequate funding for the 9/11 Commission, first giving only $3 million, after which it was finally raised to $15 million. By contrast, investigation of the Whitewater land deal in Arkansas, involving the Clintons, was allocated over $50 million,[10] and the investigation of the Challenger space shuttle disaster cost $175 million.[11] These contrasts suggest that "the most serious attack on the United States in its history" was far less important than these events.

These occurrences, especially when taken together and in conjunction with the evidence in Chapters 2 through 7, support the contention that 9/11 was a false-flag operation and hence a State Crime against Democracy.

II The Professionalization of the 9/11 Truth Movement

Further evidence that the official account of 9/11 is false is provided by the fact that thousands of professionals have joined organizations by signing petitions, which indicate their judgment that the official story is indeed false. In Chapter 2, we looked at examples of impressive members of two of these organizations: Scientists for 9/11 Truth and Architects and Engineers for 9/11 Truth. But there are many more.

Here are a few members of Intelligence Officers for 9/11 Truth:[12]

- Terrell E. Arnold, who served as an analyst in the US State Department's Office of Intelligence and Research, after which he became the Principal Deputy Director of the State Department's Office of Counterterrorism.

- William Christison, who had a 28-year career with the CIA, during which he became the National Intelligence Officer for Africa and South Asia, after which he became the Director of the CIA's Office of Regional and Political Analysis.

- Ray McGovern, 30-year Army Intelligence officer and CIA analyst, who prepared the *President's Daily Brief* for three presidents.

- Major General Albert Stubblebine, former Commanding General of US Army Intelligence and Security Command.

Here are some members of Journalists for 9/11 Truth:[13]

- Giulietto Chiesa, an Italian journalist who served for 19 years as a correspondent in Moscow, after which he became a member of the European Parliament and produced *Zero*, a documentary film about 9/11.

- Fiammetta Cucurnia, a journalist for one of Italy's leading newspapers, *La Repubblica*, who previously served for nine years as a correspondent in Moscow.

- Jean-Marie Molitor, the Paris-based director of three French magazines: *Minute*, *Monde & Vie*, and *Le Choc du mois*.

- Barrie Zwicker was a reporter for the *Detroit News*, the *Toronto*

Star, and the *Globe and Mail*, after which he became a commentator for Vision TV in Toronto.

Here are a few members of Lawyers for 9/11 Truth:[14]

- Dennis Cunningham, an attorney, was involved in legal cases arising from the Attica Prison rebellion and the 2002 prosecution of FBI agents and police officers who had framed Earth First! activists.

- Ferdinando Imposimato, formerly the senior investigative judge presiding over the trials dealing with the assassination of President Aldo Moro and the attempted assassination of Pope John Paul II.

- Dr. Christopher Pollman, Professor of Law at Université Paul Verlaine–Metz (France), who in 2001-02 was a Visiting Fellow at Harvard Law School.

- William Veale, former Chief Assistant Public Defender of Contra Costa County in California, who has also taught at the University of California School of Law.

- Dr. Burns Weston, Professor Emeritus of Law at the University of Iowa.

Here are a few members of Medical Professionals for 9/11 Truth.[15]

- Dr. Mary Ellen Bradshaw, former Chief of the Bureau of School Health Services in the US Department of Public Health, and former President of the American Association of Public Health Physicians.

- Dr. Steven Jonas, professor at Stony Brook University's School of Medicine and fellow of the New York Academy of Medicine and of the Royal Society of Medicine.

- Dr. E. J. Muñoz-Martínez, Professor and Researcher in the Department of Physiology, Biophysics, and Neuroscience of the Center for Research and Advanced Studies in the National Polytechnic Institute in Mexico City, and twice president of the Mexican Society of Physiological Sciences.

- Dr. Jonathan B. Weisbuch, Past President and Past Vice President, American Association of Public Health Physicians (AAPHP), and AAPHP's representative to the American Medical Association.

Here are a few members of Pilots for 9/11 Truth:[16]

- Captain Ross "Rusty" Aimer, retired from a 40-year career as a pilot for six airlines, including United Airlines, for which he flew Boeing 757s and 767s.

- Major Jon I. Fox, a former Marine Corps fighter pilot, with special training in interceptions, after which he had a 35-year commercial aviation career.

- John Lear, retired from a 40-year career, during which he flew over 100 types of planes. Besides holding every certificate offered by the FAA, he held 17 world records, and received the PATCO award for outstanding airmanship in 1968.

- Capt. Russ Wittenberg, who was a fighter pilot with over 100 combat missions, after which he had a 35-year career as a commercial pilot, flying the Boeing 757, 767, and 777.

Here are a few members of Political Leaders for 9/11 Truth.[17]

- Berit Ås, a former member of the Norwegian Parliament, was also Professor of Social Psychology at the University of Oslo.

- Dr. Andreas von Bülow, former State Secretary in the Federal Ministry of Defense, West Germany, was also the former Minister of Research and Technology.

- Yukihisa Fujita is a member of the House of Councilors (parallel to the US Senate) in the National Diet of Japan.

- Dr. Sergey Ivanovic Kolesnikov, who has been named a Distinguished Scientist of Russia, is a member of the State Duma and the former Deputy Director of the Russian Academy of Medical Sciences.

- Michael Meacher, a member of the British Parliament, has served as the Minister of State for the Environment.

Here are a few members of Religious Leaders for 9/11 Truth (in addition to me):[18]

- Dr. John B. Cobb, Jr., Professor Emeritus of Theology at Claremont School of Theology (California), and the author of books on religious pluralism, economic theory (with ecological economist Herman Daly), and evolutionary theory.

- Dr. Joseph C. Hough, Jr., served as the academic dean of the Claremont School of Theology and the Vanderbilt Divinity School and as the president of Union Theological Seminary.

- Dr. Gene Reeves, after serving as the dean and president of the Meadville/Lombard Theological School in Chicago, taught at Rikkyo University in Tokyo and provided a new translation of the Lotus Sutra.

Here are a few members of Veterans for 9/11 Truth.[19]

- Capt. Daniel Davis, a former US Army Air Defense Officer and NORAD Tac Director, he was decorated with the Bronze Star and the Soldiers Medal for bravery under fire in Vietnam.

- Commander Ralph Kolstad, retired from a 20-year career in the US Navy, where he was an Air Combat Instructor at the US Navy Fighter Weapons School (Topgun).

- Lt. Col. and Dr. Karen U. Kwiatkowski, retired from a 20-year career in the US Air Force, where she was a Political-Military Affairs Officer in the Office of the Secretary of Defense.

- Lt. Col. Shelton F. Lankford had a 20-year career in the US Marine Corps, where he received the Distinguished Flying Cross and 32 Air Medals.

- Col. Ronald D. Ray, retired from a career in the US Marine Corps, during which he received a Bronze Star, a Purple Heart, and two Silver Stars for service in Vietnam, and served as Deputy Assistant Secretary of Defense.

Finally, with regard to Firefighters for 9/11 Truth,[20] I will, rather than giving a list of members, quote extracts from a statement by its founder, Erik Lawyer:

> I am currently a full time firefighter, and have been assigned to Ladder 3 in the City of Seattle for the last 13 years. . . . I have 20 years experience in Emergency Services. . . . I graduated with a Bachelor's of Science in Mathematics . . . , with 2 years of elective Engineering courses. . . . I first visited Ground Zero in October of 2001 . . . . I vividly remember the anger I felt, the intense desire for vengeance. . . . I've been a conservative my entire life. . . . So when conspiracy theories quickly surfaced. . . , I chalked it up to their political beliefs and bitterness towards the Republican President. . . . I told conspiracy theorists . . . that they were insane if they thought anyone other than the terrorists did this. . . . Fast forward to March of 2008. A great friend of mine with a Business degree from West Point, as conservative and non-conspiratorial as they get, came over one night. . . . He provided some disconcerting evidence. . . . So, I looked at both sides and quickly noticed a pattern. On one side, the general media ignores some of the most compelling evidence that contradicts the "official" story. On the other side, science based conspiracy sites . . . , along with the experience based sites . . . , fully explore the evidence. . . . [M]y friends . . . thought I had lost my mind . . . . Through my research I learned that many mainstream people . . . doubt the "official" story. Yet the media still treats "Truth" seekers like they have a mental disorder. . . . To be honest, I was asleep at the wheel, and relied on what I was being told by mainstream media.[21]

Mainstream opinion-makers commonly describe members of the 9/11 Truth Movement as nuts, cranks, and idiots, as we saw in Chapters 2 and 8. The *New York Times* reviewer of Jonathan Kay's book even said, in a passage dealing with "what conspiracy theorists believe," that "even to dignify it with the word 'theory' is probably to grant them more legitimacy than they deserve."[22] That kind of snide remark may seem justified to many readers, as long as the members of the movement are simply referred to as "Truthers." But that kind of remark would seem strange about architects, engineers, intelligence officers, journalists, lawyers, medical professionals, political leaders, religious leaders, and scientists—which can explain why the movement's detractors in the press generally refer simply to "Truthers," failing to point out that the people lumped together under this name are people such as the ones in the above lists of names, along with the architects, engineers, and scientists in Chapter 2.

III Why the 9/11 Crime Has Succeeded: Psychological and Sociological Reasons

Having reviewed the fact that there is overwhelming evidence that the official story about 9/11 is false, including the fact that thousands of respected professionals have publicly declared their disbelief in that story, I now turn to the question of how, in the face of such evidence, the official story not only arose but has continued to hold the allegiance of the majority of the people (at least in this country). I will name five factors:

1. Shock and Rallying around the Flag

When the 9/11 attacks occurred, most Americans responded with shock. Only a few people were able from the first to raise critical questions. Most felt an upsurge of patriotism, and many shared Erik Lawyer's "intense desire for vengeance." In the intervening decade, many Americans have become critical of what we were told about 9/11. But it took many years: For Richard Gage, who had been a conservative Republican, this critical evaluation did not begin until 2006. For Erik Lawyer, it did not begin until 2008. In both cases, it was a chance encounter that started their critical reevaluation. For many, perhaps most, Americans, their views of 9/11 have remained essentially the same since 2001.

2. Trust the President

Most Americans tend to believe the president. At the time of 9/11, especially, it did not occur to most people to wonder if he was telling the truth about the attacks. In the intervening years, many Americans became much more suspicious of claims by the president and the vice president, especially as they learned that the White House, wanting to attack Iraq, had misled the American people with regard to "weapons of mass destruction." But a strong tendency to "take the President's word" continues. The views of Democrats would have changed, to be sure, if Barack Obama, after becoming the new president, had expressed doubt about the official story or even failed to reaffirm the story as told by the Bush-Cheney White House. But, given the fact that Obama has completely endorsed that story, most Democrats as well as other Americans maintain the official story about 9/11 because they "trust the President."

3. Nationalist Faith

Chapter 8 was devoted to one of the most powerful factors leading American citizens, even if they have come to believe that Bush and/or Obama are not trustworthy, to believe what they have said about 9/11. According to this "nationalist faith," our political leaders might sometimes lie and do immoral things, but they would not do anything *terribly* evil, something that would challenge the fundamental goodness of our country. If citizens who accept this faith learn of good evidence that 9/11 was an inside job, however, they are confronted with an enormous case of what psychologists call "cognitive dissonance." Judge Andrew Napolitano expressed this problem perfectly in his statement quoted in Chapter 4. On the one hand, referring to the question whether the US government would have itself brought down the World Trade Center, Napolitano said: "I think that it is highly unlikely that the government would do anything nefarious on a scale of this epic nature." On the other hand, he said: "[B]uilding [7] does appear to come down in a way that is reminiscent of a controlled demolition."[23] The following week, he made an even more definitive statement, saying: "It's hard for me to believe that it came down by itself."[24] Napolitano is a judge, who has been trained to consider the evidence, no matter what his personal beliefs might be. But in many Americans, their nationalist faith enables them "to believe that [Building 7] came down by itself."

4. The Big Lie

In Chapter 3, we looked at the psychological dynamic of the "Big Lie." For many Americans, this dynamic probably operates in conjunction with nationalist faith. But it can be so powerful that even people who have left behind the myth of American goodness—people such as Bill Moyers and Robert Parry—can be persuaded by the Big Lie to maintain their belief in the Bush-Cheney story about what happened on 9/11. To repeat Hitler's words:

> [Ordinary people] more readily fall victims to the big lie than the small lie, since they themselves often tell small lies in little matters but would be ashamed to resort to large-scale falsehoods. It would never come into their heads to fabricate colossal untruths, and they would not believe that others could have the impudence to distort the truth so infamously.[25]

I know the power of this dynamic, having fallen victim to it myself. Although I disliked and distrusted Bush and Cheney and thought their "election" to have been a disaster for our country, I dismissed the suggestion, when I first heard it, that they had either allowed or engineered the 9/11 attacks. This would have been *so* evil, I said, that even Bush and Cheney would not have done it.

5. The Power of Salary and Status

Upton Sinclair said something that is as true today as it was when he wrote it in 1935: "It is difficult to get a man to understand something, when his salary depends upon his *not* understanding it!"[26] In many cases, of course, people merely *pretend* to believe the official story about 9/11 in order to keep their jobs.

One likely example is provided by Van Romero, a demolitions expert who became the vice president for research and development for the New Mexico Institute of Mining and Technology. On 9/11, Romero said that there must have been "explosive devices inside the buildings that caused the towers to collapse," because the collapses appeared "too methodical" to have been a chance result of airplanes colliding with the buildings. "It would be difficult for something from the plane to trigger an event like that."[27] But ten days later, Romero stated that he now believed that "there were no explosives in the World Trade Center towers."[28] Romero claimed that he had, in the earlier statement, been misquoted; but an examination shows this to be untrue.[29] Romero was responsible for obtaining government grants for his institute, and stories in 2002 and 2003 show that by then he had become very successful.[30] It seems that Romero realized that, unless he reversed his position on the collapse of the towers, his career would suffer a reversal of fortune.

Another public person who evidently knew the truth but did not speak out was involved in the story about Charles Lewis (reported in Chapter 7), who had worked on security systems at LAX. According to Lewis, he told Captain LaPonda Fitchpatrick of the Los Angeles Airport Police, who was head of Security in the Airport Operations Area, what he had heard. Lewis wrote: "I told her that I heard everything Security was discussing on 9/11 at Guard Post II and that I did not see how the attacks could have succeeded without inside participation. She replied that LAX security was well aware that 9/11 was an inside job."[31]

Assuming that our suspicion about Romero is correct, and that Fitchpatrick did say what Lewis reported, then Romero and Fitchpatrick can serve as examples of the likely hundreds of people in business and civil service who know the official story to be false—additional examples might include members of the Fire Department of New York who reported in their oral histories that explosions went off in the Twin Towers—but who have, to protect their positions, remained silent in public.

However, although many people have concealed their true beliefs about 9/11, in many other cases Sinclair's statement is literally true—that it is difficult for people to understand something, when their salary and status depend upon their *not* understanding it. For example, imagine a woman who has landed her dream job with a major newspaper. As she becomes aware of the 9/11 Truth Movement, she becomes simultaneously aware that, if reporters were to file stories about the movement expressing understanding for its position, they would soon be fired. But she would not be able to live with herself if she were pretending to accept the official story while secretly accepting the 9/11 Truth Movement's position. She avoids this dilemma by consciously accepting the orthodox view, keeping any doubts safely in the unconscious level of her mind.

IV WHY THE 9/11 CRIME HAS SUCCEEDED: THE PRESS

I will now focus on ways in which the press has contributed to the fact that the truth concerning the attacks has not been publicly unmasked. Indeed, aside from the actual perpetrators of the false-flag attacks and their cover-up artists, there are good reasons to see the press as primarily responsible, by virtue of the fact that the media, rather than giving the public the available facts, have concealed such facts.

SIBEL EDMONDS AND SEYMOUR HERSH

Sibel Edmonds offered, at the risk of going to prison (because of a gag order), to tell a major US television network what she had learned about illegal operations while working as a translator for the FBI. But no network accepted her offer. She later gave some of her information to London's *Sunday Times*. The result was an explosive story,[32] which Chris Floyd called "one of the most important stories of the last quarter-century."[33] Dave Lindorff wrote that "there is enough in just this one *London Times* story to keep an army of investigative reporters busy for years."[34] But America's mainstream press ignored it.[35] Edmonds, not mincing words about the press's responsibilities, said in 2007:

> The only way they got away with [Executive Branch crimes] was because of the mainstream media. They are the biggest culprit for the state of our country. Whether it's Iraq, or torture or the NSA wiretapping . . . these people are the real culprit.[36]

That same year, Seymour Hersh said:

> All of the institutions we thought would protect us—particularly the press, but also the military, the bureaucracy, the Congress—they have failed. The . . . jury's not in yet on the courts. So all the things that we expect would normally carry us through didn't. The biggest failure, I would argue, is the press.[37]

2. PAUL CRAIG ROBERTS: AN ORWELLIAN TREATMENT OF "CONSPIRACY THEORY"

Having introduced the discussion of the press's responsibility by means of these brief statements by Edmonds and Hersh, I will devote most of the remainder of this section to a fascinating article by Paul Craig Roberts. Formerly an associate editor of the *Wall Street Journal* and a contributing editor for *National Review*, Roberts knows something about the publishing world. And we might expect him, with his conservative credentials (he is often considered the father of "Reaganomics"), to endorse the official story of 9/11. But anyone who expected this would be quite surprised by his recent essay "9/11 and the Orwellian Redefinition of 'Conspiracy Theory.'"

Conspiracy Theory: In talking about an "Orwellian redefinition," Roberts made a point similar to one I made in Chapter 8: that whereas a "conspiracy theory" in the normal (generic) sense of the term is a secret agreement to do something illegal, supporters of the government's position on 9/11, exploiting the recently cultivated sense that conspiracy theories are by nature ludicrous, use the term "conspiracy theory" to apply only to the view that 9/11 was an inside job. In developing his version of this distinction, Roberts wrote:

> A "conspiracy theory" no longer means an event explained by a conspiracy. Instead, it now means any explanation, or even a fact, that is out of step with the government's explanation.

In other words, Roberts said, the *New York Times* tends to use the term "conspiracy theory" for "news and opinions that the *New York Times* does not report and the US government does not endorse." So, even though what is being said may be perfectly true, Roberts stated, this "truth is redefined as conspiracy theory, by which is meant an absurd and laughable explanation that we should ignore." The *Times* "protects" us from certain truths, that is, by calling them "conspiracy theories." The purest example of how Americans are shielded from truth, Roberts suggested,

> is the media's (including many Internet sites') response to the large number of professionals who find the official explanation of September 11, 2001 inconsistent with everything they, as experts, know about physics, chemistry, structural engineering, architecture, fires, structural damage, the piloting of airplanes, the security procedures of the United States, NORAD's capabilities, air traffic control, airport security, and other matters. These experts, numbering in the thousands, have been shouted down by know-nothings in the media who brand the experts as "conspiracy theorists."[38]

To drive home the way in which the media have brought about an Orwellian reversal, Roberts pointed out that, given the way in which the term "conspiracy theory" has traditionally been understood, the official account of 9/11 involves an extraordinarily extravagant conspiracy theory. It is a conspiracy theory because the claim is that Osama bin Laden and other al-Qaeda leaders, such as Khalid Sheikh Mohammed, conspired with 19 young Muslim Arabs to orchestrate the 9/11 attacks. In explaining how this conspiracy was especially *extravagant*, Roberts wrote:

> [These] young Muslim Arabs . . . outwitted not only the CIA and the FBI, but also all 16 US intelligence agencies and all intelligence agencies of US allies. . . . In addition [they] outwitted the National Security Council, the State Department, NORAD, airport security four times in the same hour on the same morning . . . , caused the US Air Force to be unable to launch interceptor aircraft, and caused three well-built steel-structured buildings, including one not hit by an airplane, to fail suddenly in a few seconds as a result of limited structural damage and small, short-lived, low-temperature fires that burned on a few floors.[39]

However, whereas by normal standards this is a conspiracy theory, and a quite extravagant one at that, the mainstream media regard it as sober truth, and anyone who doubts it is excluded from expressing their views about it on ABC, CBS, NBC, Fox, CNN, and the "ultra liberal" MSNBC, and on the opinion pages of the *New York Times*, the *Washington Post*, and any other newspapers that want access to policy-makers. Roberts wrote:

> [Although] the official explanation endorsed by the official media is the most extravagant conspiracy theory in human history. . . , anyone who doubts this improbable conspiracy theory is defined into irrelevance by the obedient media.

9/11, Scientific Principles, and Kooks: But surely, we must think, the *New York Times* ridicules biblical fundamentalists who reject cosmic, geological, and biological evolution on the basis of their interpretation of the Bible. Given the fact that the *Times* takes science as the standard of truth on the question of the age of the earth, it must also take science as the standard of truth with regard to the events that happened on 9/11—at least in the sense that no political documents can contradict well-established scientific principles. But, Roberts indicated, this is not so:

> Anyone who believes an architect, structural engineer, or demolition expert who says that the videos show that the buildings are blowing up, not falling down, anyone who believes a Ph.D. physicist who says that the official explanation is inconsistent with known laws of physics, anyone who believes expert pilots who testify that non-pilots or poorly-qualified pilots cannot fly airplanes in such maneuvers, any-one who believes the 100 or more first-responders who testify that they not only heard explosions in the towers but personally experi-enced explosions, anyone who believes University of Copenhagen nano-chemist Niels Harrit who reports finding unreacted nano-thermite in dust samples from the WTC towers, anyone who is con-vinced by experts instead of by propaganda is dismissed as a kook.

We are familiar with, and properly amused by, biblical fundamentalists—people who measure truth, even about scientific matters, by documents written thousands of years ago. But what we now have is *9/11 fundamentalism*—my term, not Roberts'—according to which the truth about what happened on September 11, 2001, is to be settled by assertions made by the Bush-Cheney administration. So if this administration, along with its appointed commission, declared that the

World Trade Center was brought down by airplanes, then that is "truth," no matter what principles of physics and chemistry may say, and anyone who doubts this truth is a "kook." Roberts continued:

> [A]ctual facts and true explanations have been relegated to the realm of kookiness. Only people who believe lies are socially approved and accepted as patriotic citizens.

Moreover, Roberts stated, it is not merely that writers and reporters are not allowed to point out that the official account of the World Trade Center's destruction violates various scientific principles. Rather,

> a writer or newscaster is not even permitted to report the findings of 9/11 skeptics. . . . Everyone in the US print and TV media knows that he/she will be instantly fired if they report Harrit's findings, even with a laugh. Thus, although Harrit has reported his findings on European television and has lectured widely on his findings in Canadian universities, the fact that he and the international scientific research team that he led found unreacted nano-thermite in the WTC dust and have offered samples to other scientists to examine has to my knowledge never been reported in the American media.

A Terrified HuffPost Reporter: Lest people suspect that Roberts has exaggerated the extent of the media's censorship of 9/11 discussion, he reported an incident that illustrates the ludicrous degree to which the media have instilled a fear of publishing or broadcasting anything that might be taken as a disagreement with the official story. Roberts wrote:

> I myself had experience with a Huffington Post reporter who was keen to interview a Reagan presidential appointee who was in disagreement with the Republican wars in the Middle East. After he published the interview that I provided at his request, he was terrified to learn that I had reported findings of 9/11 investigators. To protect his career, he quickly inserted on the online interview that my views on the Iraq and Afghanistan invasions could be dismissed as I had reported unacceptable findings about 9/11.[40]

3. The Extraordinary Episode at Fox News

In the above discussion, I included Fox News in the list of television networks that do not allow discussions of evidence against the official view. Indeed, Fox News has been the network that has in general offered the greatest support for the official view. But an unusual exception to this policy occurred on Fox News in late 2010.

As we saw in the fourth chapter, two commentators at Fox News, after at least one of them—Geraldo Rivera—had previously maligned the 9/11 Truth Movement, took seriously the contention that WTC 7 was professionally demolished. Rivera's change of mind evidently occurred after he became aware, due to a Building What? ad, that there is a professional organization, Architects and Engineers for 9/11 Truth, containing over a thousand members supporting this view.

If then—to let our imaginations soar—Geraldo Rivera had prepared reports about members of other professional 9/11 organizations—such as firefighters, intelligence officers, journalists, lawyers, and scientists—this development could have turned much of the country around. Actually, however, if Rivera had insisted on going forward with such a story, he would have no longer worked for Fox News. The events, of course, did not move in that direction. But the issue of whether the two commentators should be fired did arise.

As mentioned in Chapter 4, Rivera's program on Building 7 inspired another Fox commentator, Judge Andrew Napolitano, to speak up, and he went even further, saying about this building: "It's hard for me to believe that it came down by itself. . . . It couldn't possibly have been done the way the government told us."[41]

This produced predictably negative responses from both conservative and liberal commentators.[42] But the most interesting comment came from former MSNBC commentator Keith Olbermann, who argued (with irony) that, given the stance that Fox News has taken toward "Truthers" in the past—Glenn Beck and Sean Hannity had both insisted that Van Jones should be fired for having signed a petition calling for a new investigation of the 9/11 attacks—Fox chief Roger Ailes must, for the sake of consistency, fire Napolitano.[43]

In any case, it should not be thought that what I have here called "the extraordinary episode at Fox News" disproves the picture of the media painted above with the aid of Paul Craig Roberts. What occurred at Fox *was* simply an "episode": Rivera and Napolitano did not continue to suggest that WTC 7 was brought down by explosives. Although Ailes obviously did not want to chastise two of his stars in public, he likely did let them know that, unless they said no more about the matter, one or both of them would be let go.

V Why the 9/11 Crime Has Succeeded:
The Academy

As Roberts has shown, the press, in its determination to defend the official account of 9/11, has become ludicrous, censoring all criticisms of the official account and even endorsing claims that contradict basic scientific principles. The press has employed a 9/11 fundamentalism that is no less absurd than biblical fundamentalism, to which it sees itself as superior. However, the press has always combined genuine information and, especially with respect to national security, propaganda. We are right to be disappointed, even disgusted, with the depths to which the mainstream press has fallen.

But it is the academy, above all the university, that has the primary responsibility to defend truth, especially in relation to important societal issues. There has been no more important issue than 9/11 in this century. And yet the academy has devoted virtually no attention to the apparent contradictions of the official account with scientific principles.

1. The Failure to Protest the Dismissal of Steven Jones
In Chapter 4, I referred to an essay, written by Professor Matthew Witt, which criticized the academy for its failure to protest the treatment of a physics professor, Steven Jones, who was forced out of his university teaching position "for merely reminding the world that physical laws, about which *there is no dissent whatsoever*, contradict the official theory of the World Trade Center Towers' collapse."[44]

As we saw in Chapter 2, there is indeed no dissent about the physical principles involved. No physics department would claim, for example, that a steel-framed high-rise building could be caused to come down in free fall. No physics department would say that, if such a building was somehow brought down by fire, its direction could be changed in mid-air. And no physics department would agree that a hydrocarbon fire could melt steel and even molybdenum.

Normally, university faculties take very seriously the principle of academic freedom. They normally defend any senior faculty members who appear to have been dismissed because their administrations disagree with their research. The faculties would protest even more strongly if professors are being forced out for political reasons. In the case of Steven Jones, there was absolutely no scientific disagreement.

His university, Brigham Young University, supported the Bush administration and hence wanted him out because his research implied that the Bush administration's claims about the World Trade Center were untrue.

So why did the academic world allow Jones to be dismissed without protest? It would appear that the academy was intimidated. And, given the fact that the academic world did not rally to Jones' defense, this set a precedent, which likely led many other academics to remain silent about their own reasons for disagreeing with the official view.

2. THE FAILURE OF PROFESSORS OF ARCHITECTURE AND ENGINEERING

Matthew Witt, in pointing out that the statements by Jones were based on principles about which there is no dissent, compared Newton's laws, such as the conservation of energy, with George Orwell's "secret doctrine that 2 + 2 = 4."[45] Although neither the press nor the academy denies that Newton's laws apply to the world of large objects, such as buildings, they both *effectively* deny that they applied to the World Trade Center buildings on September 11, 2001. Whereas the press did this by preventing people from pointing out conflicts between physical laws and the official account, the academy effectively denied that Newton's laws applied to the World Trade Center by failing, in these ten years, to hold any significant academic discussions as to whether the official account of the destruction of the World Trade Center is consistent with physical principles.

Such discussions are necessary because the official theory of the destruction of the three World Trade Center towers has serious implications for the foundations of science and engineering. Witt pointed out that, if NIST's explanation "provides the most robust account of the Towers' collapse, based on known science," then some previously accepted physical laws would need to be revised:

> [These laws] would have to succumb, at some point, to the theoretical claims purported to explain the Towers' collapse: New laws determining when steel melts and the phases at which such material loses its tensile strength would have at some point to replace existing science-based presumptions.[46]

This revision of physical laws would also have practical implications for building codes: "[T]he specifications of design for all skyscrapers *ought*, in the public interest, to be subjected to major review." The acceptance of NIST's account, therefore, creates an "obvious crisis," which should be evoking scientific and practical responses.[47]

With regard to the *practical* crisis that should have been evoked by NIST's report on WTC 7, this was previously addressed by four of the September 11th Advocates (a.k.a. the "Jersey Girls") in a statement released in September 2008, after the publication of NIST's report on WTC 7. They wrote:

> Over the past seven years, the Families of the 9/11 Victims have been repeatedly told by fire experts, engineers and architects that we should NOT FOCUS our efforts on advocating for building and fire code changes based on the collapse of the WTC 1 and 2 towers. We were continuously reminded that the crashing of airplanes into buildings was a unique event. Additionally, we were told that the design and construction of WTC Towers 1 and 2 was unique and that there were no other buildings of that particular height or design in the world. We were repeatedly told that the key was WTC 7 since this building was of conventional design and height, yet it too collapsed without the unique event of an airplane striking it. . . .
>
> Dr. Shyam Sunder of NIST . . . stated that WTC 7 met all New York City codes. Yet, WTC 7 is the first steel high-rise building of traditional construction in the United States—and the world, to completely collapse as a result of fire. According to . . . Dr. Sunder, "there were no flaws with the construction of the building."
>
> We don't know how the rest of the country is feeling about this news, but we are very scared! These findings suggest that ANY EXISTING building is prone to a progressive collapse if a fire should start and the sprinkler system fails for whatever reason. . . .
>
> The ultimate purpose of advocating for the $16 million to have NIST study this event was to determine how to make buildings safer in the future. If we are now to believe that any skyscraper is subject to total collapse from fire, why isn't NIST emphasizing the impact on EXISTING buildings? . . . NIST needs to . . . provide guidance for EXISTING buildings.
>
> NIST should put the most important conclusion in plain English and announce it to the entire country: UNCONTROLLED FIRES IN HIGH-RISE BUILDINGS CAN LEAD TO THEIR TOTAL COLLAPSE. . . . NIST must address this dangerous issue immediately. The future safety of the public and the fire services hangs in the balance."[48]

Like the SCADs symposium, this brilliant piece of satire makes clear that NIST's explanation of WTC 7's collapse should have created a crisis. Why did NIST, after releasing its report on WTC 7—according to which this flawless steel-framed building was brought down by an ordinary building fire—not alert the general public to the possibility that other steel-framed buildings may be caused to collapse entirely from fire?

The reason is that NIST knew full well that WTC 7 was *not* brought down with ordinary building fires. Knowing its fire theory to be a lie, NIST did only what it needed to do: issue its report. It was not about to try to convince people around the country—and around the world—that other steel-framed buildings were liable to be brought down by fires.

In any case, the NIST report should have been discussed immediately by the academy, especially by professors of architecture and engineering. They should have asked NIST:

How is this conceivable—that a steel-framed building, one that met the building codes and was not weakened by any flaws, was—for the first time in history—brought down by fire? And how is it conceivable that this building came down in free fall for over 2 seconds—an occurrence that normally could happen only through the use of explosives? Given these facts, must we not conclude that the building was brought down by controlled demolition, and that you, NIST, know this but cannot say it for political reasons?

Why have universities not raised these rather obvious questions? It appears that they have been intimidated, perhaps partly by fear of being accused of "accepting conspiracy theories," and partly by fear of losing government funding.

VI Because the 9/11 Crime Has Succeeded Thus Far

This book's subtitle, *When State Crimes against Democracy Succeed*, suggests that such crimes have serious consequences. And the fact that the 9/11 crime succeeded has indeed produced serious consequences.

1. Wars

The gravest undesirable result has been the wars that were allowed by the fact that the 9/11 false-flag attack was not exposed within the first month—even though it should have been exposed within a few days.

This failure allowed the US attack on Afghanistan to get started. And once US wars get started, it seems almost impossible (for various reasons) to get them stopped. This war, which is now in its tenth year, has resulted in an enormous number of Afghani deaths, with estimates running from a few hundred thousand to over four million.[49]

Moreover, the fact that the 9/11 crime was still not exposed by the end of 2002 allowed the Bush-Cheney administration to use 9/11 as a pretext to attack Iraq. Dr. Gideon Polya, who estimated the number of Afghani deaths at 4.5 million by early 2010, put the figure for Iraqi deaths at 2.3 million in 2009.[50]

Wars, besides being difficult to stop, also lead to other wars. At some point, the "Afghan war" became the "Af-Pak war," as the United States military started fighting in Pakistan, usually with drones. (In earlier decades, the Vietnam war expanded into Laos and Cambodia, all of these wars justified in the name of fighting "Communism.") Also, in addition to its wars in these three Muslim countries—Afghanistan, Iraq, and Pakistan—the United States has been fighting—justified mainly by 9/11—in Libya, Yemen, and Somalia (with the fighting in Libya alone costing $10 million a day). (The way in which all of America's wars are regarded as justified by 9/11 was illustrated by Secretary of Defense Leon Panetta's statement to American troops in Baghdad in July 2011: "The reason you guys are here is because of 9/11. The US got attacked and 3,000 human beings got killed because of Al-Qaeda."[51])

Besides the deaths—and whatever the actual figures, there has been an *enormous* amount of death in both countries—there have been countless numbers of peoples in both countries who have been permanently injured.

The costs to the United States have also been great, although much lower in terms of deaths, with roughly 1,500 Americans killed in Afghanistan and 4,500 in Iraq. But the costs also include the financial costs, which are staggering. According to a June 2011 report by Brown University's Watson Institute for International Studies: "The final bill" for the total cost of the wars in Iraq, Afghanistan, and Pakistan, said Reuters, "will run at least $3.8 trillion and could reach as high as $4.4 trillion."[52]

Absurdly, at a time when steps are being made to save a few billion dollars a year by cutting back on benefits and services to the poor, the Afghan war is costing the United States $300 million every day.[53]

2. The Assault on the US Constitution

Another major effect of 9/11, as a crime against democracy, is that the attacks have been used as a pretext to weaken the US Constitution. A central aim of the authors of the Constitution was to avoid a king who could single-handedly take the nation to war. But 9/11 was used during the Bush-Cheney years to move toward an "imperial presidency," and this movement has not been reversed during the first years of the Obama presidency.

Constitutional scholar Louis Fisher, in his 2008 book *The Constitution and 9/11*, has discussed various policies through which 9/11 has been used to replace much of the Constitution with policies of an imperial presidency. Fisher discusses a range of such policies, including:

- Military tribunals;
- Secret tribunals;
- Extraordinary rendition;
- Warrantless surveillance;
- Justification of torture;
- State secrets privilege;
- Suspension of habeas corpus; and
- The authority of the president to initiate war.[54]

Each of these points constitutes a serious restriction on the claim that the United States is a democratic system. These policies, taken together, leave us with a very crippled form of democracy.

Conclusion

It is impossible to see, apart from revealing the truth about 9/11, how American political life could ever again become more than a hollow shell of democracy. The events on 9/11 and the reports following it—especially *The 9/11 Commission Report* and the NIST reports on the Twin Towers and WTC 7—have been extremely effective attacks on the American democratic system. The effectiveness of these reports has been magnified by the refusal of the press, the academy, and the religious institutions to deal with the contradictions and provably false claims in these reports.

VII Overcoming the Success of the 9/11 Crime against Democracy

Although the 9/11 crime against democracy has been successful for ten years, there is no reason to assume that this success will be permanent. The evidence is all on the side of the 9/11 Truth Movement. Its case is so strong, while that for the government is so weak, that the government can uphold its position only by maintaining pressure to exclude spokespersons for the 9/11 Truth Movement from the mainstream media, while continuing to fill the media with false characterizations of this movement and lies about the facts. The movement itself has, moreover, continued to get stronger, now having thousands of professional members and a dozen 9/11 professional organizations.

Although the 9/11 Truth Movement does have truth on its side—even though the mainstream media, employing another Orwellian reversal, claims that "Truthers" are liars—this will not be enough: Having the truth is a necessary, but not a sufficient, condition for victory. The 9/11 crime has been a truly *enormous* crime, involving many branches of government and dozens of powerful people with reputations to protect. Most of all, the reputation of America itself is at stake. Its reputation may be considered the ultimate example of being "too big to fail." So most of our country's "wise ones"—if there are any left—would surely counsel that any attempt to reveal and prosecute the crime, to restore America's good name, would be futile.

But as a wise one of a previous age said, "a journey of a thousand miles begins with a single step." The 9/11 Truth Movement has taken a few steps in the first decade of the 9/11 era: forming 9/11 groups in cities throughout the United States and many other countries; educating millions of people in the United States and globally; creating books and websites in which the evidence is readily available; creating many 9/11 professional organizations; and establishing consensus on the best evidence against the official account of 9/11.[55]

Having taken those steps, it is now time for the movement to take some additional steps. I will here suggest two possibilities.

1. Insiders Willing to Speak Up

The movement is always greatly strengthened when people who were in some respect "on the inside" decide to speak up.

Two Examples from Earlier Years

Kevin Ryan: Now one of the leading scientists of the 9/11 Truth Movement, Kevin Ryan until 2004 had been the site manager at Environmental Health Laboratories, a division of Underwriters Laboratories (UL). He became a whistleblower by virtue of allowing a letter that he had written to Frank Gayle, the deputy chief of NIST's metallurgy division, to become public. The occasion for Ryan's letter was a conflict between an advance summary of NIST's forthcoming report about the collapse of the World Trade Center, on the one hand, and the findings of a NIST team that had been led by Gayle, on the other hand. Gayle's team, Ryan was aware, had said in 2003 that the steel in the Twin Towers "was probably exposed to temperatures of only about 500°F (250°C)," so that NIST could "rule out weak steel as a contributing factor in the collapse." However, the advance report of the NIST report seemed to ignore Gayle's findings, suggesting instead that, in spite of Gayle's reported low temperatures, the fires had caused exposed bits of the buildings' steel cores to "soften and buckle." Also, whereas Gayle's report had said that 157 of 160 perimeter columns "saw no temperature above 250°C," NIST's advance report claimed that these columns' steel had softened such as to "lead to rapid structural collapse." Ryan also pointed out that seemingly authoritative people, such as Dr. Hyman Brown of the WTC construction crew, were (absurdly) claiming that the towers collapsed because the airplane fuel caused the steel to melt. Ryan closed his letter to Gayle by saying:

> If steel from those buildings did soften or melt, I'm sure we can all agree that this was certainly not due to jet fuel fires of any kind, let alone the briefly burning fires in those towers. . . . Please do what you can to quickly eliminate the confusion regarding the ability of jet fuel fires to soften or melt structural steel.[56]

However, Gayle, who in a 2004 report supported positions that contradicted his 2003 report, was unmoved. And although Ryan had written his letter in support of UL, because it had certified the steel in the Twin Towers, whereas NIST's report implied that the steel failed, UL fired Ryan, purportedly because he had written his letter "without UL's knowledge or authorization."[56] As to why Ryan wrote his letter to Gayle, "pleading with him to clarify a report of his work," and then allowed his letter to become public, Ryan later wrote: "To me, the report in question represents a decision point, not just for the US, but for humanity as a whole. We're at a point where we must decide if we will live consciously, or literally give up our entire reality for a thin veneer of lies."[58]

A Former NIST Scientist: In 2007, a scientist who had worked for NIST until 2006 wrote and published a statement saying that NIST had become "fully hijacked from the scientific into the political realm." As a result, scientists working for NIST "lost [their] scientific independence, and became little more than 'hired guns.'" With regard to 9/11-related issues, this whistleblower said:

> By 2001, everyone in NIST leadership had been trained to pay close heed to political pressures. There was no chance that NIST people "investigating" the 9/11 situation could have been acting in the true spirit of scientific independence. . . . Everything that came from the hired guns was by then routinely filtered through the front office, and assessed for political implications before release.

In fact, this whistleblower said, all reports were examined by NIST's front office and three external oversight groups: the National Security Agency, the Department of Commerce ("which . . . wouldn't permit us to release papers . . . without changes to conform to their way of looking at things"), and the White House's Office of Management and Budget (which "had a policy person specifically delegated to provide oversight on our work").[59] Although this scientist, fearing possible retaliation, wishes to remain anonymous, his identity is known to physicist Steven Jones.[60]

This whistleblower's report has been very helpful, confirming the truth of suspicions that many of us had and giving us additional information. This report significantly informed my 2009 book, *The Mysterious Collapse of World Trade Center 7*, especially the first chapter, "NIST as a Political, Not a Scientific, Agency."[61]

A New Whistleblower

On July 8, 2011, a TV program, "The Richplanet Starship," carried an interview of Tony Farrell, who the previous year had become aware of evidence that 9/11 had been an "inside job." This discovery created a problem, because Farrell for several years had been the Principal Intelligence Analyst for the South Yorkshire Police. (South Yorkshire is the southern region of Yorkshire, a northern county,

England's largest.) As the intelligence analyst, Farrell had the duty of presenting his annual assessment to the Intelligence Strategic Management Board. In 2010, this assessment was due on July 8. But shortly before this date, he came across information on the Internet that 9/11 had been a false-flag attack. Although previously Farrell had entertained no such ideas, he found the evidence compelling.

Having been encouraged to look at the 7/7 attacks in London as well, he studied this information and concluded that it, too, was a false-flag attack.

Given his new perspective, Farrell was then convinced that the threat was internal. But he knew that his superiors would not allow him to tell the board that the most serious threat was internal. The Director of Intelligence encouraged him to just go ahead and present the report that he had planned to give before he developed his new perspective. But after having at first thought he would do this, he decided that he could not, given his strong Christian beliefs—which include, among other things, the prohibition against bearing false witness against neighbors. To make the expected threat assessment report, he concluded, would have made him complicit in the crime. Also, he was convinced that the public is becoming increasingly aware that 9/11 and 7/7 were false-flag attacks. So if the governments keep pretending to believe that these events were the products of external terrorists, there will come a "tipping point," when community adhesion will be impossible.

When it became clear to Farrell's superior that he would not agree to conceal his beliefs, he was dismissed. But his superiors expressed no animosity toward Farrell, and they did not even say that he was wrong. They said, in fact, that he might well be right. But he had to be dismissed because his beliefs were incompatible with his position as intelligence analyst: The South Yorkshire Police could not allege that 9/11 and 7/7 had been inside jobs.

Although at first Farrell was not planning to appeal his termination, he decided that he must, for at least two reasons. One was that he had been fired for truthfully expressing his beliefs—truthfulness that reflects the police force's own code of professional standards, which speaks of honesty and integrity. A second reason was that the lies about 9/11 and 7/7 involve "corruption in the highest places of a monstrous kind." So his conscience told him that he had to appeal his termination.

As this book was going to press, Farrell was waiting for the hearing on his appeal. He knew that this appeal was likely to be turned down, and he knew from the beginning that his stance might seriously harm his financial security. But he had no doubt that he had done the right thing. He hoped that his example might lead others to follow suit, with the result that somehow a "greater body" will stand up for truth.[62]

It is to be hoped that the 9/11 Truth Movement, building on the examples of Ryan, Farrell, and the former NIST scientist, will help create a "greater body" of 9/11 (and 7/7) whistleblowers—people who spoke out while in organizations that concealed evidence that the official 9/11 story is false.

2. Converting Leading Journalists

I pointed out in the second and third chapters that, although most of the peace and anti-war websites and publications have not supported the 9/11 Truth Movement, and have even criticized it, they should be natural allies. On the one hand, the 9/11 Movement's effort to fight against the war machine could be given experience and expertise through association with wise and experienced members in the peace and anti-war movements. On the other hand, a union could revitalize the peace/anti-war movements, providing them with thousands of new workers.

Most important, such a union would overcome the primary weakness from which the peace/anti-war efforts have suffered since 9/11. Paul Craig Roberts has written:

> The unwillingness or inability to entertain any view of 9/11 different from the official view dooms to impotence many Internet sites that are opposed to the wars and to the rise of the domestic US police state. These sites, for whatever the reasons, accept the government's explanation of 9/11; yet, they try to oppose the "war on terror" and the police state which are the consequences of accepting the government's explanation. Trying to oppose the consequences of an event whose explanation you accept is an impossible task.[63]

Although Roberts wrote this in terms of Internet sites, the same logic applies to any publication or organization that works to oppose war and promote peace. I discussed above many of the consequences of 9/11, from extraordinary rendition to the wars in Iraq and Afghanistan (and now Pakistan and Libya) to the ever-increasing percentage of the annual budget that goes for war. Is Roberts not right—that trying to oppose the consequences of 9/11 while accepting the government's explanation of it is an impossible task?

This would surely make sense to many peace and anti-war leaders. And because these are intelligent people, the 9/11 evidence will surely convince at least most of them, if only they will look at it. My suggestion for the next "step of a thousand miles" is that various 9/11 leaders work on various leaders of these organizations, publications, and Internet sites, trying to convince these people to examine some of the new evidence. In Chapter 3, I suggested Bill Moyers and Robert Parry, who are honest and courageous as well as intelligent, would be good places to start.

The 9/11 Truth Movement has taken great strides in its first decade. Let us set for ourselves this goal: to have the 9/11 crime against democracy exposed well before the end of the second 9/11 decade.

CONCLUSION

Getting the 9/11 lie exposed is essential. One obvious reason is simple justice. There needs to be justice for the 9/11 family members, who must be told the truth, and who must be given recompense—in whatever sense this can be done—for this crime committed by forces within the American government. There also needs to be justice in the sense of punishment for those who engineered this crime. They perhaps considered themselves patriots, because 9/11 was going to stimulate the US economy by increasing military spending and by opening up oil resources. But whether or not that plan is regarded as having worked out, those Americans, including military leaders, who engineered this operation are guilty of murder and treason.

Exposing the truth about 9/11 is also necessary for the sake of preventing further crimes against democracy. That President Kennedy and Senator Robert F. Kennedy were both assassinated by forces within the US government is obvious to most people who study the evidence. And yet neither crime was publicly exposed. This fact likely convinced people contemplating the 9/11 operation that they would be able to get away with it.

Many lines of evidence show that 9/11 was an inside job. As we saw, probably most obvious is the evidence that WTC 7 was demolished. But the destruction of the Twin Towers also cannot be explained without explosives, and the official story about the Pentagon attack is also clearly false. Likewise, the story of phone calls from the planes cannot stand up to scrutiny. If the perpetrators of this crime are not brought to justice, then they will believe that they can get away with almost anything.

So unless we want continued false-flag attacks, we should do our best to uncover the truth about 9/11.

INTRODUCTION

1. My previous nine books were: *The New Pearl Harbor: Disturbing Questions about the Bush Administration and 9/11* (2004); *The 9/11 Commission Report: Omissions and Distortions* (2005); *Christian Faith and the Truth behind 9/11: A Call to Reflection and Action* (2006); *9/11 and American Empire: Intellectuals Speak Out*, co-edited with Peter Dale Scott (2006); *Debunking 9/11 Debunking: An Answer to Popular Mechanics and Other Defenders of the Official Conspiracy Theory* (2007); *9/11 Contradictions: An Open Letter to Congress and the Press* (2008); *The New Pearl Harbor Revisited: 9/11, the Cover-Up, and the Exposé* (2008); *The Mysterious Collapse of World Trade Center: Why the Final Official 9/11 Report is Unscientific and False* (2009); *Cognitive Infiltration: An Obama Appointee's Plan to Undermine the 9/11 Conspiracy Theory* (2010). I did not include in this list *The American Empire and the Commonwealth of God: A Political, Economic, Religious Statement*, co-authored with John B. Cobb Jr., Richard Falk, and Catherine Keller (2006), because it had only a few pages about 9/11. And I did not include *Osama bin Laden: Dead or Alive?* (2008), because there is no evidence—even the FBI agrees—that Osama bid Laden had anything to do with 9/11.

2. The International Federation of Journalists has defined freedom of the press: "that freedom from restraint which is essential to enable journalists, editors, publishers and broadcasters to advance the public interest by publishing, broadcasting or circulating facts and opinions without which a democratic electorate cannot make responsible judgments"; contained in "Status of Journalists and Journalism Ethics: IFJ Principles," May 2003 (http://www.ifj.org/en/articles/status-of-journalists-and-journalism-ethics-ifj-principles). It matters little whether the "restraint" is political (as in the former Soviet Union) or financial.

3. David Ray Griffin, *Christian Faith and the Truth behind 9/11: A Call to Reflection and Action* (Louisville: Westminster John Knox, 2006).

CHAPTER 1

1 ABC/Washington Post Poll, June 2–5, 2011 (http://www.pollingreport.com/afghan.htm); (Jennifer Epstein, "Poll: Rising Number of Americans Want U.S. Out of Afghanistan," Politico, June 9, 2011 (http://www.politico.com/news/stories/0611/56623.html).

2 Marjorie Cohn, "Bombing of Afghanistan Is Illegal and Must Be Stopped," *Jurist*, November 6, 2001 (http://jurist.law.pitt.edu/forum/forumnew36.htm).

3 Marjorie Cohn, "Afghanistan: The Other Illegal War," AlterNet, August 1, 2008 (http://www.alternet.org/world/93473/afghanistan:_the_other_illegal_war). In this article, Cohn added the following observation: "Bush's justification for

attacking Afghanistan was that it was harboring Osama bin Laden and training terrorists. Iranians could have made the same argument to attack the United States after they overthrew the vicious Shah Reza Pahlavi in 1979 and he was given safe haven in the United States. The people in Latin American countries whose dictators were trained in torture techniques at the School of the Americas could likewise have attacked the torture training facility in Fort Benning, Ga., under that specious rationale."

4 President Barack Obama, "The Way Forward in Afghanistan and Pakistan" (remarks at the US Military Academy at West Point), December 1, 2009 (http://www.msnbc.msn.com/id/34231058).

5 "Security Council Condemns, 'In Strongest Terms,' Terrorist Attacks on United States," September 12, 2001 (http://www.un.org/News/Press/docs/2001/SC7143.doc.htm).

6 Brian J. Foley "Legal Analysis: U.S. Campaign Against Afghanistan Not Self-Defense Under International Law," Lawyers against the War, November 6, 2001 (http://www.counterpunch.org/foley1.html).

7 "This Constitution, and the Laws of the United States which shall be made in Pursuance thereof; and all Treaties made, or which shall be made, under the Authority of the United States, shall be the supreme Law of the Land." US Constitution, Article VI, par. 2.

8 Robert H. Reid, "August Deadliest Month for US in Afghanistan," Associated Press, August 29, 2009 (http://www.huffingtonpost.com/2009/08/28/us-firing-on-afghan-clini_n_270997.html).

9 "White House Warns Taliban: 'We Will Defeat You,'" CNN, September 21, 2001 (http://archives.cnn.com/2001/WORLD/asiapcf/central/09/21/ret.afghan.taliban).

10 David B. Ottaway and Joe Stephens, "Diplomats Met with Taliban on Bin Laden," *Washington Post* October 29, 2001 (http://www.highbeam.com/doc/1P2-486256.html).

11 "Bush Rejects Taliban Offer to Hand Bin Laden Over," *Guardian* October 14, 2001 (http://www.guardian.co.uk/world/2001/oct/14/afghanistan.terrorism5).

12 Sheryl Gay Stolberg, "Obama Defends Strategy in Afghanistan," *New York Times* August 17, 2009 (http://www.nytimes.com/2009/08/18/us/politics/18vets.html?_r=1&th&emc=th).

13 See the two chapters entitled "The New Great Game" in Ahmed Rashid, *Taliban: Militant Islam, Oil and Fundamentalism in Central Asia* (New Haven: Yale University Press, 2001), and Steve Coll, *Ghost Wars: The Secret History of the CIA, Afghanistan, and bin Laden, from the Soviet Invasion to September 10, 2001* (New York: Penguin, 2004), 330.

14 Rashid, *Taliban*, 75–79, 163, 175.

15 Quoted in Jean-Charles Brisard and Guillaume Dasquié, *Forbidden Truth: U.S.-Taliban Secret Oil Diplomacy and the Failed Hunt for Bin Laden* (New York: Thunder's Mouth Press/Nation Books, 2002).

16 George Arney, "U.S. 'Planned Attack on Taleban,'" BBC News, September 18, 2001 ("Taleban" is a spelling preferred by most British writers).

17 *Meet the Press*, NBC, September 23, 2001 (http://www.washingtonpost.com/wpsrv/nation/specials/attacked/transcripts/nbctext092301.html).

18 "Remarks by the President, Secretary of the Treasury O'Neill and Secretary of State Powell on Executive Order," White House, September 24, 2001 (http://www.whitehouse.gov/news/releases/2001/09/20010924-4.html).

19 Seymour M. Hersh, "What Went Wrong: The C.I.A. and the Failure of American Intelligence," *New Yorker* October 1, 2001 (http://cicentre.com/Documents/DOC_Hersch_OCT_01.htm).

20 Office of the Prime Minister, "The UK's Bin Laden Dossier in Full," BBC News, October 4, 2001 (http://news.bbc.co.uk/2/hi/uk_news/politics/1579043.stm). The original title for the story—"Responsibility for the Terrorist Atrocities in the United States"— made clear the government's claim.

21 "The Investigation and the Evidence," BBC News, October 5, 2001 (http://news.bbc.co.uk/2/hi/americas/1581063.stm).

22 Federal Bureau of Investigation, "Most Wanted Terrorists: Usama bin Laden" (http://www.fbi.gov/wanted/terrorists/terbinladen.htm).

23 Ed Haas, "FBI says, 'No Hard Evidence Connecting Bin Laden to 9/11,'" Muckraker Report, June 6, 2006 (http://web.archive.org/web/20090207113442/http://teamliberty.net/id267.html). For more on this episode, see my *9/11 Contradictions*, Chap. 18.

24 "Bin Laden's FBI Poster Omits Any 9/11 Connection," KSLA 12 in Shreveport, Louisiana (http://video.google.com/videoplay?docid=-6443576002087829136).

25 "Bin Laden, Most Wanted For Embassy Bombings?" *Washington Post* August 28, 2006 (http://www.washingtonpost.com/wp-dyn/content/article/2006/08/27/AR2006082700687.html).

26 Quoted in Haas, "FBI says, 'No Hard Evidence Connecting Bin Laden to 9/11.'"

27 See 9/11CR Ch. 5, notes 16, 41, and 92.

28 Kean and Hamilton, *Without Precedent*, 118.

29 Ibid., 122–24.

30 Ibid., 119.

31 Robert Windrem and Victor Limjoco, "9/11 Commission Controversy," *NBC News*, January 30, 2008 (http://911research.wtc7.net/cache/post911/commission/msnbc_commission_torture.html).

32 "Could the Bin Laden Video Be a Fake?" BBC News, December 14, 2001 (http://news.bbc.co.uk/2/hi/1711288.stm).

33 Steven Morris, "US Urged to Detail Origin of Tape," *Guardian* December 15, 2001 (http://www.guardian.co.uk/world/2001/dec/15/september11.afghanistan).

34 Ibid.; BBC, "Could the Bin Laden Video Be a Fake?"

35 Ibid.

36 Associated Press, "Bin Laden Denies Being Behind Attacks," *Milwaukee Journal Sentinel* September 16, 2001 (http://www2.jsonline.com/news/nat/sep01/binladen-denial.asp).

37 "Pakistan to Demand Handover of Bin Laden," *Guardian* September 16, 2001 (http://www.guardian.co.uk/world/2001/sep/16/september11.usa16).

38 "Interview with Usama bin Laden," *Ummat* (Karachi), September 28, 2001 (http://www.robert-fisk.com/usama_interview_ummat.htm). Bin Laden's statement about innocents repeated what he had said in an interview with John Miller of ABC News in 1998: "Our religion forbids us from killing innocent people such as women and children" (http://web.archive.org/web/

20010927151820/http://abcnews.go.com/sections/world/DailyNews/miller_
binladen_980609.html).

39 "Bin Laden's Message to the US," *Asia Times* October 10, 2001
(http://www.atimes.com/media/CJ10Ce02.html); the text of the speech can be
read at "Osama bin Laden Speeches," September11News.com
(http://www.september11news.com/OsamaSpeeches.htm).
40 For a photograph from the video of November 3, 2001, see "Bin Laden Lashes Out
at U.N., U.S. Attacks in Taped Message," CNN, November 3, 2001
(http://archives.cnn.com/2001/WORLD/asiapcf/central/11/03/ret.bin.laden.
statement/index.html). Bin Laden's appearance in the October 7 and November
3 videos can also be seen in "Osama bin Laden Speeches,"
September11News.com(http://www.september11news.com/OsamaSpeeches.htm).
41 For a video known to have been made sometime after November 16, 2001, see
either "Osama bin Laden Speeches" or "Transcript: Bin Laden Video Excerpts,"
BBC News, December 27, 2001 (http://news.bbc.co.uk/2/hi/
middle_east/1729882.stm). A portion of the November 9 video is on YouTube
(http://www.youtube.com/watch?v=x0FVeqCX6z8).
42 For a nose comparison, see "Osama bin Laden Gets a Nose Job"
(http://www.awitness.org/news/december_2001/osama_nose_job.html) or "Bruce
Lawrence," Radio Du Jour (http://www.radiodujour.com/people/lawrence_bruce).
43 Compare his hands with bin Laden's hand as shown in the post-November 16
video (http://news.bbc.co.uk/2/hi/middle_east/1729882.stm).
44 "Transcript of Usama bin Laden Video Tape."
45 Lawrence is the editor of *Messages to the World: The Statements of Osama Bin
Laden* (London and New York: Verso, 2005).
46 Lawrence made these statements on February 16, 2007, during a radio interview
conducted by Kevin Barrett of the University of Wisconsin at Madison. It can be
heard at Radio Du Jour (http://www.radiodujour.com/people/lawrence_bruce).
47 Mark Hosenball, "Bin Laden, Two Others Didn't Fire on Seals: Sources,"
Reuters, May 5, 2011; Mark Landler and Mark Mazzetti, "Account Tells of
One-Sided Battle in Bin Laden Raid," *New York Times* May 4, 2011
(http://www.nytimes.com/2011/05/05/us/politics/05binladen.html).
48 Yochi Dreazen, Aamer Madhani, Marc Ambinder, "Goal Was Never to Capture
bin Laden," *Atlantic* May 4, 2011
(http://www.theatlantic.com/politics/archive/2011/05/goal-was-never-to-
capture-bin-laden/238330/).
49 Evann Gastaldo, "Bin Laden Just a 'Suspect,' Deserved Trial: Noam Chomsky
Describes His Reaction to Osama Bin Laden Raid," Newser, May 8, 2011
(http://www.newser.com/story/118098/noam-chomsky-osama-bin-laden-was-
just-a-suspect-and-deserved-fair-trial.html).
50 Philip Rucker, Scott Wilson, and Anne E. Kornblut, "Osama bin Laden Buried
at Sea After Being Killed by U.S. Forces in Pakistan," *Washington Post* May 1,
2011 (http://www.washingtonpost.com/politics/osama-bin-laden-is-killed-by-
us-forces-in-pakistan/2011/05/01/AFXMZyVF_story.html).
51 SEALs is shorthand for the Navy's Sea, Air, and Land Teams. Another question
about the SEALs is whether this operation was executed with no deaths, as
claimed. A purported eyewitness said that one of the helicopters caught fire
and all aboard were killed. See Paul Craig Roberts, "How Many SEALs Died?"

Information Clearing House, May 21, 2011
(http://www.informationclearinghouse.info/article28156.htm).

52 As reported in David Ray Griffin, *Osama bin Laden: Dead or Alive?*
(Northampton: Olive Branch Press [Interlink Publishing], 2009), 5–6.

53 Ibid., Ch. 1.

54 With the aid of Elizabeth Woodworth, I used a press release to try to insert this
point into the public discussion. See David Ray Griffin, "Obama Says 'Justice
Has Been Done': Bin Laden Scholar Says No," PR Newswire, May 6, 2011
(http://www.prnewswire.com/news-
releases/obama-says-justice-has-been-done-bin-laden-scholar-says-no-
121381654.html).

55 Translation of passage in "Das schreit geradezu nach Aufklärung," Interview of
Federal Judge Dieter Deiseroth, by Marcus Klöckner, December 15, 2009
(http://www.heise.de/tp/artikel/31/31729/1.html). My thanks to Jens Wagner of
Hamburg, Germany, for help with the translation.

56 *The 9/11 Commission Report: Final Report of the National Commission on Terrorist
Attacks upon the United States*, Authorized Edition (New York: W. W. Norton,
2004), 154.

57 Kevin Fagan, "Agents of Terror Leave Their Mark on Sin City," *San Francisco
Chronicle* October 4, 2001 (http://sfgate.com/cgi-bin/article.cgi?file=/
chronicle/archive/2001/10/04/MN102970.DTL).

58 "Professor Dittmar Machule," Interviewed by Liz Jackson, A Mission to Die For,
Four Corners, October 18, 2001 (http://www.abc.net.au/4corners/atta/
interviews/machule.htm).

59 *The 9/11 Commission Report*, 160.

60 Evan Thomas and Mark Hosenball, "Bush: 'We're at War," *Newsweek*
September 24, 2001 (http://www.newsweek.com/id/76065).

61 Daniel Hopsicker, *Welcome to Terrorland: Mohamed Atta and the 9-11 Cover-Up in
Florida* (Eugene, OR: MadCow Press, 2004). See also Hopsicker, "The Secret
World of Mohamed Atta: An Interview With Atta's American Girlfriend,"
InformationLiberation, August 20, 2006
(http://web.archive.org/web/20090120194105/http://informationliberation.com/
?id=14738). Many of the details are summarized in my *9/11 Contradictions*,
Chap. 15, "Were Mohamed Atta and the Other Hijackers Devout Muslims?"
As I explain in that chapter, there were attempts to try to discredit Amanda
Keller's account by intimidating her into recanting and by claiming that she
lived with a different man of the same first name, but these attempts failed.

62 "Professor Dittmar Machule."

63 Kate Connolly, "Father Insists Alleged Leader Is Still Alive," *Guardian* September
2, 2002 (http://www.guardian.co.uk/world/2002/sep/02/september11.usa).

64 "Photographs Taken of Mohamed Atta during His University Years," A Mission
to Die For, Four Corners (http://www.abc.net.au/4corners/atta/resources/
photos/university.htm). Also, the differences between the (bearded) Atta in
his passport photo, which is in the FBI's evidence for the Moussaoui trial, and
the Atta of the standard FBI photo, seem greater than can be accounted for by
the fact that only the former Atta is bearded. The two photos can be compared
at 911Review (http://911review.org/JohnDoe2/Atta.html).

65 "Professor Dittmar Machule."

66 Thomas Tobin, "Florida: Terror's Launching Pad," *St. Petersburg Times*, September 1, 2002 (http://www.sptimes.com/2002/09/01/911/Florida__terror_s_lau.shtml); Elaine Allen-Emrich, "Hunt for Terrorists Reaches North Port," *Charlotte Sun-Herald* September 14, 2001 (available at http://www.madcowprod.com/keller.htm).

67 Connolly, "Father Insists Alleged Leader Is Still Alive."

68 David Bamford, "Hijack 'Suspect' Alive in Morocco," BBC, September 22, 2001 (http://news.bbc.co.uk/1/hi/world/middle_east/1558669.stm). Although some news organizations, including the BBC itself, later tried to debunk this story, they failed, as I showed in *The New Pearl Harbor Revisited: 9/11, the Cover-Up, and the Exposé* (Northampton: Olive Branch Press [Interlink Publishing], 2009), 151–53.

69 See Jay Kolar, "What We Now Know about the Alleged 9-11 Hijackers," in Paul Zarembka, ed., *The Hidden History of 9-11* (New York: Seven Stories Press, 2008), 3–44, at 22–26; and Paul Thompson, "The Two Ziad Jarrahs," History Commons (http://www.historycommons.org/essay.jsp?article=essayjarrah).

70 For types of evidence not discussed here, see Griffin, *The New Pearl Harbor Revisited*, Chap. 8, "9/11 Commission Falsehoods about Bin Laden, al-Qaeda, Pakistanis, and Saudis."

71 FBI Affidavit, signed by agent James K. Lechner, October 4, 2001 (http://www.abc.net.au/4corners/atta/resources/documents/fbiaffidavit1.htm).

72 9/11CR 451n1; FBI Director Robert S. Mueller III, "Statement for the Record," Joint Intelligence Committee Inquiry, September 26, 2002 (http://www.fas.org/irp/congress/2002_hr/092602mueller.html).

73 "Two Brothers among Hijackers," CNN, September 13, 2001 (http://english. peopledaily.com.cn/200109/13/eng20010913_80131.html).

74 "Feds Think They've Identified Some Hijackers," CNN, September 13, 2001 (http://edition.cnn.com/2001/US/09/12/investigation.terrorism).

75 Joel Achenbach, "'You Never Imagine' A Hijacker Next Door," *Washington Post* September 16, 2001 (http://www.washingtonpost.com/ac2/ wp-dyn?pagename=article&node=&contentId=A38026-2001Sep15).

76 Rowland Morgan and Ian Henshall, *9/11 Revealed: The Unanswered Questions* (New York: Carroll & Graf, 2005), 181.

77 This photo can be seen at http://www.historycommons.org/context.jsp?item=a553portlandfilmed&scale=0.

78 Associated Press, July 24, 2004. The photo with this caption can be seen in Morgan and Henshall, *9/11 Revealed*, 117–18, along with a genuine security video (with identification data), or at http://killtown.911review.org/flight77/hijackers.html (scroll half-way down).

79 Rowland and Henshall, *9/11 Revealed*, 118.

80 9/11CR 452n11.

81 Jay Kolar, "What We Now Know about the Alleged 9-11 Hijackers," in Paul Zarembka, ed., *The Hidden History of 9-11* (New York: Seven Stories, 2008), 3–44, at 8.

82 Quoted in 9/11CR 19.

83 "Summary of Air Traffic Hijack Events: September 11, 2001," FAA, September 17, 2001(http://replay.waybackmachine.org/20100728000016/http:// www.gwu.edu/~nsarchiv/NSAEBB/NSAEBB165/faa7.pdf)

84 Frank J. Murray, "Americans Feel Touch of Evil; Fury Spurs Unity," *Washington Times* September 11, 2002 (http://web.archive.org/web/20020916222620/http://www.washtimes.com/september11/americans.htm).

85 "Ashcroft Says More Attacks May Be Planned," CNN, September 18, 2001 (http://edition.cnn.com/2001/US/09/17/inv.investigation.terrorism/index.html); "Terrorist Hunt," ABC News (http://911research.wtc7.net/cache/disinfo/deceptions/abc_hunt.html).

86 Anne Karpf, "Uncle Sam's Lucky Finds," *Guardian* March 19, 2002 (http://www.guardian.co.uk/september11/story/0,11209,669961,00.html), emphasis added. Like some other articles, this one mistakenly said that the passport belonged to Mohamed Atta.

87 Statement by Susan Ginsburg, senior counsel to the 9/11 Commission, at the 9/11 Commission Hearing, January 26, 2004 (http://www.9-11commission.gov/archive/hearing7/9-11Commission_Hearing_2004-01-26.htm). The Commission's account reflected a CBS report that the passport had been found "minutes after" the attack, which was stated by the Associated Press, January 27, 2003.

88 Nick Davies, *Flat Earth News: An Award-Winning Reporter Exposes Falsehood, Distortion, and Propaganda in the Global Media* (London: Random House UK, 2009), 248.

89 Charles Lane and John Mintz, "Bid to Thwart Hijackers May Have Led to Pa. Crash," *Washington Post* September 13, 2001 (http://www.highbeam.com/doc/1P2-459249.html).

90 For a photograph of the bandana, see United States v. Zacarias Moussaoui (http://www.vaed.uscourts.gov/notablecases/moussaoui/exhibits/prosecution/PA00111.html), or 911 Research, "The Crash of Flight 93" (http://911research.wtc7.net/disinfo/deceptions/flight93.html).

91 Milt Bearden, quoted in Ross Coulthart, "Terrorists Target America," Ninemsn, September 2001 (http://sunday.ninemsn.com.au/sunday/cover_stories/transcript_923.asp). I learned of Bearden's statement in Ian Henshall, *9/11 Revealed: The New Evidence* (New York: Carroll & Graf, 2007), 106.

92 For claims about hijackers' names on the flight manifests, see Richard Clarke, *Against All Enemies: Inside America's War on Terror* (New York: Free Press, 2004), 13; George Tenet, *At the Center of the Storm: My Years at the CIA* (New York: HarperCollins, 2007), 167–69; and my discussion in Griffin, *The New Pearl Harbor Revisited*, 174–75.

93 See Griffin, *The New Pearl Harbor Revisited*, 163, 174–75.

94 His 2005 book (Terry McDermott, *Perfect Soldiers: The 9/11 Hijackers: Who They Were, Why They Did It* [New York: HarperCollins, 2005]), contains a photocopy of a portion of an apparent passenger manifest from American Flight 11, with the names of three of the alleged hijackers (photo section after page 140). In response to a query, McDermott reportedly stated that a set of flight manifests for the four flights were "amongst a set of investigative files he obtained from the FBI while researching his book," 911 Myths, "The Passengers" (http://911myths.com/html/the_passengers.html).

95 Although discussions on the Internet have often claimed that these manifests were included in the FBI's evidence for the Moussaoui trial, several researchers looking for them have failed to find them. See Jim Hoffman's discussion (http://911research.wtc7.net/planes/evidence/passengers.html).

96 For example, Ziad Jarrah's last name is spelled correctly on this "manifest," whereas in the early days after 9/11, the FBI was referring to him as "Jarrahi," as news reports from the time show ("Hijackers Linked to USS Cole Attack? Investigators Have Identified All the Hijackers; Photos to Be Released," CBS News, September 14, 2001 [http://www.cbsnews.com/stories/2001/09/12/national/main310963.shtml]; Elizabeth Neuffer, "Hijack Suspect Lived a Life, or a Lie," *Boston Globe* September 25, 2001 [http://web.archive.org/web/20010925123748/boston.com/dailyglobe2/268/nation/Hijack_suspect_lived_a_life_or_a_lie+.shtml]). Also, the "manifest" for American Flight 77 contains Hani Hanjour's name, whereas the FBI's initial list of hijackers for this flight included a name transcribed as "Mosear Caned," leading the *Washington Post* to speculate as to why Hanjour's "name was not on the American Airlines manifest for the flight" ("Four Planes, Four Coordinated Teams," *Washington Post*, September 16, 2001 [http://www.washingtonpost.com/wp-srv/nation/graphics/attack/hijackers.html]). Moreover, the manifest for American Flight 11 contains the names of Wail al-Shehri, Waleed al-Shehri, Satam al-Suqami, and Abdul Aziz al-Omari, whereas the FBI's original list of hijackers included instead the names of Adnan Bukhari, Ameer Bukhari, Amer Kamfar, and Abdulrahman al-Omari (see Jay Kolar, "What We Now Know about the Alleged 9-11 Hijackers," Paul Zarembka, ed., *The Hidden History of 9-11-2001*, Elsevier [2006]; enlarged edition Seven Stories Press [2008]).

97 Thomas R. Olmsted, M.D. "Still No Arabs on Flight 77," Rense.com, June 23, 2003 (http://www.rense.com/general38/77.htm).

98 *Popular Mechanics* has claimed that hijacker names were on the Pentagon autopsy report; see *Debunking 9/11 Myths: Why Conspiracy Theories Can't Stand Up to the Facts: An In-Depth Investigation by Popular Mechanics*, ed. David Dunbar and Brad Reagan (New York: Hearst Books, 2006), 63. For my discussion, see Griffin, *Debunking 9/11 Debunking: An Answer to Popular Mechanics and Other Defenders of the Official Conspiracy Theory* (Northampton: Olive Branch Press [Interlink Publishing], 2007], 267-69.

99 Glen Johnson, "Probe Reconstruction Horror, Calculated Attacks on Planes," *Boston Globe* November 23, 2001 (http://www.boston.com/news/packages/underattack/news/planes_reconstruction.htm).

100 "America Under Attack: How Could It Happen?" CNN Live Event, September 12, 2001 (http://transcripts.cnn.com/TRANSCRIPTS/0109/12/se.60.html).

101 Richard A. Serrano, "Heroism, Fatalism Aboard Flight 93," *Los Angeles Times* April 12, 2006 (http://rednecktexan.blogspot.com/2006/04/heroism-fatalism-aboard-flight-93.html).

102 9/11CR 5.

103 See David Ray Griffin, *Christian Faith and the Truth behind 9/11* (Louisville: Westminster John Knox, 2006), Chap. 1, "9/11 and Prior False Flag Operations."

104 General Wesley Clark, *Winning Modern Wars: Iraq, Terrorism, and the American Empire* (New York: Public Affairs, 2003), 120, 130; "Gen. Wesley Clark Weighs Presidential Bid: 'I Think about It Everyday,'" *Democracy Now!* March 2, 2007 (http://www.democracynow.org/article.pl?sid=07/03/02/1440234); Joe Conason, "Seven Countries in Five Years," Salon.com, October 12, 2007 (http://www.salon.com/opinion/conason/2007/10/12/wesley_clark); Gareth Porter, "Yes, the Pentagon Did Want to Hit Iran," *Asia Times*, May 7, 2008 (http://www.atimes.com/atimes/Middle_East/JE07Ak01.html).

105 Some have seen drug profits as central. Others have focused on access to oil, natural gas, and minerals. For example, economist Michel Chossudovsky, referring to the allegedly recent discovery of huge reserves of minerals and natural gas in Afghanistan, wrote: "The issue of 'previously unknown deposits' sustains a falsehood. It excludes Afghanistan's vast mineral wealth as a justifiable casus belli. It says that the Pentagon only recently became aware that Afghanistan was among the World's most wealthy mineral economies . . . [whereas in reality] all this information was known in minute detail." See Michel Chossudovsky, "'The War is Worth Waging': Afghanistan's Vast Reserves of Minerals and Natural Gas: The War on Afghanistan is a Profit Driven 'Resource War,'" Global Research, June 17, 2010 (http://www.globalresearch.ca/index.php?context=va&aid=19769).

106 Dr. Gideon Polya, author of *Body Count: Global Avoidable Mortality Since 1950*, estimated by January 2010 that over four million Afghanis died (from both violent and non-violent causes) since the 2001 invasion who would not have died without the invasion; see "January 2010 - 4.5 Million Dead in Afghan Holocaust, Afghan Genocide," January 2, 2010, Afghan Holocaust, Afghan Genocide (http://afghangenocide.blogspot.com).

107 On US-NATO war crimes in Afghanistan, see Marc W. Herold, "Media Distortion: Killing Innocent Afghan Civilians to 'Save our Troops': Eight Years of Horror Perpetrated against the People of Afghanistan," Global Research, October 15, 2009 (http://www.globalresearch.ca/index.php?context=va&aid=15665).

CHAPTER 2

1 Alexander Cockburn, "The 9/11 Conspiracy Nuts," ZNet, September 20, 2006 (http://www.zcommunications.org/the-9-11-conspiracy-nuts-by-alexander-cockburn-1). A shorter version appeared in the September 24, 2006, issue of *The Nation*.

2 Alexander Cockburn, "The Conspiracists, Continued—Are They Getting Crazier?" *The Free Press* September 16, 2006 (http://www.freepress.org/columns/display/2/2006/1433).

3 Alexander Cockburn, "Conspiracy Disproved: Distractions from Awful Reality," *Le Monde Diplomatique* December 2006 (http://mondediplo.com/2006/12/02dconspiracy).

4 Ibid.

5 George Monbiot, "9/11 Fantasists Pose a Mortal Danger to Popular Oppositional Campaigns," *Guardian* February 20, 2007 (http://www.guardian.co.uk/commentisfree/2007/feb/20/comment.september11).

6 Matt Taibbi, "The Idiocy Behind the '9/11 Truth' Movement," AlterNet, September 26, 2006 (http://www.alternet.org/story/42181). This date, incidentally, refers to the original posting of the article at Rollingstone.com. It was not posted on AlterNet until May 7, 2008. In another article, posted on Rollingstone.com a couple of weeks earlier (September 14, 2006), Taibbi had offered a different diagnosis, saying that people who thought that the towers had been wired with explosives were "clinically insane." See Matt Taibbi, "Americans in Denial about 9/11," AlterNet June 6, 2008 (http://www.alternet.org/story/41635).

7 Christopher Hayes, "9/11: The Roots of Paranoia," *The Nation* December 8, 2006 (http://www.chrishayes.org/articles/911-roots-paranoia).

8 "Chomsky: 9/11 Truth Movement Pushes Non-Scientific Evidence," YouTube (http://www.youtube.com/watch?v=mBg3aFZVATk).

9 "Chomsky Dismisses 9/11 Conspiracy Theories As 'Dubious,'" Rense.com, December 13, 2006 (http://rense.com/general74/dismiss.htm).

10 Terry Allen, "The 9/11 Faith Movement," *In These Times* July 11, 2006 (http://www.inthesetimes.com/site/main/article/2702).

11 David Corn, "When 9/11 Conspiracy Theories Go Bad," AlterNet, March 1, 2002 (http://www.alternet.org/story/12536); "How 9/11 Conspiracy Poison Did in Van Jones," Politics Daily, September 7, 2009 (http://www.politicsdaily.com/2009/09/07/how-9-11-conspiracy-poison-did-in-van-jones).

12 Corn, "How 9/11 Conspiracy Poison Did in Van Jones."

13 David Corn, "Van Jones and the 9/11 Conspiracy Theory Poison," *Mother Jones*, September 7, 2009 (http://motherjones.com/mojo/2009/09/van-jones-and-911-conspiracy-theory-poison).

14 Matthew Rothschild, "Enough of the 9/11 Conspiracy Theories, Already," *The Progressive* September 18, 2006 (http://www.alternet.org/story/41601/).

15 See David Ray Griffin, *The Mysterious Collapse of World Trade Center 7: Why the Final Official Report about 9/11 Is Unscientific and False* (Northampton: Olive Branch Press [Interlink Publishing], 2009), Chs. 4–5.

16 This cartoon, by Sydney Harris, is contained in Science Cartoons Plus (http://www.sciencecartoonsplus.com/pages/gallery.php).

17 James Glanz, "Engineers Have a Culprit in the Strange Collapse of 7 World Trade Center: Diesel Fuel," *New York Times* November 29, 2001 (http://www.nytimes.com/2001/11/29/nyregion/nation-challenged-site-engineers-have-culprit-strange-collapse-7-world-trade.html). The original title of this story was "Engineers Suspect Diesel Fuel in Collapse of 7 World Trade Center."

18 See FEMA, *World Trade Center Building Performance Study*, Therese McAllister, ed. (Washington, DC, and New York: Federal Emergency Management Agency, 2002), Chapter 5, by Ramon Gilsanz, Edward M. Depaola, Christopher Marrion, and Harold "Bud" Nelson (http://www.fema.gov/pdf/library/fema403_ch5.pdf), 31. As the title of Glanz's article in the previous note indicates, he had already suggested that the diesel fuel might provide an explanation.

19 *Debunking 9/11 Myths: Why Conspiracy Theories Can't Stand Up to the Facts: An In-Depth Investigation by Popular Mechanics*, ed. David Dunbar and Brad Reagan (New York: Hearst Books, 2006), 53, 56.

20 Ibid., 53–54, 29.

21 Rothschild, "Enough of the 9/11 Conspiracy Theories, Already."

22 Hayes, "9/11: The Roots of Paranoia."

23 Allen, "The 9/11 Faith Movement."

24 As this example shows, Allen's rejection of the 9/11 Truth Movement's empirical claims seems to be based entirely on her taking on faith the claims of the Bush-Cheney administration as mediated through *Popular Mechanics*. It is quite ironic, therefore, that she caricatures the 9/11 Truth Movement as the "9/11 Faith Movement." But she seems to have a special knack for getting things backwards: With regard to an *In These Times* editor's question about me, "What could have transformed this sober, reflective scholar into a conspiracy theorist?" (which was his way of asking why I had rejected the government's conspiracy theory in favor of an alternative conspiracy theory), she replied: "I think part of it is that he's a theologian who operates on faith" (quoted in Salim Muwakkil, "What's the 411 on 9/11?" *In These Times*, December 21, 2005 [http://www.inthesetimes.com/article/2444]). Given the fact that the primary issue at hand was my belief "that the towers were toppled by a controlled demolition," for which there is an overwhelming amount of empirical evidence, it is especially strange that she would say that the reason I believe this must be that I am "a theologian who operates on faith" She was obviously the one who was operating on faith with regard to 9/11.

25 NIST NCSTAR 1A, *Final Report on the Collapse of World Trade Center Building 7* (brief version), National Institute of Standards and Technology, November 2008, xxxvi (http://wtc.nist.gov/NCSTAR1/PDF/NCSTAR%201A.pdf). This document is henceforth cited simply as NIST NCSTAR 1A, which will always refer to the final (November 2008) version (as distinct from the Draft for Public Comment, which was issued in August 2008).

26 Ibid., xxxvii.

27 Ibid., xxxv.

28 See Shyam Sunder, "Opening Statement," NIST Press Briefing, August 21, 2008 (http://wtc.nist.gov/media/opening_remarks_082108.html); NIST NCSTAR 1–9, *Structural Fire Response and Probable Collapse Sequence of World Trade Center Building 7*, November 2008, Volume 2: 493, 617, 618 (http://wtc.nist.gov/NCSTAR1/PDF/NCSTAR%201-9%20Vol%202.pdf).

29 "NIST WTC 7 Investigation Finds Building Fires Caused Collapse," NIST, August 21, 2008 (http://www.physorg.com/news138546437.html).

30 NIST NCSTAR 1A, xxxvii.

31 NIST NCSTAR 1–9, *Structural Fire Response and Probable Collapse Sequence of World Trade Center Building 7*, November 2008, Vol. 1 (wtc.nist.gov/NCSTAR1/PDF/NCSTAR%201-9%20Vol%201.pdf): 341.

32 Rothschild, "Enough of the 9/11 Conspiracy Theories, Already."

33 Allen, "The 9/11 Faith Movement."

34 J. Gordon Routley, Charles Jennings, and Mark Chubb, "High-Rise Office Building Fire, One Meridian Plaza, Philadelphia, Pennsylvania," FEMA (Federal Emergency Management Agency), 1991 (http://www.interfire.org/res_file/pdf/Tr-049.pdf).

35 Robin Nieto, "Fire Practically Destroys Venezuela's Tallest Building," Venezuela News, Views, and Analysis, October 18, 2004 (http://www.venezuelanalysis.com/news/741).

36 Sunder, "Opening Statement."

37 Griffin, *The Mysterious Collapse of World Trade Center 7*: 170–77.

38 David Ray Griffin, *Debunking 9/11 Debunking: An Answer to Popular Mechanics and Other Defenders of the Official Conspiracy Theory* (Northampton: Olive Branch Press [Interlink Publishing], 2007), Chap. 4.

39 Hayes, "9/11: The Roots of Paranoia."

40 Griffin, *Debunking 9/11 Debunking*, 152–63.

41 See "WTC7 Demolition on 9/11 – Video Compilation," YouTube (http://www.youtube.com/watch?v=DlTBMcxx-78). For video and analysis, see "WTC7: This Is an Orange," YouTube (http://www.youtube.com/watch?v=Zv7BImVvEyk&feature=related), and David Chandler, "WTC7: NIST Finally Admits Freefall (Part III)" (http://www.youtube.com/watch?v=v3mudruFzNw), at 2:25–4:00.

42 See Frank Legge, "9/11: Acceleration Study Proves Explosive Demolition," *Journal of 9/11 Studies* 5 (November 2006) (http://journalof911studies.com/volume/200611/911-Acceleration-Study-Proves-Explosive-Demolition.pdf).

43 Daniel Hofnung, Patriots Question 9/11 (http://patriotsquestion911.com/engineers.html#Dhofnung).

44 Chester W. Gearhart, Patriots Question 9/11 (http://patriotsquestion911.com/engineers.html#Gearhart).

45 Jack Keller, Architects and Engineers for 9/11 Truth (http://www2.ae911truth.org/signpetition.php).

46 See "Danny Jowenko on WTC 7 Controlled Demolition," YouTube (http://www.youtube.com/watch?v=877gr6xtQIc). For more of the interview, "Jowenko WTC 7 Demolition Interviews," in three parts (http://www.youtube.com/watch?v=k3DRhwRN06I&feature=related).

47 "The Myth of Implosion" (http://www.implosionworld.com/dyk2.html).

48 Liz Else, "Baltimore Blasters," *New Scientist* July 24, 2004, 48 (http://www.911research.wtc7.net/mirrors/new_scientist/BaltimoreBlast_Loizeaux.html).

49 Hayes, "9/11: The Roots of Paranoia."

50 NIST NCSTAR 1-9, Draft for Public Comment, Vol. 2 (http://wtc.nist.gov/media/NIST_NCSTAR_1-9_vol2_for_public_comment.pdf), 596.

51 "WTC 7 Technical Briefing," NIST, August 26, 2008. Although NIST originally had a video and a transcript of this briefing at its Internet website, it removed both of them. However, Nate Flach has made the video available at Vimeo (http://vimeo.com/11941571). And the transcript, under the title "NIST Technical Briefing on Its Final Draft Report on WTC 7 for Public Comment," is available at David Chandler's website: (http://911speakout.org/NIST_Tech_Briefing_Transcript.pdf).

52 Ibid.

53 David Chandler, "WTC7 in Freefall - No Longer Controversial," September 4, 2008 (http://www.youtube.com/watch?v=rVCDpL4Ax7I), at 2:45.

54 NIST NCSTAR 1-9, Vol. 2: 607.

55 Chandler, "WTC7 in Freefall—No Longer Controversial," at 3:27.

56 Chandler, "WTC7: NIST Finally Admits Freefall (Part III)," previously dated January 2, 2009, now dated February 12, 2010 (http://www.youtube.com/watch?v=v3mudruFzNw), at 1:19.

57 "Questions and Answers about the NIST WTC 7 Investigation," NIST, August
   21, 2008, updated April 21, 2009. Whereas the 2008 version of this document
   denied free fall, the updated version affirmed it. Although both versions were
   removed from NIST's website, Jim Hoffman's website has both the 2008 version (http://911research.wtc7.net/mirrors/nist/wtc_qa_082108.html) and the
   2009 version (http://911research.wtc7.net/mirrors/nist/wtc_qa_042109.html).
   Now, NIST has an updated (2010) version of the 2009 version
   (http://911research.wtc7.net/mirrors/nist/wtc_qa_042109.html).
58 Chandler, "WTC7: NIST Finally Admits Freefall (Part III)," at 2:20, 3:15.
59 NIST NCSTAR 1–9, Draft for Public Comment, Vol. 2: 595-96, 596, 610.
60 Monbiot, "9/11 Fantasists Pose a Mortal Danger to Popular Oppositional
   Campaigns."
61 Rothschild, "Enough of the 9/11 Conspiracy Theories, Already."
62 Johnson's statement is at Patriots Question 9/11
   (http://patriotsquestion911.com/engineers.html#Djohnson).
63 NIST, *Final Report on the Collapse of the World Trade Center Towers*, September
   2005 (http://wtc.nist.gov/NCSTAR1/PDF/NCSTAR%201.pdf), 146.
64 NIST, "Answers to Frequently Asked Questions," August 30, 2006
   (http://wtc.nist.gov/pubs/factsheets/faqs_8_2006.htm), Question 2.
65 NIST NCSTAR 1, *Final Report on the Collapse of the World Trade Center Towers*, 146.
66 NIST, "Answers to Frequently Asked Questions," Question 6. In the italicized
   portion of this statement, NIST was quoting NIST NCSTAR 1, *Final Report on
   the Collapse of the World Trade Center Towers*, Section 6.14.4 (page 146).
67 Jim Hoffman, "A Reply to the National Institute for Standards and Technology's
   Answers to Frequently Asked Questions"
   (http://911research.wtc7.net/reviews/nist/WTC_FAQ_reply.html).
68 William Rice's statement is quoted at Patriots Question 9/11
   (http://patriotsquestion911.com/engineers.html#Rice).
69 Steven E. Jones, Frank M. Legge, Kevin R. Ryan, Anthony F. Szamboti, and
   James R. Gourley, "Fourteen Points of Agreement with Official Government
   Reports on the World Trade Center Destruction," *Open Civil Engineering
   Journal* 2/1 (2008): 35–40 (http://911reports.wordpress.com/2008/09/17/
   fourteen-points-of-agreement-with-official-government-reports-on-the-
   world-trade-center-destruction-by-steven-e-jones-frank-m-legge-kevin-r-ryan-
   anthony-f-szamboti-and-james-r-gourley).
70 "Request for Correction Submitted to NIST," *Journal of 9/11 Studies* 12 (June
   2007) (http://www.journalof911studies.com/volume/200704/
   RFCtoNISTbyMcIlvaineDoyleJonesRyanGageSTJ.pdf). This letter, dated
   April 12, 2007, was also signed by Bob McIlvaine, Bill Doyle, and Scholars for
   9/11 Truth and Justice.
71 Gordon Ross, "Momentum Transfer Analysis of the Collapse of the Upper
   Storeys of WTC 1," *Journal of 9/11 Studies* 1 (June 2006) (http://www.
   journalof911studies.com/articles/Journal_5_PTransferRoss.pdf): 32–39, at 37.
72 NIST, "Answers to Frequently Asked Questions," Question 7.
73 Alexander Cockburn, "The 9/11 Conspiracy Nuts: How They Let the Guilty
   Parties of 9/11 Slip Off the Hook," *Counterpunch*, September 9/10, 2006
   (http://www.counterpunch.org/cockburn09092006.html); Hayes, "9/11: The
   Roots of Paranoia."

74 Thomas W. Eagar and Christopher Musso, "Why Did the World Trade Center Collapse? Science, Engineering, and Speculation," JOM 53/12 (2001) (http://www.tms.org/pubs/journals/jom/0112/eagar/eagar-0112.html).

75 NIST NCSTAR 1, *Final Report on the Collapse of the World Trade Center Towers*, 90.

76 Don Paul and Jim Hoffman, *Waking Up from Our Nightmare: The 9/11/01 Crimes in New York City* (San Francisco: Irresistible/Revolutionary, 2004), 34.

77 Steven Jones, "Why Indeed Did the WTC Buildings Completely Collapse?" *Journal of 9/11 Studies* 3 (September 2006): 1–47, at 28 (http://www.journalof911studies.com/volume/200609/Why_Indeed_Did_the_WTC_Buildings_Completely_Collapse_Jones_Thermite_World_Trade_Center.pdf).

78 Quoted in Liz Else, "Baltimore Blasters" (see note 48, above).

79 "Request for Correction Submitted to NIST."

80 The statement by Deets is at Architects and Engineers for 9/11 Truth (http://www.ae911truth.org/profile.php?uid=998819).

81 See "911 Eyewitness: Huge Steel Sections Ejected More than 600 Feet" (http://video.google.com/videoplay?docid=1807467434260776490), or "9/11 Mysteries: Demolition" (http://www.youtube.com/watch?v=Y5_tTRliTDo).

82 Sunder, "Opening Statement."

83 NIST NCSTAR 1A: xxxvi.

84 NIST NCSTAR 1–9, Vol. 1: 125.

85 NIST NCSTAR 1A: 16.

86 NIST NCSTAR 1, *Final Report on the Twin Towers*, 183, 184.

87 Jonathan Barnett, Ronald R. Biederman, and Richard D. Sisson, Jr., "An Initial Microstructural Analysis of A36 Steel from WTC Building 7," JOM 53/12 (2001), 18 (http://www.tms.org/pubs/journals/JOM/0112/Biederman/Biederman-0112.html).

88 Jonathan Barnett, Ronald R. Biederman, and R. D. Sisson, Jr., "Limited Metallurgical Examination," FEMA, *World Trade Center Building Performance Study*, Appendix C, 2002 (http://www.fema.gov/pdf/library/fema403_apc.pdf).

89 James Glanz and Eric Lipton, "A Search for Clues in Towers' Collapse," *New York Times* February 2, 2002 (http://query.nytimes.com/gst/fullpage.html?res=9C04E0DE153DF931A35751C0A9649C8B63).

90 Joan Killough-Miller, "The 'Deep Mystery' of Melted Steel," *WPI Transformations* Spring 2002 (http://www.wpi.edu/News/Transformations/2002Spring/steel.html).

91 Glanz, "Engineers Suspect Diesel Fuel in Collapse of 7 World Trade Center." I have here quoted Glanz's paraphrase of Barnett's statement.

92 See Kenneth Chang, "Scarred Steel Holds Clues, And Remedies," *New York Times* October 2, 2001 (http://query.nytimes.com/gst/fullpage.html?res=9B05E6DC123DF931A35753C1A9679C8B63).

93 WebElements: The Periodic Table on the Web: Iron (http://www.webelements.com/iron/physics.html).

94 "Questions and Answers about the NIST WTC 7 Investigation," August 21, 2008 (http://911research.wtc7.net/mirrors/nist/wtc_qa_082108.html). This

statement was repeated in a version of this document that was updated April 21, 2009 (http://911research.wtc7.net/mirrors/nist/wtc_qa_042109.html). Thanks to Jim Hoffman for preserving these documents at his website, after NIST had removed them from its own website. Now the 2009 has been updated in September 17, 2010 (http://www.nist.gov/public_affairs/factsheet/wtc_qa_082108.cfm).

95 See NIST NCSTAR 1–3C, *Damage and Failure Modes of Structural Steel Components*, September 2005 (http://wtc.nist.gov/NCSTAR1/PDF/NCSTAR%201-3C%20Damage%20and%20Failure%20Modes.pdf), in which the authors, Stephen W. Banovic and Timothy Foecke, referred to "the analysis of the steel from WTC 7 (Sample #1 from Appendix C, BPAT/FEMA study) where corrosion phases and morphologies were able to determine a possible temperature region" (233).

96 *The Conspiracy Files: 9/11—The Third Tower*, BBC, July 6, 2008 (available at http://video.google.com/videoplay?docid=9072062020229593250# and http://www.911blogger.com/node/16541); the statement by Barnett is at 48:00. I am indebted to Chris Sarns for this discovery. Barnett during this interview, incidentally, speculated that the steel had "cooked" in the underground fire. This explanation was, however, deceptive at best, for three reasons: First, the effects being discussed by Barnett could have been caused only by something producing much higher temperatures than ordinary hydrocarbon fires could have produced—fires fueled, for example, by nanothermite or some other energetic nanocomposites, as explained below in Section 8. The second and third reasons also involve facts discussed in that section: Ordinary hydrocarbon fires would not have been able to keep burning underground without oxygen; and they would, in any case, have been extinguished by the water and chemical suppressants that were pumped into the rubble.

97 "NIST WTC 7 Investigation Finds Building Fires Caused Collapse."

98 RJ Lee Group, "WTC Dust Signature," Expert Report, May 2004: 11 (http://www.nyenvirolaw.org/WTC/130%20Liberty%20Street/Mike%20Davis%20LMDC%20130%20Liberty%20Documents/Signature%20of%20WTC%20dust/WTCDustSignature_ExpertReport.051304.1646.mp.pdf).

99 RJ Lee Group, "WTC Dust Signature Study: Composition and Morphology," December 2003: 24 (http://www.nyenvirolaw.org/WTC/130%20Liberty%20Street/Mike%20Davis%20LMDC%20130%20Liberty%20Documents/Signature%20of%20WTC%20dust/WTC%20Dust%20Signature.Composition%20and%20Morphology.Final.pdf).

100 Ibid., 17.

101 See "Comments on WTC Signature Study and Peer Review from Greg Meeker, Paul Lioy and Mort Lippmann, November 3, 2005" (http://web.archive.org/web/20100508195240/http://www.epa.gov/wtc/panel/pdfs/SubGroupComments_110305.pdf). I am indebted to Kevin Ryan for this information.

102 WebElements: The Periodic Table on the Web: Iron (http://www.webelements.com/iron/physics.html).

103 Heather A. Lowers and Gregory P. Meeker, U.S. Geological Survey, US Department of the Interior, "Particle Atlas of World Trade Center Dust," 2005 (http://pubs.usgs.gov/of/2005/1165/508OF05-1165.html).

104 Steven E. Jones et al., "Extremely High Temperatures during the World Trade Center Destruction," *Journal of 9/11 Studies* 19 (January 2008): 4 (http://journalof911studies.com/articles/WTCHighTemp2.pdf).

105 Eric Lipton and Andrew C. Revkin, "The Firefighters: With Water and Sweat, Fighting the Most Stubborn Fire," *New York Times* November 19, 2001 (http://www.nytimes.com/2001/11/19/nyregion/19FIRE.html); Jonathan Beard, "Ground Zero's Fires Still Burning," *New Scientist* December 3, 2001 (http://www.newscientist.com/article.ns?id=dn1634).

106 Trudy Walsh, "Handheld APP Eased Recovery Tasks," *Government Computer News* September 11, 2002 (http://911research.wtc7.net/cache/wtc/evidence/gcn_handheldapp.html).

107 Niels H. Harrit, Jeffrey Farrer, Steven E. Jones, et al., "Active Thermitic Material Observed in Dust from the 9/11 World Trade Center Catastrophe," *The Open Chemical Physics Journal* 2 (2009): 7–31 (http://www.benthamscience.com/open/tocpj/articles/V002/7TOCPJ.htm? TOCIEJ/2008/00000002/00000001/35TOCIEJ.SGM). The quoted description of how nanothermite can be tailored was provided by Niels Harrit, email letter of June 19, 2011, to Elizabeth Woodworth for Consensus 9/11.

108 Kevin R. Ryan, James R. Gourley, and Steven E. Jones, "Environmental Anomalies at the World Trade Center: Evidence for Energetic Materials," *The Environmentalist* 29/1 (August, 2008): 56–63, at 58, 56. Also published online, August 4, 2008 (http://www.springerlink.com/content/f67q6272583h86n4/ fulltext.html). Ryan has provided experiments showing the explosive power of nanothermite; see DK1Ryan, "Experiments with Nanothermite," July 24, 2011 (http://www.youtube.com/watch?v=O66UyGNrmSI).

109 NCSTAR 1–9, Vol. 1: 330.

110 NIST, "Answers to Frequently Asked Questions," Question 2.

111 Glanz and Lipton, "A Search for Clues in Towers' Collapse."

112 Killough-Miller, "The 'Deep Mystery' of Melted Steel."

113 Barnett, Biederman, and Sisson, "Limited Metallurgical Examination."

114 Ibid., C-13.

115 Dr. Arden L. Bement, Jr., Testimony before the House Science Committee Hearing on "The Investigation of the World Trade Center Collapse," May 1, 2002 (http://911research.wtc7.net/cache/wtc/official/nist/bement.htm). In the quoted statement, the name "FEMA" replaces "BPAT," which is the abbreviation for "Building Performance Assessment Team," the name of the ASCE team that prepared this report for FEMA.

116 "Answers to Frequently Asked Questions," NIST, Question 12.

117 Jones et al., "Extremely High Temperatures during the World Trade Center Destruction," 3.

118 Email letter from Kevin Ryan, October 16, 2008.

119 Email letter from Steven Jones, October 17, 2008.

120 Personal communications from Niels Harrit, May 8, 2009, and June 25, 2010.

121 Steven E. Jones, "Revisiting 9/11/2001: Applying the Scientific Method," *Journal of 9/11 Studies* 11 (May 2007): 81 (http://www.journalof911studies.com/volume/200704/ JonesWTC911SciMethod.pdf).

122 Ibid., 75.

123 Symposium on State Crimes against Democracy, *American Behavioral Scientist* 53 (February 2010): 783–939 (http://abs.sagepub.com/content/vol53/issue6).

124 Matthew T. Witt, "Pretending Not to See or Hear, Refusing to Signify: The Farce and Tragedy of Geocentric Public Affairs Scholarship," *American Behavioral Scientist* 53 (February 2010): 921–39 (http://abs.sagepub.com/content/vol53/issue6), at 934.

125 Ibid., 932 (emphasis in original).

126 Cockburn, "The Decline of the Left," *The Free Press* September 30, 2006 (http://www.freepress.org/columns/display/2/2006/1440); Taibbi, "The Idiocy Behind the '9/11 Truth' Movement."

127 "9/11 Fantasists Pose a Mortal Danger to Popular Oppositional Campaigns."

128 Corn, "How 9/11 Conspiracy Poison Did in Van Jones."

129 Corn, "When 9/11 Conspiracy Theories Go Bad."

130 Cockburn, "The 9/11 Conspiracy Nuts: How They Let the Guilty Parties of 9/11 Slip Off the Hook."

131 "Chomsky Dismisses 9/11 Conspiracy Theories As 'Dubious.'"

132 Monbiot, "9/11 Fantasists Pose a Mortal Danger to Popular Oppositional Campaigns."

133 Charles Pigden, "Conspiracy Theories and the Conventional Wisdom," *Episteme* 4 (2007): 219–32, at 219.

134 Ibid., 222.

135 Ibid., 223.

136 Political leaders, the mainstream press, and even much of the left-leaning press have been reluctant to admit that the official account of 9/11 is a conspiracy theory (often because they like to use this label to discredit people without examining their evidence). But former Harvard law professor Cass Sunstein, who was appointed to a senior post in the Obama administration, acknowledged this fact in a co-authored essay: Cass R. Sunstein and Adrian Vermeule, "Conspiracy Theories: Causes and Cures," *Journal of Political Philosophy* 17/2 (June 2009), 202–27, at 208. Sunstein also helpfully referred to Charles Pigden's above-quoted article, which criticizes the widespread use of the "conspiracy theory" label to avoid substantive issues. I deal with the Sunstein-Vermeule essay in *Cognitive Infiltration: An Obama Appointee's Plan to Undermine the 9/11 Conspiracy Theory* (Northampton: Olive Branch Press [Interlink Publishing], 2010).

137 Quoted in "Jesse Ventura's Piece on 9/11—KILLED BY HUFFPOST!" News from the Underground, March 9, 2010 (http://markcrispinmiller.com/2010/03/jesse-venturas-piece-on-911-killed-by-huffpost).

138 "HuffPost's Absurd Stand on 'Conspiracy Theories' (David Ray Griffin)," News from the Underground, March 11, 2010 (http://markcrispinmiller.com/2010/03/huffposts-absurd-stand-on-conspiracy-theories-david-ray-griffin).

139 Taibbi, "The Idiocy Behind the '9/11 Truth' Movement."

140 See "Two Hit, Three Down—The Biggest Lie," by National Medal of Science-winner Lynn Margulis, *Rock Creek Free Press* January 24, 2010 (http://rockcreekfreepress.tumblr.com/post/353434420/two-hit-three-down-the-biggest-lie)

141 Jones et al., "Fourteen Points of Agreement with Official Government Reports on the World Trade Center Destruction."

142 Ryan, Gourley, and Jones, "Environmental Anomalies at the World Trade Center."

143 Harrit, Farrer, Jones, et al., "Active Thermitic Material."

144 Crockett Grabbe, "Discussion of 'Progressive Collapse of the World Trade Center: A Simple Analysis' by K.A. Seffen," *Journal of Engineering Mechanics* 136/4 (April 2010): 538–39 (http://dx.doi.org/10.1061/(ASCE)EM.1943-7889.0000025).

145 James R. Gourley, "Discussion of 'Mechanics of Progressive Collapse: Learning from World Trade Center and Building Demolitions' by Zdenek P. Bazant and Mathieu Verdure," *Journal of Engineering Mechanics* 134/10 (October 2008): 915–16 (http://dx.doi.org/10.1061/(ASCE)0733-9399(2008)134:10(915)).

146 Anders Björkman, "Discussion of 'What Did and Did Not Cause Collapse of World Trade Center Twin Towers in New York?' by Zdenek P. Bazant, Jia-Liang Le, Frank R. Greening, and David B. Benson," ASCE, *Journal of Engineering Mechanics*, 136/7 (July 2010): 933–34 (http://dx.doi.org/10.1061/(ASCE)EM.1943-7889.0000090).

147 Scientists for 9/11 Truth (http://www.scientistsfor911truth.org) has been formed under the leadership of Dr. John Wyndham, a former research scholar at the California Institute of Technology.

148 Information about these and other architects who question the official story can be found at Architects and Engineers for 9/11 Truth (http://www.ae911truth.org) or under "Engineers and Architects" at Patriots Question 9/11 (http://www.patriotsquestion911.com/engineers.html#Search).

149 Information about these and other engineers who question the official story can be found in Architects and Engineers for 9/11 Truth (see previous note) or under "Engineers and Architects" at Patriots Question 9/11 (http://www.patriotsquestion911.com/engineers.html#Search).

150 Firefighters for 9/11 Truth (http://firefightersfor911truth.org); Intelligence Officers for 9/11 Truth (http://IO911truth.org); Medical Professionals for 9/11 Truth (http://mp911truth.org); Military Officers for 9/11 Truth (http://www.militaryofficersfor911truth.org); Pilots for 9/11 Truth (http://pilotsfor911truth.org); Scientific Panel Investigating Nine-Eleven: Physics 911 (http://physics911.net); Veterans for 9/11 Truth (http://v911t.org).

151 Actors and Artists for 9/11 Truth (http://www.actorsandartistsfor911truth.org); Journalists and Other Media Professionals for 9/11 Truth (http://mediafor911truth.org); Lawyers for 9/11 Truth (http://l911t.com); Political Leaders for 9/11 Truth (http://pl911truth.com); Religious Leaders for 9/11 Truth (http://rl911truth.org); Scholars for 9/11 Truth and Justice (http://stj911.com).

152 Corn, "How 9/11 Conspiracy Poison Did in Van Jones."

153 Upton Sinclair, "*I, Candidate for Governor: And How I Got Licked* (1935; University of California Press, 1994), 109.

154 "9/11: Time for a Second Look." For the text, see Voltaire.net.org, April 18, 2009 (http://www.voltairenet.org/article159749.html). For the lecture as delivered in Boston, see the YouTube video at davidraygriffin.com (http://davidraygriffin.com/calendar/april-11-2009-boston). For the lecture as delivered in Hamburg, see the YouTube video at davidraygriffin.com (http://davidraygriffin.com/calendar/may-9-2009-hamburg).

154 David Ray Griffin, *The New Pearl Harbor Revisited: 9/11, the Cover-Up, and the Exposé* (Northampton: Olive Branch Press, [Interlink Publishing] 2008); henceforth *NPHR*.

155 *Publishers Weekly* November 24, 2008 (http://www.publishersweekly.com/pw/by-topic/1-legacy/15-web-exclusive-book-reviews/article/6017-web-exclusive-reviews-week-of-11-24-2008-.html).

156 Rothschild, "Enough of the 9/11 Conspiracy Theories, Already."

157 Hayes, "9/11: The Roots of Paranoia."

158 The FBI's report on the phone calls from the four flights is at United States v. Zacarias Moussaoui, Exhibit Number P200054 (http://www.vaed.uscourts.gov/notablecases/moussaoui/exhibits/prosecution/flights/P200054.html). But these documents can be more easily viewed in Jim Hoffman's "Detailed Account of Phone Calls from September 11th Flights" (http://911research.wtc7.net/planes/evidence/calldetail.html).

159 Rothschild, "Enough of the 9/11 Conspiracy Theories, Already."

160 See the graphic at Jim Hoffman's website (http://911research.wtc7.net/planes/evidence/calldetail.html) and my discussion in *NPHR* 60–62.

161 Griffin, *NPHR* 206–07.

162 See David Ray Griffin, *Osama bin Laden: Dead or Alive?* (Northampton: Olive Branch Press [Interlink Publishing], 2009), 22–36.

163 Dr. David Ray Griffin, "The Truly Distracting 9/11 Conspiracy Theory: A Reply to Alexander Cockburn," *Le Monde Diplomatique*, Nordic Edition, March 2007 (http://www.lmd.no/index.php?article=1408); a response to Alexander Cockburn, "US: The Conspiracy That Wasn't," *Le Monde Diplomatique*, December 2006 (http://mondediplo.com/2006/12/02conspiracy), which was headlined: "Distractions from Awful Reality."

164 See the obituary I wrote, "William A. ('Bill') Christison (1928-2010)," 911Truth.org, June 20, 2010 (http://911truth.org/article.php?story=20100620115516747).

165 Bill Christison, "Stop Belittling the Theories about September 11," Dissident Voice, August 14, 2006 (http://dissidentvoice.org/Aug06/Christison14.htm).

166 Paul Joseph Watson, "28-Year Career CIA Official Says 9/11 An Inside Job," Prison Planet, September 7, 2006 (http://www.prisonplanet.com/articles/september2006/070906insidejob.htm).

167 Mainstream sources estimate the total number of deaths due to the invasions and occupations at about one million for each country. But Dr. Gideon Polya, author of *Body Count: Global Avoidable Mortality Since 1950*, has put the numbers much higher. See his "Iraqi Holocaust: 2.3 Million Iraqi Excess Deaths," March 21, 2009 (http://www.countercurrents.org/polya210309.htm); and "January 2010 - 4.5 Million Dead in Afghan Holocaust, Afghan Genocide," Afghan Holocaust, Afghan Genocide, January 2, 2010 (http://afghangenocide.blogspot.com).

168 Both this statement and the Chicago version of my lecture can be seen at eddieleaks.org (http://edwardrynearson.wordpress.com/2010/05/02/is-the-war-in-afghanistan-justified-by-911/).

169 Cockburn, "The Decline of the Left"; Corn, "Van Jones and the 9/11 Conspiracy Theory Poison."

CHAPTER 3

1 "The New Pearl Harbor: A Debate On A New Book That Alleges The Bush Administration Was Behind The 9/11 Attacks," *Democracy Now!* May 26, 2004 (http://www.democracynow.org/2004/5/26/the_new_pearl_harbor_a_debate).

2 "Buying the War," *Bill Moyers Journal*, PBS, April 25, 2007 (http://www.pbs.org/moyers/journal/btw/transcript1.html).

3 Bill Moyers, "America Can't Deal With Reality—We Must Be Exposed to the Truth, Even If It Hurts," AlterNet, February 14, 2011 (http://www.alternet.org/world/149925/bill_moyers%3A_america_can't_deal_with_reality_--_we_must_be_exposed_to_the_truth,_even_if_it_hurts).

4 Ibid.

5 Robert Parry, "The 9/11 'Truth' Parlor Game," Consortiumnews.com, January 15, 2011 (Updated January 16, 2011) (http://www.consortiumnews.com/2011/011511.html).

6 Norman Solomon, "Robert Parry," AlterNet, April 26, 2000 (http://www.alternet.org/story/8012/cohen_and_solomon%3A_robert_parry).

7 Robert Parry, "A Brief History of Consortiumnews.com," Consortiumnews.com, December 21, 2004 (http://www.consortiumnews.com/2004/122104.html).

8 Barbara Honegger, *October Surprise* (Greensboro: Tudor Publishers, 1989).

9 For example, *Newsweek* and the *New Republic* declared that Casey could not have been in Madrid on July 27 and 28, because he was at a historical conference in London. The press declared this evidence proved the "October Surprise" to be a myth. However, the attendance sheet for this London conference, Parry discovered, showed that Casey did not arrive until 4:00 PM on the 28th, so he could have had meetings in Madrid on July 27 and 28, as the witnesses had testified. Although *Newsweek* and the *New Republic*, confronted with this disproof of their claims, refused to print retractions, Lee Hamilton sought a better alibi for Casey. His task force claimed that from July 25 to 27, Casey had been at the Bohemian Grove near San Francisco, after which he flew overnight to London in time to arrive at the historical conference by 4:00 PM on the 28th. However, documentary evidence showed that Casey attended the Bohemian Grove in August, not in July. Hamilton's task force, nevertheless, stuck with the Bohemian Grove alibi.

10 Ibid.

11 Parry, "A Brief History of Consortiumnews.com."

12 Robert Parry, "Key October Surprise Evidence Hidden," Consortiumnews.com, May 6, 2010 (http://www.consortiumnews.com/2010/050610.html).

13 Dan Kennedy, "Parry's Thrust," Salon.com, June 11, 1996 (http://www.salon.com/media/media960611.html). One of the *Newsweek* journalists who wrote the debunking story said that, although Parry was "a very good reporter," the October Surprise story "was his undoing," and the author of the *New Republic*'s debunking story said: "Parry's continued obsession with these delusions is a personal tragedy."

14 Ibid.

15 Technically, Hamilton was the vice chairman of the 9/11 Commission and Thomas Kean was the chairman, but the two men had agreed to function as co-chairmen; see page 68 of the book in the following note.

16 Philip Shenon, *The Commission: The Uncensored History of the 9/11 Investigation* (New York: Twelve, 2008), Chap. 10.

17 Because of his conflicts of interest, Zelikow was asked repeatedly to resign by The Family Steering Committee for the 9/11 Commission, which had been instrumental in getting the 9/11 Commission created. In 2004, this committee wrote: "Dr. Zelikow should never have been permitted to be Executive Staff Director of the Commission. . . . . The Family Steering Committee is calling for: 1. Dr. Zelikow's immediate resignation. . . . 4. The Commission to apologize to the 9/11 families and America for this massive appearance of impropriety" (Statement of the Family Steering Committee for The 9/11 Independent Commission, March 20, 2004 [www.911independentcommission.org/ mar202004.html]).

18 Shenon, *The Commission*, 388–89.

19 See FEMA, "High-Rise Office Building Fire, One Meridian Plaza, Philadelphia, Pennsylvania" (http://www.interfire.org/res_file/pdf/Tr-049.pdf).

20 James Glanz, "Engineers Have a Culprit in the Strange Collapse of 7 World Trade Center: Diesel Fuel," *New York Times* November 29, 2001 (http://www.nytimes.com/2001/11/29/nyregion/nation-challenged-site-engineers-have-culprit-strange-collapse-7-world-trade.html).

21 "The Myth of Implosion" (http://www.implosionworld.com/dyk2.html).

22 "WTC 7 Technical Briefing," NIST, August 26, 2008. Although NIST originally had a video and a transcript of this briefing at its Internet website, it recently removed both of them. However, Nate Flach has made the video available at Vimeo (http://vimeo.com/11941571), and the transcript, under the title "NIST Technical Briefing on Its Final Draft Report on WTC 7 for Public Comment," is available at David Chandler's website (http://911speakout.org/NIST_Tech_Briefing_Transcript.pdf).

23 Parry assumed that the first three features of Building 7's collapse create no problems. He wrote: "[T]he speed of the collapse should not be all that surprising because Building Seven had a large atrium. Once the atrium's supports were breached by the shock of the Twin Tower collapse and a resulting fire, Building Seven would logically fall into the open space at near freefall speed" ("The 9/11 'Truth' Parlor Game"). But if such an easy answer could be given, one must wonder why NIST's physicists and engineers did not suggest it. Also, Parry seemed not to be aware that there were fires on only a few of the building's floors; not to be aware that coming down in near free fall would have required all 82 of the building's columns to fail simultaneously; and not to be aware that for over two seconds the building came down not merely in "near freefall speed" but in absolute free fall, which requires zero resistance. Parry, a superb journalist about political matters, shows that he does not understand the problems in the official account of the destruction of the World Trade Center. In response to being "scolded [by 'truthers'] for not delving deeply enough into the intricate arguments behind their claim that 9/11 was an

'inside job,'" Parry said: "[T]he truth is that I have devoted way more time to these preposterous notions than they deserve." The real truth seems to be that, being convinced in advance that the 9/11 arguments were "preposterous," he did not spend the time needed to evaluate them.

24 NIST, *Final Report on the Collapse of the World Trade Center Towers*, September 2005 (http://wtc.nist.gov/NCSTAR1/PDF/NCSTAR%201.pdf), 146.

25 NIST, "Answers to Frequently Asked Questions," Question 6. In the italicized portion of this statement, NIST was quoting NIST NCSTAR 1, *Final Report on the Collapse of the World Trade Center Towers*, Section 6.14.4, page 146.

26 If Parry's understanding of the "collapse" of WTC 7 was uninformed, his solution to the question of why Twin Towers came down, and in the way they did, was, if anything, even more so. He wrote: "[T]he structure of the Twin Towers, with interlocking beams allowing them to have height without the weight of older skyscrapers, would have produced the falling in on itself effect once the beams were weakened by the impact of the planes and the heat from the fires." But only a few floors would have been impacted by the planes. The North Tower was impacted on the 93rd to the 98th floor, the South Tower on the 78th to the 84th floor. And the fires were restricted almost entirely to those floors and those above them. So in the South Tower, the steel in the lowest 75 floors would have been essentially unaffected, and in the North Tower the same would have been true of the lowest 90 floors. The happenings in the upper floors would not have affected the core columns of the lower floors, and these core columns were massive in the lowest floors. Unless explosives were used, only a miracle could have prevented these floors from continuing to support the floors above them.

27 These USGS scientists failed to mention in their published report the discovery of molybdenum that had melted (Heather A. Lowers and Gregory P. Meeker, U.S. Geological Survey, US Department of the Interior, "Particle Atlas of World Trade Center Dust," 2005 [http://pubs.usgs.gov/of/2005/1165/508OF05-1165.html]). But another group of scientists, having obtained the USGS team's data through a FOIA (Freedom of Information Act) request, reported evidence showing that the USGS scientists had devoted serious study to "a molybdenum-rich spherule" (Steven E. Jones et al., "Extremely High Temperatures during the World Trade Center Destruction," *Journal of 9/11 Studies* 19 (January 2008): 4 [http://journalof911studies.com/articles/WTCHighTemp2.pdf]).

28 Robert Parry, "Lies Spun into History," Consortiumnews.com, March 14, 1996 (http://www.consortiumnews.com/archive/xfile8.html).

29 Parry, "The 9/11 'Truth' Parlor Game."

30 Ibid.

31 Upton Sinclair, *I, Candidate for Governor: And How I Got Licked* (1935; University of California Press, 1994), 109.

32 Architects and Engineers for 9/11 Truth (http://www.ae911truth.org), Firefighters for 9/11 Truth (http://firefightersfor911truth.org), Intelligence Officers for 9/11 Truth (http://IO911Truth.org), Military Officers for 9/11 Truth (http://www.militaryofficersfor911truth.org), Scientists for 9/11 Truth (http://sci911truth.org).

33 Parry, "The 9/11 'Truth' Parlor Game."

34 Moyers, "America Can't Deal with Reality."

35 *Bill Moyers Journal*, PBS, February 8, 2008 (http://www.pbs.org/moyers/journal/blog/2008/02/bill_moyers_reading_recommenda_1.html).

36 David Ray Griffin, *Debunking 9/11 Debunking: An Answer to Popular Mechanics and Other Defenders of the Official Conspiracy Theory* (Northampton: Olive Branch Press [Interlink Publishing], 2007).

37 This fact was revealed on the blog for *Bill Moyers Journal* by a contributor named Jerry on February 10, 2008 (http://www.pbs.org/moyers/journal/blog/2008/02/bill_moyers_reading_recommenda_1.html).

38 The "Product Description" at Amazon.com states: "In February, 2008 Bill Moyers asked PBS viewers to recommend one book that the next president should take to the White House. More than one hundred people recommended *The Art of Non-War* by Kim Michaels, making it one of the top three choices" (http://www.amazon.com/Art-Non-war-Kim-Michaels/sim/097669719X/2).

39 Transcript, *Bill Moyers Journal*, PBS, February 15, 2008 (http://www.pbs.org/moyers/journal/02152008/transcript4.html).

40 See two notes above.

41 Moyers, "William Sloane Coffin," NOW, March 5, 2004 (http://www.pbs.org/now/society/coffin.html); Moyers, "Remembering Bill Coffin," *Religion and Ethics*, PBS, April 20, 2006 (http://www.pbs.org/wnet/religionandethics/episodes/april-20-2006/remembering-bill-coffin-bill-moyers/2954).

42 "Bill Moyers Interviews Union Theological Seminary's Joseph Hough," *NOW with Bill Moyers*, broadcast October 24, 2003 (http://www.commondreams.org/views03/1027-01.htm).

43 Parry, "The 9/11 'Truth' Parlor Game."

44 A video of the lecture,"9/11: Let's Get Empirical," is available at 911TV.org. (http://communitycurrency.org/911TV/index.html). A written version is available in *Global Outlook: Prescription for a World in Crisis*, Issue 13, Annual 2009: 87–102.

45 Adolf Hitler, *Mein Kampf*, trans. James Murphy, Vol. I, Ch. X.

46 Jonathan Kay recently published a book (*Among the Truthers: A Journey Through America's Growing Conspiracist Underground* [New York: HarperCollins, 2011]), in which he makes very negative judgments about members of the 9/11 Truth Movement—calling them, for example, "cranks"—while providing no evidence to support these judgments. In an earlier writing, Kay explained: "[T]he truth is. . . I never bothered with schooling myself on the minutae [sic] of 9/11-ology. . . . I never felt the need to because, on a purely instinctual level, I always felt the Truthers case was complete nonsense." In "Jonathan Kay on the Humbling Frustrations of Debating 9/11 Truthers," *National Post* October 27, 2008(http://network.nationalpost.com/np/blogs/fullcomment/archive/2008/10/27/jonathan-kay-on-the-humbling-frustrations-of-debating-9-11-quot-truthers-quot.aspx). It would appear that Parry and Moyers have treated 9/11 in the same way.

47 Parry, "The 9/11 'Truth' Parlor Game."

48 Ibid.

49 Robert Parry, "A Brief History of Consortiumnews.com," Consortiumnews.com, December 21, 2004 (http://www.consortiumnews.com/2004/122104.html).

CHAPTER 4

1 David Ray Griffin, *The Mysterious Collapse of World Trade Center 7: Why the Final Official Report about 9/11 Is Unscientific and False* (Northampton: Olive Branch Press [Interlink Publishing], 2009).

2 Lynn Margulis, "Two Hit, Three Down—The Biggest Lie," *Rock Creek Free Press* January 24, 2010 (http://rockcreekfreepress.tumblr.com/post/353434420/two-hit-three-down-the-biggest-lie).

3 James Glanz, "Engineers Have a Culprit in the Strange Collapse of 7 World Trade Center: Diesel Fuel," *New York Times* November 29, 2001 (http://www.nytimes.com/2001/11/29/nyregion/nation-challenged-site-engineers-have-culprit-strange-collapse-7-world-trade.html).

4 Rather's statement is available on YouTube (http://www.youtube.com/watch?v=Nvx904dAw0o).

5 See the video *911 Eyewitness* (http://video.google.com/videoplay?docid=65460757734339444) at 29:05.

6 See "Danny Jowenko on WTC 7 Controlled Demolition," YouTube (http://www.youtube.com/watch?v=877gr6xtQIc), or, for more of the interview, "Jowenko WTC 7 Demolition Interviews," in three parts (http://www.youtube.com/watch?v=k3DRhwRN06I&feature=related).

7 "Michael Hess, WTC7 Explosion Witness," YouTube (http://www.youtube.com/watch?v=BUfiLbXMa64). Hess should have said "down to the sixth floor." As Barry Jennings later clarified, the explosion that blocked their descent occurred when they reached the sixth floor, after which they walked back up to the eighth floor, where they waited to be rescued; see "Barry Jennings—9/11 WTC7 Full Uncut Interview," Part 2 (http://www.youtube.com/watch?v=kxUj6UgPODo), at 5:08–5:33.

8 See "Barry Jennings—9/11 Early Afternoon ABC 7 Interview" (http://www.youtube.com/watch?v=5LO5V2CJpzI).

9 This statement could previously be seen in "Barry Jennings—9/11 WTC7 Full Uncut Interview," Part 1, at 3:57–4:05. But at the time this essay was written, it had been blocked from the Internet, because it is now in the film *Loose Change 9/11: An American Coup*. But the footage is available at "World Exclusive: WTC7 Survivor Barry Jennings Account" (http://www.youtube.com/watch?v=kRaKHq2dfCI).

10 Quoted in Chris Bull and Sam Erman, eds., *At Ground Zero: Young Reporters Who Were There Tell Their Stories* (New York: Thunder's Mouth Press, 2002), 97.

11 Bartmer's statement is quoted in Paul Joseph Watson, "NYPD Officer Heard Building 7 Bombs," Prison Planet, February 10, 2007 (http://www.prisonplanet.com/articles/february2007/100207heardbombs.htm).

12 This unnamed medical student can be seen making this statement in *911 Eyewitness* (at 31:30).

13 James Glanz and Eric Lipton, "A Search for Clues in Towers' Collapse," *New York Times* February 2, 2002

(http://query.nytimes.com/gst/fullpage.html?res=9C04E0DE153DF931A35751
C0A9649C8B63). Joan Killough-Miller, "The 'Deep Mystery' of Melted
Steel," *WPI Transformations* Spring 2002 (http://www.wpi.edu/News/
Transformations/2002Spring/steel.html); James Glanz, "Engineers Have a
Culprit in the Strange Collapse of 7 World Trade Center: Diesel Fuel," *New
York Times* November 29, 2001 (http://www.nytimes.com/2001/11/29/
nyregion/29TOWE.html).

14 See Kenneth Change, "Scarred Steel Holds Clues, And Remedies," *New York
Times* October 2, 2001 (http://www.nytimes.com/2001/10/02/science/
scarred-steel-holds-clues-and-remedies.html).

15 WebElements: The Periodic Table on the Web: Iron
(http://www.webelements.com/iron/physics.html).

16 Ibid.

17 See FEMA, *World Trade Center Building Performance Study*
(http://www.fema.gov/pdf/library/fema403_ch5.pdf), Chap. 5, Sect. 6.2,
"Probable Collapse Sequence," at page 31.

18 "A Word about Our Poll of American Thinking Toward the 9/11 Terrorist
Attacks," Zogby International, May 24, 2006
(http://web.archive.org/web/20090422012551/http://www.zogby.com/features/
Features.cfm?ID=231).

19 In the ensuing exchange, Judge Lehner showed that he was not completely un-
aware of this building's destruction, asking if it was "the one that has been re-
built." Shortly thereafter, however, the judge confused this building with the
Twin Towers. See pages 16–19 of "Proceedings, Christopher Burke et al,
Petitioners. vs. Michael McSweeney as City Clerk of New York and Clerk of
the City Council of New York and the Board of Elections in the City of New
York, before Honorable Edward H. Lehner, J. S. C., Supreme Court of the
State of New York, September 29, 2009."

20 Glanz, "Engineers Have a Culprit in the Strange Collapse of 7 World Trade Center."

21 "National Construction Safety Team Advisory Committee 2003 Report to Congress" (http://wtc.nist.gov/media/NCSTAC2003ReporttoCongressFinal.pdf), 4.

22 NIST, "Answers to Frequently Asked Questions," , Question 14
(http://wtc.nist.gov/pubs/factsheets/faqs_8_2006.htm). This document
originally contained what was quoted in the text. But NIST, never a stickler
for retaining past statements that later prove embarrassing, changed this
statement, evidently when they "updated" it on January 28, 2008. This
"updated" version of the 2006 document gives the reader the impression that
NIST in 2006, instead of saying, "It is anticipated that a draft report will be released by early 2007," said: "It is anticipated that a draft report will be released
for public comment by July 2008 and that the final report will be released
shortly thereafter." The original document, as updated August 30, 2006, has
been preserved in Jim Hoffman, "NIST's World Trade Center FAQ"
(http://911research.wtc7.net/reviews/nist/WTC_FAQ_reply.html).

23 NIST, "WTC Investigation Overview," December 18, 2007
(http://wtc.nist.gov/media/NCSTAC_December18(Sunder).pdf). Like NIST's
2006 document discussed in the previous note, this one has also been revised, so
that it now says July and August, 2008, respectively, without giving exact dates.

24 See "WTC 7: The Smoking Gun of 9/11"
   (http://www.youtube.com/watch?v=MwSc7NPn8Ok), and Paul Joseph Watson,
   "BBC's 9/11 Yellow Journalism Backfires: Building 7 Becomes the Achilles Heel
   of the Official Conspiracy Theory," Prison Planet, March 5, 2007 (http://
   infowars.wordpress.com/2007/03/05/bbcs-911-yellow-journalism-backfires).
25 "Progress Report on the NIST Building and Fire Investigation into the World
   Trade Center Disaster," NIST, December 9, 2002
   (http://www.fire.nist.gov/bfrlpubs/build03/PDF/b03040.pdf); "Progress Report on
   the Federal Building and Fire Safety Investigation of the World Trade Center
   Disaster," NIST, May 2003
   (http://wtc.nist.gov/pubs/MediaUpdate%20_FINAL_ProgressReport051303.pdf).
26 NIST, Interim Report on WTC 7, June 2004
   (http://wtc.nist.gov/progress_report_june04/appendixl.pdf).
27 NIST, "WTC 7 Collapse," April 5, 2005
   (http://wtc.nist.gov/pubs/WTC%20Part%20IIC%20-%20WTC%207%20
   Collapse%20Final.pdf).
28 NIST, "Answers to Frequently Asked Questions," Question 14.
29 Shyam Sunder, "Opening Statement," NIST Press Briefing, August 21, 2008
   (http://wtc.nist.gov/media/opening_remarks_082108.html).
30 Associated Press, "Report: Fire, Not Bombs, Leveled WTC 7 Building," USA
   Today August 21, 2008 (http://www.usatoday.com/news/nation/2008-08-21-
   wtc-nist_N.htm).
31 National Science Foundation, Office of Inspector General, "What is Research
   Misconduct?" in New Research Misconduct Policies (http://www.nsf.gov/oig/
   session.pdf). This document is undated, but internal evidence suggests that it
   was published in 2001.
32 NIST NCSTAR 1–9, Structural Fire Response and Probable Collapse Sequence of
   World Trade Center Building 7, Vol. 1 (wtc.nist.gov/NCSTAR1/PDF/
   NCSTAR%201-9%20Vol%201.pdf): 324.
33 Jonathan Barnett, Ronald R. Biederman, and Richard D. Sisson, Jr., "Limited
   Metallurgical Examination," FEMA, World Trade Center Building Performance
   Study, Appendix C (http://wtc.nist.gov/media/AppendixC-fema403_apc.pdf),
   page 13.
34 Dr. Arden L. Bement, Jr., Testimony before the House Science Committee
   Hearing on "The Investigation of the World Trade Center Collapse," May 1,
   2002 (http://911research.wtc7.net/cache/wtc/official/nist/bement.htm). In the
   quoted statement, the name "FEMA" replaces "BPAT," which is the
   abbreviation for "Building Performance Assessment Team," the name of the
   ASCE team that prepared this report for FEMA.
35 "Questions and Answers about the NIST WTC 7 Investigation," August 21, 2008,
   updated (http://www.nist.gov/public_affairs/factsheet/wtc_qa_082108.html). In
   response to the question, "Why didn't the investigators look at actual steel
   samples from WTC 7?" NIST replied: "Steel samples were removed from the site
   before the NIST investigation began. In the immediate aftermath of Sept. 11,
   debris was removed rapidly from the site to aid in recovery efforts and facilitate
   emergency responders' efforts to work around the site. Once it was removed from
   the scene, the steel from WTC 7 could not be clearly identified. Unlike the
   pieces of steel from WTC 1 and WTC 2, which were painted red and contained

distinguishing markings, WTC 7 steel did not contain such identifying characteristics." This document was updated in 2010 (http://www.nist.gov/public_affairs/factsheet/wtc_qa_082108.cfm), but there was no change in the quoted passage.

36 Steven E. Jones et al., "Extremely High Temperatures during the World Trade Center Destruction," *Journal of 9/11 Studies* 19 (January 2008): 8 (http://journalof911studies.com/articles/WTCHighTemp2.pdf).

37 Ibid., 4–5.

38 WebElements: The Periodic Table on the Web (http://www.webelements.com/molybdenum/physics.html).

39 See the statement quoted from Niels Harrit in n. 107 of Chap. 2.

40 Niels H. Harrit, Jeffrey Farrer, Steven E. Jones, et al., "Active Thermitic Material Observed in Dust from the 9/11 World Trade Center Catastrophe," *The Open Chemical Physics Journal* 2 (2009): 7–31 (http://www.benthamscience.com/open/tocpj/articles/V002/7TOCPJ.htm? TOCIEJ/2008/00000002/00000001/35TOCIEJ.SGM).

41 According to the *Guide for Fire and Explosion Investigations*, put out by the National Fire Protection Association, investigators should, in seeking to determine the cause of a fire, look for evidence of accelerants, which are any substances that could be used to ignite a fire or accelerate its progress (National Fire Protection Association's *921 Guide for Fire and Explosion Investigations*, 1998 Edition, Section 12-2.4 (http://www.interfire.org/res_file/92112m.asp), and thermite mixtures are explicitly classified as accelerants (Section 19.2.4, "Exotic Accelerants" and "Thermite Mixtures").

42 NIST, "Answers to Frequently Asked Questions," Question 12 (http://wtc.nist.gov/pubs/factsheets/faqs_8_2006.htm).

43 Jennifer Abel, "Theories of 9/11," *Hartford Advocate*, January 29, 2008 (http://www.ae911truth.org/press/23).

44 National Science Foundation, "What is Research Misconduct?"

45 See *The Mysterious Collapse*, 150–55.

46 NIST NCSTAR 1–9, Vol. 1: 346.

47 NIST NCSTAR 1–9, Vol. 2: 462 (http://wtc.nist.gov/NCSTAR1/PDF/NCSTAR%201-9%20Vol%202.pdf).

48 See NIST, *Interim Report on WTC 7*, L-6-7, and Griffin, *The Mysterious Collapse*, 212–15.

49 NIST, *Interim Report on WTC 7*, L-26 (http://wtc.nist.gov/progress_report_june04/appendixl.pdf). This contradiction is pointed out in a video, "NIST Report on WTC7 Debunked and Exposed!" YouTube, December 28, 2008 (http://www.youtube.com/watch?v= qFpbZ-aLDLY), at 0:45 to 1:57.

50 NIST NCSTAR 1–9, Vol. 2: 384, Figure 9–11.

51 NIST, "WTC 7 Technical Briefing," August 26, 2008. Although NIST originally had a video and a transcript of this briefing at its Internet website, it removed both of them. However, Nate Flach has made the video available at Vimeo (http://vimeo.com/11941571). And the transcript, under the title "NIST Technical Briefing on Its Final Draft Report on WTC 7 for Public Comment," is available at David Chandler's website (http://911speakout.org/NIST_Tech_Briefing_Transcript.pdf).

52 NIST NCSTAR 1-9, *Structural Fire Response and Probable Collapse Sequence of World Trade Center Building 7* (wtc.nist.gov/NCSTAR1/PDF/NCSTAR% 201-9%20Vol%201.pdf): 607.

53 David Chandler, "WTC7 in Freefall - No Longer Controversial," September 4, 2008 (http://www.youtube.com/watch?v=rVCDpL4Ax7I), at 3:27.

54 NIST NCSTAR 1-9, Draft for Public Comment, Vol. 2: 595–96, 596, 610.

55 Glanz, "Engineers Have a Culprit in the Strange Collapse of 7 World Trade Center" (emphasis added).

56 Symposium on State Crimes against Democracy, *American Behavioral Scientist* 53 (February 2010): 783–939 (http://abs.sagepub.com/content/vol53/issue6). Online access is expensive, but the entire published (hardcover) issue can be purchased for $24 (journals@sagepub.com).

57 Lance deHaven-Smith, "Beyond Conspiracy Theory: Patterns of High Crime in American Government," *American Behavioral Scientist* 53 (February 2010): 795–825 (http://abs.sagepub.com/content/vol53/issue6), at 796.

58 Ibid. 797.

59 Ibid., 783.

60 Matthew T. Witt, "Pretending Not to See or Hear, Refusing to Signify: The Farce and Tragedy of Geocentric Public Affairs Scholarship," *American Behavioral Scientist* 53 (February 2010): 921–39 (http://abs.sagepub.com/ content/vol53/issue6), at 934.

61 Ibid., 932 (emphasis in original).

62 Daniel Hofnung, Patriots Question 9/11 (http://patriotsquestion911.com/ engineers.html#Dhofnung).

63 Chester W. Gearhart, Patriots Question 9/11 (http://patriotsquestion911.com/engineers.html#Gearhart).

64 "Danish Scientist Niels Harrit, on Nanothermite in the WTC Dust (English subtitles)," YouTube, April 6, 2009 (http://www.youtube.com/watch?v=8_tf25lx_3o).

65 NIST NCSTAR 1A, *Final Report on the Collapse of World Trade Center Building 7* (http://wtc.nist.gov/NCSTAR1/PDF/NCSTAR%201A.pdf) 51; NIST NCSTAR 1-9: 119.

66 Jeremy Baker, "Was WTC 7 a Dud?" Serendipity, 2005 (http://www.serendipity.li/wot/wtc7_dud.htm).

67 Jeremy Baker, "Last Building Standing," Serendipity, 2007 (http://www.serendipity.li/wot/last_building_standing.pdf). This is a revised and updated version of "Was WTC 7 a Dud?"

68 NIST NCSTAR 1-9, Vol. 1: 194, 243, 244, 247.

69 Peter Dale Scott, "9/11, Deep State Violence, and the Hope of Internet Politics," *Global Research* June 11, 2008 (http://www.globalresearch.ca/index.php?context=va&aid=9289).

70 Ibid. More recently, Scott has ceased speaking about a "deep state," because it suggests an organized entity with a location, and speaks instead only of "deep events" brought about by "deep forces." This revised language is reflected in his *American War Machine* (Lanham, MD: Rowman & Littlefield, 2010 [http://www.amazon.com/American-War-Machine-Connection-Afghanistan/dp/0742555941]), in which he refers to "deep events" as "events

that are systematically ignored, suppressed, or falsified in public (and even internal) government, military, and intelligence documents as well as in the mainstream media and public consciousness," and says that underlying these events "is frequently the involvement of deep forces linked either to the drug traffic or to agencies of surveillance (or to both together)." He then adds: "A clearly defined deep event will combine both internal features—evidence, such as a discernible cover-up, that aspects are being suppressed—and external features—an ongoing and perhaps irresoluble controversy as to what happened."

71 Laurie A. Manwell, "In Denial of Democracy: Social Psychological Implications for Public Discourse on State Crimes against Democracy Post-9/11," *American Behavioral Scientist* 53 (February 2010): 848-84 (http://abs.sagepub.com/content/vol53/issue6), at 867–70.

72 Ibid., 863.

73 Matthew T. Witt and Alexander Kouzmin, "Sense Making Under 'Holographic' Conditions: Framing SCAD Research," *American Behavioral Scientist* 53 (February 2010): 783–94 (http://abs.sagepub.com/content/vol53/issue6), at 789.

74 *Publishers Weekly*, November 24, 2008 (http://www.publishersweekly.com/pw/by-topic/1-legacy/15-web-exclusive-book-reviews/article/6017-web-exclusive-reviews-week-of-11-24-2008-.html).

75 Jennifer Harper, "Explosive News," *Washington Times* February 22, 2010 (http://www.washingtontimes.com/news/2010/feb/22/inside-the-beltway-70128635/?feat=home_columns).

76 Architects and Engineers for 9/11 Truth (http://ae911truth.org).

77 "Building *What?*" (http://www.youtube.com/watch?v=PXkiSPXvZbY).

78 "Geraldo Rivera Does 911 Truth Segment about Building 7," YouTube, November 13, 2010 (http://www.youtube.com/watch?v=kPOHs-v-uJ0).

79 "Judge Napolitano and Geraldo Rivera Discuss Building 7," November 24, 2010 (http://www.youtube.com/watch?v=wPEj2Pa1Y2g).

80 "Fox Host Napolitano is a 9-11 Truther: 'It couldn't possibly have been done the way the government told us,'" Media Matters, November 24, 2010 (http://mediamatters.org/blog/201011240019).

81 Remember Building 7.org (http://rememberbuilding7.org).

CHAPTER 5

1 Kerry Hall, "Flight Attendant Helped Fight Hijackers," *News & Record* (Greensboro, N.C.), September 21, 2001 (http://web.archive.org/web/20080302115428/http://mm.news-record.com/legacy/photo/tradecenter/bradshaw21.htm).

2 See especially Rowland Morgan. *Voices*. Self-published, 2010 (http://www.radiodujour.com/pdf/voices-book.pdf).

3 "Interview with Deena Lynne Burnett," Federal Bureau of Investigation, September 11, 2001 (http://intelfiles.egoplex.com/2001-09-11-FBI-FD302-deena-lynne-burnett.pdf).

4 Ibid.

5 "Tom Burnett: A Hero on Flight 93: An Interview with Deena Burnett," Ignatius Insight, September 2006 (http://www.ignatiusinsight.com/features2006/deenaburnett_intvw_sept06.asp)

6 9/11CR 11, 29. The FBI's interview of Deena Burnett showed that Tom's first call came at 6:30 AM PST, hence at 9:30 AM EST (http://intelfiles.egoplex.com/2001-09-11-FBI-FD302-deena-lynne-burnett.pdf). And at that time, UA 93 was said to have been at 36,000 feet. See "Flight Path Study: United Airlines Flight 93," National Transportation Safety Board, February 19, 2002 (http://www.911myths.com/images/8/84/Team8_Box15_HijackedAirplanes_Folder3_NTSB-Reports-On-UA93.pdf).

7 A.K. Dewdney, "Project Achilles Report: Parts One, Two and Three," Physics 911, April 19, 2003 (http://www.physics911.net/projectachilles); "The Cellphone and Airfone Calls from Flight UA93," Physics 911, June 2003 (physics911.net/cellphoneflight93.htm).

8 The results of Dewdney's twin-engine experiments are reported in Barrie Zwicker, Towers of Deception: The Media Cover-Up of 9/11 (Gabriola Island, BC: New Society Publishers, 2006), 375.

9 David Ray Griffin, The New Pearl Harbor Revisited: 9/11, the Cover-Up, and the Exposé (Northampton: Olive Branch Press [Interlink Publishing], 2008), 113, citing A. K. Dewdney, "The Cellphone and Airfone Calls from Flight UA93," Physics 911, June 9, 2003 (http://physics911.net/cellphoneflight93.htm).

10 Griffin, The New Pearl Harbor Revisited, 113.

11 Erik Larson, "Critique of David Ray Griffin's Fake Calls Theory," 911 Truth News, February 11, 2011 (http://911truthnews.com/critique-of-david-ray-griffins-fake-calls-theory).

12 Dewdney, "Project Achilles Report," Part 3.

13 Larson, "Critique of David Ray Griffin's Fake Calls Theory."

14 Ibid.

15 United States v. Zacarias Moussaoui, Exhibit Number P200054 (http://www.vaed.uscourts.gov/notablecases/moussaoui/exhibits/prosecution/flights/P200054.html). These documents can be more easily viewed in an article by Jim Hoffman, "Detailed Account of Phone Calls from September 11th Flights" (http://911research.wtc7.net/planes/evidence/calldetail.html).

16 Thomas Burnett, Jr., United Airlines Flight #93 Telephone Calls (http://911research.wtc7.net/planes/evidence/docs/exhibit/ThomasBurnett.png). According to this report, Burnett placed two calls from row 24 ABC and one call from row 25 ABC (although he had been assigned a seat in row 4).

17 Greg Gordon of McClatchy Newspapers reported that "a member of an FBI Joint Terrorism Task Force testified" that "13 of the terrified passengers and crew members made 35 air phone calls and two cell phone calls." See Greg Gordon, "Jurors Hear Final Struggle of Flight 93: Moussaoui Trial Plays Cockpit Tape of Jet that Crashed Sept. 11," Sacramento Bee April 13, 2006 (http://911research.wtc7.net/mirrors/sacbee/Gordon_MoussaouiTrialTape.pdf).

18 A graph labeled "US-93 Altitude Profile" (http://good-times.webshots.com/photo/2367739610098837763LtPhuo) shows the plane as having descended to 5,000 feet at 9:58 AM.

19 Karen Breslau, "The Final Moments of United Flight 93," Newsweek September 22, 2001 (http://www.newsweek.com/2001/09/21/the-final-moments-of-united-flight-93.html).

20 Dennis B. Roddy, "Flight 93: Forty Lives, One Destiny," *Pittsburgh Post-Gazette* October 28, 2001 (http://www.post-gazette.com/headlines/20011028flt93mainstoryp7.asp).

21 FBI Affidavit, signed by agent James K. Lechner, September 11, 2001 (http://www.abc.net.au/4corners/atta/resources/documents/fbiaffidavit1.htm), page 9. Sweeney and Woodward are not identified by name in the affidavit, which refers simply to Sweeney as "a flight attendant on AA11" and to Woodward as "an employee of American Airlines at Logan." But their names were revealed in an "investigative document compiled by the FBI" to which reporter Eric Lichtblau referred in "Aboard Flight 11, a Chilling Voice," *Los Angeles Times* September 20, 2001 (http://articles.latimes.com/2001/sep/20/news/mn-47829).

22 Interview of Michael Woodward by FBI Special Agent Craig Ring, Federal Bureau of Investigation, September 11, 2001 (http://www.scribd.com/doc/19131547/T7-B13-DOJ-Doc-Req-3513-Packet-6-Fdr-Entire-Contents-FBI-Reports-730). I am indebted to Eric Larson's article, "Critique of David Ray Griffin's Fake Calls Theory," for that information.

23 Gail Sheehy, "9/11 Tapes Reveal Ground Personnel Muffled Attacks," *New York Observer* June 24, 2004 (http://www.observer.com/node/49415).

24 Deena L. Burnett (with Anthony F. Giombetti), *Fighting Back: Living Life Beyond Ourselves* (Longwood, FL: Advantage Inspirational Books, 2006), 61.

25 Interview with Lorne Lyles, Federal Bureau of Investigation, September 12, 2001 (http://www.scribd.com/doc/15072623/T1A-B33-Four-Flights-Phone-Calls-and-Other-Data-Fdr-Entire-Contents-FBI-302s-843).

26 Interview with Deena Lynne Burnett, Federal Bureau of Investigation, September 11, 2001 (http://www.scribd.com/doc/15072623/T1A-B33-Four-Flights-Phone-Calls-and-Other-Data-Fdr-Entire-Contents-FBI-302s-843) (also available at http://intelfiles.egoplex.com/2001-09-11-FBI-FD302-deena-lynne-burnett.pdf).

27 *The New Pearl Harbor Revisited* (2008); *Debunking 9/11 Debunking: An Answer to Popular Mechanics and Other Defenders of the Official Conspiracy Theory* (Northampton: Olive Branch Press [Interlink Books], 2007).

28 Dewdney, "The Cellphone and Airfone Calls from Flight UA93;" Section 3; Rowland Morgan, *Voices*.

29 William M. Arkin, "When Seeing and Hearing Isn't Believing," *Washington Post* February 1, 1999 (http://www.washingtonpost.com/wp-srv/national/dotmil/arkin020199.htm).

30 Ibid.

31 Larson, "Critique of David Ray Griffin's Fake Calls Theory."

32 See Rowland Morgan, *Voices*; and Dewdney, "The Cellphone and Airfone Calls from Flight UA93," Section 3, "Operational Details."

33 Aidan Monaghan, "No Conclusive Evidence Debunking Faked 9/11 Phone Calls," 9/11 Blogger, February 24, 2011 (http://911blogger.com/news/2011-02-23/jesse-ventura-s-fake-phone-calls-claim-debunked#comment-246640).

34 George Papcun, "Voice Morphing and the Alleged 9/11 Government Conspiracy," Sound Evidence (http://soundevidence.com/voicemorphing&911_ 1.html).

35 Dewdney, "The Cellphone and Airfone Calls from Flight UA93."

36 Larson, "Critique."

37 Papcun, "Voice Morphing and the Alleged 9/11 Government Conspiracy."

38 Burnett, *Fighting Back*, 61.

39 *Portrait of Courage: The Untold Story of Flight 93*, DVD, directed by David Priest (Baker City, OR: Grizzly Adams Productions, 2006). See Shoestring 9/11, "Husband of Flight 93 Attendant: 'Cell Phones Don't Work on a Plane" (http://shoestring911.blogspot.com/2008/04/husband-of-flight-93-attendant-cell.html).

40 Dewdney, "The Cellphone and Airfone Calls from Flight UA93."

41 Ibid.

42 To be more precise, I would need to say that Tom Burnett could not possibly have made the calls unless his cell phone had been given artificial assistance, perhaps with a "repeater," as suggested by Erik Larson. I will give reasons later, however, for rejecting this as a method that might have been used on 9/11.

43 "Transcript of Tom's Last Calls to Deena," Tom Burnett Family Foundation (http://www.tomburnettfoundation.org/tomburnett_transcript.html).

44 Ibid.

45 "Court Recording of CeeCee Lyles on Flight 93—HEAR THE WHISPERS IN THE BACKGROUND," YouTube (http://www.youtube.com/watch?v=5SED 76UvuAw).

46 To confirm this point, one can check the CeeCee Lyles recording in the computer presentation of the AA 77 telephone calls. The official presentation is at http://www.vaed.uscourts.gov/notablecases/moussaoui/exhibits/prosecution/flights/P200054.html.

47 For this section, I am heavily indebted to Shoestring 9/11, "'Shockingly Calm': The Phone Calls From the Planes on 9/11," July 5, 2008 (http://shoestring911.blogspot.com/2008/07/shockingly-calm-phone-calls-from-planes.html).

48 Staff Report, 9/11 Commission, August 26, 2004: 40 (http://www.archives.gov/research/9-11/staff-report.pdf).

49 *The 9/11 Commission Report: Final Report of the National Commission on Terrorist Attacks upon the United States*, Authorized Edition (New York: W. W. Norton, 2004), 13.

50 Ibid., 6.

51 Ibid., 5.

52 Hope Yen, "Flight Attendant Calm on September 11 Tape," Associated Press, January 28, 2004 (http://www.redorbit.com/news/general/40060/flight_attendant_calm_on_sept_11_tape/index.html).

53 Public Hearing, 9/11 Commission, National Commission on Terrorist Attacks Upon the United States (http://govinfo.library.unt.edu/911/archive/hearing7/9-11Commission_Hearing_2004-01-27.htm), January 27, 2004.

54 Jennifer Julian, "One of the Last Calls," ABC11 Eyewitness News, September 11, 2002 (http://web.archive.org/web/20021107235946/http://abclocal.go.com/wtvd/news/091002_NW_LastCall.html).

55 Yen, "Flight Attendant Calm on September 11 Tape."

56 Deena Burnett, *Fighting Back*, 66.

57 David Segal, "A Red Carpet Tragedy: Grief and Glamour an Odd Mix at 'United 93' Debut," *Washington Post* April 26, 2006 (http://www.washingtonpost.com/wp-dyn/content/article/2006/04/26/ AR2006042600061.html).

58 Jere Longman, *Among the Heroes: United 93 and the Passengers and Crew Who Fought Back* (New York: HarperCollins, 2002), 128.

59 Matthew Brown, "Hero's Family Perseveres: As Spotlight Fades, Young Wife Looks Ahead," *Bergen Record* October 5, 2001 (http://www.highbeam.com/doc/1P1-47456022.html).

60 Longman, *Among the Heroes*, 129–30; Phil Hirschkorn, "More 9/11 Families Testify for Moussaoui," CNN, April 21, 2006 (http://edition.cnn.com/2006/LAW/04/21/moussaoui.families/index.html).

61 "Stories of Flight 93," *Larry King Live*, CNN, February 18, 2006 (http://transcripts.cnn.com/TRANSCRIPTS/0602/18/lkl.01.html).

62 Wendy Schuman, Interview with Lisa Jefferson, "I Promised I Wouldn't Hang Up," Beliefnet, 2006 (http://www.beliefnet.com/Inspiration/2006/06/ I-Promised-I-Wouldnt-Hang-Up.aspx).

63 Lisa D. Jefferson and Felicia Middlebrooks, *Called* (Chicago: Northfield Publishing, 2006), 33.

64 Segal, "A Red Carpet Tragedy."

65 Brown, "Hero's Family Perseveres."

66 Longman, *Among the Heroes*, 172.

67 "Calm Before the Crash," ABC News, July 18, 2002 (http://911research.wtc7.net/cache/planes/evidence/abc_fl1beforecrash.html).

68 Hirschkorn, "More 9/11 Families Testify for Moussaoui."

69 Morgan, *Voices*, 113.

70 Public Hearing, 9/11 Commission, January 27, 2004, Panel III (http://www.9-11 commission.gov/archive/hearing7/9-11Commission_Hearing_2004-01-27.htm).

71 Interview with Lyzbeth Glick, Federal Bureau of Investigation, September 12, 2001 (http://www.scribd.com/doc/14094225/T7-B17-FBI-302s-of-Interest-Flight-93-Fdr-Entire-Contents).

72 Lyz Glick and Dan Zegart, *Your Father's Voice: Letters for Emmy about Life with Jeremy—and Without Him after 9/11* (New York: St. Martin's Griffin, 2005), 195.

73 Interview with Richard Makely, Federal Bureau of Investigation, September 12, 2001 (http://www.scribd.com/doc/14094225/T7-B17-FBI-302s-of-Interest-Flight-93-Fdr-Entire-Contents).

74 9/11CR 462n168.

75 Won-Young Kim and Gerald R. Baum, "Seismic Observations during September 11, 2001, Terrorist Attack," *Maryland Geological Survey*, Spring 2002 (http://www.mgs.md.gov/esic/publications/download/911pentagon.pdf). Jonathan Silver, "Day of Terror: Outside Tiny Shanksville, a Fourth Deadly Stroke," *Pittsburgh Post-Gazette* September 12, 2001 (http://www.post-gazette.com/headlines/20010912crashnat2p2.asp); Tom Gibb, James O'Toole, and Cindi Lash, "Investigators Locate 'Black Box' from Flight 93; Widen Search Area in Somerset Crash," *Pittsburgh Post-Gazette* September 13, 2001 (http://post-gazette.com/headlines/20010913somersetp3.asp); William Bunch, "We Know it Crashed, But Not Why," *Philadelphia Daily News* November 15, 2001 (http://www.whatreallyhappened.com/flight_93_crash.html).

76 "Jeremy Glick," United Airlines Flight #93 Telephone Calls (http://911research.wtc7.net/planes/evidence/docs/exhibit/JeremyGlick.png).

77 Lisa D. Jefferson and Felicia Middlebrooks, *Called* (Chicago: Northfield Publishing, 2006).

78 Windy Schuman, Interview of Lisa Jefferson, "I Promised I Wouldn't Hang Up," Beliefnet, June 2006 (http://www.beliefnet.com/Inspiration/2006/06/I-Promised-I-Wouldnt-Hang-Up.aspx?p=1).

79 "Todd Beamer," United Airlines Flight #93 Telephone Calls (http://911research.wtc7.net/planes/evidence/docs/exhibit/ToddBeamer.png).

80 "United Flight 93 Victims at a Glance," *USA Today* September 25, 2001 (http://www.usatoday.com/news/nation/2001/09/11/victims-capsules.htm).

81 Morgan, *Voices*.

82 Peter Perl, "Hallowed Ground," *Washington Post* May 12, 2002 (http://www.washingtonpost.com/ac2/wp-dyn?pagename=article&node=&contentId=A56110-2002May8).

83 Jefferson and Middlebrooks, *Called*, 53.

84 Jim McKinnon, "13-Minute Call Bonds Her Forever with Hero," *Pittsburgh Post-Gazette* September 22, 2001 (http://www.post-gazette.com/headlines/20010922gtenat4p4.asp).

85 The name of Phyllis Johnson is publicly known only because of the aforementioned *Pittsburgh Post-Gazette* story by Jim McKinnon, "13-Minute Call Bonds Her Forever With Hero." (Lisa D. Jefferson, who became well known by writing about this call, never mentioned Johnson's name. See Jefferson and Middlebrooks, *Called*, 29; Wendy Schuman, Interview with Lisa Jefferson, "I Promised I Wouldn't Hang Up.")

86 Douglas Holt, "Call Records Detail How Passengers Foiled 2nd Washington Attack," *Chicago Tribune* September 16, 2001 (http://www.accessmylibrary.com/coms2/summary_0286-6765842_ITM).

87 Jefferson and Middlebrooks, *Called*, 47.

88 Ibid., 47-48.

89 Morgan, *Voices*.

90 Ibid.

91 Jim McKinnon, "GTE Operator Connects With, Uplifts Widow of Hero in Hijacking," *Pittsburgh Post-Gazette* September 19, 2001 (http://www.post-gazette.com/headlines/20010919gtenatp3.asp).

92 "Interview with Theodore Olsen [sic]," 9/11 Commission, FBI Source Documents, Chronological, September 11, 2001, Intelfiles.com, March 14, 2008 (http://intelfiles.egoplex.com:80/2008/03/911-commission-fbi-source-documents.html).

93 "America's New War: Recovering from Tragedy," Larry King Live, CNN, September 14, 2001 (http://edition.cnn.com/TRANSCRIPTS/0109/14/lkl.00.html).

94 Tim O'Brien, "Wife of Solicitor General Alerted Him of Hijacking from Plane," CNN, September 12, 2001 (http://archives.cnn.com/2001/US/09/11/pentagon.olson).

95 "Staff No. Statement 16: Outline of the 9/11 Plot," 9/11 Commission, June 16, 2004 (http://www.9-11commission.gov/staff_statements/staff_statement_16.pdf).

96 Shoestring 9/11, "The Flight 77 Murder Mystery: Who Really Killed Charles Burlingame?" February 2, 2008 (http://shoestring911.blogspot.com/2008/02/flight-77-murder-mystery-who-really.html).

97 "In Memoriam: Charles 'Chic' Burlingame, 1949-2001," USS Saratoga Museum Foundation (http://911research.wtc7.net/cache/planes/analysis/chic_remembered.html).

98 Alfred Goldberg et al., *Pentagon 9/11* (Washington, DC: Office of the Secretary of Defense, 2007), 12.

99 Interview of Theodore Olson, Solicitor General of the United States of America, September 11, 2001 (http://intelfiles.egoplex.com/2001-09-11-FBI-FD302-theodore-olsen.pdf).

100 O'Brien, "Wife of Solicitor General Alerted Him of Hijacking from Plane."

101 *Hannity & Colmes*, Fox News, September 14, 2001.

102 *Larry King Live*, CNN, September 14, 2001 (http://edition.cnn.com/TRANSCRIPTS/0109/14/lkl.00.html).

103 Theodore B. Olson, "Barbara K. Olson Memorial Lecture," November 16, 2001, Federalist Society, 15th Annual National Lawyers Convention (http://www.fed-soc.org/resources/id.63/default.asp); Toby Harnden, "She Asked Me How to Stop the Plane," *Daily Telegraph* March 5, 2002 (http://s3.amazonaws.com/911timeline/2002/telegraph030502.html).

104 "On September 11, Final Words of Love," CNN, September 10, 2002 (http://archives.cnn.com/2002/US/09/03/ar911.phone.calls), said: "Unbeknown to the hijackers, passenger and political commentator Barbara Olson, 45, was able to call her husband—Solicitor General Ted Olson—on her cellular phone."

105 "Flight Path Study: American Airlines Flight 77," National Transportation Safety Board, February 19, 2002 (http://www.gwu.edu/~nsarchiv/NSAEBB/NSAEBB196/doc02.pdf).

106 "T7 B12 Flight 93 Calls- General Fdr- 5-20-04 DOJ Briefing on Cell and Phone Calls From AA 77 408," Federal Bureau of Investigation, May 20, 2004 (http://www.scribd.com/doc/18886083/T7-B12-Flight-93-Calls-General-Fdr-52004-DOJ-Briefing-on-Cell-and-Phone-Calls-From-AA-77-408).

107 This exchange occurred on December 6, 2004; see Morgan and Henshall, *9/11 Revealed*. Henshall and Morgan also found this information corroborated on the AA website: As it existed at that time (2005), the section headed "Onboard Technology" indicated that telephone calls were possible on AA's Boeing 767s and 777s, but it did not mention AA's 757s.

108 See Griffin, *The New Pearl Harbor Revisited*, 60–61. A supplementary reason for holding that American Airlines 757s had no onboard phones is provided by a page in the Boeing 757 Aircraft Maintenance Manual (757 AMM), which was dated January 28, 2001. The first sentence of this page stated: "The passenger telephone system was deactivated by ECO [Engineering Change Order] FO878." This page indicates, in other words, that by January 28, 2001, the passenger phone system for the AA 757 fleet had been deactivated. Also, American Airlines public relations representative John Hotard wrote: "An Engineering Change Order to deactivate the seatback phone system on the 757 fleet had been issued by that time [9/11/2001]." Following this statement,

Hotard emphasized that photographs showing seatback phones in American 757s after 9/11 would not prove that the phones were still functioning, because: "We did two things: issued the engineering change orders to disconnect/disable the phones, but then did not physically remove the phones until the aircraft went . . . in for a complete overhaul." So, there were still seatback phones in the American 757s, but they could not be used, because they had been disconnected.

Larson stated that I distorted the evidence because I had not quoted the following statement by Hotard: "Ron, engineers at our primary Maintenance & Engineering base in Tulsa tell me that they cannot find any record that the 757 aircraft flown into the Pentagon on 9/11 had had its seatback phones deactivated by that date." However, the crucial matter was the order, which would have caused things to happen. The fact that Hotard could not find any record about "the 757 aircraft flown into the Pentagon" might simply reflect the fact that no such aircraft existed.

Larson also criticized me for not quoting this statement by Hotard: "It is our contention that the seatback phones on Flight 77 were working because there is no entry in that aircraft's records to indicate when the phones were disconnected." However, the entry in question is the statement in the Aircraft Maintenance Manual of January 28, 2001, which said: "The passenger telephone system was deactivated by ECO FO878."

109 Captain Ralph Kolstad, email letters to Rob Balsamo and David Griffin, December 22, 2009. Larson, unfortunately, tried to discredit Kolstad's testimony by resorting to guilt by association: Larson claimed that Kolstad's credibility has been undermined by his membership in Pilots for 9/11 Truth—which holds "that AA 77 didn't crash into the Pentagon" (something that evidently most of the members of the 9/11 Truth Movement hold)—and his endorsement of a particular book by a member of the 9/11 movement. I fail to see how these guilt-by-association charges, even if valid, would provide reason to doubt Kolstad's observation skills. I suspect that someone twice named a Top Gun pilot must have pretty good observation skills.

110 Letter from Ginger Gainer, February 16, 2011. She added: "I do recall stickers on the seatback phones (on the international configuration) indicating they were inoperative during the time the plane had them disabled, but had not yet gone in for a 'C-Check.' . . . As to the domestic configuration at the time, I asked several current and former Flight Attendants for American, . . . who flew domestic . . . , and they all said that they recalled the phones as having been disabled at the time, or gone (due to C-check reconfiguration)."

111 "Transcription of FBI Interview with Theodore Olson," Federal Bureau of Investigation, September 11, 2001 (http://intelfiles.egoplex.com/2001-09-11-FBI-FD302-theodore-olsen.pdf).

112 "America's New War: Recovering from Tragedy."

113 United States v. Zacarias Moussaoui, Prosecution Trial Exhibit P200054. As stated earlier, this FBI report on phone calls from AA 11 can be viewed more easily in an article by Jim Hoffman, "Detailed Account of Phone Calls from September 11th Flights" (http://911research.wtc7.net/planes/evidence/calldetail.html).

114 The FBI's summary of its interview with Helen Voss, Ted Olson's special assistant, said: "Earlier this morning Barbara Olson called the office two (2) times to speak with her husband Ted Olson. Lori Keyton was the secretary that took both of these calls. . . . Lori Keyton called to Voss to relay to Ted Olson that Barbara Olson was on the phone. Keyton said that Barbara is on the line and she's in a panic. . . . Ted Olson took the call and Voss heard him say, 'hijacked!'" See Interview with Helen Voss, Special Assistant to the Solicitor General, September 11, 2001 (http://www.scribd.com/doc/15072623/T1A-B33-Four-Flights-Phone-Calls-and-Other-Data-Fdr-Entire-Contents-FBI-302s-843).

The FBI's summary of its interview with Lori Keyton said: "Keyton was working in Ted Olson's Office this morning. She is regularly called there to cover the telephones. At approximately 9:00 AM, she received a series of approximately six (6) to eight (8) collect telephone calls. Each of the calls was an automated collect call. There was a recording advising of the collect call and requesting she hold for an operator. A short time later another recording stated that all operators were busy, please hang up and try your call later. Keyton then received a collect call from a live operator. The operator advised that there was an emergency collect call from Barbara Olsen [sic] for Ted Olsen [sic]. Keyton advised that she would accept the call. Barbara Olsen [sic] was put through and sounded hysterical. Barbara Olsen [sic] said, 'Can you tell Ted?' Keyton cut her off and said, 'I'll put him on the line.' There was a second telephone call a few to five (5) minutes later. This time Barbara Olsen [sic] was on the line when she answered. She called direct. It was not a collect call. Barbara Olsen [sic] said, 'It's Barbara.' Keyton said, 'he's on the phone with the command center, I'll put you through.' Keyton advised that there is no caller identification feature on the phone she was using." See Interview with Lori Lynn Keyton, Secretary, DOJ, September 11, 2001 (http://www.scribd.com/doc/15072623/T1A-B33-Four-Flights-Phone-Calls-and-Other-Data-Fdr-Entire-Contents-FBI-302s-843).

According to another FBI interview, Teresa Gonzalez, an operator for AT&T, telephonically contacted the FBI to report an emergency phone call received by AT&T, saying: "Mercy Lorenzo, also an operator with AT&T, received a call from a female passenger on flight 77 requesting to be transferred to telephone number 202514-2201 (which was the number for the Solicitor General's office). The female passenger advised the plane was being hi-jacked. Hi-jackers were ordering passengers to move to the back of the plane and were armed with guns and knives." Interview with Teresa Gonzalez, September 11, 2001 (http://www.911myths.com/images/9/95/265A-NY-280350-302-22170-Unredacted.pdf).

So, although these statements do not show that Barbara Olson was on American 77 and called Ted Olson from there, they do provide strong evidence that people in Ted Olson's office believed that Barbara Olson made such calls.

115 See the Flight 77 graphic for "Unknown Callers" (http://911research.wtc7.net/planes/evidence/calldetail.html#ref1).

116 9/11CR 455n.57.

117 David Ray Griffin and Rob Balsamo, "Could Barbara Olson Have Made Those Calls? An Analysis of New Evidence about Onboard Phones," Pilots for 9/11 Truth, June 26, 2007 (http://pilotsfor911truth.org/amrarticle.html); also at 9/11 Blogger (http://www.911blogger.com/node/9627).

118 Larson, "Critique."

119 Ibid.

120 See my analysis in David Ray Griffin, "Phone Calls from the 9/11 Airliners: Response to Questions Evoked by My Fifth Estate Interview," Global Research, January 12, 2010 (http://www.globalresearch.ca/index.php?context=va&aid=16924).

121 9/11CR 455 n.57.

122 Ibid., 9.

123 "DavidS" in "Comments" to "David Ray Griffin on the 9/11 Cell Phone Calls," 9/11 Blogger, December 20, 2009 (http://www.911blogger.com/node/22192).

124 Griffin, "Phone Calls from the 9/11 Airliners: Response to Questions Evoked by My Fifth Estate Interview."

125 Ibid.

126 See Elizabeth Woodworth, "Did Barbara Olson Attempt Any Calls at All from Flight 77?" COTO Report (http://coto2.wordpress.com/2011/09/07/did-barbara-olson-attempt-any-calls).

127 See Ibid.

128 Morgan, *Voices*, at the end of the section entitled "Chicanery."

129 The press has generally referred to only two passengers as having made phone calls from United 175: Lee Hanson and Brian Sweeney. However, the FBI's telephone report for the Moussaoui trial indicates that four calls home were attempted by Garnet "Ace" Bailey (http://911research.wtc7.net/planes/evidence/calldetail.html), who had been a star ice-hockey player from 1968 to 1979, during which his team, the Boston Bruins, won the Stanley Cup twice. His last year of playing was with the Edmonton Oilers in the 1978-79 season, where he took rookie Wayne Gretzky under his wing. Bailey then became a coach with the Oilers from 1981 to 1994 (during which he won five more Stanley Cups). At the time of his death, he was living in Massachusetts while serving as the director of pro scouting for the Los Angeles Kings (Garnett Bailey, Wikipedia [http://en.wikipedia.org/wiki/Garnet_Bailey]).

   This is one of the strangest episodes of the "phone calls from the planes." The evidence supplied to the FBI indicates that three of the four attempted calls to his home number were connected, with these calls lasting for 22, 25, and 9 seconds (see United Airlines Flight #175: http://911research.wtc7.net/planes/evidence/docs/exhibit/GarnetAceBailey.png). From reading these accounts, one would assume that his wife or someone else in the house had answered these calls. His wife, Kathy Bailey, said that she was at home watching the coverage of the attacks on TV with her son, Tod, but that they did not receive any of those calls. See Doug Krikorian, "'Ace' Bailey's Legacy Lives On," *Press-Telegram* (Long Beach, CA) September 10, 2007 (http://www.allbusiness.com/transportation/air-transportation-airports/15361814-1.html). How can we explain the phenomena? On the one hand, Kathy and Tod Bailey said that they received no phone calls from "Ace," so that it was a complete surprise to them later to be told that he had been on one of the planes that struck the World Trade Center. On the other hand, the telephone records indicate that someone picked up the phone in the Bailey house three times—for 22, 25, and 9 seconds (and the telephone records had the Bailey home's phone number correct). Something is clearly wrong here, even if we cannot say what.

130 Phone Call Detail, Flight 77 (http://911research.wtc7.net/planes/evidence/calldetail.html).

131 Morgan, *Voices*.

132 David Ray Griffin, *Cognitive Infiltration: An Obama Appointee's Plan to Undermine the 9/11 Conspiracy Theory* (Northampton: Olive Branch Press [Interlink Publishing], 2010), 60; emphasis added.

133 Ibid., 80; emphasis added.

134 And this fact, I have argued, leads to the conclusion that all of the 9/11 calls must have been faked.

135 Larson, "Critique," quoting James Hoffman, "The Cell Phone Repeater Hypothesis," 9-11 Research (http://911research.wtc7.net/planes/analysis/phonecalls.html#overlooked).

136 Larson, "Critique."

137 Griffin to Hoffman email, March 2, 2011.

138 Hoffman to Griffin email, March 2, 2011. Hoffman added that he is, nevertheless, certain that "it's clearly feasible given the technology." In support of his assertion about feasibility in his 2009 article, Hoffman provided this analysis: "The range of a repeater is a function of its power and the directional character of its receive-and-transmit antennae. Cell phone radios are very low power (around 2 watts peak) and have little to no directional gain on either transmit or receive. A shoebox-sized repeater could easily pack several hundred watts of power and include directional antennae to increase signal gain by orders of magnitude. A simple calculation: If a 2 watt radio is capable of transmitting to a station at 5,000 feet, then a similar 200 watt radio could reach the same station at 50,000 feet (since the strength of an omni-directional signal falls off with the square of the distance). The addition of a simple low-gain antenna like a yagi could boost distances greatly in a general direction, while an aimable high-gain antenna could punch through almost any line-of-sight path in the atmosphere."

139 Hoffman, "The Cell Phone Repeater Hypothesis."

140 Larson, "Critique."

CHAPTER 6

1 "The Vice President Appears on Meet the Press with Tim Russert," MSNBC, September 16, 2001 (http://web.archive.org/web/20040205001654/http://www.whitehouse.gov/vicepresident/news-speeches/speeches/vp20010916.html).

2 "Interview of the Vice President by Matt Lauer of NBC News," June 14, 2008 (http://web.archive.org/web/20090112111512/http://www.whitehouse.gov/news/releases/2008/06/20080614-3.html).

3 Ibid.

4 Ibid.

5 William Langley, "Revealed: What Really Went On During Bush's 'Missing Hours,'" *Telegraph* December 16, 2001 (http://www.telegraph.co.uk/news/worldnews/northamerica/usa/1365455/Revealed-what-really-went-on-during-Bush%27s-%27missing-hours%27.html), says that Bush left at 9:12. However, Bill Sammon, a strong supporter of the Republican administration, stated that Bush lingered longer (*Fighting Back: The War on Terrorism: From Inside the Bush White House* [Washington: Regnery, 2002], 89–90).

6 David E. Sanger and Don Van Natta Jr., "After the Attacks: the Events; In Four Days, a National Crisis Changes Bush's Presidency," *New York Times* September 16, 2001 (http://query.nytimes.com/gst/fullpage.html?res=9C0DE5D7163BF935A2575AC0A9679C8B63&sec=&spon=&pagewanted=print).

7 "The Vice President Appears on Meet the Press with Tim Russert."

8 The transcript has "call a PEOC," but this was surely a mistranscription for "called PEOC."

9 *The 9/11 Commission Report: Final Report of the National Commission on Terrorist Attacks upon the United States*, Authorized Edition (New York: W. W. Norton, 2004) (http://www.9-11commission.gov/report/911Report.pdf), 39–40.

10 9/11 Commission Hearing, May 23, 2003 (http://www.9-11commission.gov/archive/hearing2/9-11Commission_Hearing_2003-05-23.htm). Mineta gave this account under questioning from 9/11 Commission Vice Chair Lee Hamilton and Commissioner Timothy Roemer. Mineta's interchange with Hamilton can be viewed at http://video.google.ca/videoplay?docid=-3722436852417384871, his interchange with Roemer at http://www.911truth.org/article.php?story=20050724164122860.

11 *The 9/11 Commission Report*, 464n.209.

12 Evan Thomas, "The Story of September 11," MSNBC, December 13, 2001. Although this article can no longer be accessed through the MSNBC URL, it is available as "The Day That Changed America," Jersey Shore Today (http://web.archive.org/web/20080630093633/http://jerseyshoretoday.com/archive/day_that_changed_america.htm), which states that it appeared in the January 7 issue of *Newsweek*.

13 Richard A. Clarke, *Against All Enemies: Inside America's War on Terror* (New York: Free Press, 2004), 1–4.

14 Ibid., 2–4. Clarke a few pages later reported that he used this line to make requests shortly after 9:30 and was "amazed at the speed of the decisions coming from Cheney" (8).

15 Ibid., 5.

16 "9/11: Interviews by Peter Jennings," ABC News, September 11, 2002 (http://s3.amazonaws.com/911timeline/2002/abcnews091102.html).

17 "Sept. 11's Moments of Crisis: Part 2: Scramble," ABC News, September 14, 2002 (http://web.archive.org/web/20021003222152/http:/abcnews.go.com/onair/DailyNews/sept11_moments_2.html).

18 Thomas, "The Story of September 11" (published by MSNBC, December 13, 2001, and "The Day That Changed America" by *Newsweek* January 7, 2002).

19 9/11 Commission Hearing, May 23, 2003.

20 Ibid.

21 "9/11 Seattle Truth Meets Norm Mineta" (http://www.youtube.com/v/
u-5PKQTUz5o).

22 Sylvia Adcock, Brian Donovan and Craig Gordon, "Air Attack on Pentagon
Indicates Weaknesses," *Newsday* September 23, 2001
(http://s3.amazonaws.com/911timeline/2001/newsday092301.html).

23 See Gregor Holland, "The Mineta Testimony: 9/11 Commission Exposed,"
911truthmovement.org, November 1, 2005
(http://www.911truthmovement.org/archives/2005/11/post.php).

24 *The 9/11 Commission Report*, 41.

25 In this revised timeline, Cheney's order also could have had no relevance to
another controversial issue: Whether the US military had shot down United
Flight 93 over Pennsylvania (which, according to the 9/11 Commission,
crashed at 10:03). There were reports that this indeed had occurred. For
example, Major Daniel Nash, one of the F-15 pilots sent to fly over New York
City that morning, reported that when he returned to base, he was told that a
military F-16 had shot down an airliner in Pennsylvania (Kevin Dennehy, "I
Thought It Was the Start of World War III," *Cape Cod Times* August 21, 2002
[http://web.archive.org/web/20080420173904/http://archive.capecodonline.
com/special/terror/ithought21.html]). This rumor became so sufficiently
widespread that it came up during General Richard Myers's confirmation
hearing with the Senate Armed Services Committee on September 13, 2001.
Chairman Carl Levin, saying that "there have been statements that the aircraft
that crashed in Pennsylvania was shot down," added: "Those stories continue
to exist" (General Myers Confirmation Hearing, Senate Armed Services
Committee, September 13, 2001 [http://emperors-clothes.com/911backups/
mycon.html]). Myers denied that it had occurred, but several other military
officers would later state that their fighters were in position to do it (see
Griffin, *9/11 Contradictions*, Chap. 13, "Could the Military Have Shot Down
Flight 93?"). Richard Clarke would later state, moreover, that Cheney had
given the authorization at approximately 9:50 (see ibid., Chap. 5, "When Did
Cheney Issue the Shootdown Authorization?"), which would have been early
enough for the military to have shot it down at 10:03. According to the
Commission, the incoming flight, which elicited Cheney's shoot-down
authorization at some time after 10:10, was indeed United 93, but,
unbeknownst to Cheney and the military, this flight had already crashed at
10:03 (*The 9/11 Commission Report*, 41). This story entailed that the military
could not, under Cheney's orders, have shot down United 93.

26 "Interview of the Vice President by Matt Lauer of NBC News."

27 Letter to Aiden [sic] Monaghan from Keith L. Prewitt, Deputy Director, United
States Secret Service (U.S. Department of Homeland Security), April 23,
2010 (http://www.scribd.com/doc/30764772/Monaghan-FOIA-USSS-Memos-
and-Timelines).

CHAPTER 7

1 Frank Legge, "What Hit the Pentagon? Misinformation and its Effect on the Credibility of 9/11 Truth," *Journal of 9/11 Studies* 26 (July 2009) (http://www.journalof911studies.com/volume/2009/WhatHitPentagon DrLeggeAug.pdf); "Joint Statement on the Pentagon: David Chandler and Jon Cole," 911Blogger, January 7, 2011 (http://911blogger.com/news/2011-01-01/joint-statement-pentagon-david-chandler-and-jon-cole).

    For a statement by one who has long held a view similar to that of Legge, Chandler, and Cole, see Jim Hoffman, "The Pentagon Attack: What the Physical Evidence Shows," Version 0.9, March 28, 2006 (http://911research.wtc7.net/essays/pentagon/index.html).

2 Legge, "What Hit the Pentagon?"

3 Chandler and Cole, "Joint Statement on the Pentagon."

4 Legge, "What Hit?"

5 Chandler and Cole, "Joint Statement on the Pentagon."

6 Jim Yardley, "A Trainee Noted for Incompetence," *New York Times* May 4, 2002 (http://newsmine.org/content.php?ol=9-11/suspects/flying-skills/pilot-trainee-noted-for-incompetence.txt).

7 *The 9/11 Commission Report: Final Report of the National Commission on Terrorist Attacks upon the United States*, Authorized Edition (New York: W. W. Norton, 2004), 242.

8 Marc Fisher and Don Phillips, "On Flight 77: 'Our Plane Is Being Hijacked,'" *Washington Post* September 12, 2001 (http://www.washingtonpost.com/ac2/wp-dyn?pagename=article&node=&contentId=A14365-2001Sep11).

9 Steve Fainaru and Alia Ibrahim, "Mysterious Trip to Flight 77 Cockpit," *Washington Post* September 10, 2002 (http://www.washingtonpost.com/wp-dyn/content/article/2007/08/13/AR2007081300752_pf.html).

10 Legge, "What Hit?"

11 Chandler and Cole, "Joint Statement."

12 Alan Miller, "U.S. Navy 'Top Gun' Pilot Questions 911 Pentagon Story," Op EdNews.com, September 6, 2007 (http://www.rense.com/general78/pent.htm).

13 National Transportation Safety Board (NTSB), "Flight Path Study—American Airlines Flight 77," February 19, 2002 (http://www.gwu.edu/~nsarchiv/NSAEBB/NSAEBB196/doc02.pdf). The NTSB video is available on YouTube (http://www.youtube.com/watch?v=DzR-q0ijbV0&).

14 Legge, "What Hit?"

15 Chandler and Cole, "Joint Statement."

16 "The Pentagon," GlobalSecurity.org (http://www.globalsecurity.org/military/facility/pentagon.htm).

17 Chandler and Cole, "Joint Statement."

18 Legge, "What Hit?"

19 Steve Vogel, *The Pentagon: A History* (New York: Random House, 2007), 450.

20 Patrick Creed and Rick Newman, *Firefight: Inside the Battle to Save the Pentagon on 9/11* (San Francisco: Presidio Books, 2008), 171–72.

21 Richard A. Clarke, *Against All Enemies: Inside America's War on Terror* (New York: Free Press, 2004), 3.

22 Ibid., 7.

23 Ibid., 8–9.

24 9/11 Commission Hearing (Day One Transcript), March 23, 2004 (http://www.washingtonpost.com/wp-dyn/articles/A17798-2004Mar23.html).

25 *The 9/11 Commission Report*, 37, 43. In a statement alluding to both Donald Rumsfeld and General Richard Myers (to be discussed next), the 9/11 Commission said: "We do not know who from Defense participated, but we know that in the first hour none of the personnel involved in managing the crisis did" (*The 9/11 Commission Report*, 36).

26 Barbara Honegger, "The Pentagon Attack Papers," originally published as an appendix to Jim Marrs, *The Terror Conspiracy: Deception, 9/11, and the Loss of Liberty* (New York: Disinformation Company, 2006), 439-65, at 443. But I am using a version updated May 2011 (http://bit.ly/PENTAGON_ATTACK_PAPERS).

27 Quoted in Barbara Honegger, "Special Operations Policy Expert and Veteran Robert Andrews Gives Distinguished Visiting Guest Lectures at NPS [Naval Postgraduate School]," interview of Andrews by Honegger, September 4, 2004. Because Honegger cannot publish this interview (it belongs to NPS, her former employer), she prepared a notarized statement, in which she made this statement and two others in this chapter: California Jurat with Affiant Statement, signed by Barbara Honegger and Notary Public Kelly Harlow of Monterey County, May 25, 2011.

28 Ibid.

29 Clarke, *Against All Enemies*, 3.

30 Ibid., 5.

31 Ibid., 7–9.

32 "Interview: General Richard B. Myers," Armed Forces Radio and Television Services, October 17, 2001 (http://web.archive.org/web/20011118060728/http://www.dtic.mil/jcs/chairman/AFRTS_Interview.htm).

33 *The 9/11 Commission Report*, 463n.199, citing an interview of February 17, 2004.

34 *The 9/11 Commission Report*, 38.

35 General Myers Confirmation Hearing, Senate Armed Services Committee, September 13, 2001 (http://emperors-clothes.com/9-11backups/mycon.htm).

36 "Interview: General Richard B. Myers," Armed Forces Radio and Television Services.

37 9/11 Commission Hearing, June 17, 2004 (http://www.9-11commission.gov/archive/hearing12/9-11Commission_Hearing_2004-06-17.htm#two).

38 Sylvia Adcock, Brian Donovan and Craig Gordon, "Air Attack on Pentagon Indicates Weaknesses," *Newsday* September 23, 2001 (http://emperors-clothes.com/9-11backups/nd923.htm).

39 Mark Gaffney, who has written a book about the E-4B (*The 9/11 Mystery Plane: And the Vanishing of America* [Walterville, OR, TrineDay, 2008]), has said that, assuming that AA 77 did indeed turn around in the Midwest and come back to Washington (as the official story holds), the E-4B "could have tracked AA 77 during its entire flight." There would have been no surprises. On the motto *Videmus Omnia*, see page 48 of Gaffney's book.

40 John King segment, *Anderson Cooper 360°* September 12, 2007
(http://transcripts.cnn.com/TRANSCRIPTS/0709/12/acd.01.html). The John
King segment is available on YouTube: "New details of 9/11 Mystery plane over
Washington D.C." (http://www.youtube.com/watch?v=oOhdU2BTT5o). It is
also available elsewhere (http://anderson-cooper-
effects.blogspot.com/2007/09/mystery-plane.html).

41 Alfred Goldberg et al., *Pentagon 9/11* (Washington, DC: Office of the Secretary
of Defense, 2007), 115–16.

42 "Terrorism Strikes in the United States in a Massive Attack," CNN, September
11, 2001 (http://edition.cnn.com/TRANSCRIPTS/0109/11/bn.03.html); "A
Constant Reminder," *Washington Post* September 5, 2002
(http://www.highbeam.com/doc/1P2-368536.html).

43 Jeffrey Mark Parsons, interview by John Darrell Sherwood, US Naval Historical
Center, December 13, 2001 (http://www.scribd.com/doc/51087013/GSA-B114-
RDOD03012797-Fdr-Entire-Contents-NHC-Intvw-Parsons-Jeff-CBP-041).

44 Shoestring 9/11, "The Mystery of the Helicopter Flying Around the Pentagon
Before the Attack There on 9/11," June 11, 2011
(http://shoestring911.blogspot.com/2011/06/mystery-of-helicopter-flying-
around.html).

45 Ibid.

46 Ibid.

47 Goldberg et al., *Pentagon 9/11*, 23.

48 Charles E. Lewis, "What I Heard LAX Security Officials Say During the 9/11
Attacks" 911Truth.org, September 7, 2008
(http://www.911truth.org/article_for_printing.php?story=2008071025531345).

49 Goldberg et al., *Pentagon 9/11*, 23.

50 Secretary of Defense Rumsfeld, "DOD Acquisition and Logistics Excellence
Week Kickoff: Bureaucracy to Battlefield," Department of Defense, September
10, 2001 (http://www.defenselink.mil/speeches/speech.aspx?speechid=430).

51 Chandler and Cole, "Joint Statement."

52 See Milan Simonich, "Army Unit Piecing Together Accounts of Pentagon
Attack," *Pittsburgh Post-Gazette* December 20, 2001
(http://whatreallyhappened.com/WRHARTICLES/pentagon_accounts.html).

53 Honegger, "The Pentagon Attack Papers." Email from Honegger, July 4, 2008.

54 See "Casualties at the Pentagon: September 11th, 2001," The Pentagon
(http://www.classbrain.com/artfree/publish/article_62.shtml), or Goldberg et
al., *Pentagon 9/11*, Appendix A, "List of 9/11 Pentagon Fatalities."

55 Jim Hoffman, "Pentagon Victims: Who was Killed in the 9/11/01 Attack on the
Pentagon" (http://911research.wtc7.net/sept11/victims/pentagonkilled.html).

56 Honegger, "The Pentagon Attack Papers." She added that Navy Lt. Kevin
Shaeffer, the only person who survived the attack, had burns over 60 percent
of his body.

57 E.P. Heidner, "Collateral Damage: U.S. Covert Operations and the Terrorist
Attacks on September 11, 2001" (http://www.wanttoknow.info/911/Collateral-
Damage-911-black_eagle_fund_trust.pdf). Heidner reports that 39 of the 40
employees of the Office of Naval Intelligence were killed.

58 Legge, "What Hit?"

59 Frank Legge letter to David Griffin, June 23, 2011.

60 Ibid.

61 Chandler and Cole, "Joint Statement."

62 Jim Hoffman, "Pentagon Eyewitnesses: Analysis of the Pentagon Attack Eyewitness Accounts" (http://911research.wtc7.net/pentagon/analysis/witnesses.html).

63 Legge, "What Hit the Pentagon?"

64 Chandler and Cole, "Joint Statement."

65 Frank Legge letter.

66 Jim Hoffman, "The Pentagon Attack: What the Physical Evidence Shows," March 28, 2006 (http://911research.wtc7.net/essays/pentagon/index.html).

67 Ibid.

68 Frank Legge letter.

69 Hoffman, "The Pentagon Attack"

70 Ibid.

71 Ibid.

72 Ibid.

73 Frank Legge letter.

74 Legge, "What Hit the Pentagon?" When he published that article (in 2010), Legge had reason to be suspicious about the FDR file in particular, because the data seemed to show the plane finished too high to have hit the Pentagon. But in the meantime, Legge came to believe that the problem had resulted from difficulties in decoding the file (Letter from Legge, June 24, 2011).

75 Legge, "What Hit the Pentagon?"

76 "The Ultimate 9/11 'Truth' Showdown: David Ray Griffin vs. Matt Taibbi," AlterNet, October 6, 2008 (http://www.alternet.org/rights/100688/the_ultimate_9_11_'truth'_showdown:_david_ray_griffin_vs._matt_taibbi/?page=entire).

77 Popular Mechanics, Debunking 9/11 Myths, 59.

78 "Eric Bart's Pentagon Attack Eyewitness Accounts," which is contained in Jim Hoffman's 9-11 Research (http://911research.wtc7.net/pentagon/evidence/witnesses/bart.html). Henceforth "Eric Bart's."

79 See the testimonies of Don Wright, D.S. Khavkin, Steve Patterson, Lon Rains, Meseidy Rodriguez, and Tom Seibert.

80 See the testimonies of John Bowman, Victor Correa, Don Perkal, and Mike Slater.

81 Jerry Russell, "Eyewitnesses and the Plane-Bomb Theories," 911-Strike.com, March 19, 2005 (http://www.911-strike.com/PlaneBomb.htm).

82 Ibid.

83 Jim Hoffman points out that there is nothing strange about the fact that many of the witnesses were Pentagon employees, because they were right there, nor about the high percentage of USA Today employees, because their office is very close to the Pentagon. The fact remains, however, that the list of witnesses is heavily biased by these witnesses, especially "elite" Pentagon employees.

84 "Eric Bart's."

85 Ibid.

86 See Probst's testimony in "Eric Bart's" or in Vince Crawley, "Fortress Report," MilitaryCity.com, September 11, 2002 (http://web.archive.org/web/20090313064358/http://www.militarycity.com/sept11/fortress1.html).

87 Dave McGowan, "September 11, 2001 Revisited: The Series: Act II," Center for an Informed America, October 2, 2004 (www.davesweb.cnchost.com/nwsltr68.html).

88 Jamie McIntyre interviewed by Judy Woodruff. Some people have claimed that McIntyre later, in supporting the view that the building was hit by a 757, contradicted his earlier statement that all the pieces he saw were "very small." The strongest evidence for this claim seems to be his statement, "I was there on September 11, and I saw the wreckage of a plane, including large pieces" (see "Jamie McIntyre Contradiction #3" at http://www.youtube.com/watch?v= KV0XRVL2vrw). In his interview with Judy Woodruff on 9/11, however, he had said: "The biggest piece I saw was about three feet long, it was silver and had been painted green and red . . . . I also saw a large piece of shattered glass. It appeared to be a cockpit windshield or other window from the plane" (http://transcripts.cnn.com/TRANSCRIPTS/0109/11/bn.35.html). There is, therefore, no contradiction, because the "large pieces" he saw were "small enough that you can pick [them] up in your hand." Thus understood, his later affirmation of "large pieces" does not contradict his earlier report that there were "no large tail sections, wing sections, fuselage, nothing like that anywhere around."

89 McWethy's statement is quoted in Allison Gilbert et al., *Covering Catastrophe: Broadcast Journalists Report September 11* (New York: Bonus Books, 2002), 187.

90 Karen Kwiatkowski, "Assessing the Official 9/11 Conspiracy Theory," in David Ray Griffin and Peter Dale Scott, ed., *9/11 and American Empire: Intellectuals Speak Out* (Northampton: Olive Branch Press [Interlink Publishing], 2006). For a more technical discussion of the debris, see "The Missing Wings" (http://www.physics911.net/missingwings.htm), in which A. K. Dewdney and G. W. Longspaugh argue that the absence of wing debris alone is sufficient to disprove the claim that a huge airliner hit the Pentagon.

91 "Responding in the Pentagon," Office of Medical History (http://web.archive.org/web/20090205064229/http://history.amedd.army.mil/ memoirs/soldiers/responding.pdf), 119.

92 Christopher Hilton, *The Women's War: Voices from September 11* (Charlston, History Press, 2002), 143.

93 "Responding in the Pentagon," Office of Medical History (http://web.archive.org/web/20090205064229/http://history.amedd.army.mil/ memoirs/soldiers/responding.pdf), 96.

94 See "Eric Bart's."

95 "Barbara Honegger Interviews April Gallop," a videotaped, under-oath interview that took place on March 11, 2007.

96 Ibid.

97 Ibid.

98 Dean E. Murphy, *September 11: An Oral History* (New York: Doubleday, 2002), 212.

99 "Barbara Honegger Interviews April Gallop."

100 Gallop's view is consistent, however, with photographs showing that in the first few minutes after the attack, there was no big fire at the alleged crash site. See Ralph Omholt, "9-11 and the Impossible: The Pentagon: Part One of an Online Journal of 9-11" (http://www.physics911.net/omholt.htm). Referring to a photograph of the first fire trucks to the scene, former pilot Omholt wrote:

"There is no suggestion of an aircraft crash and the expected fuel fire—NONE! The firemen should be in aluminum-clad suits, with hand-lines extended to the building, to 'penetrate' the fire . . . . The clue is in the background smoke; indicative of a structural fire, coming from the interior rings" (Omholt, "9-11 and the Impossible").

101 Russell, "Eyewitnesses and the Plane-Bomb Theories."

102 All of these are in "Eric Bart's."

103 Photos of the lawn can be seen in Omholt, "9-11 and the Impossible."

104 Both quoted in "Eric Bart's."

105 Russell, "Eyewitnesses."

106 Goldberg et al., *Pentagon 9/11*, 68.

107 Ibid., 69.

108 Ibid., 70.

109 "DOD News Briefing," Defense Link, Department of Defense, September 12, 2001. This briefing was removed from the DOD, but it has been preserved by Yale Law School's Avalon Project (http://avalon.law.yale.edu/sept11/dod_brief01.asp).

110 "Ed Plaugher: La Mémoire à rebours," *Digipresse* May 22, 2002. Translated in Thierry Meyssan, *Pentagate* (London: Carnot, 2002), 21.

111 Leslie Filson, *Air War over America: Sept. 11 Alters Face of Air Defense Mission*, foreword by Larry K. Arnold (Public Affairs: Tyndall Air Force Base, 2003), 66.

112 Jack Sullivan, "Fargo Pilots remember Sept. 11 Duty," Associated Press, August 19, 2002 (http://s3.amazonaws.com/911timeline/2002/ap081902c.html).

113 Sgt. Keith Bohn, Interviewed for Pentagon Terrorist Attack Incident, November 19, 2001, Naval Historical Center (http://www.scribd.com/doc/51154485/GSA-B115-RDOD03012868-Fdr-Entire-Contents-NHC-Intvw-2001-11-19-Bohn-Keith-Park-Pol-Huey-065).

114 Sgt. Ronald Alan Galey, Interviewed for Pentagon Terrorist Attack Incident, November 20, 2001, Naval Historical Center (http://www.scribd.com/doc/51087018/GSA-B115-RDOD03012845-Fdr-Entire-Contents-NHC-Intvw-2001-11-20-Galey-Ron-Park-Police-Aviation-055). I am indebted to Matthew Everett for these quotations from Galey and Bohn.

115 Randy Dockendorf, "Tyndall Native Relives 9/11," *Yankton Press & Dakotan* September 11, 2003 (https://docs.google.com/Doc?id=dc52kcvf_311f283grd2&pli=1).

116 Eric Bart's Witness Accounts (http://web.archive.org/web/20040501101751/http://eric-bart.net/iwpb/witness.html).

117 Scott P. Cook, "September 11, 2001," Cloth Monkey (http://www.abovetopsecret.com/forum/thread378783/pg80). Although Cook wrote "missed," he obviously meant "saw."

118 "Eric Bart's."

119 Goldberg et al., *Pentagon 9/11*, 31.

120 Vogel, *The Pentagon*, 434.

121 Nielsen gave this report in an interview with Barbara Honegger. Although Honegger used Nielsen's experience in the 2006 version of "The Pentagon Attack Papers" (included in Jim Marrs' book), without revealing his name, she later gave his name to me with permission to use it (email July 4, 2008).

122 Timothy McSweeney "The Works of Humankind: A Dispatch by Don Perkal" (http://www.mcsweeneys.net/2001/09/19perkal.html).

123 "Eric Bart's."

124 Barbara Vobejda, "'Extensive Casualties' in Wake of Pentagon Attack," Washingtonpost.com, September 11, 2001, 4:59 PM (http://www.washingtonpost.com/wp-srv/metro/daily/sep01/attack.html).

125 Honegger, "The Pentagon Attack Papers."

126 Barbara Honegger, California Jurat with Affiant Statement, signed by Notary Public Kelly Harlow of Monterey County, May 25, 2011.

127 "Images Show September 11 Pentagon Crash," CNN.com, March 8, 2001 (http://archives.cnn.com/2002/US/03/07/gen.pentagon.pictures/index.html).

128 See, e.g., "5 Frame Analysis Pentagon & Flight 77," YouTube, October 19, 2009 (http://www.youtube.com/watch?v=ZYKpSUN_J1A), or "9/11 Pentagon Attack: A Closer Look," YouTube (http://www.youtube.com/watch?v=lsWZHKIg3Cs&feature=fvwrel).

129 Thierry Meyssan, "Pentagon 911 Images Released by the DOD Do Not Prove that a Boeing 757 Hit the Pentagon," Global Research (http://www.globalresearch.ca/index.php?context=va&aid=2463).

130 "New Pentagon Video from Judicial Watch FOIA Request" (http://911review.org/Reports/NEW_VIDEO.html).

131 Massimo Mazzucco, *The Pentagon Videos Are Doctored* (video, available at http://www.consensus911.org). Mazzucco is an award-winning filmmaker, screenwriter, and journalist. His 2005 documentary, *Inganno Globale* ("Global Deceit"), argued that the official 9/11 story has major faults. In 2006, it was broadcast on Italian TV (Berlusconi's Canale 5), serving as a platform for a full-fledged national debate—which made Italy the only country to have thoroughly discussed 9/11 in the mainstream media. His later film, *The New American Century*, was presented at the 2008 Sao Paulo Film Festival in Brazil and some European film festivals. Supported by world famous filmmakers such as Costa-Gavras, Wim Wenders, and Ken Loach, this documentary premiered in the US at the 2009 Oakland 9/11 Film Festival.

132 Pier Paolo Murru is a cinematographer, editor, compositor, and digital video expert in 3D modeling and film animations. He has worked on several award-winning films and has taught the technical aspects of film-making.

133 Mazzucco, *The Pentagon Videos Are Doctored.*

134 Marilyn Adams, Alan Levin, and Blake Morrison, "Part II: No One Was Sure if Hijackers Were on Board," *USA Today* August 12, 2002 (http://www.usatoday.com/news/sept11/2002-08-12-hijacker-daytwo_x.htm).

135 "Timeline for the Day of the September 11 Attacks," Wikipedia (http://en.wikipedia.org/wiki/Timeline_for_the_day_of_the_September_11_attacks#cite_note-14).

136 Jerry Schwartz, "World Trade Center Collapses in Terrorist Attack; Washington Hit by Coordinated Attacks," Associated Press, September 11, 2001 (http://newsmine.org/content.php?ol=9-11/flight77-aa-pentagon/helicopter-hits-pentagon-on-september-11.txt).

137 "Minute by Minute with the Broadcast News," PoynterOnline, September 11, 2001.

138 Gerry J. Gilmore, "Alleged Terrorist Airliner Attack Targets Pentagon," American Forces Press Service, September 11, 2001 (http://old.911digitalarchive.org/crr/documents/2861.pdf).

139 Geraldine Baum and Maggie Farley, "Terror Attack: Hijacked Jets Fly into Trade Center, Pentagon," *Los Angeles Times* September 11, 2001 (http://emuseum.icp.org/view/objects/asitem/People$00401967/ 2;jsessionid=75E9B537C24F294B47B2443CD0DA8DEB?t:state:flow= 4d6bf745-862c-4026-b98d-66806ec34f79).

140 FBI, "Interview with Theodore Olsen [sic]," *9/11 Commission, FBI Source Documents, Chronological, September 11,* 2001, Intelfiles.com, March 14, 2008 (http://intelfiles.egoplex.com:80/2008/03/911-commission-fbi-source-documents.html).

141 *Larry King Live,* CNN, September 14, 2001 (http://edition.cnn.com/ TRANSCRIPTS/0109/14/lkl.00.html).

142 "T7 B12 Flight 93 Calls- General Fdr- 5-20-04 DOJ Briefing on Cell and Phone Calls From AA 77 408," Federal Bureau of Investigation, May 20, 2004 (http://www.scribd.com/doc/18886083/T7-B12-Flight-93-Calls-General-Fdr-52004-DOJ-Briefing-on-Cell-and-Phone-Calls-From-AA-77-408).

143 United States v. Zacarias Moussaoui, Exhibit Number P200054 (http://www.vaed.uscourts.gov/notablecases/moussaoui/exhibits/prosecution/ flights/P200054.html). These documents can be more easily viewed in Jim Hoffman, "Detailed Account of Phone Calls from September 11th Flights" (http://911research.wtc7.net/planes/evidence/calldetail.html).

144 "'Get These Planes on the Ground': Air Traffic Controllers Recall Sept. 11," ABCNews.com, October 24, 2001 (http://web.archive.org/web/20011025074733/http://abcnews.go.com/ sections/2020/2020/2020_011024_atc_feature.html).

145 *Good Morning America,* ABC, September 13, 2001.

146 Pentagon News Briefing, September 15, 2001. This briefing has apparently been removed from the Pentagon's website. But it has been preserved by the Wisdom Fund (http://www.twf.org/News/Y2009/0101-DODnews.html).

147 Thierry Meyssan, *Pentagate* (London: Carnot Publishing, 2002), 60.

148 *Arlington County After-Action Report on the Response to the September 11 Attack on the Pentagon,* 2002 (http://web.archive.org/web/20080227173846/http://www.arlingtonva.us/ departments/Fire/edu/about/docs/after_report.pdf), A-8.

149 ASCE (American Society of Civil Engineers), *Pentagon Building Performance Report,* January 2003 (http://fire.nist.gov/bfrlpubs/build03/PDF/b03017.pdf), 40.

150 Popular Mechanics, *Debunking 9/11 Myths,* 70.

151 Vogel, *The Pentagon,* 431.

152 Goldberg et al., *Pentagon 9/11,* 17.

153 Legge, "What Hit?"

154 Ibid.

155 Quoted on Patriots Question 9/11 (http://www.patriotsquestion911.com/#Wittenberg).

156 Dave McGowan, "September 11, 2001 Revisited: The Series: Act II" (http://www.davesweb.cnchost.com/nwsltr68.html).

157 One can see a letter requesting 85 videos that had been mentioned by an FBI agent (http://web.archive.org/web/20100508192537/http://www.flight77.info/85tapes.gif), and one can also see a DOJ letter saying: "The material you requested is located in an investigative file which is exempt from disclosure" (http://web.archive.org/web/20100508192535/http://www.flight77.info/00new/n85reply.jpg).

158 See Judicial Watch, "CITGO Gas Station Cameras Near Pentagon Evidently Did Not Capture Attack," September 15, 2006 (http://web.archive.org/web/20100616195426/http://www.judicialwatch.org/printer_5965.shtml), and a video on You Tube (http://www.youtube.com/watch?v=2LJvFjsl6zk). Another video was released in November 2006 (http://www.youtube.com/watch?v=H285_DWX_bQ).

159 Legge, "What Hit?"

160 Colonel George Nelson, USAF (ret.), "Impossible to Prove a Falsehood True: Aircraft Parts as a Clue to Their Identity," Physics 911, April 23, 2005 (http://www.physics911.net/georgenelson.htm).

161 Legge, "What Hit?" Chandler and Cole have made a similar argument ("Joint Statement"). Stating that "the physical evidence does not rule out that [sic] possibility that it was American Airlines Flight 77 that actually crashed into the Pentagon," they continue: "Confidently asserting otherwise, then being proven wrong and discredited for sloppy research, would be disastrous for the credibility of the solid science-based research at the World Trade Center." But who among us would "rule out the possibility that it was American Airlines Flight 77"? Reasonable people would simply say something such as: "Given the evidence we now have, it seems unlikely that it was AA 77." If the government were, after all these years, to release evidence that this "unlikely possibility" had been the truth, what would this prove? It would not say anything negative about those who had expressed this view because the DOD had hidden evidence. It would only show that the government had been concealing evidence that should have been revealed many years earlier.

162 Aidan Monaghan, "9/11 Aircraft 'Black Box' Serial Numbers Mysteriously Absent," 911Blogger, February 26, 2008 (http://911blogger.com/node/14081).

163 One can see the NTSB's FDR report on AA 77 (http://www.911myths.com/AAL77_fdr.pdf), and one can also see the NTSB's FDR report on United Flight 93 (http://www.gwu.edu/~nsarchiv/NSAEBB/NSAEBB196/doc04.pdf).

164 Aidan Monaghan, "FBI Records Chief Describes Unsuccessful Search for Identifying Records of 9/11 Aircraft Wreckage & Flight Data Recorders," 9/11 Blogger, August 26, 2008 (http://911blogger.com/node/17363).

165 Aidan Monaghan, "F.B.I. Elaborates On Reportedly Absent 9/11 Aircraft Wreckage Recovery & Identification Records," 911 Blogger, March 18, 2008 (http://www.911blogger.com/node/14422).

166 This FBI statement also indicated that it has no records proving that UA 93 crashed near Shanksville, Pennsylvania, or that the World Trade Center was struck by AA 11 and UA 175.

167 "Searchers Find Pentagon Black Boxes," USA Today September 14, 2001 (http://www.usatoday.com/news/nation/2001/09/14/pentagon-fire.htm#more).

168 Ibid.

169 "Washington's Heroes: On the Ground at the Pentagon on Sept. 11," *Newsweek* September 28, 2003. It said: "Early Friday morning [9/14], shortly before 4 a.m., [search-and-rescue specialist Carlton] Burkhammer and another firefighter, Brian Moravitz, were combing through debris near the impact site. Peering at the wreckage with their helmet lights, the two spotted an intact seat from the plane's cockpit with a chunk of the floor still attached. Then they saw two odd-shaped dark boxes, about 1.5 by 2 feet long. They'd been told the plane's 'black boxes' would in fact be bright orange, but these were charred black. The boxes had handles on one end and one was torn open. They cordoned off the area and called for an FBI agent, who in turn called for someone from the NTSB who confirmed the find: the black boxes from Flight 77" (Peace Plant's Blog [http://www.myspace.com/paulstc44/blog/542589584]).

170 Aidan Monaghan, "Pentagon 9/11 Flight 'Black Box' Data File Created Before Actual 'Black Box' Was Recovered?" 911 Blogger, May 18, 2008 (http://www.911blogger.com/node/15636).

171 See the *Newsweek* story cited two notes above.

172 *Pentagon Building Performance Report*, Section 6.2.

173 Popular Mechanics, *Debunking 9/11 Myths*, 70.

174 "YouTube - 9/11 Truth: Pentagon Eyewitness Bob Pugh Tells His Story," YouTube (http://www.google.com/search?client=safari&rls=en&q=9/11,+Bob+Pugh+video&ie=UTF-8&oe=UTF-8).

175 Omholt, "9-11 and the Impossible."

176 Won-Young Kim and G. R. Baum, "Seismic Observations during September 11, 2001, Terrorist Attack," Spring 2002 [http://www.mgs.md.gov/esic/publications/download/911pentagon.pdf]).

177 David Ray Griffin, *The New Pearl Harbor Revisited: 9/11, the Cover-Up, and the Exposé* (Northampton: Olive Branch Press [Interlink Publishing], 2008), 71.

178 Wallace's comment can be found in "The Damage Inside the Building: Bomb or Not Bomb?" August 2004 (http://jpdesm.pagesperso-orange.fr/pentagon/archive0704/dam-inside.html).

179 "Damage To Buildings Near World Trade Center Towers Caused By Falling Debris and Air Pressure Wave, Not Ground Shaking, Seismologists Report," *ScienceDaily* November 16, 2001 (http://www.sciencedaily.com/releases/2001/11/011116064642.htm).

180 *After-Action Report on the Response to the September 11 Attack on the Pentagon.*

181 Ibid., C-45.

182 Some people have said that this would be "too gruesome." It would indeed have been gruesome. But so was the deliberate killing of 39 of the 40 employees of the Office of Naval Intelligence and the killing of a majority of the employees of the Army's financial management/audit area. Was killing almost three thousand workers of the World Trade Center, many of whom burned to death or jumped to their deaths, not gruesome? In such operations, gruesomeness or the lack thereof is not a criterion of truth.

183 Col. H. Theodore Harcke, Major Joseph A. Bifano, and Capt. Kelly K. Koeller, "Forensic Radiology: Response to the Pentagon Attack on September 11, 2001," *Radiology* 223 (April 2002): 7–8 (http://radiology.rsnajnls.org/cgi/content/full/223/1/7).

184 Frank Legge and Warren Stutt, "Flight AA77 on 9/11: New FDR Analysis Supports the Official Flight Path Leading to Impact with the Pentagon," *Journal of 9/11 Studies* 30 (January 2011) (http://www.journalof911studies.com/volume/2010/Calibration%20of%20altimeter_92.pdf).
185 See an Image Shack photo (http://img35.imageshack.us/img35/650/pole5.jpg) and a Photo Bucket photo (http://i14.photobucket.com/albums/a327/lytetrip/187b.jpg).
186 Navy, Pentagon Clock (http://www.news.navy.mil/view_single.asp?id=2480Pentagonclock_BBC).
187 "September 11: Bearing Witness to History. Pentagon Helipad Clock" (http://www.americanhistory.si.edu/september11/collection/search.asp?search=1&keywords=Wall+clock&location=).
188 Barbara Honegger, "The Pentagon Attack Papers," note 2B.
189 Navy, Pentagon Clock.
190 This point is included in Barbara Honegger's notarized statement.

CHAPTER 8

1 This chapter is a revised version of a lecture that was delivered October 19, 2007, at Iliff School of Theology in Denver, Colorado.
2 David Ray Griffin, *Debunking 9/11 Debunking: An Answer to Popular Mechanics and Other Defenders of the Official Conspiracy Theory* (Northampton: Olive Branch Press [Interlink Publishing], 2007), 1.
3 Richard Falk, "Foreword" to David Ray Griffin, *The New Pearl Harbor: Disturbing Questions About the Bush Administration and 9/11* (Northampton: Olive Branch Press, [Interlink Publishing], 2004), vii.
4 On the Mukden incident, see Walter LaFeber, *The Clash: U.S.-Japanese Relations throughout History* (New York: Norton, 1997), 164–66; Louise Young, *Japan's Total Empire: Manchuria and the Culture of Wartime Imperialism* (Berkeley: University of California Press, 1999), 40; or "Mukden Incident," *Encyclopedia Britannica*, 2006 (http://www.britannica.com/eb/article-9054193).
5 Proof that the Nazis themselves set the fire was confirmed in 2001 with the publication of *Der Reichstagbrand: Wie Geschichte Gemacht Wird*, by Alexander Bahar and Wilfried Kugel (Berlin: Edition Q, 2001). For a review of this book, see Wilhelm Klein, "The Reichstag Fire, 68 Years On," World Socialist Website, July 5, 2001 (http://www.wsws.org/articles/2001/jul2001/reic-j05.shtml).
6 See "Nazi Conspiracy and Aggression, Vol. II: Criminality of Groups and Organizations" (http://www.nizkor.org/hweb/imt/nca/nca-02/nca-02-15-criminality-06-05.html); Ian Kershaw, *Hitler: 1936-45: Nemesis* (New York: Norton, 2001), 221; and "Gleiwitz Incident," Wikipedia (http://en.wikipedia.org/wiki/Gleiwitz_incident#References).
7 Howard Zinn, *A People's History of the United States* (1980; New York: HarperPerennial, 1990), 150. Richard Van Alstyne, *The Rising American Empire* (1960; New York, Norton, 1974), 143.
8 Stuart Creighton Miller, *Benevolent Assimilation: The American Conquest of the Philippines, 1899-1903* (New Haven: Yale University Press, 1982), 11.
9 Ibid., 57–62.

10 George McT. Kahin, *Intervention: How America Became Involved in Vietnam* (Garden City: Anchor Press/Doubleday, 1987), 220; Marilyn B. Young, *The Vietnam Wars 1945-1990* (New York: HarperCollins, 1991), 119.

11 Daniele Ganser, *NATO's Secret Armies: Operation Gladio and Terrorism in Western Europe* (New York: Frank Cass, 2005).

12 This memorandum can be found at the National Security Archive, April 30, 2001 (http://www.gwu.edu/~nsarchiv/news/20010430). It was revealed to US readers by James Bamford in *Body of Secrets: Anatomy of the Ultra-secret National Security Agency* (2001: New York: Anchor Books, 2002), 82–91.

13 See David Ray Griffin, *The New Pearl Harbor: Disturbing Questions about the Bush Administration and 9/11* (Northampton: Olive Branch Press [Interlink Publishing], 2004), 89–92.

14 See Ron Susskind, *The Price of Loyalty: George W. Bush, the White House, and the Education of Paul O'Neill* (New York: Simon & Schuster, 2004), and "Bush Sought 'Way' to Invade Iraq?" Rebecca Leung, CBS News, January 11, 2004 (www.cbsnews.com/stories/2004/01/09/60minutes/main592330.shtml). See also Richard Clarke, *Against All Enemies: Inside America's War on Terror* (New York: Free Press, 2004), 264.

15 Wesley K. Clark, *Winning Modern Wars: Iraq, Terrorism, and the American Empire* (New York: Public Affairs, 2003), 120, 130. Clark later stated this on *Democracy Now!* See "General Wesley Clark Weighs Presidential Bid," March 2, 2007 (http://www.democracynow.org/article.pl?sid=07/03/02/1440234), and also in *A Time to Lead: For Duty, Honor and Country* (New York: Palgrave Macmillan, 2007).

16 Union of Concerned Scientists, "Restoring Scientific Integrity in Policymaking" (http://www.ucsusa.org/scientific_integrity/abuses_of_science/scientists-sign-on-statement.html).

17 See "NIST Whistleblower," George Washington's Blog, October 3, 2007 (http://georgewashington.blogspot.com/2007/10/former-nist-employee-blows-whistle.html).

18 Quoted in Dennis Smith, *Report from Ground Zero: The Story of the Rescue Efforts at the World Trade Center* (New York: Penguin, 2002), 18.

19 John Bussey, "Eye of the Storm: One Journey Through Desperation and Chaos," *Wall Street Journal*, September 12, 2001 (http://online.wsj.com/public/resources/documents/040802pulitzer5.htm).

20 Jim Yardley, "A Trainee Noted for Incompetence," *New York Times* May 4, 2002 (http://web.archive.org/web/20071005175951/http://newsmine.org/archive/9-11/suspects/flying-skills/pilot-trainee-noted-for-incompetence.txt).

21 Marc Fisher and Don Phillips, "On Flight 77: 'Our Plane Is Being Hijacked,'" *Washington Post* September 12, 2001 (http://www.washingtonpost.com/ac2/wp-dyn?pagename=article&node=&contentId=A14365-2001Sep11).

22 Email from Ralph Omholt, October 27, 2006.

23 John B. Cobb, Jr., "Truth, 'Faith,' and 9/11." This essay is posted at Religious Leaders for 9/11 Truth (http://rl911truth.org/index.php?option=com_content&view=article&id=65:cobb-john-b-truth-faith-and-911&catid=37:911-articles&Itemid=69).

24 Ibid.

25 Ibid.

26 *The American Heritage Dictionary of the English Language* (The American Heritage Publishing Co., 1969).

27 Jim Dwyer, "2 U.S. Reports Seek to Counter Conspiracy Theories About 9/11," *New York Times* September 2, 2006 (http://www.911review.com/reviews/nyt/markup/02conspiracy.html).

28 Salim Muwakkil, "What's the 411 on 9/11?" *In These Times* December 21, 2005 (http://www.inthesetimes.com/article/2444).

29 Ibid. One of the errors in Allen's diagnosis is that she assumed that, because I am "a theologian," I must operate in the way she assumes all theologians operate. But since the 18th-century Enlightenment, there has been a great methodological divide within theology. Many theologians still do operate on the traditional basis, in which questions of truth are settled by appeals to authority, the pronouncements of which are taken on faith. But I have always practiced the Enlightenment-based type of theology, which, as I explained in a book subtitled *A New Synthesis of Scientific Naturalism and Christian Faith*, rejects the "method of authority" in favor of the method of "settling questions of truth and falsity on the basis of common experience and reason—that is, by reasoning on the basis of experience that is at least potentially common to all people." See David Ray Griffin, *Two Great Truths: A New Synthesis of Scientific Naturalism and Christian Faith* (Louisville: Westminster John Knox Press, 2004), 62. Central to this type of theology is the rejection of "miracles" in the sense of "supernatural interruptions of the world's most fundamental causal processes" (ibid., 98). The centrality of this element in my theology is illustrated by the titles of two of my other books, *Religion and Scientific Naturalism: Overcoming the Conflicts* (Albany: State University of New York Press, 2000), and *Reenchantment without Supernaturalism: A Process Philosophy of Religion* (Ithaca: Cornell University Press, 2001).

30 President George W. Bush, "Address to the General Assembly of the United Nations," November 10, 2001.

31 Jacob Heilbrunn, "Inside the World of Conspiracy Theorists," *New York Times*, review of Jonathan Kay, *Among the Truthers*, May 13, 2011 (http://www.nytimes.com/2011/05/15/books/review/book-review-among-the-truthers-by-jonathan-kay.html).

32 Sonny Bunch, "Beyond the Lunatic Fringe," *Wall Street Journal*, review of Jonathan Kay, *Among the Truthers*, May 10, 2011 (http://911blogger.com/news/2011-05-10/beyond-lunatic-fringe-wall-street-journal-book-review-among-truthers-jonathan-kay).

33 Architects and Engineers for 9/11 Truth (ae911truth.org).

34 "Jonathan Kay on the Humbling Frustrations of Debating 9/11 Truthers," (http://network.nationalpost.com/np/blogs/fullcomment/archive/2008/10/27/jonathan-kay-on-the-humbling-frustrations-of-debating-9-11-quot-truthers-quot.aspx); quoted in Anthony J. Hall, "Jonathan Kay Defends the Sacred Myth of 9/11," Veterans Today, May 27, 2001 (http://www.veteranstoday.com/2011/05/27/jonathan-kay-defends-the-sacred-myth-of-911/#_ednref). In addition to Hall's illuminating essay, see Donald Benham, "Conspiracy Hunt Doesn't Always Uncover the Truth," *Winnipeg*

Free Press May 31, 2011 (http://www.winnipegfreepress.com/arts-and-life/ entertainment/books/conspiracy-hunt-doesnt-always-uncover-the-truth-122765389.html?device=mobile), and see the comment by Physicsandreason.

35 "911—David Ray Griffin on Tucker Carlson's Aug. 9, 2006," MSNBC, August 9, 2005 (http://www.youtube.com/watch?v=AxKW3EqbfRE).

36 Richard A. Horsley, *Jesus and Empire: The Kingdom of God and the New World Disorder* (Minneapolis: Fortress, 2003), 27.

37 Lord Acton, *Essays*, ed. Rufus F. Fears (Liberty Classics, 1985), Vol. II: 383. Acton's statement is quoted in Garry Wills, *Papal Sin: Structures of Deceit* (New York: Doubleday, 2000), 2.

38 Andrew J. Bacevich, *The New American Militarism: How Americans Are Seduced by War* (Oxford: Oxford University Press, 2005), 133.

39 David Ray Griffin, "Neocon Imperialism, 9/11, and the Attacks on Afghanistan and Iraq," Information Clearing House, February 27, 2007 (http://www.informationclearinghouse.info/article17194.htm). Published in revised form as "Imperial Motives for a 'New Pearl Harbor'" in *Christian Faith and the Truth behind 9/11*.

40 Ian Markham, "Did Bush Cooperate with Terrorists? Making Conspiracy Theories Respectable Can Be Dangerous," was originally published in *Zion's Herald* November/December 2004. (http://web.archive.org/web/20050222013622/http://zionsherald.org/Nov2004_perspective2.html). Markham's essay and my response are contained in "Two Theologians Debate 9/11: David Ray Griffin and Ian Markham," AnthonyFlood.com (http://www.anthonyflood.com/griffinmarkhamdebate911.htm).

41 Email from Ian Markham to David Griffin, March 24, 2005; quoted with permission.

42 David Heim, "Whodunit? A 9/11 Conspiracy Theory," *Christian Century* September 5, 2006: 8–9.

43 Ibid.

44 See note 16, above.

45 Heim, "Whodunit?"

46 Institute of Religion and Democracy, Press Release: "IRD: Presbyterian-Published 9/11 Conspiracy Book is Absurd," September 26, 2006 (http://www.irdrenew.org/site/apps/nl/content2.asp?c=fvKVLfMVIsG&b=390529&ct=2925837).

47 Quoted in Juli Cragg Hilliard, "9/11 Book Stirs Church Controversy," Religion BookLine, *Publishers Weekly*, August 16, 2006.

48 Quoted in Daniel Burke, "September 11 Conspiracy Book from Presbyterian Publishing Corporation Raises Eyebrows," Religion News Service, August 9, 2006 (http://web.archive.org/web/20090212230918/http://www.pcusa.org/pcnews/2006/06402.htm).

49 Quoted in Jason Bailey, "Official Presbyterian Publisher Issues 9/11 Conspiracy Book," *Christianity Today* July 31, 2006 (http://www.christianitytoday.com/ct/2006/131/12.0.html). This review by Bailey in *Christianity Today*, incidentally, was one of the most responsible reviews in a Christian publication that I have seen.

50 Jason Bailey, "Presbyterian Publisher Seeks Distance from 9/11 Conspiracy Book," *Christianity Today* November 15, 2006 (http://www.christianitytoday.com/ct/2006/novemberweb-only/146-22.0.html).

51 Quoted in Heather Wilhelm, "Anything Goes: The Presbyterian Church Gets into the 9/11 Conspiracy Business," *Wall Street Journal* September 8, 2006 (http://web.archive.org/web/20070423220043/http://www.opinionjournal.com/taste/?id=110008914). Wilhelm's article, incidentally, was the source of some of the misinformation about my views that has been circulated. She falsely claimed, for example, that I said that having a global democratic government "would bring the kingdom of God to earth" and that I believe that Jesus "was a political activist who wanted to overthrow the Roman Empire." Given these mischaracterizations, combined with her suggestion that I am "irresponsible" and a "total wingnut," I wonder if her title, "Anything Goes," gives away her view about what is permissible when a reporter's intent is to defame someone.

52 "Statement of the Board of Directors of the Presbyterian Publishing Corporation: Comments on David Ray Griffin's *Christian Faith and the Truth Behind 9/11*," November 8, 2006.

53 Peter Smith, "Church Publishers Criticize Own Book: Author Says Bush Planned 9/11 Terror," *Louisville Courier-Journal* November 18, 2006 (http://www.religionnewsblog.com/16595/church-publishers-criticize-own-book).

54 "9/11: Debunking the Myths," *Popular Mechanics* March 2005. The title of the online version is "Debunking The 9/11 Myths" (http://web.archive.org/web/20090228075427/http://www.popularmechanics.com/science/defense/1227842.html?page=1&c=y).

55 *Christian Faith and the Truth behind 9/11: A Call to Reflection and Action* (Louisville: Westminster John Knox, 2006), 43–44.

56 Ibid., 207-08,n.58.

57 Smith, "Church Publishers Criticize Own Book."

58 After the editorial board of PPC, led by Ken Godshall, published its statement apologizing for the publication of my book, Alan Wisdom, an IRD spokesman, said: "Let us hope that the (corporation) editors will learn a lesson and refrain from future dalliances with the loony left" (quoted in Smith, "Church Publishers Criticize Own Book). Will you ever see IRD criticizing any Christian publishers for their alliance with the rabid right?

59 See Griffin, *Christian Faith and the Truth behind 9/11*, Chap. 7, "Jesus and the Roman Empire."

CHAPTER 9

1 Symposium on State Crimes against Democracy, *American Behavioral Scientist* 53 (February 2010): 783–939 (http://abs.sagepub.com/content/vol53/issue6). Online access is expensive, but the entire published (hardcover) issue can be purchased for $24 (journals@sagepub.com).

2 "Silverstein Properties and Westfield Win $3.2B World Trade Center Lease," International Council of Shopping Centers, April 27, 2001 (http://www.icsc.org/srch/front/200104270803.htm); "Governor Pataki, Acting Governor DiFrancesco Laud Historic Port Authority Agreement to Privatize World Trade Center," Port Authority of New York and New Jersey, July 24, 2001 (http://www.panynj.gov/press-room/press-item.cfm?headLine_id=81).

3 Bill Manning, editor, "Selling Out the Investigation," *Fire Engineering* January 2002 (http://www.globalresearch.ca/articles/MAN309A.html).

4 Philip Shenon, *The Commission: The Uncensored History of the 9/11 Investigation* (New York: Twelve, 2008), 29, 26; "The 9/11 Commission Primer," Center for American Progress, July 20, 2004 (http://www.americanprogress.org/issues/2004/07/b124722.html).

5 Shenon, *The Commission*, 10–15.

6 "The Kissinger commission," *New York Times*, November 30, 2002 (as republished by the *International Herald Tribune*) (http://web.archive.org/web/20030225131602/http://www.iht.com/articles/78598.htm).

7 Shaun Waterman, UPI, "Victim Families Glad Kissinger to Quit 911 Panel," December 14, 2002 (http://www.rense.com/general32/glad.htm).

8 Shenon, *The Commission*, 18–19, 25.

9 Ibid., 28-29, 59; Griffin, *The New Pearl Harbor Revisited: 9/11, the Cover-Up, and the Exposé* (Northampton: Olive Branch Press [Interlink Publishing], 2008), 238-51.

10 "Whitewater: Case Closed," CBS News, September 20, 2000 (http://www.cbsnews.com/stories/2000/09/20/national/main234848.shtml).

11 "Cost of Columbia Accident Inquiry Is Soaring," *Los Angeles Times* March 15, 2003 (http://articles.latimes.com/2003/mar/15/nation/na-probe15).

12 Intelligence Officers for 9/11 Truth (http://IO911Truth.org).

13 Journalists and Other Media Professionals for 9/11 Truth (http://mediafor911truth.org).

14 Lawyers for 9/11 Truth (http://l911t.com).

15 Medical Professionals for 9/11 Truth (http://mp911truth.org).

16 Pilots for 9/11 Truth (http://pilotsfor911truth.org).

17 Political Leaders for 9/11 Truth (http://pl911truth.com).

18 Religious Leaders for 9/11 Truth (http://rl911truth.org).

19 Veterans for 9/11 Truth (http://v911t.org).

20 Firefighters for 9/11 Truth (http://firefightersfor911truth.org).

21 Erik Lawyer, "Mayday . . . Mayday . . . Mayday," Firefighters for 9/11 Truth, August 23, 2008 (http://firefightersfor911truth.org/?p=300).

22 Jacob Heilbrunn, "Inside the World of Conspiracy Theorists," *New York Times* review of Jonathan Kay, *Among the Truthers*, May 13, 2011 (http://www.nytimes.com/2011/05/15/books/review/book-review-among-the-truthers-by-jonathan-kay.html).

23 "Judge Napolitano and Geraldo Rivera Discuss Building 7," YouTube, November 24, 2010 (http://www.youtube.com/watch?v=wPEj2Pa1Y2g).

24 "Fox Host Napolitano is a 9-11 Truther: 'It couldn't possibly have been done the way the government told us,'" Media Matters, November 24, 2010 (http://mediamatters.org/blog/201011240019).

25 Adolf Hitler, *Mein Kampf*, trans. James Murphy, Vol. I, Ch. X.

26 Upton Sinclair, *I, Candidate for Governor: And How I Got Licked* (1935; Berkeley: University of California Press, 1994), 109.

27 Olivier Uyttebrouck, "Explosives Planted In Towers, N.M. Tech Expert Says," *Albuquerque Journal*, September 11, 2001 (http://www.public-action.com/911/jmcm/ABQjournal), scroll down.

28 John Fleck, "Fire, Not Extra Explosives, Doomed Buildings, Expert Says," *Albuquerque Journal* Sept. 21, 2001 (http://www.public-action.com/911/jmcm/ABQjournal).

29 On Romero's claim that he was misquoted, see ibid.; on the falsity of Romero's claim, see David Ray Griffin, *Debunking 9/11 Debunking: An Answer to Popular Mechanics and Other Defenders of the Official Conspiracy Theory* (Northampton: Olive Branch Press [Interlink Publishing], 2007), 255.

30 "Tech Receives $15 M for Anti-Terrorism Program," September 25, 2002 (http://infohost.nmt.edu/mainpage/news/2002/25sept03.html); George Zamora, "New Mexico Tech Vice President Romero Named a Top Lobbyist," December 18, 2003 (http://infohost.nmt.edu/mainpage/news/2003/18dec01.html). ("New Mexico Tech" is the common informal name for the New Mexico Institute of Mining and Technology.)

31 Fitchpatrick made this statement, Lewis reported, on June 8, 2006, while the two of them were discussing solutions to security problems he had observed while working at LAX.

32 Chris Gourlay, Jonathan Calvert, and Joe Lauria, "For Sale: West's Deadly Nuclear Secrets," *Sunday Times* January 6, 2008 (http://www.timesonline.co.uk/tol/news/world/middle_east/article3137695.ece).

33 Chris Floyd, "The Bomb in the Shadows: Proliferation, Corruption and the Way of the World," Empire Burlesque, January 8, 2008 (http://www.chris-floyd.com/component/content/article/3/1401-the-bomb-in-the-shadows-proliferation-corruption-and-the-way-of-the-world.html).

34 Dave Lindorff, "Sibel Edmonds, Turkey and the Bomb: A Real 9/11 Cover-Up?" *Counterpunch* January 7, 2008 (http://www.counterpunch.org/lindorff01072008.html).

35 See my discussion in *The New Pearl Harbor Revisited*, 148–49.

36 Brad Friedman, "Exclusive: Daniel Ellsberg Says Sibel Edmonds Case 'Far More Explosive Than Pentagon Papers,'" Huffington Post, November 25, 2007 (http://www.huffingtonpost.com/brad-friedman/exclusive-daniel-ellsberg_b_74022.html).

37 Matt Taibbi, "Cheney's Nemesis," *Rolling Stone* April 16, 2007 (http://www.informationclearinghouse.info/article17542.htm).

38 Paul Craig Roberts, "9/11 and the Orwellian Redefinition of 'Conspiracy Theory,'" June 20, 2011 (http://www.globalresearch.ca/index.php?context=va&aid=25339).

39 Ibid.

40 Ibid.

41 Napolitano made his comments during an interview on the Alex Jones show; see "Fox host Napolitano is a 9-11 Truther: 'It couldn't possibly have been done the way the government told us,'" Media Matters, November 24, 2010 (http://mediamatters.org/blog/201011240019).

42 From the right, Lachlan Markay of *Dialog New Media* assured readers that the idea that there was a conspiracy behind the collapse of WTC 7 had been "thoroughly debunked a number of times," after which he said: "The physics of the incident . . . and moral repugnance of the suggestion that the American government would deliberately slaughter thousands of its own citizens as a

pretext for war are generally enough to dissuade thinking Americans from these sorts of theories" (Lachlan Markay, "Judge Andrew Napolitano: Another 9/11 Truther on Fox's Staff?" Newsbusters, November 30, 2010 [http://news-busters.org/blogs/lachlan-markay/2010/11/30/judge-andrew-napolitano-another-911-truther-foxs-staff]). From a more liberal perspective, Joe Strupp of Media Matters wrote an article entitled "9-11 Victim Families Criticize Napolitano Comments," thereby suggesting that such criticism, which was based on four family members, was universal (Joe Strupp, "9-11 Victim Families Criticize Napolitano Comments," November 29, 2010 (http://www.mediamattersinstitute.org/blog/201011290030). But this title ignores the fact that many 9/11 family members support the 9/11 Truth Movement—including Bob McIlvaine, who appeared with Geraldo Rivera on the Fox program that initiated the debate about Fox News. Strupp also claimed, citing *Popular Mechanics*, that "[e]xperts have debunked this myth [that WTC 7 was brought down with explosives]," thereby ignoring not only that none of the people who produced the *Popular Mechanics* book were experts, but also that over 1,500 genuine experts—architects, engineers, and physicists—say that Building 7 was brought down with explosives.

43 "Olbermann Says Fox Must Fire Judge Napolitano for Being a 9/11 Truther," Infowars.com, November 26, 2010 (http://www.infowars.com/olbermann-says-fox-must-fire-judge-napolitano-for-being-a-911-truther/).

44 Matthew T. Witt, "Pretending Not to See or Hear, Refusing to Signify: The Farce and Tragedy of Geocentric Public Affairs Scholarship," *American Behavioral Scientist* 53 (February 2010): 921–39 (http://abs.sagepub.com/content/vol53/issue6), at 932 (emphasis in original).

45 Ibid., 935.

46 Ibid., 932.

47 Ibid.

48 "Statement of September 11th Advocates Regarding the Release of the NIST Final Draft of Collapse of WTC7" (signed by Patty Casazza, Monica Gabrielle, Mindy Kleinberg, and Lorie Van Auken), September 26, 2008 (http://www.911truth.org/article.php?story=20080927030009489).

49 Dr. Gideon Polya estimated in January 2010 that by then, over four million Afghanis had died (from both violent and non-violent causes) who would not have died without the invasion. See "January 2010 - 4.5 Million Dead in Afghan Holocaust, Afghan Genocide," January 2, 2010, Afghan Holocaust, Afghan Genocide (http://afghangenocide.blogspot.com).

50 Dr. Gideon Polya, "Iraqi Holocaust, 2.3 Million Iraqi Excess Deaths," International News, March 21, 2009 (http://internationalnews.over-blog.com/article-29310829.html).

51 "Panetta Makes 9/11 Gaffe in Iraq," AFP, July 11, 2011 (http://www.activistpost.com/2011/07/panetta-makes-911-gaffe-in-iraq.html). Panetta's "gaffe" cannot be explained by the fact that he had just become the secretary of defense, because he had previously been the director of the CIA.

52 "Cost of War at Least $3.7 Trillion and Counting," *New York Times* June 29, 2011 (http://www.nytimes.com/reuters/2011/06/29/us/politics/politics-us-usa-war.html?_r=1).

53 Afghan War Costs $300 million a Day: Pentagon," AFP, February 14, 2011 (http://www.google.com/hostednews/afp/article/ALeqM5gNQ3JbWwd6t-PzkuECkRJvsAlNkA).

54 See Louis Fisher, *The Constitution and 9/11: Recurring Threats to America's Freedom* (Lawrence, KS: University Press of Kansas, 2008).

55 See 9/11 Consensus (http://www.consensus911.org).

56 See "UL Executive Speaks Out on WTC Study," 911Truth.org, November 12, 2004 (http://www.911truth.org/article.php?story=20041112144051451), or "Text of E-mail Letter from Kevin Ryan to Frank Gayle," 911Review.com, November 11, 2004 (http://911review.com/articles/ryan/letter.html).

57 John Dobberstein, "Area Man Stirs Debate on WTC Collapse: South Bend Firm's Lab Director Fired after Questioning Federal Probe," *South Bend Tribune* November 22, 2004 (http://www.wanttoknow.info/911kevinrryanfired).

58 Kevin Ryan, "A Personal Decision," DemocraticUnderground.com, June 9, 2005 (http://www.democraticunderground.com/discuss/duboard.php?az=view_ all&address=125x42811).

59 This former NIST scientist's written statement, dated October 1, 2007, is contained in "NIST Whistleblower" (http://georgewashington.blogspot.com/2007/ 10/former-nist-employee-blows-whistle.html).

60 Email letter from Steven Jones, December 3, 2007.

61 David Ray Griffin, *The Mysterious Collapse of World Trade Center 7: Why the Final Official Report about 9/11 Is Unscientific and False* (Northampton: Olive Branch Press [Interlink Publishing], 2009).

62 Richard D. Hall's interview of Tony Farrell on the "Richplanet Starship" on July 8, 2011, is available in three parts: Part 1 (http://www.richplanet.net/starship_main.php?ref=65&part=1); Part 2 (http://www.richplanet.net/starship_main.php?ref=65&part=2); and Part 3 (http://www.richplanet.net/starship_main.php?ref=65&part=3).

63 Roberts, "9/11 and the Orwellian Redefinition of 'Conspiracy Theory.'"